WISDOM IN ACTION

Other Theosophy Trust Books

The Dawning of Wisdom
Essays on Walking the Path
by Raghavan Iyer

Teachers of the Eternal Doctrine
From Tsong-Ka-Pa to Nostradamus
by Elton Hall

Symbols of the Eternal Doctrine
From Shamballa to Paradise
by Helen Valborg

The Key to Theosophy
An Exposition of the
Ethics, Science, and Philosophy
by H. P. Blavatsky

Evolution and Intelligent Design
in *The Secret Doctrine*
The Synthesis of Science, Religion and Philosophy
by H.P. Blavatsky
compiled by The Editorial Board of Theosophy Trust

If thou would'st have that stream of hard-earn'd knowledge, of Wisdom heaven-born, remain sweet running waters, thou should'st not leave it to become a stagnant pond.

Know, if of Amitabha, the "Boundless Age," thou would'st become co-worker, then must thou shed the light acquired, like to the Bodhisattvas twain, upon the span of all three worlds.

Know that the stream of superhuman knowledge and the Deva-Wisdom thou hast won, must, from thyself, the channel of *Alaya*, be poured forth into another bed.

Know, O Narjol, thou of the Secret Path, its pure fresh waters must be used to sweeter make the Ocean's bitter waves — that mighty sea of sorrow formed of the tears of men.

Alas! when once thou hast become like the fix'd star in highest heaven, that bright celestial orb must shine from out the spatial depths for all — save for itself; give light to all, but take from none.

Alas! when once thou hast become like the pure snow in mountain vales, cold and unfeeling to the touch, warm and protective to the seed that sleepeth deep beneath its bosom — 'tis now that snow which must receive the biting frost, the northern blasts, thus shielding from their sharp and cruel tooth the earth that holds the promised harvest, the harvest that will feed the hungry.

Self-doomed to live through future Kalpas, unthanked and unperceived by man; wedged as a stone with countless other stones which form the "Guardian Wall", such is thy future if the seventh gate thou passest. Built by the hands of many Masters of Compassion, raised by their tortures, by their blood cemented, it shields mankind, since man is man, protecting it from further and far greater misery and sorrow.

Withal man sees it not, will not perceive it, nor will he heed the word of Wisdom . . . for he knows it not.

But thou hast heard it, thou knowest all, O thou of eager guileless Soul. . . . and thou must choose. Then hearken yet again.

On Sowan's Path, O Srotapatti, thou art secure. Aye, on that *Marga*, where nought but darkness meets the weary pilgrim, where torn by thorns the hands drip blood, the feet are cut by sharp unyielding flints, and Mara wields his strongest arms — there lies a great reward immediately beyond.

The Seven Portals
H. P. Blavatsky

WISDOM IN ACTION
ESSAYS ON THE SPIRITUAL LIFE

BY

RAGHAVAN IYER

COMPILED BY
THE EDITORIAL BOARD OF THEOSOPHY TRUST

THEOSOPHY TRUST BOOKS
WASHINGTON, D.C.

Wisdom in Action
Essays on the Spiritual Life

Theosophy Trust books may be ordered through
BookSurge, Amazon.com, and other booksellers, or by visiting:

http://www.theosophytrust.org/online_books.php

ISBN 978-0-9793205-3-8
ISBN 0-9793205-3-4

Library of Congress Control Number 2008903617

Printed in the United States of America

Dedicated to

Tenzin Gyatso

His Holiness The 14th Dalai Lama

Exemplar of Wisdom in Action

CONTENTS

INTRODUCTION

The title of this book, *Wisdom in Action*, indicates the slightly different emphasis in this second volume of Raghavan Iyer's *Hermes* essays from the first volume, *The Dawning of Wisdom*. In truth, these jeweled essays in *Buddhi Yoga* could be gathered together into any number of configurations simply because the writings themselves are so multifaceted and universal in scope. As they embody Universal Good, so too they lend themselves to the purposes of the highest good under whatever name or form. These particular writings, however, were selected for this second volume with an eye to their bearing upon the crucial and thorny problem of translating *theoria* into *praxis*, and the light they shed upon the obstacles and difficulties encountered by every aspirant who self-consciously chooses to tread the Path of Renunciation.

The constant, underlying theme of all these essays is the crucial need for unconditional devotion to the good of all as a prerequisite for traveling on the spiritual Path. There is simply nothing else that could serve as a substitute for this highest of noble motives for living the spiritual life. Indeed, in the very first line of the first essay in this volume, Prof. Iyer makes a startling statement about the perspective required, and he puts the whole of human life into the following context: Every human soul is an apprentice in the sacrificial art of applying cosmic energies for the sake of universal good. These words are a statement of fact about every human being and not simply a conditional aspiration or wish. Prof. Iyer stakes a claim to the highest perspective available to us in his assertion that every human soul **is** an apprentice . . . This statement embodies the most practical idealism, and it points to the underlying metaphysical truth so beautifully expressed by Prof. Iyer in the essay, "The Eye of Self-Existence":

> It is only by developing a taste for silence in sound, for the unmanifest within the manifest, for the unspoken within the spoken, the unrecorded within a world of frail and fugitive and often false

recordings – that we come closer to the heartbeat that makes us human. The Absolute is characterized as the Supreme Eternal Heart of all existence because, although it is ever present, it is at the same time never fathomable by thought or word. It is closer to us than anything we can ever say or think, just as there is nothing more fundamental than the beating of the heart, and there is nothing around us that is more palpable, if only we would listen, than the beating of the cosmic heart.

What is at the core of the human being is also at the core of the cosmos, and there is no real separation between the two. The *apparent* separation, all too real for most of us, is dealt with especially in the essay, "Metaphysics and Ethics", through an analysis of the term *attavada*, the great dire heresy of Separateness. There, it is described as the root illusion of the reality of the separative self which all human beings, caught in the webs of *maya* and *moha*, *illusion* and *delusion*, must overcome in the process of realization of their one true nature: "Until we are free from the dire heresy of separateness (*attavada*), we cannot claim to have grasped the doctrine of *samvriti* or of the *nidanas* that teaches us about the origins of delusions and chains of causation. To know is to become, and to become is truly to know."

Not only is the apparent sense of separation of the individual self from the heart of the universe an illusion, the very idea of the reality of a persisting, separate personal entity named Mr. This or Ms. That is fundamentally illusory. In "Buddha and the Path to Enlightenment", Prof. Iyer points to the core of this problem:

> What the ignorant individual mistakes as the self, the enduring and unchanging unity of a being or object, is a persisting illusion. A person, seemingly constituted of mind and body, is actually a mutable composite of *skandhas*, heaps or aggregates, which come together and coalesce, only to separate after a time. When they come together, the person or object comes into being as a seeming entity, and when they radically separate, death is said to have intervened.

What should be apparent to the living from watching the process of dissolution of the aged and dying is inexplicably missed by many who might in fact be devoted to the practical applications of the secret wisdom. The reason behind the inability of the personal mind to grasp the solution to this puzzle is put with remarkable clarity:

Buddha's Doctrine of Anatta, No-self, is daunting and elusive even at higher levels of apprehension. This is partly because the apprehending mind which seeks to seize upon the doctrine and make sense of it is itself a constituent of the composite *skandhas*. A contrived illusion cannot construe itself as illusory any more than a dream can negate itself.

All of these psychological tenets may be fascinating, but what, one might ask, do they have to do with the practical needs of wisdom in action? Further, why include an article about "Meditation and Self-Study" in a book dealing with practical wisdom? As Prof. Iyer explains, the knowledge to be gained by the seeker about and through meditation and self-study ". . . is the knowledge that will help him to balance his life and to gain, in a chaotic time, enough calm and sufficient continuity of will-energy, to be able to survive without succumbing to the constant threat and danger of disintegration, ever looming large like a nightmare. Even the rudimentary philosophical knowledge of the instruments, practices and conditions of these mental disciplines is of immense practical importance to the struggling soul."

Like Arjuna in Chapter III of the *Bhagavad-Gita*, when he asks Krishna to choose one method by which he might live a life of spiritual purpose and obtain happiness, there will be those who hope to see some "practical" advice in the form of easily understandable "guidelines" or "rules". They will not be disappointed with their study of this work. There are innumerable such guidelines that deal with the most basic human activities, such as eating, sleeping, breathing, working, and maintaining consciousness, given throughout these essays, especially toward the end of the book in the article "The Healing of Elementals":

Yet, if any Aquarian pioneer wishes to begin to learn how to exercise a calming, controlling influence over masses of disturbed elementals – while eating, sleeping and going about the daily round – the first thing to focus upon is silence. A simple rule would be to talk little, if at all, during meals. Whether or not one mutters words of grace, it is most important to eat food calmly and gratefully without words. That would be a definite step forward for most people.

Each of the articles in this book will be found to contain priceless jewels of great philosophical insight and practical advice, and both linked together at every point, provided by one who has long ago passed through and emerged victorious in "this glorious unsought fight which only fortune's favored soldiers may obtain".

It was the wish of Professor Iyer that his *Hermes* writings would someday be made available to the widest reading audience possible. This book is a partial realization of that wish. It is to be hoped that the remainder of those golden writings find their way into print soon. In the meantime, these two small volumes - each with 28 essays - will provide abundant food for thought, meditation, and sheer enjoyment. Those readers who find themselves wanting to read more of Prof. Iyer's *Hermes* writings can find the complete collection online, easily and freely accessible at the Theosophy Trust website (http://www.theosophytrust. org); those who wish to learn more about the remarkable human being known to the world as Raghavan Iyer, and to gain a just and expansive view of what an extraordinary philosophical mind Prof. Iyer wielded, are urged to read the excellent Introduction to the first volume, *The Dawning of Wisdom*, written by one of Prof. Iyer's life-long students, as well as the very excellent short Biographical Sketch, along with his Curriculum Vitae and Publications list, also available at the Theosophy Trust website (found simply by clicking on the 'Sri Raghavan Iyer' just under his picture).

All who come to these writings in the spirit of the true *shravaka* will find their deepest unasked questions illuminated by the light of the *Sanatana Dharma*, the Eternal Wisdom, and answered with the oldest and most practical spiritual advice:

> "Seek this wisdom by doing service, by strong search, by questions, and by humility; the wise who see the truth will communicate it unto thee, and knowing which thou shalt never again fall into error, O son of Bharata."

Editor,
Theosophy Trust Books

WISDOM IN ACTION

The atoms emanated from the Central Point emanate in their turn new centres of energy, which, under the potential breath of Fohat, begin their work from within without, and multiply other minor centres. These, in the course of evolution and involution, form in their turn the roots or developing causes of new effects, from worlds and 'man-bearing' globes, down to the genera, species, and classes of all the seven kingdoms (of which we know only four). For 'the blessed workers have received the Thyan-kam, in the eternity' (Book of The Aphorisms of Tson-ka-pa).

'Thyan-kam' is the power or knowledge of guiding the impulses of cosmic energy in the right direction.

The Secret Doctrine, i 635

Every human soul is an apprentice in the sacrificial art of applying cosmic energies for the sake of universal good. Thus, all human evolution is a record of lessons learnt, lost and rediscovered in the arduous practice of *Karma Yoga*. The ragged and uneven tale of recorded history and the glamour of current events are nothing but the distorted image of the pilgrimage of humanity reflected in the inverted lens of egotism. As a result, individuals oscillate between a sense of starvation for meaning in events and a sense of being overwhelmed by their magnitude. Nevertheless, there must be true *Karma Yogins* in disguise on the stage of the world's theatre, individuals with a measure of maturity, from whose sacrificial examples earnest students of human life may learn. Unfortunately, the energy of action is most easily stimulated by egotism, engendering a momentum that is sometimes linked to a grandiose conception of the world and of history, seemingly independent of self. Then through subsuming one's false sense of identity under some vague notion like national destiny, one can view one's life in terms of a false drama. Very often figures in public life are caught up in just such a melodramatic response to chaotic events; they regard their own choices as unique, unprecedented, momentous, fraught with extreme consequences for the future. There

1

is in all of this, of course, an absurd element of unreality. Such illusion is conveyed in the story of the French writer who imagined a poignant meeting of some of the great women of history, including Cleopatra. Gathering together in their old age, and looking back upon their lives, they recognize their relative irrelevance. Plato in his dialogues made much the same point by putting into perspective the presumed importance of what happened in Troy.

In a world of imperfect beings, certain events and actions inevitably assume a much greater magnitude than they truly deserve in the longer view of history. Nature moves gradually, working silently and gestating invisibly under the soil. This is true of the work of sun and fire, sky and earth, air and water; all mirror in time the archetypal realm of *Aether-Akasha*. As Kropotkin pointed out, one could hardly recognize from a study of earthquakes and volcanic explosions the vast geological changes that take place over millions of years, proceeding through minute imperceptible increments. These almost invisible changes can accumulate to set off a shifting in the continents. Thus, massive volcanic eruptions, for example, are the result of a long series of tremors, though they come about as abrupt precipitations filled with fury and force. So long as human beings remain trapped in the realm of effects, seeing only with the physical eye and considering only a very narrow view of time, they will have no sense of the majesty and symphonic resonance of Nature, nor will they feel its resonance in their lives. Instead, they will be caught in what Thoreau called a life of quiet desperation. They will react only to whatever seems to be titanic, dramatic or volcanic, and so reinforce their subservience to the illusion of effects.

Although true of human beings in general, it is especially true of those figures in history who are powerful in a conventional sense. Whether one considers a figure like Alexander or a Genghis Khan, or a more contemporary figure like General Douglas MacArthur, one can see that it is easy for such dedicated and determined individuals to become suddenly caught in the *maya* of the magnification of importance of events. There may have been an element of truth in what General MacArthur saw, at the time of the Korean War, as the tremendous effect upon China of the actions of the United States. At the same time, his judgement isolated China and the United States from the rest of the world. Unlike the more discerning Lord Louis Mountbatten, he was insensitive to the aspirations of millions of souls in many burgeoning nations, great and small.

Whatever the details of an historical judgement, once one leaves out of account large portions of humanity, one can be right at a certain level, though at the expense of being caught in an exaggeration. Yet it was this same sense of the enormity of events that made MacArthur the man he was, a man capable of rendering a far greater service to the nation of Japan than he himself ever realized. As a nation stultified by its immense but wounded pride, Japan required extraordinarily delicate handling. Not only that, it needed to be shown a way out. In doing this, it was necessary to act with a true humanitarian instinct, free from any taint of racism and based on a genuine love for the Japanese people. Out of his soldier's ability to distinguish between the Japanese people and their defeated generals, it was possible for MacArthur to assist in the greatest transformation of Japanese history since the Meiji restoration. If this was evident at the time to some, though perhaps less so now to many observers, its long run and fundamental importance will not emerge until after the end of the present century, when Japan shall have fully worked out all the implications of the route it has taken — breaking with elements of its own tradition, gaining an unprecedented economic ascendancy, and yet feeling itself weighed down by the anxiety that accompanies frenetic success.

The karmic lesson to be drawn is that even the most remarkable figures in history, whether statesmen, military figures or politicians, often cannot gauge the significance of the events they seem to initiate. That man is wise in his time who, without exaggerating or underestimating his own role, understands something of Tolstoy's view in *War and Peace* — that the commanding generals are irrelevant and that in a sense even the vast masses of soldiers are acted upon. There is a mighty force at work in history, moving in mysterious ways through myriad wills. How they all clash and combine and resolve themselves is difficult indeed to know. It certainly cannot be understood if one subscribes to some simplistic Great Man theory of history or military strategy. Here one may learn from the example of General George C. Marshall. As a man, he no doubt took his profession as seriously as did General MacArthur; yet he was fortunate not to have had any other advantage save loyalty to his family, loyalty to what had been done before and loyalty to his teachers. Working hard and well, he at no point found spectacular success, yet he acquired a considerable wisdom in action. For a general or anyone involved in strategic planning, wisdom in action is crucial, less in regard to one's own sphere than in reference to understanding other human beings and in choosing and drawing out their hidden potential. The ability to groom talent innately presupposes some measure of self-confidence and selflessness.

This may be seen clearly in the extraordinary choice made silently and far-sightedly by Marshall of his supreme commander in Europe. At the time Marshall's eye fell on him, Dwight D. Eisenhower was in a position to become the commandant of a military college, in which capacity he could have developed his own deep interest in the profession of military strategy. Marshall wrote to him, suggesting that he might, if he liked, come to Washington and serve in a thoroughly unimportant role as a kind of attache; Eisenhower wrote frankly of this, remarking that the position of commandant was extremely tempting, but that, out of pure and simple respect for General Marshall, he would take up his offer. What Marshall knew relatively early in the war, but kept to himself, was that there would one day come an extraordinary challenge to selfless coordination among the different allied nations. It would require a quality for which America does not prepare its people — letting others take the credit while standing behind the visible scene. It requires the ability in repetitive and protracted arenas of conflict to be cool and constructive. Marshall knew that any officer who could eventually play this role in the most crucial engagements at the end of the war would have to be trained in anonymity.

If it required a certain karmic insight on the part of Marshall to choose Eisenhower, it required a certain Buddhic intuition on the part of Eisenhower to respond to the call. Hence, he embarked upon a long apprenticeship which featured little of the excitement that he would have enjoyed had he been commandant of a college teaching military strategy. In fact, most of his duties were chores. In effect, Eisenhower merely polished the shoes of his commander, but he was happy to stay put, to watch and learn. Marshall knew that it would require an extraordinary wisdom, when the time came, to match up to the brilliance and force of personality of men like Harold Alexander, Alanbrooke and the other English generals. Most of them were well schooled in a philosophy of true sportsmanship, selflessness and disinterestedness; but at the same time it would also be necessary to cope with MacArthur-like figures on the British side such as General Bernard Law Montgomery. Remarkably, when Eisenhower was appointed as supreme commander, he quickly won the respect of Alexander and all the others, who saw that he could not be drawn into competitive games, let alone the nationalistic rivalries that were part of the high command.

Instead, they found in Eisenhower someone who was willing to learn, willing to stay quiet, but at the same time extremely strong; he was waiting to act and to act with a decisiveness born of deliberation. Eisenhower worked as karma works. When there were critical choices to be made at the end of the war, decisions affecting millions of lives and the concerted effort to bring the war to a close, the last-minute freedom of decision was left in Eisenhower's hands. Under karma he was able to initiate the final move so that World War II in Europe ended on the eighth of May, White Lotus Day, 1945. Here one may discern the *Nirmanakaya* influence at work, affecting selfless and open-minded individuals through their dreams and intuitions, their imagination and ideals. That larger force may also be discerned in the closure of World War II in Asia on the twelfth of August, 1945, the birth anniversary of H.P. Blavatsky. Thus one finds the most remarkable karma quietly at work; for those who were truly awake and alive to the meaning of events in 1945, it was a time of extraordinary tension, far greater than anything that has taken place since. In the intervening years lesser persons have been dislodged by relatively minor crises. None of them had had a preparation in living through crises, making distinctions and learning from events. Such is the mark of the *Karma Yogin* in the realm of public affairs.

Promethean foresight must be earned through a thorough study of the mistakes, as well as the wise moves, of all who have gone before. Every great military commander has the utmost respect and fascination both for the successful moves but also the avoidable mistakes made by his precursors in the field of battle. This true learning from the past means putting Epimethean wisdom in the service of Promethean forces with reference to the future. What it comes to in practice is that one must study the lives of others well enough to learn how easy it is to be mistake-prone oneself. At the same time, however, one must not let the fear of mistakes come in the way of doing the best that one knows. One's motivation can and should be to lay down as a sacrifice all that one has in the best way one can for the sake of the whole, without drawing attention to oneself. When one can do this, one can become an instrument of a higher law or collective force. In a karmic field, wherein high ideals may be intact but threatened by pollution, such as the peace that follows a horrendous war, it is possible for many people to be touched by such motivations. But to become one with an ideal and so free oneself from all pettiness and residues of personal egotism is to prepare oneself to be used by the wisdom operating through karma. Such detached ardour towards ideals was epitomized by Louis Claude de Saint-Martin at the time of the French Revolution:

> The society of the world in general appeared to me as a theatre where one is continually passing one's time playing one's role and where there is never a moment to learn. The society of wisdom, on the contrary, is a school where one is continually passing one's time learning one's role and where one waits for the curtain to rise before playing, that is to say, for the veil which covers the universe to disappear.... We are only here in order to choose.

Mon portrait historique et philosophique

Foresight at that level requires the courage to negate time, the judgements of the present and also the judgements of posterity. Too many politicians dance with an eye to posterity. This is foolish. The greatest men, like Lincoln, were not obsessed with posterity but with rightness; they understood something of the timeless nature of the enactment of right in the name of an ideal. At the same time, one must make full allowance for all the imperfections in oneself, in the moment and in the act of embodying an ideal. Therefore, *Karma Yoga* requires a balance between a capacity to be strong in a timeless and universal field and a simultaneous ability to be courageous in that sphere wherein, as Krishna says, no act is without blame. Put in another way, one must combine a macro-perspective with a micro-application, see events both in the large and in the small. The more one is able, through detachment, to infinitize and so negate the finitizing tendencies of the human mind, the more one empties oneself into the boundless, unknown, uncertain and indeterminate ocean of space. At the same time, to gain efficiency and precision, skill in the performance of action, one must master concentration, the ability to bring things to a centre, to an intense, sharp focus. If one can fuse together this sense of infinitude and a sense of laser-like precision, one will gain much more than a sense of what is immediately relevant and essential. One will begin to see the equilibrizing forces of karma as centered upon an invisible point. It is like saying that to be able to master attention in reference to three things, for example, one must focus on some invisible fourth thing that one may think of as either inside or outside the triad, but which is, in reality, entirely beyond it.

Karma Yoga depends upon a sense of depth, a sense of that which is infinitesimal and hidden. This is known by the greatest dancers, archetypally represented by Shiva Nataraj, who are concerned not with position but motion, and who at the same time know that there is something mayavic about motion in relation to a field that is homogeneous and immobile. Its pure existence is in the realm of the mind. It is the etheric empyrean of the poets. It is like the sky in which the bird takes wing and floats in a refulgent majesty, remaining in motion, but when seen from a great distance, seemingly motionless. It is difficult indeed to understand or experience this fusion of motion and motionlessness, action and inaction, the micro-perception and the macro-perspective. When one looks at the night sky, one recognizes that boundless space itself is vastly greater than all the possible galaxies and systems. Even the immense voids in intergalactic space that have recently been discovered only give a relative sense of the metaphysical void of absolute space. And when astronomers speculate along the vague lines of the so-called Big Bang theory, this is nothing but a materialized shadow of the teaching of *Gupta Vidya* regarding the emanation from within without, a version of the Central Point — the one Cosmic atom — of all the myriad centres of activity in the incipient cosmos.

Without becoming caught up in the unresolved disputes of contemporary cosmology concerning questions of the expanding universe, continuous creation and other mysteries, the ordinary person may learn to look at the sky using the mind's eye. Directing the vision of the hidden eye of the soul through continuous concentration, one will find that what one sees above in the heavens is mirrored within the heart. In particular, one may develop a sense of space in reference to the *Akasha* within the heart. Just as there are chambers in the heart and empty cavities in the brain, so too there is voidness throughout the human body. That voidness, however, cannot be understood in a two-dimensional or three-dimensional sense. Instead, one needs a sense of another level of matter which is consubstantial with the great universal matrix, *Mulaprakriti*, the Divine Darkness or primordial ground and substratum of all manifested matter. On that plane the distinction between matter and mind has no meaning; *Mulaprakriti* is mirrored as the *Akasha* within the heart. It may be symbolized as radiant matter or as a dark luminosity, and mystics have noted the striking analogies between the solar system within which the earth revolves and the miniature solar system within man. As Kropotkin said, every human being is a cosmos of organs, and each organ is itself a cosmos of cells. To be able to experience the cosmos within the empty space in the heart is to discover the seed point or bindhu within the lotus of the heart. But to experience it, one must experience the depth of introverted vision. Those who do so are actually much farther from the ordinary terrestrial realm than could ever be reached by traversing what is called outer space.

To reach the heart of action one must rethink one's view of space and time and motion. In the seventeenth chapter of the *Bhagavad Gita*, Krishna gives the mystical key to this meditation upon the heart of action. Having explained to Arjuna the application of the complex doctrine of the gunas, or qualities affecting all action, Krishna gives to Arjuna the talismanic *mantra*m vitalizing all true faith and sacrifice:

> OM TAT SAT, these are said to be the threefold designation of the Supreme Being. By these in the beginning were sanctified the knowers of *Brahma*, the *Vedas*, and sacrifices.

This is the ancient and sacred mode of consecration of karma or action. The more disinterested one's practice of *Karma Yoga*, the more that action is itself a disinterested flow of benevolence, the more one begins to gain clues into the magical connections of the workings of karma in the large. Freed from a concern with one's own karma, one may begin to discern the karma of nations, continents, races and human beings whom one wishes to serve and help. As one makes inevitable discoveries regarding the cyclic working of karma, one will begin to recognize that the more complex the karmic mathematics, the more one's practice of benevolence depends upon strength of mind and clarity of perception in taking hold of a set of karmic curves and releasing potent seeds of action.

> Therefore the sacrifices, the giving of alms, and the practising of austerities are always, among those who expound Holy Writ, preceded by the word *OM*.

OM is the Soundless Sound in boundless space — space beyond all subjects and objects, beyond all qualities, space which is no-thing and the fullness of the void. But *OM* is also in every atom, stirring within the minutest centres imaginable and in all the interstices of empty space. It is also a reverberation of one's own being, omnipresent in all the vestures, the great keynote of Nature. To be able to bring it before consciousness and to consecrate oneself to it as the *Atman* or eternal spirit is to reduce oneself to a zero, a sphere of light filled with the oceanic pulsation of the *OM* at the cosmic level. It encompasses all beginnings, middles and endings. It includes all creative, supportive and regenerative action. Most human action is not creative, but mechanical and routinized, half-hearted and preoccupied, based upon indirect calculations of consequences in the future or guilt over the past. Such action is neither free nor one-pointed. Therefore, it is significant for beings who do not normally experience creative action to set aside certain times of the day to engage in action in a deliberate spirit of sacrifice and charity — *yajna* and *dana* — for the good of all.

Since all beings must act out of internal necessity or *dharma*, it makes sense to set aside certain actions — *kriya* — as creative contributions to the universal good. Far from being grudging or mechanical, such performance of duty through action flows with a serene and steady rhythm, rooted in an ability to abstract from the outward particulars of acts and a freedom from illusion that is gained through meditation upon the *OM*. There is an element of illusion in all action, and hence there are always retrospective painful lessons to be learnt from it. *OM* is the destroyer of illusions. Through it one may learn from the flow of action, from past mistakes and illusions. By making oneself a zero, one can regenerate oneself through the *OM*. The *OM* is all this and much more. Through it one may get away from particulars, apprehending the whole, entering into the ocean of space and absolute darkness pregnant with the luminosity that contains universes. Reaching beyond the mind, it ouches the deepest core of one's being connected with the immortal Self in eternity. Thus Krishna taught:

> Among those who long for immortality and who do not consider the reward for their actions, the word *TAT* precedes their rites of sacrifice, their austerities, and giving of alms.

The moment one consecrates with the *OM*, one says *TAT* — That — without past, without limits, the boundless and nameless. To name anything is to limit it. It is not this, it is not that — *neti, neti*. It can never be made an object or a subject. It is prior, and yet also posterior, to the rise of all possible objects and subjects, all possible constellations of entities and atoms, all possible worlds and minds of beings. Thus having in the moment consecrated through the *OM*, one goes into *TAT*, totally negating oneself. Having heightened the significance of what one is going to do, one negates it, relinquishing every wish for any fruit of a sacrifice. Through the power of *tapas* one makes the sacrificial act disappear into the totality of *TAT*. This is a dialectical activity requiring the highest practice and exercise in self-consciousness, self-reference and the interplay of the individuality of the sacrificer and the universality of the cosmic sacrifice. As human beings will naturally experience a sense of satisfaction in an authentic act of creative sacrifice, Krishna pointed to this experience of inner fulfilment, inner freedom and inner recognition of truth:

> The word *SAT* is used for qualities that are true and holy, and likewise is applied to laudable actions, O son of Pritha. The state of mental sacrifice when actions are at rest is also called *SAT*. Whatever is done without faith, whether it be sacrifice, alms-giving, or austerities, is called *ASAT*, that which is devoid of truth and goodness, O son of Pritha, and is not of any benefit either in this life or after death.

SAT is not a truth, but rather ALL-TRUTH. It may be experienced as truth, goodness, purity, love or a number of other modes familiar to those who are experienced in *tapas*. Thus, having begun by consecrating with the *OM*, and then emptied all into *TAT*, which is beyond all possible concepts, worlds, definitions and beings, one reaffirms Being at the level of invisible unity, the level of the One Light of the One Spirit. Through the trinitarian *mantra*m of *OM TAT SAT*, one may consecrate activity, negate the personal self, and at the same time realize a state of self-consciousness which will give contentment, substance and continuity to a life of service. When this mode of yajna becomes as natural as breathing, it infuses creativity, sustenance and regeneration into every action.

Metaphysically, the entire cosmos of manifestation is sacrificial. All existence is sacrifice. All descent from homogeneous planes into planes of greater differentiation is a sacrifice, a kind of grace, an avataric descent of the *Logos*. The primordial compassion in the One initiates and inaugurates the many. The one white light breaks up into the spectrum and then into the myriads upon myriads of hues that are implicit in the hebdomadic worlds. The entire universe may be understood as a great act of compassion. If this is true of the whole, then by identifying oneself totally, in one's deepest identity, with the *Logos*, one may find that everything is sacrifice. Once one is attuned to the *Logos* in this way, then all the tiredness of calculation vanishes, to be replaced by fearlessness with facts and freedom from illusion. One can learn to live in the world, and yet live outside it; one can learn to live only for the sake of sacrifice and benefit to others. By accepting this and cooperating with the cosmic Logoic sacrifice, one frees oneself from virtually all the tension, anxiety and fear that arise out of pseudo-agnosticism, false pride and the inability to recognize that one does not know the karmic mathematics of the universe. One learns to admire the good in others and to adore the wisdom of those who are greater than oneself. As presumption falls away, so too do envy, craving and irritation.

At some point, one can come directly to grips with the twin demons of craving and contempt, like and dislike, attraction and repulsion. Every time one falls prey to the demon of craving, one is equally in the grip of the demon of contempt. So too in the reverse. Once one begins to understand the operation of these shadowy forces in the realm of shadowy selves, one may cut through the pall of murk and gloom that they induce and establish one's mind in the realm of pure light. The shadow world of interaction and action of shadowy fears and hopes is a lie obscuring the dynamic light of true action. That light moves through a dynamic field of endless sacrifice and perpetual motion. It is difficult to root oneself in a consciousness of that realm, but it can be done through training oneself to hold fast to a sense of the heart and a sense of that which is between the eyes. It is possible to create an alignment between the eye of time and the eye of eternity, between the microcosmic and the macrocosmic, between the field of specific sacrificial karma and the boundless fields of universal sacrifice — *Adhiyajna*. To do this is to discover wisdom in action, *Karma Yoga*. If one sets out in dead earnest, one may be confident that things will get worse before they get better. It simply means that each individual has a measure of karma to be worked out. The intense discomfort that one feels in this process is a sign that one is being tested by karma. In fact, one should be grateful that forces are rushing in. It is better to have them precipitate together than to be spread out over a protracted period. And as this happens, one should not advertise it, because it is something that everyone has to do.

Each human being must seize his or her birth, just as, in the Japanese fable, each human being must recognize the donkey of stupidity that he or she is carrying and quietly put it down. These are all elements of past egotism, thoughtlessness, envy, contempt and insensitivity. In the past, one saw people who were blind, deaf and dumb, and instead of saying, "May that be my burden and may I help", one said, "There but for the grace of God go I."

Having separated oneself from those who have mysterious karma to bear, these failures will come back to one, and one will have to live out future lives in blindness, deafness and muteness. Whatever the karmic consequences of one's actions, one must accept them as that which is best for the soul, that alone from which one may learn. It requires extraordinary fearlessness, but when one measures up to the test of accepting the truth, one will discover authentic freedom and true humility. Letting go of pride, one will see that everything is a lesson and that one is glad to learn. As one learns this true patience, one will become grateful when one can pause to look through the eyes of other human beings. One will start to feel something about the total saga of the human enterprise, encompassing all the souls living and learning and somewhere in their hearts unconsciously loving.

Inserting one's life into the vast human enterprise, one can become a serene instrument of the cosmic sacrifice, consciously throwing all sense of self and separateness into the fire to be burnt. In the end, this is far wiser than being burnt out because of frenetic action, perversity and allegiance to the tired machinations of the false persona. Instead of being an incessant and repetitive victim to excess and deficiency, one may become like the quiet tender of a fire. Discerning the illusive elements in actions, one may gently cast them into the flames of sacrifice, receiving the warmth and joy and light of the fire and freeing oneself from the burden of ignorance. If one can make this a natural way of thinking and breathing, then one will burn out all the dross that would otherwise have formed, at the moment of death, a grotesque *kama rupa*.

Through the initial mastery of sacrificial skill in action, one may purify one's will and desire, minimally assuring oneself that one's actions in life will not be a source of pollution to the human race. When this healthy tropism of the soul has been restored, one is in a position to learn about the positive applications of the Fohatic power of desire. Instead of making an unconscious form or *rupa* out of *kama*, one may enter into the current of joy that accompanies sacrificial participation through meditation and action in the pilgrimage of humanity. One learns to engage in self-study solely for the sake of helping others. One learns to sleep and remain awake, to eat and bathe, to sit and walk, to breathe and think and feel for the sake of others. As this grows natural, one becomes like a station beaming vibrations to vast numbers of human beings in need. Serving as an instrument of the *Logos* far more than one will ever know, one remains free of the distraction of thinking about how much one may have done. Instead, one is concerned only with maintaining the mental stance and spiritual posture of sacrificial action. This is the central teaching of *Karma Yoga*, which brings about whatever joy, meaning and hope in life is supportable by the universe and is compatible with the joy and hopes of all other beings. *Karma Yoga* is action in accord with the great wheel of the Law, and it is the rightful inheritance of those who have the courage to make experiments with truth on behalf of humanity.

Instead of wasting time in daydreams about others, or about one's regrets and mistakes, one should quicken one's sense of what is necessary to do now. One must learn to stay still and do it. If one can become a one-pointed, whole-hearted person in two or three things done each day, one has embarked on the path of *Karma Yoga*, and the instances will increase with time. The higher cosmic energies guided by the true *Karma Yogin* are the energies of the highest Self — the *Atman* — and they are released only by the power of constructive vows. The mysteries of action and inaction are revealed only to those who bind themselves by sacred vows and commit themselves to the judgement and impartiality of Nature. The selflessness and integrity of Nature is the inward and invisible strength of the *Karma Yogin*. The secret is to work with the Silence residing in the unmanifest, courageously holding to the sacrificial current and welcoming the adjustment whereby distractions are dissolved and one's heart and mind are drawn back to the invisible centre. The more one can learn to shackle the unruly vestures, making them instruments of *Atma-Buddhi-Manas*, the more one can create a stronger karmic matrix for a more glorious future.

Hermes, June 1985

THE EYE OF SELF-EXISTENCE

The Secret Doctrine establishes three fundamental propositions: An omnipresent, Eternal, Boundless, and Immutable PRINCIPLE on which all speculation is impossible, since it transcends the power of human conception and could only be dwarfed by any human expression or similitude. It is beyond the range and reach of thought – in the words of Mandukya, "unthinkable" and "unspeakable".

To render these ideas clearer to the general reader, let him set out with the postulate that there is one absolute Reality which antecedes all manifested, conditioned being. This Infinite and Eternal Cause – dimly formulated in the Unknowable of current European philosophy – is the rootless root of "all that was, is, or ever shall be". It is of course devoid of all attributes and is essentially without any relation to manifested, finite Being. It is "Beness" rather than Being (in Sanskrit, Sat), and is beyond all thought or speculation.

H. P. Blavatsky

In the magical phrase of the *Book of Dzyan*, the oldest book of revelation kept in the secret sanctuaries of the sacred Mystery Temples, the Rootless Root symbolizes the First Fundamental of the Sacred Science of *Gupta Vidya*, the Wisdom Religion or *Theosophia*. It is the unknowable but for humankind; it is also the unthinkable and unspeakable, especially in the Mysteries, for those who have apprehended the unknowable, those who have gone beyond all scattered thoughts to the supernal realm of Divine Thought, transcended even that, and become one with *TAT*. It is THAT, beyond all names and forms, which includes all, cancelling and superceding all beginnings and endings. It is that which is beginningless, ever existing and never dying. It is the fountainhead and origin of all Life, and of all life in the seven kingdoms of Nature in all worlds and systems, in all stars, planets and galaxies.

It is the origin of all life during *manvantara*, the 'Day' of the great universe, which is the period of activity for every single being throughout the cosmos. It is also equally and exactly the same during the 'Night' of non-manifestation in which every being is reabsorbed, without knowing it, into the great bosom of the Divine Ground, that which includes all and yet itself is No-thing, which is everything and nothing. Unthinkable, unspeakable, it is the Soundless Sound in the eternal Silence that transcends all sounds and silences in the manifested worlds of Nature, both visible and invisible. It encompasses the entire human kingdom and all the lives of all gods, monads and atoms, beings of every kind at whatever degree of awareness, knowledge, self – knowledge, universal knowledge, universal self-knowledge or universal self-consciousness.

Beyond and behind all of these is *TAT*, which is ever full, and which, though boundless, is capable of emanating countless universes, and yet remains totally undepleted. One of the most magnificent stanzas in Sanskrit declares: That which is ever full has taken away from it that which is ever full, and yet, it remains ever full. It transcends all infinities and all sum totals, and therefore it is known to the man of meditation, and sometimes in speech, as that which is No-thing or No-being. It is No-thing in space and time, nothing that is ever manifested, because it is eternally beyond manifest and non-manifest, being and non-being, day and night. It is beyond all contrast, beyond all divisions and dichotomies, beyond Spirit-Matter and the very division and contrast between concretized spirit and sublimated matter on all planes of existence. It has also been sometimes referred to as the One Universal Existence, as in the eighth *shloka* of the *Stanzas of Dzyan*:

> Alone the One form of existence stretched boundless, infinite, causeless, in dreamless sleep; and life pulsated unconscious in universal space, throughout that All-Presence which is sensed by the opened *Eye of the Dangma*.

It is the attributeless Absolute, whose only predication is attribute -lessness. This, though a paradox of thought and of language, is a poetical and metaphorical way of conveying what the *Mandukya Upanishad* calls "unthinkable and unspeakable".

And yet, as the thirteenth chapter of the *Bhagavad Gita* declares, "That which is remoter than the remotest is closer than the closest." Few fitter poetical depictions of it were offered than these lines of William Blake:

To see a World in a Grain of Sand,
And a Heaven in a Wild Flower,
Hold Infinity in the palm of your hand,
And Eternity in an hour.

Here is a way of recognizing, revering, honouring and saluting, but also conceiving, the Absolute without attempting to 'nail it down' by leaden attributes. That which is attributeless has as many attributes as there are dainty flowers and diverse trees. It has, in fact, itself been sometimes shown in relation to the Tree of Life, which includes all possible trees and all actual trees, in all possible worlds. This mighty metaphor is older than that of Blake. It is as old as thinking man. Everything represented by the hidden roots, the shoots, the trunk, the myriad branches, the myriads upon myriads of leaves, the flowers and fruits of the tree – deeply rooted in the earth and extending upward to the heavens – is significant in this sacred metaphor. It signifies the sacred function of the entire manifested cosmos. It is like a suspended bridge between the Divine Ground and all beings, and is itself expressed throughout the gamut of all existence.

The term 'Be-ness', though better than the term 'Being', is still only a poor English equivalent to the rich Sanskrit term *SAT*, which embraces the concepts of Being, Be-ness and Absolute Truth. *SAT* also encompasses the concept of Universal Absolute Consciousness, because the Absolute, though it has neither consciousness nor desire, neither wish nor thought, is absolute thought, absolute desire, absolute consciousness, absolutely all. It is each of these, and yet it is beyond them all, which is why it cannot be limited by any single being or thing in relation to its vast, immemorial, variegated perception or perspective, vital experience or vocal description. It is beyond all of these, inexplicable, inexhaustible and impossible of definition.

This is implicit in the etymology of the English term 'absolute', which is derived from the Latin *absolutus*, "that which is completed", "that which is complete in itself". Therefore it excludes nothing, it wants nothing, it lacks nothing, it needs nothing. It is all-complete and it is unfettered. Neither earthquakes nor wars, nor the ever-present cycle of destruction can have any mark or trace on it, or in any way fetter the Absolute. It is unconditional and beyond all conditions, and yet it is in all conditions intact, complete, self-sufficient, and utterly incapable of being touched or tainted, circumscribed or narrowed. It surpasses the vastest, infinite sum totals of objects and subjects in all possible worlds. The Latin *absolutus* is itself derived from the past participle of the verb *absolvere*, 'to free from', 'to complete', an etymology which shows that it is not a static concept, nor indeed is it dynamic, for it is that which is endlessly at work, behind anything and everything, and therefore to be identified with the ultimate, unknowable mystery of the one Law ceaselessly operating throughout the cosmos.

It is ever behind every single change, every single movement, all the rhythms and patterns of all of Nature in its intricate, inexhaustible vastness on the invisible causal as well as the visible plane. Therefore, it is ever capable of liberating anything and everything from conditionality. That liberation is known – if indeed we can talk of such knowledge – as the ending of embodied life, as a kind of death, yet in the Absolute there is neither birth nor death. Nothing is ever lost, nothing is ever saved, nothing is ever begun, and nothing is ever ended, because everything that comes to be already exists in the Absolute. Everything that ceases to be continues to remain in the Absolute, otherwise there would be no continuity between *manvantaras*, immense, immeasurable periods of time, epochs in galactic space. That which is unconditional, inexhaustible, all-complete and omnipresent is also by its inherent nature that which both seemingly binds and effectually liberates.

To the highest minds of meditation, the greatest lovers of true wisdom, who have reached the pinnacle and summit of the loftiest conceivable altitude of philosophic thought, it is impossible to think about it except with reverence. It is unapproachable except by cancelling all divisions between thought, will and feeling, between head and heart, and every category of every school. All of them are dim, feeble, and at best logically limited representations of existence and reality, which is itself only an irrelevant aspect of that which Ever Is and, therefore, by definition can never emerge into existence and never cease to be. Hence the term 'Be-ness'. The Latin term *solvere*, implying an alchemical sense of negation, comes from the Indo-European root *leu*, which means 'to loosen', 'to divide', 'to cut apart', as with a pair of scissors. In conversation, human beings cut apart themselves, other human beings and the world, dividing endlessly but feebly, compared with the way Nature divides all things with a daily magnificence. All our efforts to cut up, to divide and analyze the Absolute will fail because it is that which can never be divided, can never be cut up. It cannot be extended, contracted, shrunk or swallowed. No spatial metaphor can begin to characterize its essential indestructible property rooted in ever-existing self-existence. It is not only the sole Self-Existent, but it is also inclusive of all that is existent at all levels. If that is so, all words are merely invocations or petitions to burst the barriers and boundaries of finitude, fragmentation and limitation. To move towards the Absolute is continually to cancel and transcend every possible limit or characterization .

That is why the Self-Existent is apprehended by human beings more readily in silence than in speech, in states of non-being rather than in what seem to be modes of being in a body. Spatial terms obviously can have no possible reference to the Absolute. And yet, on the visible plane, both in the sky and in the sea, we have two conspicuous, all-powerful representations of that which is incapable of limitation, that which is so deep and homogeneous that it is incapable of being understood in terms of visible motion, movements and waves. No human being who has ever reflected upon the sky or sea can fail to have some sense of what the Absolute is like. No one who has ever reflected upon all the trees, all the birds upon this earth, all the animals, plants and minerals of every kind, all the millions upon millions of elementals that ceaselessly dance in the three kingdoms below the four visible kingdoms, can fail to recognize the immensity and richness of the Absolute even in the realm of the manifest.

Few human beings make the effort of thought and imagination which is the privilege and prerogative of being human and think of the births of all babies on earth, not in numbers, but in terms of monad-souls taking bodies as part of one great pilgrimage. The ceaseless, eternal, endless pilgrimage of all humanity is older than universes and will go on long after this universe has been destroyed. This cannot, after a point, be understood numerically in a linear way. Some other dialectical mode must be used. Minimally, one could think in a Shakespearean way about all tongues, all breaths, all eyes, all hands, all fingers as intimated in many magnificent statues of the Hindu gods. One would have to think in terms of myriads of humanities, and all of them gathering meaning and dignity through the experience of finitude, pain, conditionality and ignorance. At the same time, their sheer persistence through all of these limitations represents the indestructible core of divine discontent in the human soul, seeing beyond all possible experiences, ceaselessly continuing a pilgrimage through innumerable worlds. And yet, these pilgrimages themselves are like the winking of an eye in the ceaseless Life of the Eye of Self-Existence of the Absolute.

Clearly, there is no insuperable difficulty in thinking seriously about the First Fundamental of *Gupta Vidya*. But in thinking of boundless vastitude, if one tries to do so in terms of numbers or in terms of spatial concepts of largeness, one encounters a problem. For example, if one thought of all the grains of sand upon this earth, one might as well call them infinite. And yet, one has common sense and intelligence enough to know that actually there is a finite limit to the number of all the grains of sand upon all the beaches upon this globe. And indeed, one does not have to know very much astronomy to know that there must be a finite limit to everything that is manifested, whether they be planets, stars, galaxies, galactic systems or even grains of sand. No wonder the latter is a favourite metaphor of enlightened beings like Gautama Buddha. There is no human being who cannot understand the notion of the immensity involved in what is so infinitesimally small to the naked eye, a grain of sand. The infinite in the infinitesimal can be experienced by a thinking being not just with reference to the sky and sea, but also with reference to trillions upon trillions of grains of sand. And yet, however unutterable these are in magnitude, they must ultimately be finite. They exist, then, in every noble yet imperfect attempt of any soul to characterize the Absolute, the God beyond all gods.

From this it is also clear that any attempt to begin to understand the Absolute in terms of an image or icon, let alone in terms of something which is outside the cosmos and which is crudely anthropomorphic, would be absurd. It would be the surest way of caricaturing the notion of Deity since, if there is any deity less than the Absolute, that would not be the highest conceivable source worthy of human adoration. Can there be a deity which is equivalent to the Absolute? 'Deity' itself is an abstract notion, and the word 'Absolute' is an imperfect term which has relativity built into it. This can be seen clearly from the use of 'absolute' in ordinary speech: any references to something that we call 'absolutely true' or 'absolutely correct', like any measure of 'absolute heat' or 'absolute cold', are relative to a particular scale of measurements or a particular system of concepts. One does not have to be highly trained in informal logic or formal mathematics to realize that these are necessary notions, but still notions that are man-made, notions that have limitation built into them.

If this is so, we can appreciate the assistance given by enlightened beings to limited and imperfect minds in helping them to get beyond mere spatial or numerical magnitudes and metaphors by invoking poetical speech. Poetical speech is truer, less faulty, more evocative, even though it may involve the imagery of the visible, tangible and spatial. But man is capable of coining and formulating imagery, in art as in science, in poetry as in mathematics, which points beyond itself. And that is why many of the greatest Rishis and Sages have come as Kavis, Divine Poets. They have chosen, instead of characterizing or conceptualizing the Absolute, to celebrate it, to adore it. Therefore, all the great hymns are magnificent acts of celebration – celebrations of life, celebrations of the dignity of death, celebrations of the integrity as well as the compassion of all the laws that work throughout manifestation. The Absolute extends our view of what is known and unknown, pointing beyond all possible pathways, to what is essentially unknowable, transcending all knowledge and cognition.

If there is an Eternal Wisdom in this universe, hidden in the very depths of manifestation, that Eternal Wisdom can only be one aspect of the Absolute. If there is universal ideation, ceaseless ideation by the very greatest beings in all evolution, that universal ideation would be seen because of their greatness merely as a mode of participation in only a tiny portion of the Absolute. And yet, any notion of the Absolute, with all its vastness, its transcendence and its grandeur, would be meaningless if it denied significance to the very least being, to the shortest-lived insect. If the Absolute could not itself be invoked for the sake of giving meaning and beauty, dignity and truth, to the least particle, to whatever existed for the most fleeting second, it would not really afford a proper understanding either of life or the cosmos. It would not be a proper function of the exercise of the human capacity for comprehension through knowledge of life, and therefore it would fail. All human efforts to include, as to exclude, will necessarily fall far short of any attempt to characterize the Absolute. The Absolute summons that in us which does not merely want to characterize or describe, but to understand ceaselessly, to make understanding an eternal process of ceaseless learning, coeval with ceaseless living in a world of ceaseless change, under which remains an indestructible core of changelessness. That core is in every atom, in every being, in every second, in every moment, everywhere and always.

Given this, we can see why the great metaphors of the ancient scriptures are really invitations to deep, calm and continuous reflection upon everything that is. The 'Boundless All', 'that which is and yet is not', 'Eternal Non-being', 'the One Form of Existence', 'the Eternal Parent' and 'the All-Presence' are all expressions that help us because of the beauty of language, and because of the beauty of the concepts they evoke. The ubiquitous presence of Deity can no more be denied than we can deny the existence of the sun and its omnipresent light. Even if there were myriad suns and myriad worlds, the process of the diffusion of light must be analogous to what makes our living possible on this earth and our experience of the visible sun at dawn, midday and dusk. The wise celebrate the ever-present Invisible Sun even in the light of the physical world that surrounds us in our physical bodies. They thereby recognize the ever-existing, invisible Spiritual Sun that gives spiritual and mental illumination ceaselessly. The notion of life is inseparable from the notion of light, but also inseparable from divine cosmic electricity. There is a pulsation thrilling and throbbing even in the darkest period of non-manifestation, and that has sometimes been saluted as the Eternal Great Breath. The breathing in and breathing out of worlds and universes would itself have no meaning if there were not a ceaseless breathing at the very core of all life and light, and of all cosmic electricity.

Yet every one of these poetic notions gets tainted and tortured by the intrinsic limitations of human beings who must start with the limits of the known and extend them. To do this, they must emulate the greatest human beings who always, the more they know, become even more aware of what they do not know. The more gnostic they are, the more agnostic they become and the more they rejoice in the fact that the mathematics of the cosmos transcends the greatest possible representations in laws and equations, in theorems and theories. The authentic beginning of advanced thinking in philosophy of science is the recognition, through the study of mathematical logic, set theory and mathematics, that this is intrinsically so. This is especially true today because of the impressive work in the nineteenth century of outstanding minds who demonstrated conclusively how many infinities one could find in mathematics. One can even construct modes of non-Euclidean geometry in which an infinitude of points can still be related to what is capable of being mapped.

Impressive though this may be, it is but a small part of human knowledge, only a small representation in recent history within a limited field of a knowledge that is as old as thinking man. Many human beings have experienced this in the realm of feeling even more grandly than they have experienced it in the realm of thought. Consider the ecstasy of a child. Consider the sadness of a human being who is ready to finish a single day in the endless series of days that makes up the wheel of existence. Consider the poignancy felt when nearing the moment of death, which is really no more than a trivial hour in a ceaseless journey. All of these are universal experiences of the transcendence of feeling. In all cultures, civilizations and societies, among human beings who are highly sensitive to the deeper levels and subtler vibrations of feeling, there is a firm recognition that more is said through intimation than through explicit representation in external speech or form. This is part of the poetry of human life, part of the poetry of cosmic existence.

What is unsaid is more significant and more real than what is said, because it brings us closer to the Absolute. What is thought by human beings, but thought in a way that they are not even aware of, is often closer and truer to the intrinsic nature of life itself, of consciousness and of the Absolute, than all the thoughts that they bring to the forefront of their attention, let alone the thoughts they articulate and share. There is, therefore, no sense in which a human being can expect to begin to understand the Absolute except by accepting the fact that one is born alone, dies alone and lives alone. So does everything in Nature. And yet, there is nothing in Nature that is not bound up with everything else that exists. This is true in the realm of atoms, true in the realm of plants, true in the realm of human beings. Still, there is a secret solitude to the life journey of every ant, of every fly, of every flower and also of every human being.

The Absolute, then, is the very ground of all reality. All denials of it are meaningless, because they simply trap one in the unreal, which itself is only like a minor shadow of what is an ever-present veil upon the Absolute. To have a sense of the meaning of sacred metaphors such as the 'All-Presence' or the 'Boundless All' is to make come alive infinitude within finitude, transcendence within immanence, boundless space within visible space, eternal duration within limited time. The Absolute is the only conceivable ground of all experience, and it must lie continuously before our physical eyes, as well as our mind's eye and our soul's eye. To make the Absolute the ground of our being, our thinking, our living and our feeling is to recognize that everything which is by its very nature limited because of language, because of gesture, because of definition, because of its captivity within space-time, is merely a kind of apologetic, imperfect representation of that which is beyond representation in the realm of thought and the realm of feeling.

This is not difficult to understand. We are only speaking of what we already know, and what we know that we know. But we cannot bring what we know that we know in the depth of our being – which has sometimes been called the 'I am I' consciousness – into the realm of that which is limited. Therefore, the Absolute is that from which we are self-alienated, owing to our needlessly self-devised limitations. Ultimately, in a Platonic sense or as Shankaracharya pointed out, there is only one error, and that is the root of all errors. It is the treating of that which is ever changing as enduring, that which is unreal as real, or that which is finite as if it had a kind of indefinite extension in the realm of time. This applies to all worlds, all lives, all acts and all relationships. It applies to all religions, all philosophies, all sciences and all systems of thought. That is why it applies to the entire gamut of what we call civilization, which is only at best like a mask upon the great secret, unspeakable, unthinkable pilgrimage of the immortal soul of all Humanity. In other words, in consciousness we can dare further and go beyond what we can construct through thoughts, words, formulations and expressions. We all know this, and that is because most of our life is spent either in sleep or in states of consciousness where we are in no position to articulate our thoughts to anyone, or even to ourselves. Thus philosophers in the East have said that you cannot even begin to pronounce upon human nature until you can first address yourself to Being in all states of non-manifestation, which actually far exceed, in their impact upon our being, what we regard as visible and temporal states.

The central truth in relation to consciousness has already been sensed in relation to matter itself in contemporary science and it was always known to the greatest philosophers. When you think of Absolute Abstract Space, Eternal Duration and Perpetual Motion, there is no manifest motion, no measurable time, no extended space which is not trivial in relation to Duration which is eternal, Motion which is ceaseless, Space which is boundless. We all have a sense of Abstract Space, Eternal Duration and Perpetual Motion; otherwise, we would not be able to live. There would be no light in our eyes, no power to give life. There would be no will, no capability of what Spinoza called *conatus* – self-sustenance of living on and surviving, from day through night into the next day, from one life into the next life through the intermediate states between lives, let alone being able to cross the bridge between our boundaries of existence and those of all other beings now alive in worlds of embodied existence. There would be no way to cross those barriers if we absolutized our finite concepts, making them the sole basis of all knowing. The concepts to which we are ordinarily attached are trivial reflections only of the elementary needs and evanescent wants of what is shadowy in comparison with the immortal, indestructible story of human consciousness. That is why, even though the notion of consciousness would be misleading in relation to the Absolute (which is better seen as a state of unconsciousness or dreamless sleep), yet consciousness itself, like space, duration and motion, is a useful working symbol for the Absolute. But by its nature it is a conditioned symbol, because to the entire gamut of consciousness of all the greatest beings in all the worlds there is still a boundary in matter, in embodiment, and the Absolute must surely far transcend all boundaries.

Thus, when certain ideas are pushed far enough, we get a sense which helps to correct the finitizing tendency of the human mind, its self-imprisonment, its conditioned, habitual bondage to limiting and deceptive notions. Such notions cannot have any basis in reality or in thought when thought is sustained and truly rigorous, thorough and logical, and when philosophy is fearless and daring, questioning and searching in every possible direction. But if all our concepts are conditional, how then can the Absolute be conceived? The simple answer is that it cannot be conceived. The *Mandukya Upanishad* declares it to be inconceivable, unthinkable and unspeakable. Yet what is so daunting in this? There are many things in ordinary life that we find unspeakable because of their ineffable grandeur, but we often attach a much deeper and stronger sense of reality to what is unspeakable than what is spoken. This is a very common experience. Certainly we did this almost constantly until we learnt to lisp and speak in the first two or three years of life. Surely, then, to make this a peculiar problem in relation to the Absolute is itself artificial. It is, in philosophy, a pseudo-problem. Because something is infinite, it does not mean that the human mind cannot set up series, find out ratios and factors, rates of change, and try to understand what is meant by the notion of the infinite.

In relation to the Absolute, we have the greatest scriptures, the most beautiful poetry which elevates our sights, our senses, our sensitivity and feelings. Though inconceivable, there is nothing that is worth conceiving other than the Absolute. And we are conceiving it all the time, because it is the root of the very process of conceiving. If it is the root of the process of conceiving, then we can see how we may get artificially caught in mental cobwebs, which is the ancient description of most human thought and language.

To deny or attempt to ignore the ubiquitous importance of the Absolute is to contradict what we know when we are asleep. Cognition of the Absolute must, by its inherent nature, only be possible to that core in us which itself is unconditional and capable of conceiving to the point where we transcend the limits of conceiving. We are capable of using words like music, which reminds us of the ever-present ground of speech, the interstices, the spaces, the silences between and within words. It is only by developing a taste for silence in sound, for the unmanifest within the manifest, for the unspoken within the spoken, the unrecorded within a world of frail and fugitive and often false recordings – that we come closer to the heartbeat that makes us human. The Absolute is characterized as the Supreme Eternal Heart of all existence because, although it is ever present, it is at the same time never fathomable by thought or word. It is closer to us than anything we can ever say or think, just as there is nothing more fundamental than the beating of the heart, and there is nothing around us that is more palpable, if only we would listen, than the beating of the cosmic heart. Great beings have always shown us how to tune ourselves to the great heart of the cosmos. That is called meditation. They are in ceaseless meditation at all times, in a state of supreme total spiritual wakefulness known as *turiya*. Even if most human beings, by comparison, are like lisping, faltering adolescents because of their inability to contain and continue thought and consciousness to a point where the boundaries are burst, this state of *turiya* is accessible to each and every person.

Just as we took a lot of trouble to learn how to walk and talk, we cannot expect, without a lot of effort, to reverse all the habits of the imprisoning sensorium and the imprisoning finitude of embodiment. We cannot develop a taste for the sheer joy of the exhilarating experience of the Absolute without earnestly availing ourselves in meditation of the finest philosophical and poetical characterizations of the Absolute. These are always found in abundance in Sanskrit literature, wherein the Absolute is seen as not only *Sat* and *Chit*, all consciousness and all reality, but *Ananda*, all joy – but at a level where you cannot separate any one from the others. The joy is in the *Sat*, the *Sat* is in the *Ananda*, the *Sat* and the *Ananda* are in the *Chit*. It is a ceaseless, joyous reality affirming ideation, which is only a kind of sharing of those who are the Builders, making manifestation possible and maintaining it, and Those who within that world of manifestation have transcended all barriers and become totally enlightened, more powerful than all the gods, than the Demiurge, than even the highest beings who maintain manifestation.

It is certainly possible for us, if only we would have the necessary courage, tremendous whole-heartedness and single-mindedness, to break through the fundamental illusion of form, and awaken the subtler senses. It is possible to open the doors and the avenues of true cognition by the immortal monad, which is dateless and deathless and which has little to do with any particular embodiment or any particular set of acts. At this point, we come to see that to revere the Absolute is to revere life itself. It is to revere all humanity and all that exists. It is to revere Nature itself, which through change, death and destruction ceaselessly regenerates itself. Thus, it is to revere the quintessential principle of continuity, the vital principle of self-regeneration which is as potent in every atom as in the Absolute itself.

The Absolute, to those who see it as *Satchitananda*, is most perceptible in the *Anu*, the Atom, but the atom spoken of is more fundamental than those atoms which are purely conceptual devices of modern thought. The *Atman* is the atom. *Brahman* is in the infinitesimal point of timeless, spaceless Duration-Existence, but which itself is at the heart of that which makes space and time not multi-dimensional, but actually without any dimension. This we can understand by considering the mathematics of a point, which has no extension, no length, no breadth or thickness. And this idea itself only reflects the activity of the Absolute, which ceaselessly mirrors itself in billions upon billions upon billions of points, in a transcendental manner applicable to mind or matter, to space or time, to all possible cycles and patterns of causation and to all possible worlds.

Thus it is that the greatest and the wisest beings have always known that the way to recognize and revere the Absolute is by revering the Absolute in the here and now – in every hair on every head, in every blade of grass and everything that breathes. The God beyond all gods is in every pair of eyes. Reverence for the Absolute is a whole way of life in which we totally cooperate with the eternal heartbeat of the universe, cooperate with it through spiritual breathing, mental breathing, through a certain conscious, constant, ceaseless, boundless pulsation of eternal prostration and eternal reverence. To live in this way is to dare to challenge the unknowable and to give dignity to the process of eternal knowing and learning – which is the dialogue of the soul with itself. This is true philosophy, true speech, the true dialogue of the Self with itself. We can only talk about the Absolute when we talk to the God in ourselves, and we cannot do it suddenly if we do not do it daily. Actually, we do it all the time, but we are not aware of this. But when we do it consciously, and not just with a limited notion of ourselves but with a notion of divine Selfhood that has a place for everything that exists, the whole of life becomes a dialogue with the

Absolute. That dialogue becomes the life of Soul itself. The richer it is, the more rooted in the non-manifest. And when words are spoken or acts are performed, it makes them sacred and meaningful, giving them the beauty and dignity of the Divine Dance. If this, then, is our understanding of it, there is nothing which could be solely relevant to the Absolute, and at the same time there is nothing which is not so relevant.

This brings us closer, then, to the Eye of the *Dangma*, the Eye of the Sage, who breathes the Absolute, fully and self-consciously – who is name and form and without name and form, who is each and every other being and yet beyond all, and who sees worlds by analogy with the day and night of every being on the physical plane. In it he sees the Day and Night of worlds and universes. To him there is no difference. It is the same process. Every time the Sage sees a human being asleep, whether a baby or an old person, it is all the same. He sees all beings asleep, all worlds asleep – because the Sage is incapable of limitation through the perceptual realm. Long ago he went far beyond the unfolding of all the subtler senses, where there is simultaneous, instantaneous transmission of thought. Nothing can happen on a star which does not affect us, say the poets, and nothing could happen to a star which the Sage does not instantly feel.

We have, then, in the Sage a concept of living and breathing which so far transcends all possible human conceptions of perfection and enlightenment that no Sage could ever convey it fully by words or acts, gestures or postures. When Sages have spoken, whether it be Adi Shankara speaking of the *Tattvamasi mantram*, or Gautama Buddha speaking of experiencing *nirvana* in *samsara*, or K'ung Fu Tzu speaking of the Great Extreme, all they have done is essentially what we would do to children: provide pregnant analogies to make souls question and think. Above all, individuals must be encouraged to turn within themselves, wherein there is a richer experience, a greater realm of living, loving and knowing than they could ever find in the external realm. To begin to become sagely is to awaken the memory of the immortal soul, which has had myriads of parents, myriads of friends, myriads of co-workers, and to make all of that deeply, powerfully relevant to each and every moment, in each and every context.

Thus, Dakshinamurti, the Initiator of Initiates, the paradigm of all Sages, the supreme incarnation of Maheshvara, is himself unthinkable and unspeakable like the Absolute. To speak of the one is to speak of the other, which is why wise human beings use meditation upon the *Guruparampara*, the sacred lineage of true Sages, as a way of coming closer to the Absolute. Every child uses the help of its mother or father or an adult to learn how to walk. That is Nature's way. That is what comes naturally to the human being, and it is that which is ultimately the Only Way, the only door to greater knowledge, greater experience, profounder apprehension, deeper comprehension and, even more, to a taste or a foretaste of *Satchitananda*. If a person understood all of this, he or she would quickly see that to limit the unmanifest by the manifested, or the inexhaustible Absolute by any possible notion of a first cause or any particular limited God, would indeed be to limit Man. To limit Humanity, whether in terms of two thousand years or eighteen million years, would be equally irrelevant. It would truly be to deny the very visible facts of the cosmos and human life, thereby cutting oneself off from one's truest life, which is no other than the Divine Ground of the attributeless Absolute, the blissful state of silent, ceaseless contemplation (*SAT-CHIT-ANANDA*).

Hermes, July 1989

DEITY IN ACTION

Absolute Unity cannot pass to infinity; for infinity presupposes the limitless extension of something, and the duration of that 'something, and that One All is like Space – which is its only mental and physical representation on this Earth, on our plane of existence – neither an object of, nor a subject to, perception. If one could suppose the Eternal Infinite All, the Omnipresent Unity, instead of being in Eternity, becoming through periodical manifestation a manifold Universe or a multiple personality, that Unity would cease to be one. Locke's idea that "pure Space is capable of neither resistance nor Motion" – is incorrect. Space is neither a "limitless void", nor a "conditioned fullness" but both: being, on the plane of absolute abstraction, the ever-incognisable Deity, which is void only to finite minds, and on that of mayavic perception, the Plenum, the absolute Container of all that is, whether manifested or un-manifested: it IS therefore, that Absolute ALL.

The Secret Doctrine, i 8

It is fruitful to consider the Ever-existent Absolute and everything that is intrinsically relative in the light of the distinction between unity and infinity, eternity and periodicity, the relationless and that which is inextricably bound by relations. First of all, absolute unity is beyond infinity as spatial or temporal extension, even if boundless and endless, for it transcends polarization into infinite and finite, unbounded and bounded, which are correlative terms. It is important to grasp this truth fully and clearly, and to assimilate it completely, so that anyone can readily acknowledge the Rootless Root which is beyond perception and conception, images and ideas, beyond the fleeting and fickle awareness of objects and subjects, and even beyond the Creative *Logos*, the One Source and Ground of all manifestation. Each and every human being can say truly within the silence of the inmost heart:

I am I. I am the perceiver, the spectator, the eternal witness, intact and unmodified, attributeless, *sui generis. I am Brahman, Brahman am I.* I and the Absolute are one, always and forever, in all spaces and conditions and contexts. I am No-Thing, absolute voidness, *shunyata, nirguna brahman,* in a constant state of *nir-vikalpa samadhi,* changeless amidst all change, beginningless and endless even amidst births and deaths, in a state of *parinishpanna,* supreme self-awareness as the One Self-Existent.

Oral Instruction, Maitreya Seminar, September 25, 1987

Secondly, Universal Kosmic Mind ever abides, both during *pralaya* and *manvantara.* It is immutable, unmodifiable – the *plenum* of infinite potentials. This unconditioned consciousness becomes relative consciousness or *mahat* periodically at every manvantaric dawn. The Mahatma, who is not only one with *mahat* – the mind of the cosmos – but also attuned beyond *mahat* and primordial *ahankara* to the Universal Mind, is in a state of serene *turiya,* supreme, total, spiritual wakefulness. He is undistracted during *manvantaras,* undisturbed during *pralayas,* ever retentive – *smartava* – of the pristine vibration of the manvantaric dawn during cosmic and human evolution. This state of serene, absolute awareness is beyond the relativities and polarities of consciousness, which are merely modifications and manifestations of the One *chit,* the Supreme Ideation behind and beyond all creation, all change and all transformation.

Thirdly, if one of the ways in which we can distinguish the Absolute from everything relative is that the Absolute always stands out of all relation to anything, and the relative is always in some relationship or the other, then mind at any level of manifestation will be inextricably involved in relations and relativities. Thus, understanding and mastery of the nature of those networks of relations matters a great deal to one's effective capacity for self-transcendence. True knowledge or the highest wisdom ever sees what is essential among hosts of inessential, secondary and tertiary emanations, whilst rejecting nothing and assigning a proper place and new significance to each and every form, colour and number, polarity and relativity. Always aware of the quintessential distinction between internal and external relations, and the continuous modification of each through the other, which determines the regulated flow of *kundalini shakti* within the etheric astral spine, the Mahatma is fully able to overcome the process of transmigration, as well as to transmute it during voluntary and partial incarnations into this world. This is *tattvajnana* – the knowledge of *tatvas* or essences – but especially in relation to the *adhitatva*, the one Supreme Element, the one Fohatic Force behind all forces, the one Reality behind and beyond all appearances, from the most sublime, the most rarefied, the most ethereal, to the most mundane, the most tangible, and the most immediate.

Given all this, anyone can see how human consciousness must move to higher levels through a steady increase in its reflective awareness of its own relations and relativities, as well as through the progressive awakening of its own fundamentally unmodified nature. In practice, these two processes are inseparable. The Immortal Spectator goes through a series of progressive awakenings from lesser to greater horizons of awareness, from derivative causes through primary causes to the Ceaseless, Causeless Cause, and from primary relations to the Three-in-One, which radiates from the Ever-concealed One. The Self-moving Soul graduates through identification and attachment to the transient to greater identification with the "One without a second", beyond form, beyond colour and beyond all limitation. The sovereign means of egoic self-mastery is through threefold meditation upon indivisible *mulaprakriti* – the indestructible Root Substance – upon the unmanifested *Logos*, the source and synthesis of the primary seven *Logoi*, and upon the one Fohatic Force of universal ideation behind and beyond cosmic electricity and cosmic *eros*, cosmic magnetism and cosmic radiation. Such meditation is a constant abidance in the never manifested but ever-existent Three-in-One, beyond the divine dance of the One *Logos* or Krishna-Shiva-Christos, and the seven planes or forty-nine states of conscious existence.

Karma is Deity in action – the eternal, divine pulsation and breathing of the Absolute. It is the Unknowable at its Rootless Root, but it is partly cognizable as a law of eternal causation and ethical retribution, mirroring and maintaining the universal unity and total interdependence of all gods, monads and atoms. On the three formless *arupa* planes, and on the four planes of conditioned consciousness and modified ever-changing matter, it reflects absolute harmony, justice and compassion. These are ceaselessly mirrored in the workings and manifestations of karmic sub-totals, embodied in the vestures, the ideational causation of all beings, the networks of interrelations between the seven kingdoms and all the beings therein. Karma is the progressive driving force behind cosmic and human evolution and involution, and, as such, it is inexorable, impersonal, universal, irresistible, omnipresent and omnipotent. Self-conscious monads can cooperate with this Law, but they cannot cancel or supersede it. Every instance of working against the Law, consciously or unconsciously, is an inevitable precursor of pain and suffering, disillusionment and disappointment, persisting ignorance and delusion, which must eventually culminate in self-alienation and the doom of total self-destruction. For finite minds, the operation of karma must be understood as relative to past and to future, to context and condition, to planes of consciousness and states of matter. This intrinsic relativity is due to the subject-object relationship, which must vary with all planes and sub-planes, with all states and sub-states, with all globes and vestures, with all degrees of apprehension, and all levels of awareness, ranging from atoms to worlds, from infusoria and living organisms to the myriad stars and galaxies. Thus, the vast order of relations is inclusive of all possible worlds, all orders of being, and also the cosmic hierarchies extending downward from *Dhyanis* to *devas* and *devatas*, from the Demiurge and the Divine Host of Builders to all the elementals that belong to the invisible cosmos behind the visible universe.

Anyone's understanding of the Absolute and the relative, as it applies to the philosophy of perfection, depends upon the grasp of this fundamental theory, difficult and abstract though it may be. Perfection must be relative to the vestures and conditions experienced by monads, as well as the degrees of unconsciousness, partial self-consciousness, and even universal self-consciousness of thinking beings – ideating selves – in a world of differentiating objects and multiple agents and selves. There can be no static final perfection. Humanity can and should understand and enjoy the host of perfections as consummations of the repeated use of skills, of faculties, and of instruments of cognition and action. Such growth and maturation come through self-correction, through learning from the lessons of life, and as the result of experiments with limited truth in changing contexts. Absolute perfection must pertain to universal self-consciousness in the highest possible and conceivable sense. It is meaningful precisely because of the existence and living reality of Those who have attained to that state. But even such Beings, when embodied in available vestures at any given time, and when working with the available materials on any globe or in any period of evolution, must take on the relative imperfections of the race or the age in which they incarnate. At the same time, Their voluntary incarnations vindicate the promise and the possibility open to all egos of perfecting conditions and vestures, whilst honouring, serving and reaching out to the Knowers of the Three-in-One.

Even the mention of absolute perfection requires one to take several steps upward, metaphysically, to consider Absolute Being, Divine Thought and the ideal Kosmos. Firstly, all are helped to consider Absolute Being by an extraordinary and challenging question raised by H.P. Blavatsky in *The Secret Doctrine*:

> As the highest Dhyan Chohan, however, can but bow in ignorance before the awful mystery of Absolute Being; and since, even in that culmination of conscious existence – "the merging of the individual in the universal consciousness" – to use a phrase of Fichte's – the Finite cannot conceive the Infinite, nor can it apply to its own standard of mental experiences, how can it be said that the "Unconscious" and the Absolute can have even an instinctive impulse or hope of attaining clear self-consciousness?

Here is an important reference to the error of absolute idealism in its modern form, which has tinctured philosophical thought for the past three centuries. The error of absolute idealism consists in the view that the Absolute, being equivalent to absolute mind and absolute freedom, can be known by thought and emulated by the conscious ego, which is wholly autonomous as a mirror of the Absolute. Even Fichte fell into this error, though he saw that the infinite cannot conceive the finite, and also that, compared to what we call consciousness, the Absolute must be the Supreme Unconscious.

Schelling, on the other hand, stressed the inconceivability of the Absolute, even though he felt it must be the object of true philosophy in its search for a science of the Absolute. Hegel criticized Schelling's view as an empty abstraction, whilst Schelling in turn dismissed Hegel's attempt to ascribe absolute attributes to the Absolute as panlogicism. Hegel was concerned to distinguish between different phases in the

Absolute, from supreme unconsciousness to self-consciousness. If God is asleep, how to wake him up? If the Absolute is unconscious, how to get things moving and produce self-consciousness in itself, let alone in the world? This concern of Hegel, to distinguish between different phases in the Absolute from supreme unconsciousness to self-conscious alienation from itself in the world of appearances, was prompted by his wish to describe its recovery of full self-consciousness, in history and in the world, through all its emanated rays. Hence, he felt compelled to speak unphilosophically of the Absolute as capable of becoming self-conscious, or at least of having an impulse towards self-consciousness, and he used this conception to explain the dialectical unfoldment in time and history of various phases of the Absolute.

By contrast, the highest *Dhyanis* and all Mahatmas, who are tribeless and raceless and belong to no single religion except the religion of the One, recognize the absolute transcendence by the Absolute of even absolute consciousness or Divine Thought. They therefore show that the highest gnosis heightens the joyous sense of wonder and reverence, the ever deepening of states of Silence, and an open-ended agnosticism that sees beyond all worlds, all systems of thought, and even the highest possible conceptions of even perfected human beings. The finest statement of this Teaching given in eighteen million years is by Rishi Sanatsujata, the Initiator of Initiates, in the *Mahabharata*. He explains that Silence is meditation, Silence is the *Atman*, Silence is the *AUM*. There are clearly depths upon depths in the highest meditations and the deepest silences, and the Soundless Sound points beyond itself, just as all sounds point beyond themselves, to the Silence of the Soundless Sound. This is the unknown darkness of the Absolute, the Divine Darkness that is beyond worlds and must ever surround the Absolute in its absoluteness. Its absoluteness is known as *parabrahman*, the emphasis being on *para* – beyond – as the *shloka* said of Buddha at the close of the *Heart Sutra*:

> *gate gate paragate parasamgate bodhi svaha*
> Gone, gone, gone beyond,
> Gone to the other shore, O Bodhi!
> So let it be.

Secondly, in relation to the exalted conceptions of Divine Thought and the ideal Kosmos, H.P. Blavatsky explained in *The Secret Doctrine* that:

> It is only with reference to the intra-cosmic soul, the ideal Kosmos in the immutable Divine Thought, that we may say: "It never had a beginning nor will it have an end." With regard to its body or Cosmic organization, though it cannot be said that it had a first, or will ever have a last construction, yet at each new *Manvantara*, its organization may be regarded as the first and the last of its kind, as it evolutes every time on a higher plane.

Whilst there is no first or last in the appearance of worlds, epochs of manifestation and subsequent periods of nonmanifestation, the cosmic process is not a mechanical repetition of cyclical recurrence for two important reasons. First of all, the ideal Kosmos can only be partially and imperfectly reflected in any series of actual universes. And at the same time, secondly, there is a progression in awareness and in modes of substance between *manvantaras*, owing to the inexhaustible potential contained in the all-sufficient ideal Kosmos. Yet, whilst the intra-cosmic soul, the ideal Kosmos in all-comprehending Divine Thought, is beginningless and endless, it is not the Absolute. Divine Thought itself represents the highest knowledge accessible, beyond which lies the unknown darkness of the Absolute.

Thus, one of the highest mysteries lies in the fact that the Absolute finds its highest expression in its greatest Knowers, the wisest Beings throughout the ages. Further, this mystery is reflected in the relativity of time itself, wherein each time-bound epoch of embodied existence is dependent upon a prior cause. It also represents a unique manifestation that can never be exactly duplicated. In this sense, even the relative reality of each epoch of manifestation must have an immense sanctity, one which is in no way diminished by the consideration of preceding and succeeding epochs, or even by the contrast between actual manifestation and the ideal Kosmos in the Divine Thought. This is important, because when most people think of progression, they tend to think in a utilitarian and time-bound manner of succession as supersession. The latest must be the best, apparently, and yet is itself only a means to an end, a higher state in the future. To think in this self-contradictory way is to misunderstand completely the Absolute, the realm of the relative, and also the mysterious concepts of mirroring and inevitably incomplete incarnation. This persistent error arises out of the failure to see that the supremely transcendent Absolute is also ever present in anything and everything existent. The Absolute is universally immanent.

To take a time-honoured example, much favoured by all the Rishis and Sages, who are poets and seers as well as philosophers and renouncers, the leaves of a tree are similar and also subtly different, each radiating, especially when newly sprouted, the freshness of its uniqueness. Each tree is also unique, and one can imagine that from the seed of each healthy evergreen tree there may arise trees that are even finer or grander than those before. But the quintessential sap in every tree that springs from the seeds of its predecessor is the same. It is the primordial sap, which is inexhaustibly potent. Similarly, seekers of enlightenment have to recognize and revere the all-potent sap of the Absolute, as well as the inexhaustible fecundity of the ideal Kosmos, potentially present in the Absolute. They must venerate the inconceivable richness and diversity of unique expressions of ideal forms, as well as the ever-expanding and ever-deepening awareness of all the myriad hosts of hierarchies, from the highest and most homogeneous to the lowest and most heterogeneous, from *manvantara* to *manvantara*. This is what Plato meant by the statement that time is the moving image of eternity. It is a celebration of endless continuity as well as infinite diversity amidst the seeming discontinuities in the realm of appearances. To know this is to live in the Eternal Now. Every atom is sacred, and so too is every grain of dust. Just as the Absolute beyond all absolutes is sacred, so too are all the omniscient Knowers of *Brahma Vach*, regardless of all the variations among them, and even differences of degree in universal self-consciousness.

This sense of limitless sanctity throughout all manifestation brings the true seeker of the *OM* to the mystical and powerful idea of the Diamond Soul of the Avatar. One could think of and see the Avatar as a shining Jewel, precipitated from the Absolute into the realm of the relative, a Jewel so multi-faceted that all sentient beings may find means of approach by some aspect of the Light that it compassionately radiates in every direction. As Krishna, the Purna Avatar and the paradigm of all Avatars – who are all one and the same – states, "In whatever way men approach Me, in that way do I assist them." Sacred texts speak of the alchemical and therapeutic influence of the Avatar upon all three worlds, and upon all beings belonging to all the seven kingdoms of Nature, as well as upon the entire host of three hundred and thirty million *devas* and *devatas*. At the same time, they also speak of the Avatar as *achyuta* – as inseparable from the mysterious Spiritual Sun, with its immaculate seven primordial rays. Despite the divine Avataric descent and the universal diffusion of supernal light, there is that which neither descends nor differentiates, but is close to the inmost fiery core of the One that never comes or goes but Ever Is, the Self-Existent. There is also the statement in the *Bhagavad Gita* that all Rishis and Mahatmas, all *Dhyanis* and *devas*, are contained within the Divine sphere of the invisible universal form, the *vishvarupa* of the Avatar.

> Behold, O son of Pritha, My myriad divine forms in their hundreds and thousands of variegated colours and shapes.
>
> Behold the Adityas and Vasus, Rudras and Ashvins, and also the Maruts. Behold myriad wonders never seen before, O son of Bharata.
>
> Behold here and now the whole world comprising the moving and motionless, abiding as a unity within My body, O Gudakesha, and whatever else thou wishes to see.
>
> Thou canst not see Me with this thine eye alone. I give thee the Divine Eye (*divya chakshu*). Behold My yoga as the God of all.
>
> *Bhagavad Gita* XI. 5-8

This Sacred Teaching helps one to understand, at some level, the beautiful image of the Diamond Soul, the divine essence of absolute truth, who is *Vajradhara*, the holder of the weapon of righteousness, and also *Vajrapani*, especially to his close disciples. He is the compassionate holder of the Jewel of Wisdom, which becomes the Way and the Path for those who are willing and in earnest, as well as the elixir of immortality and the philosopher's stone for highly developed souls who are ready for further initiations into the Mysteries. The same esoteric teaching is also behind the *trikaya* doctrine of Mahayana, the three vestures of *dharmakaya*, *sambhogakaya* and *nirmanakaya*. The first corresponds to the state of *nirguna brahman*, the second to the state of *saguna brahman*, and the third to the state of Mahatmas and Bodhisattvas, who live in this world, unseen and unknown but ever helpful to all souls who are ready to receive the light of truth, wisdom and compassion. At another level, there is also a similar secret teaching in regard to the simultaneous triple incarnation of a perfected enlightened being, as a transcendental Buddha, a mediating Bodhisattva, and an incarnated Teacher of Enlightenment. All point to the ineffable, inconceivable and inexpressible Absolute, the supreme, transcendental Source of all light, all life and all love.

Now, the intuitive today must look at the Absolute Godhead and relative self-consciousness because the Avatar is a fact. What about the Avatar or the Mahatmas as an ideal? There is the priceless instruction:

> "*Paramartha*" is self-consciousness in Sanskrit, *Svasamvedana*, or "the self-analysing reflection" – from two words, *parama* (above everything) and *artha* (comprehension), *Satya* meaning absolute true being, or Esse. In Tibetan *Paramarthasatya* is *Dondampaidenpa*. The opposite of this absolute reality, or actuality, is *Samvritisatya* – the relative truth only – "*Samvriti*" meaning "false conception" and being the origin of illusion, *Maya*; in Tibetan *Kundzabchi-denpa*, " illusion-creating appearance".

> *The Secret Doctrine*, i 48

Paramarthasatya, like the Absolute, is supreme, transcendent, universal self-consciousness, the One and Only Self-Existent beyond all worlds and beings, all states and conditions. But *paramarthasatya* is correlative with *samvrittisatya*, and thus refers to the continual cancelling of all that is evanescent, fascinating and enslaving. It refers to the transcendence of all that is deceptive and alluring in the realm of appearances, relativities and relations, the realm of relative truths, partial truths and falsehoods, of unrealities and illusions. All these elements of *samvritti* can give rise to errors, but nowhere more persistently and poignantly than in relation to the sin of partial and partisan selfhood, the sin of separateness from the whole and from all other parts. This can be countered by a vigorous dialectic of continual negation, such as that taught by Nagarjuna. It ever demands the voiding of all false conceptions, entities and selves, coupled with the ready willingness to enter the Supreme Void, the Divine Darkness, wherein is hidden the ineffable light that is nameless and formless, signless and shadowless. That light of the *Logos, Daiviprakriti*, is best worshipped in the silence of the secret sanctuary of the spiritual heart, which mirrors the compassion of the *vajrasattva*, the Diamond Soul.

Jnanayoga, the path of Divine Wisdom, involves ever-deepening levels of vision attained by the Seer, but Divine Wisdom cannot be a subject for study in any ordinary intellectual sense. It may be an object for search, however, once one awakens in oneself the desire to begin the search and learns how to sustain the light of enquiry. True enquiry must begin in self-enquiry and must persist until, as veil upon veil lifts, there is an acceptance that there will be veils upon veils behind. The pupil must persist in the progressive discovery of the distinction between the Self and non-self, willing to see that seeming life is really death, and that what seems to be non-being leads to true being. This painful and persistent search for the one Self hidden in each and all beings, worlds and conditions will eventually lead to the recognition, at some stage of one's quest, that one is both the subject and the object of the search, because transcendent Divine Wisdom is within oneself and it is also in each and every noetic soul on its great "pilgrimage of necessity." Within oneself is the entrance to the sanctuary of the cosmic Heart, the Supreme Self, the omnipresent *AUM* who is *Ishvara*, the *paramatman*, known ultimately as *parabrahman*, the sole source and *sine qua non* of Deity in action in the manifested cosmos.

The mysterious mirroring of the Ultimate Reality is itself the mighty and magical power of *maya*, the creative capacity of the *Logos*, and the source of illusory manifestation. This means that the polarity of *paramartha* and *samvritti*, of *nirvana* and *samsara*, is ultimately mayavic, and that the true path of Divine Wisdom cannot be a mere negation of manifestation as illusion. Thus the twentieth century Tamil poet Muruganar states:

> To cling to the void and neglect compassion is to fall short of the highest path. To practice compassion is not to abandon the toils of existence. He who is mighty in the practice of both passes beyond *nirvana* and *samsara*.

This Sacred Teaching is the Secret Heart of *Gupta Vidya*, and is central to the purest and highest Mahayana teaching of the Gelukpa tradition in Tibet. It was reaffirmed in this century through silence and speech by Shri Ramana Maharshi, who urged one and all who came to him to keep searching for the origin of the 'I-thought' in asking the age-old question "Who am I?" until it dissolves in the attributeless Supreme Self in the Silence, which is Wisdom-Compassion. It alone can give the true strength to do one's *dharma*, the best one can in this world of *samsara*, whilst abiding alone, aloof and apart in the blissful awareness of the vestureless state of *nirvana*, supreme non-doing, or pure being.

Once one sees that *samsara* can be equated to *samvrittisatya*, and that *nirvana* can be equated to *paramarthasatya*, one may apprehend the nature of the Highest Path. Both *samsara* and *nirvana* are states of mind. What humanoids call this world is a state of mind. Because both *samsara* and *nirvana* are states of mind, they may therefore be seen as contrasting states of consciousness – *samvrittisatya* corresponding to the realm of relativities and relative truths, and *paramarthasatya* to the realm of the Absolute, the transcendental, the dateless and deathless, the ever existent. In deep sleep, in meditation, in times of the deepest silence and stillness and during the calm of ceaseless contemplation, anyone who is pure and patient can touch the threshold and have a taste of nirvanic completeness. While in waking consciousness and in chaotic sleep, souls are tossed upon the tempestuous waves of samsaric existence, which is transient, conditioned, provisional and probationary. It is solely meant for the soul's learning of the lessons of life.

The Highest Path must represent the dissolution of all dichotomies and dualities, and the transcendence of the very contrast between two worlds – the world of time and the world of eternity, the world of matter and the world of spirit, the world of temporal change and the world of timeless duration. If the former is only a veil upon the latter, mortality is a mask for the immortal ray of the Supreme *Logos* in the cosmos, and the world of appearance serves merely as a School of ceaseless renunciation and disinterested performance of duties. In it all disciples may learn the relinquishment of the acquisitive karma of results, as well as skilful means, in the sacrificial application of Divine Wisdom to each and every atom in every sphere of ever-moving life. The Path to serene enlightenment is secret and sacred because it cannot be seen from the outside, and cannot be told by words or conveyed through acts. Yet it is that to which everything points. Anything can intimate the *AUM* to the meditative soul in the Silence of the spiritual comradeship of those who have chosen Krishna-Christos, saluting and emulating the Knowers and Exemplars of *Brahma Vach*.

Hermes, September 1989

BUDDHA AND THE PATH
TO ENLIGHTENMENT

II. The Message of Buddha

When in deep silent hours of thought
The Holy Sage to Truth attains,
Then is he free from joy and sorrow,
Released from Form and the Formless Realm.

Udana

The course of Buddha's prolonged vigil is often portrayed as a progressive ascent through a series of luminous states of being, rather like the gradual lifting of shrouds of darkness and the rapturous unveiling of the roseate dawn. Tradition testifies that in the first watch of the night he witnessed all his former incarnations and comprehended the poignant pilgrimage of humanity and the strenuous path of full emancipation. During the second watch, his spiritual insight, unbounded by space and untrammelled by time, expanded, opening the Divine Eye (*divya chakshu*), which sees the inevitable dissolution of form and the involuntary rebirth of beings, yielding direct apprehension of the most difficult of themes, the intricate workings of the Law of Karma. During the third watch of the night, Buddha directed his attention to the invisible and visible worlds and grasped the immense implications of the Four Noble Truths, *chattari ariya sachchani* (Skt. *chatvari arya satyani*), the central core of all his subsequent teaching. Thus Buddha attained complete Enlightenment on the full moon night of *Vesakha* at the place which came to be known as Bodh Gaya.

If *shunyata* is initially apprehended as the "voidness of the seeming full", the radical negation of ignorance (*avidya*), *shunyata* is then positively experienced as a boundless *plenum*, the "fullness of the seeming void".

Nirvana is supreme bliss, *parama sukha*, utterly unconditioned, free from sickness (*aroga*), free from fear (*abhaya*), free from taint (*anashrava*). It is pure joy (*shiva*), deep peace (*shanta*) and calm assurance (*kshema*), unsullied by ageing (*ajara*), and untouched by death (*amata*). *The Voice of the Silence* provides a memorable portrait of one who has attained perfect insight:

> He standeth now like a white pillar to the west, upon whose face the rising Sun of thought eternal poureth forth its first most glorious waves. His mind, like a becalmed and boundless ocean, spreadeth out in shoreless space. He holdeth life and death in his strong hand.

Buddha chose to set aside the joyous outcome of his complete Enlightenment. He deliberately postponed his entry into *Parinirvana*, the primordial source of all derivative states of consciousness on lesser planes of being – and so, from one point of view, severance from the variegated field of *maya*. He had initially vowed to find a solution to the problem of universal involvement in inexorable suffering. This meant that he had resolved from the first to translate the wisdom he gained, even if it be equivalent to the ultimate gnosis, into an accessible means which any honest seeker could employ in the quest for self-emancipation. So Buddha continued to contemplate under the Bodhi Tree for several weeks, crystallizing his insights into a compact, yet compelling, message that he could transmit to others. And he deeply pondered whether or not it was truly possible to convey his profound insights with sufficient clarity and urgency to inspire many to pursue the solitary path he had trod. It is said that, before his birth and after his Enlightenment, he reflected upon the lotus and likened its phases of growth to the human odyssey. Many lotuses under water are so entangled in the mire at the bottom of the pond that they cannot rise to the surface; analogously, many human beings are so submerged in ignorance that they would remain deaf to all alternatives. A few lotuses are already close to the light of the sun; such individuals need no counsel. But alas, there are those in the middle, desperately needing the assurance of sunlight and the hope of approaching its radiant warmth. For the sake of reaching as many of these as possible, Buddha rose from his meditation and returned to a world he had renounced, attempting the formidable task of communicating the possibility and promise of universal emancipation.

Buddha recalled with affection his original mentors, Arada Kalama and Udraka Ramaputra, but both had died since he left them to take up his austere life in the forest. He then proceeded to proclaim his message to the five ascetics who had once shared his severe asceticism and then been repelled by his sudden repudiation of their mode of life. He saw them at Isipatana (now called Sarnath) near Varanasi, but when they beheld him at a distance, they agreed amongst themselves to avoid him and to ignore his presence. As he calmly approached them, however, the serene beauty of his noble countenance, the lustrous aura of inner peace which shone around him and his transparent assurance compelled their attention. Declaring that he had discovered the means to Enlightenment and was now fully awakened (*samma sambuddha*), he proclaimed the Four Noble Truths. His first sermon has come down through the centuries, appropriately called the *Dhammachakka Pavattana Sutta* (Setting in Motion the Wheel of Dharma).

The First Noble Truth is that all existence is enmeshed in suffering, *duhkha*. Whatsoever exists comes into being and must eventually pass away. Constant change is inescapable and entails much pain. Birth initiates suffering, growth means suffering, sickness and old age cause pain, and death brings sorrow. Psychologically, the past, present and future entail suffering, for recollection breeds remorse and anticipation engenders anxiety. Human consciousness is caught in a contest between inexplicable fear and ineradicable hope. Its imaginative capacity to visualize a better condition induces further pain, owing to the glaring gap between "what is" and "what might be". Suffering is indeed the concomitant of human existence and the piteous plight of all sentient creatures.

The Second Noble Truth is that all suffering has a basic cause (*samudaya*). If this were not so, there could be no means of release from the bondage of sensate existence. The entire assemblage of proximate causes of misery may be traced through a long chain of causation to a single source: *tanha* or *trishna*, "thirst". This continual thirst or deep-seated craving for embodied existence is not simply the pure, objectless desire to be, which is Nirvana, for no impure desire can summon or penetrate that unqualified and unquantified state of peace. As all craving is for sentient life in manifest form – mental, physical, even spiritual – and form necessitates limitation, coming to be and passing away, so this craving is unceasing. The Third Noble Truth is that this ubiquitous cause, which initiates the entire chain of causation, can be countered, transcended and negated (*nirodha*).

The Fourth Noble Truth affirms that the well-tested means by which all misery is ended is the Noble Eightfold Path (*atthangikamagga*, Skt. *ashtangikamarga*). It is the *majjhima patipada*, the Middle Way between self-indulgence and self-mortification, neither of which is edifying. The eightfold series of interrelated stages of spiritual awakening leads to the fullness of freedom. It begins with right perception and understanding, a clear and firm grasp of the Four Noble Truths, combining mental discipline and open-textured conceptualization. Right thought is the deliberate resolve, the confident release of the volition, to follow the Eightfold Path to its farthest end. Right speech infuses non-violence, benevolence and harmony into the individual's most potent means of interaction with others, and also fosters tranquillity of thought and feeling. "Never a harsh truth", Buddha said, "and never a falsehood, however pleasing." Right action exemplifies conservation of energy, timeliness and economy, calming and cleansing the emotions. Although many Buddhists have drawn up diverse lists of prohibitions over the centuries, the basic principle of right action is that appropriation and expropriation are improper. Right action is facilitated in daily life by right livelihood. If action should not injure others, one's means of livelihood should not exploit anyone, and one's work in this world should contribute, however modestly, to universal well-being and welfare. Right effort would be marked by continuity of endeavour and thus conduce to the maintenance of right mindfulness, vigilant attention in regard to one's thoughts, feelings and acts, and their interaction with the intentions of others as well as the psycho-physical environment. Right meditation requires concentrated one-pointedness at all times and regular periods of intense absorption in exalted states of consciousness.

The Four Noble Truths are starkly simple, yet far-reaching and profound. They subsume observable facts under broader laws of noetic psychology, fusing an acute awareness of the human condition with the testable promise of self-redemption and effective service of others. The Eightfold Path is formulated as a series of steps, but these are intertwined and recurrent stages of growth at greater levels of apprehension. Wisdom, *prajna*, commences and completes the journey, whilst righteous conduct, *shila*, becomes the stimulus as well as the outcome of deep meditation, *samadhi*, which in turn refines compassion, strengthens morality and ripens wisdom into a wholeness that makes one's breathing benevolent. Thus, one ascends a spiral stairway of being, returning to the same point at a greater elevation, but moving at an assured pace towards an ever-widening horizon. Eventually one is stripped of all one's fetters and effortlessly merges with the empyrean. "The dewdrop slips into the shining sea." This ideal of Buddhahood can be mirrored in mental states that precede complete Enlightenment.

The five ascetics who were fortunate to hear Buddha's first sermon readily accepted his message without reservation, for it gave coherence to their own experiments and endeavours. They became the earliest members of the Sangha, and thus honoured the Triple Gem (*triratna*) of Buddhist tradition. A few days after his first sermon Buddha delivered the *Anatta Lakkhana Sutta*, propounding the Doctrine of No-Self. What the ignorant individual mistakes as the self, the enduring and unchanging unity of a being or object, is a persisting illusion. A person, seemingly constituted of mind and body, is actually a mutable composite of *skandhas*, heaps or aggregates, which come together and coalesce, only to separate after a time. When they come together, the person or object comes into being as a seeming entity, and when they radically separate, death is said to have intervened. These volatile aggregates can be broadly categorized into five classes: *rupa* or form, *vedana*, feeling or sensation, *sanjna* or perception, *sanskara* or mental impulses, tendencies and predilections, and *vijnana* or sensory consciousness. Owing to the fact that these *skandhas* come together in a certain order, proportion and combination, one not only comes to believe that an impartite self is there, but also that this self is wholly unique and separate from all others. Eventual decay and death should show the living that such thoughts are delusive, but the illusion of a self is continually reinforced and consolidated by *tanha*, the craving for embodied existence and sensory indulgence, so that one may vainly imagine that this ever-changing self somehow survives the dissolution of the aggregates in some disembodied, ghostly reflection of the composite collection of *skandhas*.

If the Four Noble Truths are relatively easy to grasp at a preliminary level, however rich and recondite their fuller implications, Buddha's Doctrine of *Anatta,* No-self, is daunting and elusive even at higher levels of apprehension. This is partly because the apprehending mind which seeks to seize upon the doctrine and make sense of it is itself a constituent of the composite *skandhas.* A contrived illusion cannot construe itself as illusory any more than a dream can negate itself. Most modern scholars and, unfortunately, some nihilistic Buddhists have insisted that Buddha held that *anatta* implies the non-existence of any self whatsoever. It is instead the explicit denial of the reality of any self conceived in terms of the mutable *skandhas.* Whatever can be qualified, quantified, formalized or described cannot be the noumenal self. But if Nirvana is possible, that in oneself which can become Buddha is beyond quality and number, unformulatable and indescribable. It is what remains when everything is stripped away. It is that which experiences Nirvana because it is not essentially different from Nirvana. And it can never be understood in terms of what comes into being, is composite and subject to measure, alteration and particularization. The five ascetics understood Buddha's meaning, for upon hearing it they became *arhants,* faithfully following him and disseminating his Teaching.

Buddha also taught the Doctrine of Dependent Origination, *patichchasamuppada* (Skt. *pratityasamutpada*), which displaces ordinary notions of causality as an explanation of the operative principle in the cycles of *Samsara.* Long before Hume, Buddha recognized that thinking of causation in terms of necessary connections between sequential events involved extraneous assumptions unwarranted by strict observation. He also saw that reducing macrocosmic causation to isolated generalizations derived from sensory or time-bound experience obscured the all-pervasive Law of Karma, or universal determination. He dispensed altogether with the idea of temporal causation and synthesized his profound insights in the powerful conception of Dependent Origination, wherein one condition or set of conditions is seen as arising out of some other condition or set, forming a chain which can account for the uninterrupted flow of phenomenal and transient existence. Such a bold leap recognizes and preserves the insight expressed in the doctrine of *skandhas,* whilst avoiding the problem of the self which deeply vexed Hume, Bellamy and others.

Every condition can be traced to some anticipatory condition, and for the sake of radical understanding Buddha started with the common condition of fundamental ignorance, *avijja* (*avidya*). Ignorance or nescience gives rise to aggregates or compounds, including mental qualities, *sankharas* (*sanskaras*), which in turn foster differentiated consciousness, *vinnana* (*vijnana*). This consciousness induces name and form, *namarupa*, from which arise the senses and mind, *chalayatana* (*shadayatana*), inducing contact, *phassa* (*sparsha*). Contact induces responses to sense-objects, *vedana*, and these mental and emotional reactions generate craving or thirst for sensory experience, *tanha* (*trishna*). This is persisting attachment, *upadana*, which directly produces coming into existence, *bhava*, which involves birth, *jati*, and consequently, *jaramarana*, ageing and death. Hence, suffering is a fact of embodied existence and not an adventitious or malign feature of life, for it is bound up with the ceaseless change of dependent origination which makes embodied existence possible.

During his stay in Varanasi, a wealthy youth joined the Sangha and his parents became Buddha's first lay followers who took refuge in the Triple Gem – Buddha, Dharma and Sangha. Soon enough, the basic codes for ordained monks and lay disciples were set down so that the prime requirements of cooperative effort were met and maintained. Although Buddha's many discourses provided extensive elaboration and suggested varied applications, the vital core of his message was conveyed in the first two sermons. When Buddha decided to go to Uruvela, he did not take all his monks with him. Rather, those who had become proficient were sent forth in every direction – "Let not two of you go by the same road", he said – to spread the gospel of hope. Encountering a group of ascetics on the road to Uruvela, he delivered the *Aditta Pariyaya Sutta*, the Fire Sermon, in which he likened the world and everything in it to a burning house. Since these ascetics already grasped a great deal about the nature of *Samsara*, they needed only to identify clearly the root cause of suffering. By showing how *tanha* or craving smoulders in all sentient existence, Buddha freed them from its spell and they gladly entered the Sangha.

Buddha then fulfilled his promise to King Bimbisara by journeying to Rajagriha, and the king gave his own park, Veluvana, to the Sangha as a monastic retreat. It was there that the two remarkable ascetics Shariputra and Maudgalyayana, who later became Buddha's outstanding disciples, first met their Teacher. Shariputra had come to Rajagriha to find Buddha because he had first heard of the Four Noble Truths from Ashvajit, one of the original disciples who had followed the injunction to take a different road and promulgate the Dharma. When King Shuddhodana, Buddha's earthly father, heard amazing stories about his visit to Rajagriha, he promptly sent a message entreating Buddha to return to Kapilavastu. As soon as Buddha and his disciples arrived in the capital city he had renounced, King Shuddhodana was shocked to see his son joining the other monks in the daily round of alms-seeking. Buddha expounded his teachings before the king and his court, and soon his father, Shuddhodana, his aunt, Mahaprajapati, who had raised Siddhartha as a child, his beloved former wife, Yashodhara, his half-brother, Nanda, and a few days later, his son, Rahula, became his followers. Ananda, a cousin who became Buddha's constant attendant and cheerful companion, interceded on behalf of women followers, and Buddha blest the formation of the *bhikkhuni Sangha*, the Order of nuns. Mahaprajapati and her friends became the first nuns of the Sangha.

After spending some time at Kapilavastu, Buddha received an invitation from Anathapindika, a rich banker of Shravasti, the capital city of Koshala. He had met Buddha at Rajagriha and became such a devoted follower that he donated the famous Jetavana Grove to the Sangha. Buddha moved to Jetavana, and it became the chief centre of his work for almost half a century. During that time monastic centres were established in most of the flourishing cities in the Gangetic plain – Varanasi, Rajagriha, Pataliputra, Vaishali, Kushinagara, Pava – as well as in numerous hamlets and villages, but most of Buddha's great discourses were delivered in the Jetavana Grove. Since no caste (*jati*) or social distinctions were recognized or tolerated in the Sangha, Buddha admitted male and female disciples from every sector of society. Although his initial converts were from affluent and cultured and even aristocratic families, all classes of seekers were welcomed into the Sangha without any predilection or prejudice. As several discourses in the *Dhammapada* show, Buddha was not primarily concerned with the external reform of the prevailing social order, for any social order can become corrupt in the absence of a vital spiritual and ethical foundation. His revolution was fundamental, and it included the radical redefinition of the very basis of social esteem, stressing the exemplary virtues and graces which were originally extolled in the *Vedas*, the epics and the forest hermitages of antiquity.

There were, of course, militant groups of orthodox individuals who were hostile to Buddha's message and monastic Order, and various desultory attempts were made to vilify him. The main focus of opposition was Devadatta, a jealous cousin who had grown up with Buddha. An ambitious and impetuous individual, Devadatta had found his own accomplishments eclipsed by Prince Siddhartha's rare gifts and excellences, and Devadatta had sadly succumbed to a competitive spirit in which he lost every encounter to a magnanimous man who knew nothing of rivalry in his own generous nature, though he was well aware of every human weakness that hinders the spiritual will. When Buddha returned to teach in Kapilavastu, Devadatta joined the Sangha but could not assimilate its redemptive spirit of unconditional, universal benevolence. After Buddha had already taught for three decades, Devadatta rashly sought to assume the leadership of the Order, invoking a principle of personal ascendancy which would have been repugnant to highly respected elders like Shariputra and Maudgalyayana. Just as the Teachings (*dharma*) had been orally transmitted by Buddha, so too the monastic code (*vinaya*) had been evolved under his guidance, and he entrusted the ethical continuity of the Sangha to the entire fellowship of older and younger monks.

When Devadatta's sudden offer to 'relieve' Buddha of the onerous task of guiding the Sangha and to tighten the rules was rejected, tradition suggests that he made three crafty attempts to assassinate his spiritual benefactor. The mad and drunken elephant he unleashed upon Buddha fell before the feet of the Master. The avalanche he diverted towards Buddha receded before his presence. And the hired assassin he dispatched into Buddha's vicinity was converted and entered the Sangha. Having repeatedly failed, Devadatta then fomented a schism in the Sangha by withdrawing with some disciples he had flattered, but Shariputra and Maudgalyayana went to each of them and won them back into the fold. Having exhausted every means of eliminating or undermining Buddha, Devadatta was eventually overcome by the accumulated karma of his lifelong animosity, fell gravely ill and died. One tradition declares that even whilst dying he sought out Buddha in order to beg his forgiveness, but that he perished before he could reach his Master. Nonetheless, this account suggests that Buddha knew of his belated remorse and announced his death to the monks around him, stating that a reconciliation had indeed occurred on the mental plane. Another account suggests that Devadatta lived after Buddha and died in a penitential state.

It would be impossible to reconstruct the details of Buddha's journeys back and forth across the Gangetic plain during the nearly fifty years that he taught. He freely taught in many places, and though each sermon was fresh and adapted skilfully to the mental faculties and predilections of his listeners, his main message was always the same: the Four Noble Truths provide the basis of proper understanding, the Noble Eightfold Path is the assured means to freedom, and the common conception of a separative self, "the great dire heresy of separateness", is a costly delusion. When he was about eighty years old, he set out on his last journey, travelling north from Rajagriha. Reaching Vaishali, he accepted a park donated to him by the courtesan Ambapali, but he spent the rainy season in a nearby village called Beluvagama. He fell ill and came close to death, but willed his own recovery in order to prepare his disciples for his imminent departure. Announcing to the assembled monks that he would die in three months, he left and continued on his journey. When he reached Pava he took up residence in the park of Chunda, a blacksmith who was a lay devotee.

Chunda invited Buddha and his monks to a meal at his house, and he prepared many delicacies for them. Amongst the dishes he set before the gathering was one called *sukaramaddava*. There are different interpretations of the nature of this dish, but it was most probably a sweetened concoction of local mushrooms called 'pigs' feet', owing to their appearance. When Buddha was served the dish, he requested that it be given to him alone and that the uneaten portion be buried, since none but a Tathagata could assimilate it. Unknown to Chunda, the dish was poisonous, and Buddha saw it as the karmic indication for his departure from the world of men, upon which he had already deliberated. After this last meal, Buddha became ill and suffered acute pains. He at once set out for Kushinagara and, after resting twice on the way, he settled on a low couch between two sala trees which stood in Upavattana Park, belonging to the clan of Mallas. He asked

Ananda to reassure Chunda that he need feel no remorse for the meal he offered Buddha and his companions. "There are two offerings of food", he explained, "which are of equal fruition, of equal outcome, exceeding in grandeur the fruition and result of any other offerings in food. Which two? The one partaken of by the Tathagata on becoming fully enlightened, in supreme, unsurpassed Enlightenment; and the one partaken of by the Tathagata on coming to pass into the state of Nirvana wherein the elements of clinging do not arise. By his deed has the venerable Chunda accumulated that which makes for long life, beauty, well-being, glory, heavenly rebirth and sovereignty."

The scene under the sala trees was one of intense sadness, but Buddha calmed the weeping Ananda by reminding him that separation must inevitably occur in transient existence. "Of that which is born, come to being, put together, and so is subject to dissolution, how can it be said that it must not depart?" The Mallas paid homage to Buddha, and a wandering ascetic named Subhadra listened to his instruction. Subhadra was the last direct disciple of Buddha to enter the Sangha. Buddha called upon his disciples to take the Dharma as their Master, for Buddha himself is ever present in it. They were to be guided by the monastic code (*vinaya*), even though they could modify its minor precepts to suit changing conditions. Together, the Dharma and the discipline (*vinaya*) would meet all their needs. Calling on them to be lamps unto themselves, he enjoined them to seek the goal with diligence. Thus on the full moon day of *Vesakha* – the day of his birth and his Enlightenment – Buddha entered *Parinirvana*. His body was cremated and the ashes were divided into eight portions by a revered *brahmana* named Dona and taken to the centres where Buddha had taught, so that *stupas* could be erected to enshrine them. Recent excavations at a site identified by some archaeologists as Kapilavastu have revealed an ancient *stupa* which contains a casket of ashes on which is an inscription suggesting that they are a portion of the original division of relics. Despite their grief, monks and lay disciples joined together in holding great feasts to honour Buddha and the Teaching of universal peace, moral concord and full Enlightenment that he bequeathed to suffering humanity.

Hermes, June 1986

THE REBIRTH OF HUMANITY

We are only in the Fourth Round, and it is in the Fifth that the full development of Manas, as a direct ray from the Universal MAHAT − a ray unimpeded by matter − will be finally reached. Nevertheless, as every sub-race and nation have their cycles and stages of developmental evolution repeated on a smaller scale, it must be the more so in the case of a Root-Race. Our race then has, as a Root-race, crossed the equatorial line and is cycling onward on the Spiritual side; but some of our sub-races still find themselves on the shadowy descending arc of their respective national cycles; while others again − the oldest − having crossed their crucial point, which alone decides whether a race, a nation, or a tribe will live or perish, are at the apex of spiritual development as sub-races.

The Secret Doctrine, ii 301

Ranging from the minutest circles of daily life to the massive arcs of cosmic evolution, the spiralling progress of spiritual humanity has successive phases and synchronous aspects, marked by critical turns and decisive epochs. There are fateful times of birth and death, of transfiguration and rebirth, for individuals as well as civilizations. The majestic beating of the karmic heart of the cosmos resonates within the breast of every intrepid pilgrim-soul so that none is exempt from the challenge of the hour nor impervious to the clarion call of the Mahabharatan "war between the living and the dead". Days and hours are marked by moments of going forth (*pravritti*) and going within (*nivritti*), whilst decades and centuries have their own coded rhythms of activity and rest. In a universe of inexorable law and ceaseless transformation, no two moments in the life of any being are exactly alike. Similarly, in the lifetimes of races the accumulated karma of the past converges with the archetypal logic of cycles to precipitate climacteric moments.

At the present historical moment there is a rapid descent of *Dharmakshetra* into *Kurukshetra* and an awesome re-enactment, before the soul's eye, of the titanic struggle between Kronos and Zeus. To serve the Mahatmas and their Avatar, and through them all of humanity, is the most meaningful and precious privilege open to any person. The readiness to serve is helped by the fusion of an altruistic motive with skill in timely action. These may be gestated through deep meditation on behalf of the good of all beings and an authentic renunciation of earthly concerns for the sake of the many who are lost. One must lay one's heart open to the present plight of millions of souls who are wandering adrift and are much afflicted by the psychological terror prophesied in Tibet. Not even affording the visible reference of an external cataclysm, this psychological convulsion is needed for the transformation of the humanity of the past into the humanity of the future.

The ramifications of this crucial transition were anticipated and provided for by the Brotherhood of Bodhisattvas. The Avataric descent of the Seventh Impulsion into the moral chaos consequent upon two World Wars and the world weariness of the present epoch marks the culmination of a seven hundred-year cycle extending back to Tsong-Kha-Pa. Whilst this may be more than can be encompassed in the cribbed and cabined conceptions of mortals, it is scarcely an instant in the eyes of those who ever reside on the plane of Shamballa. Sages are fully aware that the voluntary descent of a spiritual Teacher into Myalba merely provides the outward illusion of passage through various phases of earthly life, using but a small portion of an essentially unmanifest Self. Impervious to containment by form, the true being of the Avatar abides in timeless duration, always honouring the One without a second, *Tad ekam*, that which as the central Spiritual Sun is the single source of all that lives and breathes throughout the seven kingdoms of nature, and of all that is lit up at any level of reflected intelligence from the tiniest atom to the mightiest star in this vast cosmos which extends far beyond the solar system and this earth. One with the unmanifest *Logos*, Dakshinamurti remains poised at the threshold of the realm of boundless Light, the mathematical circle dividing infinity from finitude, and reposes as *achutya* – unfallen. As H. P. Blavatsky declared:

> The first lesson taught in Esoteric philosophy is that the incognizable Cause does not put forth evolution, whether consciously or

unconsciously, but only exhibits periodically different aspects of itself to the perception of finite Minds.

The Secret Doctrine, ii 487

In the *Bhagavad Gita*, Krishna disclosed that he incarnates on earth periodically for the preservation of the just, the destruction of the wicked and the establishment of righteousness. In Hindu iconography Narayana holds the conch shell, symbolizing his ability to rock the earth through sound, the potency of the *Logos* as *Shabdabrahman*, the Soundless Sound of the indestructible *Akshara* behind and beyond and within all the spaces of "the *AUM* throughout eternal ages". This clarion call has gone out to heroic souls incarnated in the last half century for the solemn purpose of gathering together those spread out across the globe who readily recognize the immense danger to humanity from itself, the spiritual danger of self-destruction. It is a summons to halt the desecration of the sacred soil of the good earth upon which all human beings must find their common ground, regardless of race, sex, religion, creed, atheistic philosophy, indifferentism, or any set of beliefs and values. Regardless of whatsoever labels and idiosyncracies of form, all human beings are sharers of the Nur of Allah, the Light that lighteth up every soul that cometh into the world, that Light which is beyond Darkness itself. It is the One Light which has been known by diverse names amongst the many forgotten peoples of our globe over millions and millions of years, in civilizations long buried under deserts and mountains or slipped beneath the sea before existing continents emerged. Infinitely resplendent in eternal duration, it is the Light which was transmitted over eighteen million years ago when the *Manas* of humanity was lit up by divine beings of one lip, one race, one mind, one heart, seers of whom the *Vedas* speak.

> The mysteries of Heaven and Earth, revealed to the Third Race by their celestial teachers in the days of their purity, became a great focus of light, the rays from which became necessarily weakened as they were diffused and shed upon an uncongenial, because too material soil.
>
> *The Secret Doctrine, ii, 281*

Truly God is one, but manifold are its names. As the *Koran* teaches, there are as many ways to God as there are children of the breaths of men. Tragically, as mankind became progressively enwrapped in the illusion of material existence, its eyes and ears dimmed, though the light within remained inviolate. Outside the circle of ever-vigilant custodians of the Mysteries, the arcane teaching of the universal sound and light of the *Logos* was obscured, distorted and lost. Today those who call themselves Muslims, Christians, Jews, Hindus, Jains, Sikhs, Buddhists or Zoroastrians, men and women of every sect and nation throughout every continent of the globe, are bereft of the lost Word, *Shabdabrahman*. Although lost, it has yet been fervently sought by many more millions in our time than ever before in recorded history or even in earlier epochs of antiquity shrouded in myth and mist. The unseen tablets of nature, which are a vast reservoir of enigmatic glyphs and symbols and eternal verities, record the unknown strivings of innumerable human beings, groping in their gloom, sometimes with shame but often with nothing else to support them than the *pathos* of their search. It is a search to find one's way back home, out of exile from the kingdom of God, the land of the midnight sun.

In order to gather together the afflicted, the Divine Cowherd summons all awakened souls, wherever and however disguised, through the sounding of the mighty conch. Independent of all modes of external communication, and relying upon the oldest mode of communication known to the Ancient of Days – controlled transference of benevolent thought and ineffable sound – the call is heard by scattered volunteers "in the fierce strife between the living and the dead". As with Jacob's ladder in his dream, heaven and earth are reunited, even if momentarily. In this manner, over the next eighteen years the world will move through the darkness, yet mysteriously, step by step, faltering and failing yet persisting, it will move towards that moment when Anno Domini has ceased to be, and a new era will dawn with a new name. There will then be no U.S.A. but a new Republic of Conscience which will take its place in the community of mankind which would have come of age and declared itself as one family.

This is a grand prospect for which there can be inherently no empirical or merely rational proof. Yet it may be tested by any intuitive individual who is courageous enough to pour his or her deepest unspoken feelings, unarticulated dreams and unexpressed inner agony into the alchemical crucible of spiritual striving on behalf of others. It is a tryst that such souls make with destiny, but also with the grandchildren of persons yet unborn. It is a tryst with the humanity of the future, and with the full promise of the Aquarian Age which dawned on the nineteenth of June, 1902, seventy-nine years ago, with mathematical precision. This has an exact relationship to that moment five thousand and eighty-three years ago, in 3102 B.C., when Krishna, having witnessed the outcome of the Mahabharatan war between the greedy Kauravas and the foolish Pandavas, was able to end his seeming life on earth and withdraw from the terrestrial scene. Thus standing apart from this universe, into which he never really enters, he creates therein his *mayavi rupas* through the mighty magic of *prakriti*, the seminal potency of mystic thought in the eternal life of self-ideation. Again and again, under different names, it is the same being behind every divine incarnation, whether past or future.

As Dakshinamurti, the Initiator of Initiates, he is seated immovable above Mount Kailas, in mystic meditation since over eighteen million years ago from the time when there was no Mount Kailas and no Himalayas as presently understood. Coming down through all the subsequent recorded and unrecorded eras, he carries forth in unbroken continuity the onward spiritual current which is the irresistible, unconquerable, ineluctable forward march of humanity. He is Shiva-Mahadeva, reborn as the four *Kumaras* in the successive races of humanity, and that still more mysterious and solitary Being alluded to in the secret Teachings.

> The inner man of the first * * * only changes his body from time to time; he is ever the same, knowing neither rest nor Nirvana, spurning *Devachan* and remaining constantly on Earth for the salvation of mankind.
>
> *The Secret Doctrine, ii 281*

Attuned to the rhythms of the cosmic ocean of Divine Thought, he is the still motionless centre in its depths around which revolve, like myriad mathematical points in spinning circles, the scattered hosts of humanity. Amidst the larger and larger circles of ripples upon ripples, waves upon waves, all souls are citizens of that universe which is much vaster than the disordered kingdom which, as earthlings, they may seem to inherit but to which they have no claim except as members of a single family.

This mystic vision can only be fleetingly glimpsed and partially understood by beginning to ask sincere if faulty, searching if somewhat confused, questions. Herein lies the starting-point of the dialectical method taught by Krishna in the fourth chapter of the *Gita*. The sacred teaching of the kingly science was originally given by Krishna to Vivasvat, who in turn imparted it to Manu. Then Vaivaswat Manu, sometimes known as Morya, taught it to Ikshvaku, who stands for all the regal Initiates of forgotten antiquity in the golden ages of myth and fable. Thus the vigilant preservers and magnanimous rulers of this world, without abdicating from their essential state of Mahatmic wisdom, assumed the guise of visible corporeality to descend on earth and reign upon it as King-Hierophants and Divine Instructors of the humanity then incarnated upon the globe. It is this self-same eternal wisdom that Krishna gives unto Arjuna, an unhappy warrior, not for his own sake, especially when he was not entirely ready to assimilate the Teaching, but for the sake of his work in the world and his help in concluding the Mahabharatan war.

In the great summation of the eighteenth chapter of the *Gita*, Krishna reveals secrets upon secrets, wrapped in each other in seemingly unending layers, like a Chinese treasure. Every time a secret is revealed, there is more and yet more, because in the end one is speaking of that which is part of the secret of every human soul in its repeated strivings and recurrent lives upon earth. Amidst the chaos and obscuration of misplayed roles, faded memories and fragmented consciousness, coupled with the fatigue of mental confusion, there is also the power of persistence, the *sutratman* and its *connatus* which enables every person to breathe from day to day and through each night. In deep sleep, as in profound meditation and the intervals between incarnations, the immortal soul enters into the orbit of the midnight sun and emerges out of the muddle of mundane life and mangled dreams. There it discerns the melody of the flute of Krishna, the music of the spheres, and the hidden magic of the ages which, when heard self-consciously, frees the soul from the fatuous burden of self-imposed delusions. It is the priceless prerogative of every Arjuna in our time to seek once more the pristine wisdom, the sovereign purifier, through unremitting search, through fearless questions, through grateful devotion and selfless service.

Surveying the wreckage of this century in bewilderment and dismay, many have sought an understanding of events in the oft-quoted, though little understood, remarks of H. P. Blavatsky concerning the role of the New World in the evolution of the races of humanity. Too many have submitted to the delusion, to the strange idea, that spiritual evolution is possible only for a few. The idea that any single people out of the globe's teeming millions, selected at random and fed on the fat of the land, weighted down by the gifts of blind fortune, should be preferred by Krishna must be firmly repudiated. No instrument of the real work of the Lodge of Mahatmas can ever be permitted to become the refuge of the few, the chosen avenue for the exclusive salvation or cloistered comfort of any elite. Now, thanks to many benefactors and blessings in disguise, Americans are being made to slow down to the point where they may hear some of the echoes of what the pilgrim fathers heard when they landed in Plymouth over three centuries ago. In a way which could not have been known clearly to them, their setting out upon a long and difficult sea voyage was reminiscent of far more ancient voyages of seed-pilgrims across the waters of floods guided by Manu. These pilgrims to the New World had set out after having formed a compact with each other, which was a pure act of faith in themselves and in the future and in whatever their God had to offer them. This was one of many precious moments in the long and unwritten history of this mighty continent, whose vastness extends from the Arctic Circle to the Straits of Magellan, encompassing great rivers, the Grand Canyon, and awesome ranges of mountains girdling a third of the globe.

There is much more in the civilizations and peoples of pre-Columbian history than can ever be garnered through perfunctory reading of post-Columbian events. The brief journey of Columbus from Spain to the Caribbean, in search of India, but resulting in the rediscovery of America, could foretell little of the future birth in these lands of old Hindus from the India of a million years ago. It could convey few hints of the far-flung variety of spiritual strivings that would occur on the American continent, or of the enormous blasphemy, pride and temerity of inscribing the Third Eye upon the dollar bill. Yet somewhere, past all the humbug of petty educators, pompous bureaucrats and self-serving politicians, an impartial witness can only feel a genuine empathy with the series of lonely men carrying a strenuous burden of leadership in the emerging American republics.

Men such as Lincoln defined the ideal of action "with malice towards none and charity for all" and spoke for all mankind in affirming that "government of the people, by the people, and for the people, shall not perish from the earth". Much earlier, a perceptive person like President Everett of Harvard could clearly see that the death of Jefferson and Adams on the fourth of July in 1826 was an event that had nothing to do with the destiny of one nation alone, but rather with the whole of humanity. Alas, it now seems paradoxical to some Americans that few people have honoured Jefferson as highly as Ho Chi Minh, and it is a mark of the myopia of educated Americans that they could not honour Eisenhower as much as the humble villagers of India who came in millions to greet this self-effacing soldier. Humanity recognizes its own, just as millions of Americans since the thirties have seen in Gandhi the enduring re-enactment which was once seen in Christ. This is a very different world from that of fifty years ago, and it is still changing rapidly. America is now much less imposing, fortunately for all, than it was threatening to be after the Second World War. Through omission and commission, through misspent and lost opportunities, as well as outright misdeeds, more lives have been lost since World War II owing to the U.S.A. than during World War II, more lives lost than even those due to the Soviet Union, with its barbaric despotism but its immense potential for good.

This is a curious world in which there are few major actors or authentic mandates, but in which there are millions of awakened human souls who are like unto sad-eyed veterans of history, but who are also coolly waiting to strike when the iron is hot so that the City of Man, now like an embryo hidden in the dark, like Venus before the dawn, will make its timely descent. Thanks to the ineffable grace of *Daiviprakriti*, which alone can act as a midwife to the rebirth of humanity, there could suddenly emerge a successful sequel to the aborted birth of the United Nations in 1945, so that the world may find itself and retrace its pathways to a more honourable prospect than anything cogitated since that time. The teeming lands and rich resources of the earth, like the seeds of the spiritual harvest of mankind, do not belong to any single tribe and cannot be handed on by any legal system of inheritance. Just as some governments and groups have already done more to protect the environments of the earth than individuals alone could accomplish, so too will future networks and agencies initiate efforts to pool natural and human resources, the seeds and skills that creative pioneers may bring to fruition in the age of micro-electronics, so that the whole world could move into a new era of global solidarity. It will be an era of self-conscious interdependence, promoting the global discovery of the richness and immensity of the potentials in the human brain, matching the vast imaginative potentials for creative longings in the human heart.

This daunting prospect is no less magnanimous than the mandate and the vision of the Brotherhood of Mahatmas and Bodhisattvas, who stand in relation to drifting mortals as they are in relation to the black beetle, in T. H. Huxley's telling metaphor. Mahatmas are always present in the orbit of the Avatar and his true disciples on earth. They ever move in their invisible forms and are known by infallible signs. This is an arena wherein there is no room for delusion or pretense. It may well be that the Bodhisattvas are recognized only by a few, but this does not alter the fact that they are sometimes more numerous as shining witnesses to the critical events of history than the visible and volatile participants. It is high time that creedal religion catches up with contemporary science, which already knows that in every supposed physical object there is only a mere one-quadrillionth part that is, even by any stretch of the imagination, capable of being called matter. All the rest is empty space, the Akashic empyrean of Adepts, gods and elementals.

The multitudinous sense perceptions of human beings, as Heraclitus recognized, are liars. Eyes and ears are bad witnesses for the human soul unless one looks with the awakened eye and hears with humble and receptive eardrums that are tuned to the proper vibrations, the music of the Hierophants, the great Compassionaters, the true lovers and friends and servers, but also the fathers and elder brothers, of the entire human race. It is in their name that the Avatar speaks, as no divine incarnation can be separated from the Logoic host which is with and behind the Magus-Teacher. At this critical point in cosmic evolution, after more than eighteen million years, when the human race has already passed the mid-point and is approaching a climactic phase, it is only He who was present at the beginning and who will prevail at the end who can redeem humanity. Whilst the *Logos* in *esse* is outside the solar system, it is only through its accredited and self-authenticated agency in the world that it performs its Paracletic function, which was sensed both by those around Buddha and Christ as well as by those like the blind king in the presence of Krishna. Only He who can shake the earth by sound is in a position to save it, with the help of all those who are willing to stand up and be counted, especially as the *pralaya* of the West begins to envelop the globe. Already, even those who can see but dimly can discern the grim fate that awaits those minute minorities which perversely block the way to the welfare of the vast majority of mankind.

The earth must go back to the ultimate democracy of the immense majority, and no one can be excluded. All men and women, in the far corners of the earth, as well as in the first land of the common man, must inwardly pledge themselves to work for their spiritual ancestors and also for their unseen descendants who will constitute the humanity of the future. This is the original meaning and future promise of the American Dream, which has little to do with the institutionalized gains of the past two centuries, but is vitally relevant to the embryonic world civilization to be founded upon a brave declaration of human solidarity and global interdependence. Whereas Thomas Paine once welcomed mysterious messengers of thought, and later statesmen ascribed their intimations of the ever-expanding American Dream to the inspiration of God, the time has come when all true promptings of theophilanthropists must be consecrated to the Brotherhood of Bodhisattvas, the Society of Sages, the Benefactors of mankind.

Just as the global rebirth of humanity mirrors the archetypal birth of humanity in the Third Root Race, so too the authentic spiritual renewal of every human being reflects and resonates with the wider cycle of the race. Prior to physical birth each Monad has had the meta-psychological experience of being catapulted into what the Orphics called the tomb of the soul, but also that which the Ionians regarded as the temple of the human body. And whilst every baby enters the world voicing the *AUM*, each with a unique accent and intonation, it is given to very few to end their lives with the sacred Sound. This is the difference which human life makes, with its saga of fantasy and forgetfulness. What one sensed in one's pristine innocence at the moment of birth and which is witnessed through the enigmatic sounding of the Word becomes wholly obscured by the time of death unless one has deliberately and self-consciously sought out the path leading to spiritual rebirth. Through the complex processes of karmic precipitation and conscious and unconscious exercise of the powers of choice, each human being differentiates from others, self-selecting his or her own destiny. To minimize the dangers to the soul and to maximize the continuity of spiritual self-consciousness between the commencement and close of incarnation, one must learn to look back and forwards over the entire span of a lifetime, breaking it up into successive septenary cycles and their sub-phases. All cycles participate in birth, in adolescence, in slow and painful maturation, in the shedding of illusions, and in a sort of death or disintegration leading to new beginnings. In some portions of the globe the wheel revolves so rapidly that most human beings have been through many lives within one lifetime, and though this poignant fact is little understood by other persons, even those who experience it acutely do not think through its implications.

One cannot really comprehend such primal verities without silent contemplation. As Krishna hinted in the *Uttara Gita*, every time one opens one's mouth, the astral shadow is lengthened. In the demanding discipline of preparation for spiritual rebirth, there are very few who could hope to match or even approach the example of the Kanchipuram Shankaracharya, who perfected his *svadharma* over the past half century, provided sagely counsel to myriad devotees, and then retreated under a lasting vow of silence. There is evidently a Himalayan difference between mighty Men of Meditation and the motley host of deluded mortals called fools by Puck in *A Midsummer Night's Dream*. Nevertheless, the folly of mortals is largely a protected illusion. If a human being knew from the age of seven everything that was going to happen in his or her life from that moment to the time of death, life would be intolerably difficult. Similarly, if one knew exactly what tortures one had committed or connived at in the time of the Inquisition or elsewhere in the history of the world – and there is no portion of the globe which has not witnessed terrible misdeeds – it would be very hard to avoid being overwhelmed by such knowledge. Every human being has at times, like Pilate, opted out of responsibilities upon the unrecorded scenes of history. Whilst all, like Ivan in Dostoevsky's *The Brothers Karamazov*, would like to think of themselves as holding to the principle that it is never justifiable to harm even a single child, each person bears the heavy burden of karmic debts, every one of which will have to be repaid in full before the irreversible attainment of conscious immortality is feasible.

To begin to raise such questions about oneself is to realize that they cannot be answered in the utilitarian calculus of the age of commerce, which is only the crude morality of the market-place. Many people simply refuse to be priced, bought and sold or even appraised, in terms of market values or competitive criteria, especially in a time of spurious inflation. One has indeed to find out what is one's own true value. One must gain an inward recognition of the elusive truth of the axiom, "To thine own self be true . . . and thou canst not then be false to any man." Looking at the whole of one's life in terms of what one feels is the truest thing about oneself, one must search out the deepest, most abiding hope that one holds, apart from all fantasy myths. For most human beings, this hope is much the same. It is the hope to conclude one's life without being a nuisance or hindrance to others. It is the wish to finish one's life without harming other human beings, but making some small contribution to the sum-total of good, so that at the moment of death one may look back over life and feel that one has lived the best one knew how.

Broadly, too many human beings torture themselves with an appalling amount of useless guilt, owing to their utter lack of knowledge of the mathematics of the soul. Just as it is useless and unconstructive to become guilty or evasive about one's checkbook balance, because the figures do not lie and the facts cannot be denied, it is equally fruitless and destructive to become immersed in guilt-fantasies with regard to one's whole life. Even a little knowledge of the relevance of simple mathematics to the realm of meta-psychology can save one from recurring though needless despair. Every attempt to blot out awareness of responsibility for karma through giving way to emotional reactions obscures the impersonal continuity of one's real existence and is an insult to the divine origin of one's self-consciousness.

In each of us that golden thread of continuous life – periodically broken into active and passive cycles of sensuous existence on Earth, and super-sensuous in *Devachan* – is from the beginning of our appearance upon this earth. It is the *Sutratma*, the luminous thread of immortal impersonal monadship, on which our earthly lives or evanescent Egos are strung as so many beads – according to the beautiful expression of Vedantic philosophy . . . Without this principle – the emanation of the very essence of the pure divine principle *Mahat* (Intelligence), which radiates direct from the Divine mind – we would be surely no better than animals.

The Secret Doctrine, ii 513

In order to insert one's own efforts to recover this Mahatic awareness into the regeneration of humanity by the Mahatmas and the Avatar, one must learn to work first with the cycles of the seasons of nature. The period of fourteen days beginning with the winter solstice and culminating on the fourth of January, which is sacred to Hermes-Budha, may be used as a period of *tapas* for the sake of generating calm and sacrificial resolves. The precious time between January and March may be spent in quiet inward gestation of the seeds of the coming year. Care needs to be taken if one is to avoid excess and idle excitement at the time of the vernal equinox and deceptive dreams about the carefree, indolent summer. From March until June there is an inevitable and necessary descent into manifestation, but if the summer solstice is to find one prepared for the season of flourishing, one must not give way to the extravagances of anticipation and memory. If one observes this solstice with one's resolves intact, then one is in a good position to maintain inward continuity, free from wastefulness and fatigue, until the onset of autumn. Then arriving at the autumnal equinox, not having accumulated a series of debts and liabilities owing to lost opportunities and forgotten resolves, one will be able to maintain the critical detachment needed to participate in the season of withdrawal and regeneration, culminating in the return of the winter solstice.

By setting oneself realistic goals and working with the rhythms of nature, it is possible over a period of seven years to nurture within oneself the seedlings of the virtues – "the nurslings of immortality" – needed to become a true servant of the Servants of Humanity. Because of the dual nature assumed by *Mahat* when it manifests and falls into matter as self-consciousness, it is necessary to correct for the terrestrial attractions of the moon of the mind if one would recover the illumination of the solar power of understanding. As Longfellow said, one may hit the mark by aiming a little bit above the mark because every arrow feels the earth's gravity. One must allow for the sagging or declination of the curve, but whilst one allows for it, one must not hesitate to resolve with inner strength and cool confidence. Spiritual rebirth initially means being born again with new eyes and with the ability to see each successive year and cycle as truly new. This noetic perspective can be gained only by linking each year or cycle with its predecessors, not in detail but in essence. And infallibly, if one is able to live consciously and self-consciously throughout the cycles and seasons of life, one will be able to use the thread of continuity at the moment of death. *Sutratma-Buddhi* thus becomes *Manas-Sutratman*, and both arise through the fiery, Fohatic energy of the *Mahat-Atman*.

Those who are serious about engaging in spiritual self-regeneration in the service of others could begin with the simplest assumption: death is inevitable but the moment of death is uncertain. This is in no wise a morbid or gloomy assumption, for death always comes as a deliverer and a friend to the immortal soul. If one can remotely resonate to the words of Krishna and feel in the invisible heart the ceaseless vibration of one's essential immortality, then one will understand that being born is like putting on clothes and dying is like taking them off. At this point in human evolution it is too late to indulge in body identification along with its consequent denial of the ubiquity of death and suffering for mortal vestures. It is a mark of spiritual maturity to recognize that human life involves risk and pain. Were it otherwise, it could hold no promise. Even if one is not yet prepared for the Himalayan heights of spiritual mountain climbing, nonetheless, one may begin to discern and hearken to the light of daring that burns in the heart. Whatever one's mode of self-measurement, that measure should be in favour of what is strong, what is true, what is noble and what is beautiful in oneself. All the Avatars concur in the strength of affirmation that the spirit is willing, even though the flesh is weak. Unlike the preachers of discouragement who emphasize the element of weakness in the flesh, the true Prophets of the divine destiny of mankind place the stress upon the willingness of the spirit.

In this difficult time of collective death and regeneration, signified by the entry of Uranus into Scorpio, the whole host of Bodhisattvas bears witness to the Avataric message that this is a propitious time of opportunity for all souls to protect, to nurture and fructify the seeds of futurity that sleep deep beneath the astral soil of the earth. It is a time of silent burgeoning growth, and there is a supple softness and mellowness in the astral light as at the dawn of Venus. It is also a time rather like the crimson sunset because it is the twilight hour for the devouring demons of recorded history. It is the sacred hour of the dawn of the humanity of the future in which there will be neither East nor West, neither North nor South, neither black nor brown nor white nor yellow. Though all this will not materialize in eighteen years of Mahabharatan struggles, the time has surely come for the sacred reaffirmation of true learning, of the supernal light of the transcendent *Logos*, such that myriad souls may rekindle the divine spark of creativity and compassion (*Agni-Soma*) and seek the hidden cornerstone of the City of Man.

Hermes, December 1981

DATELESS AND DEATHLESS

Having taken as a bow the great weapon of the Secret Teaching, one should fix in it the arrow sharpened by constant Meditation. Drawing it with a mind filled with That (Brahman) penetrate, O bright youth, that Immutable Mark.

The pranava (AUM) is the bow; the arrow is the self; Brahman is said to be the mark. With heedfulness It is to be penetrated. Become one with It as the arrow in the mark.

Mundaka Upanishad

Dateless and deathless, the intricate impulse works its will.

Rupert Brooke

To become a man of meditation is to master the Science of Spirituality, which may be approached by any aspirant who is in earnest pursuit of the ageless truth. All human beings are consubstantial with the very highest in the cosmos. All human beings are also continuously interacting, through the ceaseless flux and efflux of life-atoms in their enveloping vestures, with everything that exists. This dual participation in time and timelessness is central to the attempt of any person to raise his or her sights, to arouse the power of spiritual awakening, to go beyond all categories, including even the subtlest intellectual conceptions. The essence of the inmost core of being, the self, is inseparable from the Self of the whole and the Self in each and all. Whenever a person makes such an attempt, he is not in the same position as at any other moment. No human being can be sundered from other human selves owing to the constant interaction of life-atoms, and every human soul participates, in principle and in practice, in all the states of being of all beings that are now alive, or were embodied upon this earth.

From this enormous universal perspective, one can see that most ordinary thinking, even concerning spiritual life, is way off centre, what the Hopi Indians called *koyaanisqatsi*, out of balance, reeling, badly requiring radical readjustment. It is based upon an emphasis on a minute portion of oneself bound up with present preoccupations and feelings, passing emotions and desires. Owing to limited specific aims, people hold extremely foreshortened, fragmented and distorted conceptions of themselves. When this fact is coupled with the endemic tendency to manufacture a delusive personality out of habits, wants, memories and fears, one comes to see that most so-called human life is a sorry disappointment to the immortal soul. Yet, whilst every human being must live in the world for the sake of spiritual growth – for there can be no growth without participation – no human being need be lost. Every human being must to some extent participate in the world of illusion, in the whirl of change, and therefore in the realm of ever-conflicting and ever-changing thoughts, feelings and desires. This does not, however, alter the fundamental fact that every human being is perpetually rooted in That which is beyond all time and worlds.

In the *Upanishads* this paradox is portrayed by the metaphor of two birds in a tree – the one busily pecking at the tree's fruits, the other serenely watching from above. One's true Self is a spectator in eternity, seeing everything from a universal and eternal standpoint that is unmodified by mental conceptions and undisturbed by fleeting emotions. It is witness to the captivity of the other bird in the world of illusions, a participating and fragmented mind, which is by turns passive and assertive, frightened and aggressive, grasping and gasping. Once one recognizes that there is a deeper core in one's being which does not become involved in the world of time, change and reaction, but is able to reflect upon the entirety of what happens to all the lower vestures, then one begins to recognize in oneself a principle of transcendence and a true basis of aspiration.

There is no unbridgeable gap between the two perspectives. The potential awareness in the bird that is caught in illusions of the other bird as its true Self will make a crucial difference in its ability to relativate its plane of perception. From the perspective of the Science of Spirituality, which is grounded in the ontology of objective idealism, everything in the universe is the result of ideation. All forms, at every level, are, at root, expressions or manifestations of pure ideas. Two important consequences follow from this: first of all, there is an interpenetration of all worlds through ideas; and secondly, there is in every human being a power to step aside from self. Through ideation, one can abstract and remove oneself from seeming captivity to the world, and instead of doing this involuntarily through sleep or death, or intermittently through emotional or intellectual ecstasy, one can learn to do this consciously, constructively and as a matter of spiritual discipline.

If one can think this through, not merely in relation to specific contexts and particular situations, but in terms of all manifested existence and the entire sphere of objective phenomena, one will come to see that there is an illusion inherent in the manifested world itself, and that its relative reality is only the result of ideational participation, involvement through a lesser ideation, by the Self in that world. In other words, though the metaphor of the two birds or selves is helpful, one is, in reality, only one being with the power of ideation. The concept of the scale of ideation, ranging from the absolute and abstract to the particular and concrete, is directly reflected in the constitution of the human mind. The distinction between the divine intelligence of higher *Manas* and the personal ray of the same mind is really a difference between sets or classes of perceptions. One can look at anything passively by comparing and contrasting, obsessively, and from within a narrow spatio-temporal framework. Or one can loosen the framework and look at the same thing from a larger perspective, in relation to the distant past and what may be in the dawning future, in relation to what is deceptively near or far, but also in relation to certain intimate feelings and enduring convictions that are actually much closer to oneself than the dominant emotions or *idée fixe* of any particular context.

These capacities to alter perspectives, to expand horizons and to deepen perceptions all spring from the fundamental capacity to ideate. At its very deepest core, the Self is eternally ideating and eternally watching, but this vital truth is obscured by the extent to which one becomes wholly identified with the participating and reacting self. The projected ray, itself the product and proof of the power of ideation, becomes permeable to external sights and forces which appear to be inescapable because they affect one's inner feelings, states of mind and persisting moods. Affecting one's astral system and the extent to which it is stretched or strained or loosened, this immersion in and identification with lesser planes of ideation distorts one's tone of voice and spreads a film over one's vision, clouding everything one sees.

All of this represents an obscuration of one's true Self that is the effect of complex karma. But when one begins to be able to recognize this and understand what one has done to oneself through neglect of true meditation over lifetimes, one can move away from this initial duality and seek the beginnings of authentic meditation upon the *OM*. Celebration of the *OM* is the central thread of the spiritual path and of the quintessential hermetic current. Celebration of hymns of praise to the *OM* is the axis around which the entire work of the Great Lodge of Mahatmas turns, and it is a celebration on behalf of and among intrepid individuals who are willing to become men and women of meditation, consciously very aware of what the highest level of *OM* represents. The *OM* is the highest that one can conceive. The unbroken current of meditation of the true Self is also the supreme resource behind the whole of manifestation and THAT which is beyond manifestation itself. It is *Nada Brahman*, the divine resonance that becomes the vibrant vesture of the divine radiance of the Light of the unmanifested *Logos*.

At its highest level, *AUM* is the Soundless Sound which becomes the medium of transmission for the Ineffable Light. The *AUM* is also the origin of sound in the world of manifestation, the most sacred syllable, the hierophantic leader of all prayers and chants, and the most important subject of all meditation. Thus, it may be seen in two ways. As a single letter uttered with one articulation, it is the *OM*, the symbol of the Supreme Spirit. One should imagine this as a constant, omnipresent sounding, capable of being consciously sounded within the consecrated temple of the human form. One should imagine it superimposed on all other sounds, all other vibrations, all other thoughts and feelings. To do so is to cooperate consciously with the great cosmic sounding of the One Resonance, but within the sphere and temple of one's own invisible vestures. *OM* is the Supreme Spirit, *Ishvara*, the Most High.

Considered as the triliteral word *AUM*, consisting of the three letters A, U and M, as well as the crucial silent stoppage, it implies all the archetypal trinities and triplicities inherent in the manifesting

Tetraktys. It is the three *Vedas* and the Vedanta. It is the three primary states of human consciousness, which are at one simple level waking, sleeping and deep sleep; it is also *turiya*, the state of supreme spiritual wakefulness. It is the three divisions of the universe invoked in the *Gayatri* – *bhur*, which is the most material and visible realm; *bhuvah*, which is the indwelling, invisible counterpart of the visible; and *svah*, which is transcendental, ethereal and celestial in comparison with all that is astral and earthy. It is also the *trimurti*, the three ruling deities Brahma, Vishnu and Shiva, the mighty agents of creation, preservation and destruction, the three principal attributes of the One Supreme Reality, which is *Sat-Chit-Ananda*, the fusion of Truth, Ideation and Bliss. In this sense, the *AUM* embraces the entire cosmos as emanated and controlled by the Supreme Spirit, the *Paramatman,* which is a pristine, primeval radiation from the Divine Ground, *Parabrahman.*

At the highest, most para-cosmic and universal level, the Sacred Word is both the One and the Three-in-One. It is the *OM*, the single homogeneous sound which, whether uttered or unuttered, is the supreme sound, the One Sound behind all other sounds. Because it is a vesture of the one unmanifested Logoic Light, it is the source of all vibrations. It can also be seen as the triune *AUM* because, as human beings, all individuals are triune in nature and connected with the triune aspects of the cosmos – the physical, the astral and the ethereal. But the *AUM* can also be related to the three aspects or interpenetrating phases of one single continuous activity which involves creation, preservation, destruction and regeneration. Just as one can postulate that Deity is independent of and prior to all worlds, and the universe itself, so too one can cognize the mirroring of Deity in Nature, in the cosmos, in the process of manifestation, as a triune *AUM*, which is then the source of all the many variegated combinations, permutations, collections and associations of vibrations that are involved on all planes of life. By deliberately moving away from the dualism of two selves, and towards the interrelated vibrations of the two *AUM*s, which are really one and the same, one may come to cognize the unmanifest behind the manifest, the substratum behind the mutable, and the indwelling, unmanifest, ever-existing spiritual source of life, light and energy behind the cosmic dance of Deity. It is ceaselessly at play, continually working through vast, immense multiplicity, constantly harmonizing, sifting and selecting, but also perpetually dissolving and destroying forms, and reaffirming endlessly the inmost, imperishable essence of Life.

Thus, the *Maitrayana Brahmana Upanishad* speaks of the *OM* as:

> The *Udgitha*, called *Pranava*, the leader, the bright, the sleepless, free from old age and death, three-footed, consisting of three letters and likewise to be known as fivefold, placed in the cave of the heart.

It is the end and aim of the deepest undercurrent of constant meditation, beyond all borrowed vestures and finite faculties, and one with the Highest Self. As an ardent apprentice in the science of meditation upon the *AUM*, one might start one's day by thinking of it in relation to the dawn of manifestation, corresponding to the moment when one awakens, arises from sleep and begins one's duties in waking existence. One could return to it around midday, again at sunset and again before going to sleep. Thus, one could give oneself four significant moments during the day, four precious opportunities to reaffirm the dateless and deathless, the bright, the bodiless, the indestructible, the immortal and invulnerable as one's inmost Self and the inmost Self of all that exists, but also as THAT which transcends the cosmos. If one aspires to adore the *AUM*, worship it, commune with it and become one with it, then the more one can contemplate it, chant it, feel with it and for it, the more one could think about it – thinking until one loses oneself in the thought and feeling of its nature – the better for one's constant current of meditation.

The *Maitrayana Brahmana Upanishad* gives further food for reflection upon the object of worship, explaining that:

> In the beginning *Brahman* was all this. He was one, and infinite. . . . The Highest Self is not to be fixed, he is unlimited, unborn, not to be reasoned about, not to be conceived. He is like the ether, everywhere, and at the destruction of the Universe, he alone is awake. Thus from that ether he wakes all this world, which consists of thought only, and by him alone is all this meditated on, and in him it is dissolved.

In other words, thinking about that Highest Self, one can fuse the three functions of the meditator, the act of meditating and the object of meditation. He is the object of meditation, but He is also the subject of meditation who gives the power to meditate. His self-subsisting essence is the sustenance of the power of meditation. The way in which the subject, the object and the activity of meditation are fused in Him as the Three-in-One represents the entire invisible, unmanifest universe veiled by the manifest cosmos. And that is true of each and every human being. Once one begins to focus on THAT which is all that exists, as in the wonderful songs of the poet-sage Namalvar, one will be drowned in Him. These people, those people, this man, that man, this woman, that woman – none of these have any meaning other than Him. All hands are His hands, all feet are His feet, all eyes are His eyes, all minds are His mind. Everything thrills and throbs in the *AUM* because of the one indwelling, universal, ever-existent Light of the *Logos*. As the *Upanishad* says:

> His is that luminous form which shines in the sun, and the manifold light in the smokeless fire. . . . He who is in the fire, and he who is in the heart, and he who is in the sun, they are one and the same. He who knows this becomes one with the One.

The sole prerogative and higher privilege of being human is the possibility of knowing, celebrating and adoring the Universal Self and beholding its triune nature within and behind all subjects and objects, as well as all their interconnections. To know that Self is to fuse everything ceaselessly and yet remain apart, alone and ever awake in the Night of Non-Manifestation, apart from the entire masquerade of manifestation. W.Q. Judge states, in commenting upon these passages from the *Maitrayana Brahmana Upanishad*, that

> 'to know' this does not mean to merely apprehend the statement, but actually become personally acquainted with it by interior experience. And this is difficult. But it is to be sought after. And the first step is to attempt to realize universal brotherhood, for when one becomes identified with the One, who is all, he 'participates in the souls of all creatures'; surely then the first step in the path is universal brotherhood.

The Path, May 1886

To experience the elusive ideal of universal brotherhood as actual conscious participation in the souls of all creatures means thinking through as many lives as possible from the standpoint of the soul going through the school of experience and seeing all of them within a single universal pilgrimage. In another place, Judge underscores the intimate connection between ethically and psychologically inserting oneself into the pilgrimage of Humanity and the quickening of the power of meditation in the awakened soul:

> If we do all our acts, small and great, every moment, for the sake of the whole human race, as representing the Supreme Spirit, then every cell and fibre of the body and inner man will be turned in one direction, resulting in perfect concentration.
>
> *Irish Theosophist*, July 1883

This fusion of thought, will and feeling, cognition and concentration, volition and empathy, so crucial to the activation of the true potency of meditation, is virtually impossible when predicated upon the nebulous notion of the personal self. But when seen as the living solidarity of all souls, all selves, all beings, in the one universal pilgrimage, it becomes buoyant and effortless, joyous and expansive.

This is the golden thread inspiring and sustaining alchemical self-regeneration through meditation, and it lies at the core of the sacred meaning of the *Gayatri*, the holiest of all *mantras*, which begins with the deathless *AUM* and ends with the dateless *OM*.

> The object of this prayer is that we may carry out our whole duty, after becoming acquainted with the truth, while we are on our journey to thy Sacred Seat. This is our pilgrimage, not of one, not selfishly, not alone, but the whole of humanity. For the sacred seat is that place where all meet, where alone are all one. It is when and where the three great sounds of the first word of the prayer merge into one soundless sound. This is the only proper prayer, the sole saving aspiration.
>
> *The Path*, January 1893

One can thus see that the very stance of an individual soul trying to become one with the Higher Self is only a way of stating what could equally be stated from the other side. The same process could also be seen as that of the universal Self entering into the receptive seeker, more fully suffusing every cell and atom of the surrendering devotee. The *Gayatri* invokes the True Sun of the Highest Self to unveil itself and illumine one's entire being. This hidden element of divine grace is vital to the operation of consecration, prayer and meditation because one's determination to learn the truth includes a fearless recognition that there is that which hides or veils it from one's vision. Only when the projected ray subordinates and surrenders itself to its divine parent can there be a release of intense, ardent, longing aspiration for the Supreme Truth, for the one Source, for the sacred seat of the ever-invisible, ever-existent Fire, which is the fountainhead of all Mystery Fires, ceaselessly burning throughout *manvantara* and *pralaya*, unaltered by the whole universe and unmodified by all conditioned existence.

If this is inaccessible, it arises from the karma of past deeds, which have left the brain substance and fibres of one's being too opaque and too sluggish to respond to higher vibrations. If one is mired in a life of careless indifference and recalcitrant ignorance, unable to cooperate with the universal processes of Divine Life, it means that in the past one did not cooperate with and adore the Greater Mysteries, but settled instead for something small and tawdry, a delusive spell of self-adoration. Such a life creates a film or veil that estranges one's own feelings from the feelings of others, one's own concerns from the concerns of the universal pilgrimage of humanity. Failing in the custody and care of the divine flame within, one falls into that fickle carelessness which produces endemic passivity, extinguishing full awareness and plunging one into irresponsibility and the aimless drift of self-indulgence amidst the highs and lows of the insecure self. One becomes blinded and bound by a fundamental ignorance of the self-destructive, self-doomed nature of such an episodic existence, where the sacred power of mind is dragged down and made to enlist in the slavery of consciousness to the passions, to false distinctions between inner and outer, and also to an extremely narrow, ephemeral and unreal conception of space and time. Far from aiding the *persona* in its desperate plight, this infusion of a volatile mentality only serves to feed the vultures of the insatiable passions, and stokes the fires of multiplicity which can only produce a kind of chaotic screen that fogs, confuses and smokes out the light of true reason, hindering the hearing of the Soundless Sound. At best, there lingers a subliminal echo which can haunt but cannot heal. Thus all past karma has created a kind of captivity and a failure to understand illusions as illusions, yet this bondage is masked by a pessimistic pseudo-objectivity that declares a false finality to the conditioning of consciousness and a depressing fixity to the state of enslavement to delusion.

That is why it is so crucial that in the very act of adoration, using the *Gayatri*, one utters a tremendous cry of the soul, which is a cry of spiritual freedom. But such a cry is useless at the moment of death. It is to be made now or never, by those who use the *Gayatri* unfailingly; it is a cry for clarity, a cry that the veil may fall, that the scales may drop from one's eyes, and that the obscuration of one's being may be dispelled. Therefore, it takes the form of the sound Unveil! Judge, in translating the *Gayatri*, has deliberately fused its actual meaning with a very powerful *mantra* in the *Isha Upanishad*, producing a ringing rendition which conveys the full force of the invocation:

> *AUM*. Unveil, O Thou who givest sustenance to the Universe, from whom all proceed, to whom all must return, that face of the True Sun now hidden by a vase of golden light, that we may see the truth and do our whole duty on our journey to thy sacred seat. *OM*.

The vase of golden light is the *Hiranyagarbha*, the cosmic sphere of Light around the secret, sacred Sun which is the true source of all enlightenment, all ideation, and all divine and supra-mental energy. It is only reflected at a very limited level in the physical sun, which is the source of what people call physical life or pranic vitality, and also what they call light. That light, however, appears bright only in contrast to physical darkness, and it is only an illusory light compared with the ineffable Light of the Divine Darkness that is the essential nature of the unmanifest *Logos*. Whilst the physical sun gives all the energy that people ordinarily understand, that pervasive energy must necessarily participate in the law of conservation and must also be subject to the law of entropy. The ineffable Light of the *Logos*, by contrast, is inconsumable and inexhaustible: it can only be the object of the highest ideation of a *Manasa*, an immortal thinking being who can light up the flame that is its priceless share in the universal fire of *Mahat*.

The *Gayatri* can be extremely potent if it is used regularly every day, but it can only work when it is invoked on behalf of all living beings.

It can become daily more intense as a regular act, a request or prayer, a kind of petition for grace arising out of the depths of the hidden hearts of the human race. Then it becomes a form of manifestation capable of summoning and activating the sacrificial ladder, along which travel the high *Dhyanis, Devas* and Hierarchies that move up and down the great rainbow bridge invoked by all the Vedic hymns. Being the *Matriveda*, the mother of the *Vedas*, the *Gayatri* is venerated as the highest possible *mantra*. It enables every human being to reach out on behalf of all Humanity, ardently to the One Source. By doing this again and again, one becomes attuned to that to which one appeals, and familiar with the avataric descent of the Divine Light and the shedding of its supernal grace.

If human beings start to use the *Gayatri* daily whilst their motives are yet sullied, they are in awesome danger. They risk summoning forces that will be too strong to resist or to regulate, and they will need the ever-present protection of the Rishis and Mahatmas, who are likened in Upanishadic metaphor to the ribs of an umbrella sheltering all beneath. Every human being holds the handle of this umbrella, but its ribs belong to all Humanity, for they represent the highest hierarchies of enlightened human beings who are conscious instruments of the Cosmic Will. They are the supreme divine agents of the One Law, the One Life and the One Light, and through their boundless compassion they can protect and provide opportunities to human beings, who suffer from glaring gaps between their moral stature and their mental aspiration, between their spiritual strength and their emotional stamina, between their longing for union and their communion with the One. The compassion of perfected human beings gives strength to the weak. And it gives hope to those who are sometimes awed or made afraid by the enormity of their undertaking.

Yet, whilst this allegorical umbrella provides a measure of assured protection to the fallible aspirant, enlightened beings cannot vicariously substitute for the self-conscious effort each individual must make for himself or herself to maintain the mysterious thread of life's meditation as a constant vibration. There must, however, be honesty and moral courage in recognizing the avoidable gaps in one's practice, and a clarity in discerning tendencies that make one vulnerable to delusion through likes and dislikes, delusive affections and false dependencies.

One must become vigilant against the simian tricks that memory plays, and against the perverse tendency to misuse the power of thought to produce rationales which only consolidate the discontinuities in oneself. All of these persist as concessions to that part of oneself which is drowsy, lazy, cowardly and terrified of the Light; that part which is terrified of standing up confidently and moving apart from the inert mass of most beings. Before one can become a true man or woman of meditation, and so a true servant of Humanity, one must first become, in a Pauline sense, separated out of the astral and psychic plane – a being without external signs of slavish connections with human beings. One must go through the Isolation of the immortal soul, a painful period of withdrawal from lesser supports. Only then can one attain the height of what is possible, reaching the pristine source that is above the head, and that, once touched, eventually sets aflame the thousands of latent centres that are in the head, the legendary Tree of Light, Life and Cosmic Electricity in Man.

Long before this turning-point is reached, one must render reliable the steady effort to meditate. Thus it is said that if one cannot initially meditate upon the most abstract themes, one should begin by meditating upon meditation itself. Meditate upon the great Masters of Meditation, enjoying the very thought of the Buddhas of Contemplation, self-luminous beings who are masters of compassion and ceaselessly radiate currents of beneficence. In the very enjoyment of meditating upon the galaxy of *Dhyanis* and the host of Mahatmas, one will elevate oneself, expanding one's horizon, one's sense of kinship and one's conception of the human family. One will be thrilled that the human family can include such a vast array of self-resplendent beings, and one will begin to see this world anew.

Then, when one earnestly meditates and finds multiple obstructions arising, one will be able to see them for what they are and honestly trace them to their origins in forgetfulness, indolence and cowardice. At the same time, one will understand that the very ability one has gained to stand apart from these shadows is itself rooted in a recognition of that which is all-knowing, unforgetful, ever awake, courageous, free, untrammelled and universally self-conscious. Even though one's deeper Self must be repeatedly invoked, one will still find a certain joy arising in oneself, a certain natural desire flowing out of deep love for that universal Self. This is the true source of all other loves and the only thing that can ultimately give meaning to all one's other altruistic urges. It is the well-spring of one's empathy for all life, for all the kingdoms of Nature, for what is in every stone and plant and tree. It is that in oneself which can resonate to the rising sun, can respond to the setting sun, and can echo back to the invisible Midnight Sun. All these are but veiled expressions of a deeper universal current of energy which is compassionate, which is sacrificial, and which is consciously emanated by the Masters of Light and Love, Compassion and Wisdom.

When one begins to develop a natural joy, hunger, longing and love for this mystic meditation, one will find that it acts as an eliminator. Many of one's lesser longings will simply fall away, and one's vanity, delusion and ego-projection will be revealed and emptied out. Yet, what was good and true at the core of them will never be lost, for that is an outflow of the fount of universal love which belongs to the *Paramatman*, the universal Self. If this meditation is real, it should arouse and deepen one's capacity to be one-pointed – single-minded and single-hearted – able to concentrate upon the appointed task at hand and able to consecrate it for the good of all. Letting go of all results, reducing one's participation in fantasy, anticipation and regret, one will become more fully engaged, more fully active and wide awake. With this, a great deal of what before looked to be oneself will become exteriorized, come out and fall away. It will all show itself for what it is – a mask, a veil. And layer by layer, veil upon veil of false selfhood will fall away until nothing remains but the one ineffable Light. It is beginningless and endless. It is the Light that is hidden in the Divine Darkness, behind all worlds, beings and manifestations. It is the One Light behind every spark of aspiration and every spark of truth, beauty and goodness in each and every being in existence. It is the Light of which Jesus spoke when he said, "If thine eye be single, thy body shall be full of Light", and it is the Light spoken of by Krishna as the lighting up in oneself of the Supreme Saviour, who then becomes visible. Let each fearless pilgrim soul meditate upon that Light which lives in all as the Highest Self. Let each devotee concentrate upon it in adoration, surrendering and subordinating all to that one fiery Self. And let each heroic seeker after undying truth will to work for its eternal habitation in every human heart.

> And now thy Self is lost in SELF, Thyself unto THYSELF, merged in THAT SELF from which thou first didst radiate.
>
> Where is thy individuality, Lanoo, where the Lanoo himself? It is the spark lost in the fire, the drop within the ocean, the ever present ray become the All and the eternal radiance.
>
> And now, Lanoo, thou art the doer and the witness, the radiator and the radiation, Light in the Sound, and the Sound in the Light.

The Voice of the Silence

Hermes, October 1987

THE MYSTERY OF THE EGO

*If we feel not our spiritual death, how should we dream of
invoking life?*

Claude de St.-Martin

The sure test that individuals have begun to ascend to higher planes of consciousness is that they find an increasing fusion of their ideas and their sympathies. Breadth of mental vision is supported by the depth of inmost feeling. Words are inadequate to convey these modes of awareness. Mystics cannot readily communicate the ineffable union of head and heart which has sometimes been called a mystic marriage. Such veiled metaphorical language may often refer to specific centres of consciousness in the human body. If the body is the living temple of an imprisoned divine intelligence, the metaphorical language of the mystics points to a tuning and activation of interrelated centres in the body. There is a mystical heart that is different in location and function from the physical heart. There is also a seed of higher intellection, "the place between thine eyes", which is distinct from those centres of the brain that are involved in ordinary cerebration. The more a person is able to hold consciousness on a plane that is vaster in relation to time and space, subtler in relation to cause and motion, than normal sensory awareness, the more these higher centres are activated. Since this cannot take place without also arousing deeper feelings, the original meaning of the term 'philosophy' – "love of wisdom" – is suggestive and significant. There is a level of energy released by love that is conjoined with a profound reverence for truth *per se*. This energy releases a greater capacity to experience self-conscious attunement to what is behind the visible phantasmagoria of the whole of life, drawing one closer to what is gestating under the soil in the hidden roots of being and closer to the unarticulated longings of all other human beings. Everyone senses this kinship at critical moments. Sometimes, in the context of a shared tragedy or at a time of crisis caused by a sudden catastrophe, many people experience an authentic oneness with each other despite the absence of any tokens of tangible expression.

To bring the disciplined and developed creative imagination into full play is to do much more than merely to have a passive awareness of sporadic moments of human solidarity. These moments are only intermittent, imperfect and partial expressions of vaster capacities in the realms of thought and feeling. To draw out these capacities fully requires that we withdraw support from everything that is restrictive. The higher *Eros* presupposes a kind of negative *Eros*, a withdrawal of exaggerated emotional involvement in the things of this world, in sensations and sense-objects, in name and form and in ever-changing personalities. This withdrawal is based upon a recognition that there is a lie involved in superficial emotion, and a calm awareness of a noumenal reality which is unmanifest. To realize this is to prepare for the potential release of the higher *Eros*, but this is truly difficult because to negate means to come to a void. There is no way to withdraw from the froth of psychic emotion and the tangles of discursive reasoning without experiencing a haunting loneliness and immense void wherein everything appears meaningless. Though painful and even terrifying, this is the necessary condition through which the seeker must pass if he is to die so that he may be reborn. *The Voice of the Silence* teaches that "the mind needs breadth and depth and points to draw it towards the Diamond Soul". It must actively generate these mental linkages through deep meditation upon the suffering of humanity, seeing all individual strivings as part of a collective quest for enlightenment, focussing with compassion upon the universal suffering that transcends yet includes all the pains and agonies of all living beings.

When a person can connect and coordinate these periods of deliberate meditation and conscious cultivation of universal compassion, and experiences ordinary life through these contacts with the realm of non-being, then the purification and renovation of the temple has begun. There is a starving out of entire clusters of elementals, minute constellations of matter that have been given a murky colouring and destructive impress, and which make up the astral vesture. These matrices of frustration, limitation, anger and self-hatred are gradually replaced by new clusters of life-energy – readily available throughout nature – which are more attuned to the highest abstract conceptions of space, time and motion. Thus there is a greater incarnation of the indwelling divine nature. Every human body may be seen as a mystic cross upon which the *Christos* within is being crucified. To nurture radical renovations in the vestures through the concentrated mind and disciplined imagination, by forging connections between points touched in meditation and in everyday life, is to make possible, after the Gethsemane necessitated by collective Karma, a fuller manifestation of the *Christos*, the god within. This long journey is coeval and coequal with the whole of life and the entirety of mankind. When individuals discern in their own quest a cosmic dimension, impersonality and selflessness in their endeavours become an authentic affirmation of what is potentially within all. It is impossible to grow in awareness of what one truly is without finding that the barrier between oneself and other beings weakens. There is an internal integrity to this quest, and, therefore, it is pointless to pretend that all at once, simply by words, gestures and rituals, one can suddenly come to a universal love of all mankind. Of course, some desperate people, through drugs or other adventitious aids, experience enthralling intimations of the wonder of life or of its unity. These are the result of temporarily loosening the screws in the complex psychophysical organism called the human body and should not be mistaken for true wisdom. The crucial difference lies in continuity.

The more consciously one is able to sense the universal presence of the true Self, the more one can maintain continuity. The more one can see the moment of death and its connection with the present moment, the more one can participate in the unmanifest core of the universal quest. While the mystical capacity for sensing cosmic *Eros* grows, the desire to express it declines. Those who are caught up in external appearances crave messianic miracles and want to treat the universe as if they could manipulate it. This is a stumbling block to the quest. The real quest has an integrity that can be tested continuously because it must release an energy of commitment to the whole. Just as it is only through the cessation of the repetitive revolutions of the lower mind that higher thought is released, it is only by the cessation of limiting desires on the heterogeneous plane of perception that the true *Eros* may be released.

The Voice of the Silence teaches: "Shun ignorance, and likewise shun illusion. Avert thy face from world deceptions: mistrust thy senses; they are false. But within thy body – the shrine of thy sensations, seek in the Impersonal for the 'Eternal Man'; and having sought him out, look inward: thou art Buddha." Tragically, the divine origin of human consciousness is all too often forgotten by individuals who permit themselves to become entrapped in "world deceptions". Just as people in a room with artificial light forget the light of the sun, consciousness, when it is focussed through a lucid zone that points in the realm of externals in one direction, is in the very activity of awareness shutting off a larger consciousness. Human beings reinforce each other in assigning reality to the visible tip of the whole of life, to that which is maintained and activated by words, names and desires which have public criteria of recognition that can be fulfilled on the plane of external events. On the other hand, an individual who senses the rays of the Spiritual Sun, enfolded in the blackness of the midnight sky, comes closer to wisdom. Participating in the reflections of lesser lights, while retaining an inward reverence for the cosmic ocean of light, is living within the moment with a calm awareness of eternity. *The Secret Doctrine* suggests that what is called light is a shadowy illusion and that beyond what are normally called light and darkness there is noumenal Darkness which is eternally radiant.

In the focussing of consciousness on the plane of differentiation, the process is broken into forms and colours, moments of time, fields of space. In the breaking up of consciousness, something gets caught, causing mental inertia. Cosmic spirit can only manifest in and through a material matrix, but it cannot manifest without mind, or without the energy that brings about the fusion of the matrix and what is potentially present in spirit. This is why, in all spiritual disciplines, the battleground is the mind. The fact that the mind becomes dual is the price paid for self-consciousness and this price involves both self-limitation and the limiting of other selves. This limitation is reinforced by religious beliefs that foreshorten the age of man and the earth, and also by constricting fears of death and decay, whether applied to human lives or collectively to a culture. There is a consequent increase in the inability of consciousness to free itself from its frozen identification with a particular aspect of the differentiated field, which is at best only a veil cast over the greater life process. At the very core of the life process all worlds are potentially present. In addition to a particular differentiated field, an infinite number of potentially differentiated fields lie latent in a pregenetically differentiated state. This is the core of reality in the realm of divine thought called *Mahat,* the realm in which Mahatmas abide. It is also at the heart of cosmic *Eros* or *Fohat.*

Whether one examines the collective structure of society or an individual in a nuclear family, one will find myriad ways in which human beings transfer anxiety and limitations to each other. Not all human beings are equally trapped, nor are they all prey to the same kinds of illusions. Some individuals are perpetually subject to delusive expectations of worldly success. Their experience is painful and it seems they never truly learn. There are others who experience violent reactions, and just because there is so much violence in their reaction, they are bound equally at the extreme points in the oscillation between optimism and pessimism. Still others seem to be shrewd and subtle in leaving possibilities open by negating their involvements intuitively and unconsciously, even though they may not have any metaphysical map to guide them. There are always a few everywhere who are reminiscent of the great galaxy of beings who are awake during the long night of non-manifestation. They self-consciously begin with a certain thread of awareness, and those who know them from an early age may sense how calmly they are going to lay aside their mortal vestures in the end. Theirs is a beautiful, self-conscious reflection, though guarded and veiled, within the lesser vehicles and ordinary orbits of profane existence. While other human beings are cursing life and themselves, these heroic pioneers move as if they are constantly making an inward advance towards that which they knew early in life, and to which they will be true until the end.

The difference between human beings has to do with previous lives, and with the sad fact that many human beings seem to gravitate again and again in the same direction in which they had formerly been trapped. Given a sufficiently vast period of evolution, all human beings require in some sense to be where they are and need their illusions. This is true metaphysically and in regard to evolution as a whole. But under the law of cycles, in certain periods of history and at crucial moments in the present, people come to a parting of the ways, a moment of choice. It is as if they sense that if they do not do something, they are going to be left behind. One cannot hold down high souls who have work to do in regard to human evolution, who are going to sow the seeds for the harvest of tomorrow. One cannot expect them to be held back by those who are born then under karma, even though unwilling or unready to put themselves in that posture where they confidently affirm their right to belong to a larger life. This is part of the complex process of the dying of a civilization or an epoch, and of the coming to birth of a new order through a long and painful gestation. Ultimately, then, fragmentation and entrapment of consciousness cannot be understood solely in terms of the interdependence between human beings, or the differences between people bound up with the same illusions and those with the courage to break them. The missing term in such an account is the confrontation between self-consciousness and the void.

If life after life every time one starts to negate and encounters the void, one flees back into the world, a pattern is established which cannot be sustained indefinitely. Suppose that such an individual comes into contact with beings who have gone through the void and see no difference between the void, themselves and all other beings. Such Men of Meditation do not entertain any emotions below the level of cosmic *Eros*, and they do not engender any thought-currents except those in the context of *Mahat*, the universal mind. Contact with such beings is an immense opportunity but also an immense challenge, an instrument of precipitation. The entire riddle of the entrapment of consciousness, when moved from the general plane to a particular person, can only be solved by the individual. The perspective can be given, the metaphysical maps provided, but each person must examine why he or she is in a particular condition in terms of memories, feelings or ideas. By keeping in the forefront of awareness a conception that is larger than any habitual view of self, and with the assurance that there are those who have been able to resolve for all what individuals find so difficult to resolve for themselves, each will be helped. In the end, each must plunge into the stream. All must engage in individual self-study, asking again and again, "What is important to me? What am I prepared to let go? Have I the courage to die and be reborn?" A person who is in earnest will, without losing a sense of proportion and humour, set aside periods in which to take specific steps in the direction towards the Path. This centres upon what H. P. Blavatsky called the mystery of the human ego, the mystery of each human being.

The need for self-study bears directly upon the discovery of the thread of individual continuity, the *sutratman*. This thread of consciousness in every person is only an aspect of the monadic essence of which one is a ray. It is what makes of a person a monad, a particular being or an individual, separate only in the functional capacity to reflect the universal. Every human being is a unique lens capable of self-consciously reflecting universal light. If that is what all individuals are in essence, when they are manifesting through personalities bound up with name and form and involved in the world of differentiated matter, they become caught up in a psychic fog that obscures the clarity of the monadic vision of the true meaning and purpose of the pilgrimage of life. Nevertheless, in that fog there remains a residual reflection of what the monad in its fullness knows. This is what may be called the golden sutratmic thread within every human being. The thread is activated during deep sleep, but during waking life it cannot very easily be activated. It is involved in the baby's first cry at birth, and is glimpsed at the moment of death. It can be self-consciously activated in meditation. The true, sacrificial meaning of the Theosophical Movement is to give human beings in waking life points of contact with what they truly know themselves to be in deep sleep, and to do this in a manner that can give to each the strength of a collective affirmation. "To live and reap experience, the mind needs breadth and depth and points to draw it towards the Diamond Soul. Seek not these points in Maya's realm." The golden thread can only be lit up as a constant basis of light by each one individually. Every person must clean out the mirror-like mind which gathers dust while it reflects. Each person by self-study and self-examination helps to mitigate the obscuration of the golden thread-light which is broken up into details, lost in the externals, caught up in particular events, through memories looking backwards and through wish-fulfilment producing unreal psychic states. All must banish this obscuration on their own.

In the end, however, one cannot activate that golden cord, as Plato called it, without the exhilaration of self-transcendence. Paradoxically, when you are truly yourself, you forget yourself. To be calmly engaged in the manifestation of the golden thread is to increase awareness of all other beings and the whole of life. Self-study, then, has further depths of meaning. When a person in a period of true contemplation has a vision of the sutratmic Self, brought down from above and enriching consciousness through the activation of divine thought, then suddenly there will be a kickback arising from the resistance of the lesser self. One will painfully discover that the mind cannot stay for very long on a sufficiently abstract and impersonal level, and that the heart cannot continuously hold that which is the collective misery of mankind and bear love to all beings. It falls back to lesser concerns. Self-study becomes a way of studying the lesser self with firmness and honesty, together with a sense of humour towards the ridiculousness of the lesser self, the impostor that shuts out the richness and potentiality of the Self. True self-study takes the form of studying those periods of waking life where there is a forgetting and therefore a denial of the Self. Self-study is a way of minimizing the propensity to forget and the need for too many reminders, and above all, safeguarding against the need to have one's knuckles rapped by admonitions that come from the life process. To choose one's reminders rather than have them come from outside is to adjust the ratios of moments of time that are well spent to those that are wasted through being caught in forgetfulness of the golden thread. These wasted moments constitute the tragedy of the crucifixion of the *Christos*. The more one finds this happening, the greater the necessity to get to the root of the problem. Self-study can never be made the object of schemata because it must vary for every individual, and any person may find that repeated efforts yield only limited results. There may be particular moments when there is a brilliant flash, and one sees through so much in the masquerade that one is freed. But this is something about which no general rules can be made because it involves the interaction of complex variables and the emanations of consciousness in the life of every man, and so it constitutes part of the mystery of the ego itself.

As taught and exemplified by Socrates, philosophic self-study during life is an integral part of a continual preparation for the moment of death. A fruitful source for study and reflection is the *Bhagavad Gita*. Robert Crosbie suggests, in his remarks on the eighth chapter, that there is a real danger that fruits of effort will not carry over to the next life. The measure of difficulty in truly availing oneself of the teaching is identical to that involved in becoming immortal. Those for whom the teaching becomes a reality are able to reverse the false image given by the *maya* of the life process and by the moulds of interaction of men in terms of the reality they assign to the finite, the ever-fleeting and the false. They are able to reverse it so completely that they see with the eyes of pity and participate in the illusions of men with a constant inward awareness of *Mahat* and cosmic *Eros*. Such men display an existential consciousness of immortality which goes beyond external tokens and marks, beyond forms, words and concepts. It is that consciousness which ultimately must become the basis by which one thinks, and therefore by which one lives, and each one must cultivate this independently. Few individuals will reach that point in life before the moment of death where they have gained the power to slay their lunar form at will. After death every human being has to linger in a state in which there is a purgatorial dissipation of the lunar form made up of illusions, fears and anxieties engendered during life. All of these constitute the substance of what people call "living" and "the self", and to dissipate them in life means to have periods where one can see right through oneself. Most human beings are blocked in this because they have developed the tendency of seeing through others more than they see through themselves.

On the Path, one is not concerned to see through anything in anyone else without an appropriate compassion that can only be real if based upon knowledge gained by having broken through comparable illusions in oneself. One must first build into daily life an awareness that negates illusions, sifting and selecting between what is quintessential and what is not in every experience. Until this becomes a steady current, one is not going to be able to dissipate the lunar form at will before death, but for those who have done this, dying is like the discarding of clothes. Life in the ordinary sense has no hold over them and therefore their coming into the world is not involuntary. This is very difficult for most human beings to understand. As they go through a painful process of acting in one direction, reacting in another direction, they may suddenly hope that by some confession or ritual they can wipe out the past, but since that is impossible, the wheel of life is extraordinarily painful, monotonous and meaningless for them. They keep being propelled back into life, repeating the same oscillations of illusion. This is graphically described by Plato in the "Myth of Er". There is a sense in which conventionally good people choose the life that they envied. If their goodness is caught up in appearances, they are going to be misled by external trappings. To be above the realm of appearances is to see to the very core of life, to see the essential justice of all things, and to be able to handle such insight one will need true compassion. To exemplify this authentically and continuously is in fact to be able to ceaselessly negate one's own self and to see that self as being ultimately linked up with every other being on every plane. At its root it is no-thing; it is not conditioned, it is not in the process, it is beyond.

This is a long and difficult process, but given the mystery of the ego, people do not really know why they failed in the past when they made such attempts, and they have no right to despair in advance. They do not know, through what seem to be small steps taken with integrity, that great results might accrue to them. Sometimes the first earnest steps may be taken very late in life. Fortunate is the man who begins this very early in life. But whether early or late, it can be tested in relation to reduction of fears and an elevation of all encounters with other beings. The Theosophical Movement seeks to maximize the opportunity for human beings to gain strength, support, inspiration and instruction in working upon the maintenance of conscious continuity of awareness. That awareness helps them to develop an eye for essentials in daily life, enabling them to distinguish the everlasting from the ever-fleeting and not to mistake the ephemeral for the enduring, not to mistake appearances and forms for archetypal realities. To do this again and again and to make it ultimately a line of life's meditation is the only constructive way in which a person can prepare for the moment of death. This is to put the issue in psychological terms. It could also be put in terms of the sound that a human being can utter at the moment of death. That sound can be chosen only in a limited sense, because the whole of life is going to determine a dominant thought and feeling, and these will determine what sound is uttered at the moment of death. The line of life's meditation is reflected in the particular aperture in the human body through which the life-current withdraws. A very wise being who looks at a corpse will see straightaway through which orifice life departed, and hence will know a great deal about the consciousness of the soul.

The wisest beings during life gather up all their energies, like the shy and watchful tortoise, into that which is within and above them.

At the moment of death they will have a sublime gnostic experience which is an affirmation of immortality, a joyous discarding of all awareness of conditions. Having put themselves beyond conditions, they are able to experience not only immortal longings, but through the continuity of unconditioned cosmic *Eros* and through the continuity of an unconditional awareness of *Mahat*, they experience spiritual freedom. This detachment may look at times austere, but it is combined with an inexhaustible compassion and immense vitality. If they live right, without being caught in the process, every burden lies lightly upon them. They are constantly stripping away even as other men are draining themselves in the gardens of illusion. They constantly affirm on behalf of all the Upanishadic invocation: "Lead me from the unreal to the real. Lead me from darkness into light. Lead me from death to immortality." When one can make a positive inner affirmation of the Divine within, this becomes a potent current of thought and feeling, energy and life. Without words, all one's actions will convey to others a sense that behind the games of life there is a deeper reality of pure joy in which there is dignity to every individual. As a preliminary training in making this invocation, every night before going to sleep one should renounce all identification with the body and the brain, with form, with all likes and dislikes, with all memories and anticipations. One should invoke the same affirmation upon rising, as well as at other chosen times and spontaneously whenever possible. If it is to be meaningful in the context of a universe governed by the boundless ideation of *Mahat* and suffused by the beneficence of cosmic *Eros*, this invocation must be made not only for oneself, but for all.

Hermes, April 1979

THE GOLDEN THREAD

When we read what H.P. Blavatsky has written of her predecessors, those true transmitters acting in strict obedience to the Brotherhood of Bodhisattvas – Wise Men, Initiates, Mahatmas belonging to all mankind – we are naturally led to think of what she herself experienced in the nineteenth century on behalf of us all. She founded the Theosophical Society in New York with three objects, the first of which was the formation of a nucleus of Universal Brotherhood – Brotherhood *in actu* and not only in name. The second object was a comparative study of the religions, sciences and philosophies of every part of the world so that all men and women, including Americans, might come to salute every true witness in a long, largely unknown but unbroken history of accumulated wisdom. She taught the perennial philosophy and invited her true students to find in it an Ariadne's thread, a golden thread hidden behind the veil of form and symbol in every great tradition of thought, philosophy, religious aspiration and myth. It is the very basis of real science, and it is the inspiration behind the founding of the Royal Society as well as much of the significant work of men like Edison, a Fellow of the Theosophical Society, and many other scientists indirectly influenced by the wisdom of the Secret Doctrine.

When we consider the efforts of sincere Theosophists to apply this philosophy to their lives, in conformance with the third object of the Theosophical Society, we must think of those moments which are the first concern of any person of any age involved in finding meaning within the flux of experiences: the moment of birth and the moment of death. We can also think of the line that threads these moments. Each of us discovers this entirely for himself, exercising the supreme prerogative of a human being, the privilege of self-reflective consciousness, the gift of the gods, the *Dhyanis* and the *Manasaputras,* seeking out what in his or her whole life was most quintessentially sacred. A great deal happens every day, from morn to night. But even in a small town or in beautiful natural settings, much energy is dissipated. We live in a culture where fragmentation of consciousness is widespread and confusion prevails. In such times of trouble, students of *Theosophia* or *Brahma Vach* are wise in following the advice given by Merlin to Arthur: "Go back to the original moment."

Beginnings are important, endings are inevitable and change is constant in a universe of ceaseless transformation. The wheel revolves constantly faster in the Age of Iron, and everything changes so rapidly that irrelevant analyses and outmoded diagnoses crowd the scene. There are many learned tomes on the pace of change in technological society, but they are not needed by those who understand the winds of change because they recognize the timeless truth of the teachings of Lord Krishna: that a man is wise to meditate upon birth, death, decay, sickness and error. This is the most ancient wisdom, and it is as fresh today as it was five thousand years ago, thanks to the sacrificial ideation of the mighty Brotherhood of silent and eternal Teachers who worship the Nameless and Ineffable. They work in perfect harmony through willing and cheerful obedience to the Maha Chohan, who wanted a Brotherhood of Humanity to be initiated and knew that it would not happen at once, but that the line must and would be kept unbroken. In all theosophical assemblies and associations there are those self-determining agents who are self-elected to serve as the compassionate custodians of the living tradition of the primordial Teaching for the sake of all.

Theosophia is like that ancient Banyan tree. Some come to sit in its shade, while others come to exchange words and seek friends. Still others come to pick fruit. Nature is generous. Some come to sit in the presence of teachers to receive instruction in the mighty power of real meditation, to secure help in self-examination. All are welcome. The antiquity and enormity of the tree are beyond the capacity of any person in any period of history to enclose in a definition or formulation. Great Teachers point beyond themselves to that which is beyond formulation, which is ineffable and indefinable. They seek to make alive and to make real for every man "the priceless boon of learning truth" spoken of in *The Voice of the Silence*.

Pythagoras, in 530 B.C., with the precision of a man who had prepared himself through twenty-two years of training in the Egyptian Mysteries, came to the small town of Krotona. He spent twenty years there laying the foundations of a school and a college for the sake of establishing in the Near East, and in what subsequently became the western world, science (symbolized by the Pythagorean sphere), religion (symbolized by the *tetraktis*), and philosophy (a term that he devised). When asked, "Are you a wise man?" he said, "I am a man who is in love with wisdom, a philosopher, *philosophos*." Any man who loves – like a child, like a teenager, like all human beings – but loves with a wisdom sufficient to care for love itself, to treasure it, and to prize it, becomes like the blooming lotus. So he exercises the privilege and the right extended to every human being. Independent of authorities and experts, independent of the clash of rival and changing fashions, fads, isms, sects and systems, he may exercise the privilege of becoming a true philosopher, of reflecting upon the long journey. Every man is a nomad. The journey begins we know not where. It leads we know not whither. In a world which is like a stage, in which all the players are pilgrims, the pilgrimage is the thing. What is unique, precious and private to each one can only be partly known or shared imperfectly with even the closest friends. *Light on the Path* teaches that no man is our enemy, no man is our friend, but that all alike are our teachers. Our enemy is a mystery, a problem that must be solved even though it take ages. Our friend is an extension of ourself, a riddle hard to read. Only one thing is even more difficult to know, and that is one's own self. Not until the bonds of personality – the mask under which all men masquerade – is loosened, shall that Self be truly known.

Hence the great cry of the ancients, "Know thyself," and the sacred teaching in relation to self-knowledge and self-reference: that they involve and include a real love of wisdom – unmanifest and manifested, in books and brooks, in stones where there are stones, and everywhere for those who have eyes to see, and ears to listen. One of the Mahatmas spoke of music as the most abstract of the arts and mathematics as the most abstract of the sciences. Pythagoras was concerned with both music and mathematics. He fused in himself active and passive contemplation. This is the subject of a conversation in *The Merchant of Venice* between the newlyweds Lorenzo and Jessica, where Jessica, a Jewish girl of the time with a kind of hippie background, experiences what Lorenzo formulates. It is Lorenzo who says that the man who has no music in his soul is fit for stratagems and spoils.

We are very fortunate to have had from the beginning of the Theosophical Society a great plan laid down in the letter of the Maha Chohan. He spoke of the Theosophical Society as the cornerstone, the foundation of the future religions of humanity. There is a grandeur, a magnitude, a magnificence and a breadth of love and compassion in that sacred document which few who call themselves students of Theosophy can remotely hope to emulate, but which every man or woman is invited to attempt to honour in daily life. H.P. Blavatsky said that we must honour every truth by its use, and that this is the archetypal ritual of any theosophical society. When we use those statements of the Great Master, we discover that the great plan laid down was not irrelevant then, never has been irrelevant since, nor could it ever be. Today it rings with a freshness and a contemporary relevance – especially in its reference to the struggle for existence. Everything is known to the master mathematician Hermes, who is an old man and a young boy at the same time. It is a magnanimous letter, helpful to any of us at this point of time in relation to our fellow human beings.

Each of us is potentially perfect, but each of us is like an iceberg and a mystery to himself and to everyone else. Each of us knows many marvellous volumes of mystical philosophy. When so much is known, to so little avail, clearly then what we are faced with requires more than the knowledge of the mind. It involves more than what we, as inheritors of the methods and modes of Aristotle and Bacon, regard as head-learning. We need soul-wisdom. Here we might well think of simple people walking the streets with waiting, wanting lips. Some are very old, some of them so poor in the wealth of the world that they only have what Lord Buddha called the greatest wealth – contentment. This is the simple man's golden thread. Have some of us lost that simplicity, being so overburdened with our divine discontent which sometimes takes less than human forms? Have we overlooked perhaps the importance of that which is so obvious – a measure of contentment?

We are Promethean beings. We have gaps between our limitations and our potentialities. Every one of us knows that he might have been much more than what he is or what he can show on the surface. In this society the surface has become excessively important. Appearances are lies, but we are caught in the *Mahamaya* of these lies, which then become delusions. The Buddha taught that each man makes his own prison and that within ourselves deliverance must be sought. No man can be saved by himself, and yet no man can be saved by another. In fact, the very notion of 'saving' needs re-thinking. We are taught in *The Voice of the Silence* that salvation for one man has no meaning apart from the salvation of the whole of mankind and all living beings. The Maha Chohan spoke of mystical Christianity, of the mystical in every religion, and of self-redemption through one's own seventh principle, the liberated *paramatma*. Etymologically, it is this which ceaselessly moves and which in its movement is the source of light, and life, and joy.

If a man asks, "How can we see the Golden Thread in relation to God, Law and Man?" we might say that theosophically, God is formless, beyond colours and sounds, yet immanent in all of them. God is to be found in each of the colours of the riddle of the spectrum, which are in turn puzzles in themselves. They hide subtler hues which may only be seen by those who have the appropriate senses developed and controlled on the planes where alone those senses operate. But all can salute *Tat* – that which is like the one white colourless light, like the sacred white in rice or in the semen which gives birth to a human body within a holy receptacle. Every human being can understand that which is in the heavens, even if only in the realm of appearances, well enough to realize that there will be always some counteraction between solar wisdom – Mercury close to the Sun – and the Moon that waxes and wanes. Every human being finds that he participates in this waxing and waning, albeit not self-consciously enough since his knowledge of cyclic law is limited, his capacity to use it is less, and he usually forgets to look at the heavens. Theosophy appeals to no less an authority than the authority of the heavens, the universal wisdom from which all religions, sciences and philosophies sprang. The greatest founders of all faiths spoke in accents of great awe before That which could not be spoken about.

This profound message is relevant to seeking the Golden Thread that binds all monadic minds in the great universal pilgrimage, and to looking for that common storehouse in *akasa* where alone lies the universal solvent which no man can use unless he wishes to use it for all. In seeking the larger good, a man is able to insert his own good into the good of all – *lokasangraha*. Every man is entitled to be concerned, directly and squarely, with his own good. But his good is only supportable by the law of the universe when it is compatible with universal good. We do not fully know this. Therefore, to the extent to which either we do not know – or knowing, forget it – we have to look for clues. These clues are in the process of life, in nature and in the working of *prana*. When the force of this good comes from outside, it seems like *dharma* or fate, but when we understand it and it works within, it is always seen as our very best friend.

The Golden Thread that binds the cosmos is unveiled only in partial ways. Arising in the realm of the unmanifest, it participates in the Light of the *Logos, daiviprakriti,* which is like a veil upon the Absolute. The Absolute is beyond all relativities or absolutizations of the relative, and, in the words of the *Mandukya Upanishad,* is "unthinkable and unspeakable." But if it is unthinkable and unspeakable, can men recognize it in each other? Can men greet each other with an inward thought and an authentic reference to the absolute centre of a boundless circle within the consciousness of another man inhabiting that holy temple we call the human body? Is this possible for a human being, in the midst of the primary activities of life, in one's respect for one's parents, in one's respect for one's husband or wife, ex-husband or ex-wife, future husband or future wife? Is it possible, in relation to one's own children and the children of others, to remember, where it counts and where it hurts, but where it matters most, that all are children, all are old souls, all are fallen gods, all are men who have made mistakes, but who in the making of them deserve a chance to become self-conscious in relation to survival. Theosophy, warned the Maha Chohan, is for all, not for a few.

The story of the Theosophical Movement and of every group that came together in the name of the Wisdom-Religion, is that each fell below the grandeur of the universality and catholicity of the pre-ecumenical, primordial and eternal revelation which remains always in the hands of its great and mighty custodians. Though its breadth is boundless, its height is relevant throughout history and in every religion. It is relevant to every man because every man is entitled to seek and to become worthy of relationship with those men of spiritual stature whom we treat as real Teachers. They cannot be known by external marks. The Buddha's thirty-two marks were always invisible, and as *Kali Yuga* proceeds, it is only from within without that anything worthwhile may be known. All else is a kind of tomfoolery, a concession to Wall Street and Madison Avenue which the Brotherhood has never made and does not now propose to make. "Are not our beards grown?" wrote one of Them. Humanity is mature to a point where it must observe with a wise eye, with a loving heart, and with a compassion that thrills and pulses with the heart of every human being. The Theosophical Movement is for all. The contented simple man who walks the valley of life with very little, and yet smiles and laughs, is one of the teachers of the Theosophical Movement.

The Wisdom-Religion is everywhere, it assumes strange and manifold guises, but it is always sacrificial. Self-reliance is not to be thrown at others like a weapon, but rather, to be gently exemplified through love. Appeals to lesser authorities are mutually destructive, cancelled by the boundless authority of the universe, with which every man is directly linked without need of intermediary. Every man has his own access to God, as was known by the Puritans who spoke of the civil war within the breast of every human being. When we think of the very idea of God, we know that we have to negate and negate. We must negate until we begin to recognize the relevance of *No-thing* to *everything*. To see this in nature with the mind's eye takes time, but once seen, it is the Golden Thread. It shows itself in human affairs as partial representations of the mighty workings of the great wheel of the Law, which is no protector of the illusions of classes, groups, or nations, but which, as the Founding Fathers of the American Republic sensed, can ultimately be understood by all.

The American Constitution is at once a noble document and a threatening one. It is noble because it arose out of the same divine inspiration which is recalled by the third eye on the dollar bill. It is threatening to a country threatened by the magnitude of the Grand Canyon, but which offers every one of its children opportunities which they could use for the sake of all and exemplifies the meaning of the statement, "The whole of nature lies before you. Take what you can." In taking we should not forget to be thankful, not only on Thanksgiving Day, but every day. Then, Theosophy becomes a living power in the life of a man, who can ascend into the hidden realm of occultism in daily life. What is true of scientists like Einstein is even more true of the Brotherhood – that their knowledge cannot be communicated except when preliminary conditions are met. Primary among them, as Shankaracharya pointed out, is gratitude. But any and every man at any time could seek to meet them. Therefore, one of our Masters said, "Take one step in our direction and we will take one in yours."

A man may seek the Golden Thread that binds all religions, sciences and philosophies, and yet never be wholly successful unless he becomes a universal man, a Renaissance man, a man of all cultures. This is a task that is coeval with a whole lifetime. It would be good to begin it in childhood. It is never too late to start, but once started, it is not easy to pursue. Above all, it must be kept in mind with continuity of consciousness if we are to unravel the mystery of mysteries, the mystery of individuality. Who am I? Am I this or that? Am I the person who can be identified in terms of fears and hopes? Am I to be known by my likes and dislikes? Am I the person who masquerades behind a physical form of a certain age and sex, with advantages and disadvantages inherited from a whole line of remote ancestors? We know that over a thousand years every man has had a million ancestors. If a million ancestors have entered into the making of each human being, surely in the complex maze of psycho-physical ancestry there is no clue comparable to the Ariadne's Thread that Theseus used to escape the labyrinth.

Each of us is a labyrinth of complexity today. Everything is in print, but there is scarcely enough time to read or enjoy anything. We suffer from such a surfeit that it is tempting to become nominalists. Yet we know better than that, because we know that refinement of the soul and the culture of the man of the future have nothing to do with class. Therefore, Theosophy can speak to men of all kinds. It cannot be identified with the aristocracy, though H.P. Blavatsky helped them in the nineteenth century. It cannot be identified with the so-called working class, though it benefitted through the laying of the foundations of Theosophical socialism. Annie Besant founded the first trade union for girls in England, while B.P. Wadia founded the first trade union in India. Theosophists who must work in different ways must above all learn to respect diversity. We cannot have a secular fundamentalism wherein each one claims that his is the only diet, the only way. This merely creates more walls that divide men. Each must enjoy his own mode and make his own changes. A Theosophist who learns to set out on his own as an individual cannot make concessions to the conformities of a culture that is now dying. Its death throes, as well as its labour pains, are already evident both in the establishment and elsewhere. The young, with their hungers, sense that something is changing and that something has got to change. Sometimes, even though they love their parents, they cannot outwardly express their respect. In turn, sometimes parents love children so much that they cannot communicate to them the difficulty of the human enterprise. Many a man – almost every great American – knows at some level that God is not mocked, that, "As ye sow, so shall ye also reap." Nature is a teacher here. No man can teach this to another man except by the power of love and the force of example.

The modes of the future will require giving paramount emphasis to that greatest gift possessed by every human being – the most divine gift in the hands of man, treasured in the oral traditions of the past – the gift of sounding the *Logos* within the frame of the human body. It is the gift of making sound, of speech, of articulation. Appropriate articulation, with intrinsic negations, touches that which transcends all verbalization and is beyond verbal expression, that which must always baffle analysis and defy imitation. If we do not appreciate and respond to these opportunities in relation to self-discovery, it is because of the game of externalization, which people play when they come together in a variety of roles and contexts. We are all violating so constantly the most sacred commandment of the Master Jesus, "Judge not, lest ye be judged," that we are not even aware of it. Ceaseless judgment of other human beings – in small towns, in large cities, and in villages – pursued with loveless intransigence in small companionships and groups, makes us think that there is much we all have yet to do if our divine gifts are to become the basis of permanent well-being. What can we do – but not 'do' in the sense in which 'doing' is usually understood in a society which runs around too much? Can we feel what is in the hearts of the young? Of those who are aging? Can we draw larger circles? Can we learn to come together not to analyze why we cannot cooperate but to forget ourselves and to see beyond ourselves? In simple ways, can we accommodate human foibles for the sake of enhancing the good of all?

The good of all is the key to the Golden Thread. No wonder Pythagoras' disciple Plato taught that the best subject for meditation is the universal Good – *to agathon.* He who wishes to meditate on the universal Sun, the source of life and light, is invited to dwell on the sacred *mantram,* the *Gayatri*:

Aum bhur bhuvah svah
tatsaviturvarenyam bhargo devasya dhimahi
dhiyo yo nah prachodayat. Om.

Let us adore the supremacy of that divine sun who illuminates all, from whom all proceed, to whom all must return, whom we invoke to direct our understandings aright in our progress towards his holy seat.

Anyone who wishes to meditate upon the Sun must see beyond the planets, beyond the diversity of the myriads of galaxies, to the midnight sun in the darkness of the firmament. He must see the Sun as the source of one flame from which shoots a ray of light that kindles every spark in every atom. It is that which is differentiated into innumerable monads and is the only line that persists through its reflection within the human being. Therefore, this is the thread upon which hang like pearls all the personalities of human beings over an immensity of lives in the long journey already extending over some eighteen million years of human existence on this planet.

Every human being has played every role from Puck to Prospero. There is hardly a person who has not held the burden of kingly office. There is no human being who has not known the iniquity of poverty and deprivation. Thoreau understood this when he said, "I was in Judea once, in Greece, in Egypt, everywhere." Whitman knew this and sang of it with love in his heart in the *Song of the Open Road* so that we may all become compassionaters, brothers and lovers of all men, nations and races. It is a teaching sung throughout the history of this Republic. Theosophy is an integral part of the inheritance of the American Republic, originally conceived as a Republic of Conscience.

It has been forgotten. Men have tried to limit America. Men have tried to say that this is a three-religion country, and that each American has to choose between being a Catholic, a Protestant, or a Jew. Now, there is a great deal to learn from the Jewish tradition. It speaks of justice. It speaks of the joy of God when a man and woman come together. It is linked up with the honesty of the psychiatric tradition. Every human being is an honorary wandering Jew. But every human being can also learn from the Catholic tradition, in terms of its current emphasis upon simple decency and the beauty of simple things that can be made sacramental. Just as every boy who is born Jewish has the right of choosing to be as Jewish as he pleases, so every Catholic boy or girl must choose his or her own ways of making moments in daily life sacramental. Also, we are all Protestants because we are all protesting against the views of authority. This was at the very basis of the inspiration of the Constitution. It is imperfect, but it is too late merely to condemn the Protestant tradition. Perhaps it is not three cheers, but it is surely at least two, for the Protestant ethic. It came with the Reformation as a part of the work of Tsong-Kha-Pa and the Brotherhood for the sake of a spiritual reformation within Christianity, comparable to a concurrent spiritual reformation within Hinduism and Buddhism and earlier work within the Catholic church. The last Adept actually to work within the church was Nicolas of Cusa.

No religion or institution is exempt from the all-seeing gaze of *Migmar*, whose eye sweeps over slumbering Earth. Every sincere human being who seeks to become a true disciple of the divine discipline of the Wisdom-Religion has the protective aura of the hand of *Lhagpa* over his head. When things go wrong we cannot blame our Teachers. Accepting or assuming our own limitations, we must not limit the Brotherhood. Men have often limited and crucified those the Brotherhood sent. They did it again in a subtle psychological way in the nineteenth century. They will surely attempt to do it in this century and in the future, but will always fail because a great galaxy of Beings is involved, within a carefully designed plan providing lines of retreat to one and all. It was only the Buddha who could take the sacred decision in *Kali Yuga*, where all men have failed and no man can condemn another as a sinner, that although the rules cannot be changed (since occult laws are inviolable), nonetheless access could be made easier for more souls in every part of the world to the wisdom and its mystery temple.

The key always lies within. Tom Paine was prophetic when he anticipated the religion of the future as a trimming away of all the excrescences upon the original substratum. In the beginning was the Word, the *Verbum*. That was *Theosophia*. Students of Theosophy should not be sensitive to ill-considered criticisms by those non-Theosophists who are also non-everything else, due to the fear of belonging to anything. This fear has become an obsession among human beings consumed with fear for themselves and therefore of others. Instead of worrying about the opinions of others, Theosophists should display the courage of the lion wed to the gentleness of the dove.

Because Theosophy is ultimately beyond names, the Wisdom-Religion is known by many names in all times. Today, the largeness and magnificence of the Wisdom-Religion is a Golden Thread of retreat for any man who wishes to make his own contributions to the future or who wishes to come out and become separate from the cycles of the past which must run their course. He should learn from the old man in the Japanese film *Ikiru,* who, when suddenly told that he had only another week to live, said "Good heavens, what can I do in a week?" He tried everything he had tried before – drinking, doing this, doing that – but time was running out. Suddenly it occurred to him that he had never really lived, or at least that there was still something fundamental he had yet to learn about living. There was no time to make a trip to Tibet or Timbuctu. He had to find his inspiration where he was. He sat sadly, very sadly, until he saw some children playing. He saw how they were doing what Buckminster Fuller teaches – making a little go far – getting a great deal of fun out of very little. They did not even have a proper children's park, but they were having a whale of a time. Then he knew he had something which he could use, that he had tremendous gifts in certain areas. He rushed like a man on a mission and organized with all his wisdom a park where these and many more children might play and enjoy themselves. In effect, he followed the advice that the inventor of supermarkets, Edward Bellamy, gave in the nineteenth century as the secret of self-transcendence. Bellamy felt that the time would come when the only self-transcendence that people would know – and he said it would not work – would be the lesser mystery, sexual love. He predicted that men would desperately want some other mode of seeing beyond themselves, and advised that there is a joy and a thrill which every human being knows in losing himself within the welfare of others. Without this, mothers would not have brought their children to birth and suffered the trials that all mothers have suffered to see their children grow.

Life is a great teacher of the Self and of the teaching about the Self. The Golden Thread binds the various centres within the human constitution. In every human being the *sutratman,* the thread-soul, is *sutratma buddhi.* It is reflected in an innate sense of intuitive recognition, decency, fairness, kindness and minimum self-transcendence. In our culture *minima* have become profoundly important. They will be the foundations for the *maxima* of the future. Anyone who has contacted the Path of the Wisdom-Religion can, at the minimum, grasp the simple message, a reminder of what everyone already knows, that it is possible at *this* moment to make a difference to the moment of death. Follow the injunction of *The Voice of the Silence:*

> 'Great Sifter' is the name of the 'Heart Doctrine,' O Disciple. The wheel of the Good Law moves swiftly on. It grinds by night and day. The worthless husks it drives from out the golden grain, the refuse from the flour.

Every man can sift from experience what is worth saving from what cannot be taken or must later be discarded. This was part of the training of the disciples of Pythagoras. It is part of the American Dream. Every human being can, with psychological as well as social mobility, rearrange his critical luggage in the realm of the mind. This has to do with chains of self-reproductive thought, which cannot be stilled suddenly by a dramatic attempt at meditation. Meditation involves the hindering of hindrances. Patanjali's *Yoga Sutra* defines meditation as the hindering of the modifications of the thinking principle. Each must do this in his own way. In the old traditions of Tibet, where all the various schools of Buddhism respected each other and tolerance and civility were shown between the different orders, the distinctive teaching of the Gelukpa Yellow Cap tradition was that the best thing to meditate upon is meditation.

The Golden Thread eludes us when we try too hard to think about it. At the same time, when we do make the attempt we must think seriously about what it is and what it is not. The Golden Thread cannot be discerned in the realm of the physical body which lives through food – the *annamaya kosha*, the lowest, grossest sheath. The Golden Thread cannot be discerned in the *pranamaya kosha*, the sheath in which the lower currents of energy circulate. The Golden Thread is not to be picked up from those portions of the *manomaya kosha* which are made up of thought-patterns that come from outside and that do not originate from above. The Golden Thread can be picked up in that aspect of the *manomaya* sheath which negates externals and seeks the sheath of *Atman*, the *vignanamaya kosha*, having to do with *vignam*, discrimination or *buddhi*.

The Golden Thread can only be genuinely picked up in the realm of discriminative insight, available to every man. When it is picked up, then one must seek by negation to become self-conscious in one's awareness of continuity of consciousness. Thereby, *manas* itself can shine and then in turn illuminate the *sutratma* thread, which is *sutratma buddhi*. This, then, can become *manas sutratman*. A person could become self-consciously a being who knows "I am I" and could proudly take his place in the cosmic scheme of things. Every human being is a unit ray reflecting the light of the *Logos*. It is the light with which every man was born, according to the gospel of St. John, and with which he may become resplendent in its fullness. It may be found by all men who choose the heroic steps outlined in the *Book of the Golden Precepts*:

> Shun ignorance, and likewise shun illusion. Avert thy face from world deceptions: mistrust thy senses; they are false. But within thy body – the shrine of thy sensations – seek in the Impersonal for the 'Eternal Man'; and having sought him out, look inward: thou art Buddha.

Ojai, April 25, 1972

Hermes, November 1976

THE SCOPE OF SELF-CONSCIOUSNESS

In sober truth, ... every 'Spirit' so-called is either a disembodied or a future man. As from the highest Archangel (Dhyan Chohan) down to the last conscious 'Builder' (the inferior class of Spiritual Entities), all such are men, having lived aeons ago, in other Manvantaras, on this or other Spheres; so the inferior, semi-intelligent and non-intelligent Elementals – are all future men. That fact alone – that a Spirit is endowed with intelligence – is a proof to the Occultist that that Being must have been a man, and acquired his knowledge and intelligence throughout the human cycle. There is but one indivisible and absolute Omniscience and Intelligence in the Universe, and this thrills throughout every atom and infinitesimal point of the whole finite Kosmos which bath no bounds, and which people call SPACE, considered independently of anything contained in it.

The Secret Doctrine, i 277

Self-consciousness is the Gordian knot of both philosophical psychology and arcane metaphysics. Its paradoxes can be unravelled only through a discipline that combines sacrificial action and meditation. As the aspirant proceeds along these parallel lines, recondite evolutionary mysteries will reveal themselves to the awakening spiritual sight. Beyond and beneath all of these, present both at the beginning and at the end of the quest, lies the riddle of Being and Non-Being, the crux of the process of infinite perfectibility within eternal divine harmony. Each stage along the way reveals fresh beginnings and tentative illuminations, all revolving around the talismanic question, "Who am I?" and its ever-enigmatic response from the depths of divine consciousness, "THAT thou art." This timeless dialogue between the divine soul and its projected ray is repeated over myriad lives in countless diverse forms. It is the quintessential enquiry of enquiries, comprehending the divine and the mundane while serving as the archetype of every science and every symbolic system. Although this enquiry is perennially and universally relevant, it truly demands an ever-deepening sense of detachment and an ever-expanding feeling of compassion for all humanity. The restoration of the dual sense of individual dignity and human solidarity is a primary object of the Aquarian Age and a necessary prelude to participation in the succeeding age of *Makara*, of magical creativity.

The development of self-conscious humanity on earth began well over eighteen million years ago, following a much longer period of development during the first three-and-a-half Rounds of the earth chain. Throughout this vast period, successive ethereal hierarchies fashioned the sentient but non-intelligent vestures of future mankind. With each succeeding Round and globe, a different class of Builders evolved out of itself more and more dense shadowy projections. During the early portion of the present Fourth Round, the sixth group or hierarchy, counting downward from spirit, evolved out of itself the filmy astral vestures of the future physical man. The seventh, or lowest, hierarchy then gradually formed and condensed the physical body of animal man upon the ethereal frame. Neither the sixth hierarchy, which is connected with ethereal gods, nor the seventh hierarchy, which is connected with vast numbers of terrestrial spirits or elementals, was capable of completing self-conscious intelligent man. Thus, it became the task of the fifth hierarchy, the mysterious beings that preside over the constellation *Makara*, to inform the empty and ethereal animal form, creating out of it the rational man. This in itself is an awesome mystery which may be understood only through meditation and, ultimately, initiation.

At a preliminary level the quintessential aspect of self-consciousness is conveyed in a statement from *The Voice of the Silence* which compares disciples to the strings of the soul-echoing *vina*, and mankind as a whole to its sounding board. The hand that plucks the string of the *vina* is likened to the great World-Soul. The simultaneous attunement of the disciples to the World-Soul and to all humanity intimates the essential characteristic of Manasic self-consciousness. One may view human beings as links in a chain or members of an orchestra, each having a separate function. All are complementary and interdependent in their functions, yet none are equivalent in their degrees of consciousness or concentration. The third violinist in the orchestra might, for example, be an inspiration in his selflessness and concentration although musically he performs only a modest role within the whole. Indeed, the being who is high in self-consciousness is distinguished by a regular and refined ability to think of the whole. Through the powers of concentration and choice any self-conscious being can heighten the essential function of being human, which is the crystalline capacity to mirror the cosmos. Thus, whilst all human beings participate to some extent in a vague sense of solidarity, some become such effortless exemplars of cosmic solidarity that they release a potent force for human brotherhood. This capacity derives from meditation and altruism over many previous lives. The more lives devoted through meditation to heightening the power of *Manas*, the more lives devoted through renunciation to suffusing *Manas* with Buddhic compassion, the greater the degree of noetic discernment. The deeper this discernment, the stronger the sense of duty in the world, and the willingness in finite time to summon one's best and highest energies.

Employing the powers of individuality for the sake of universal unity depends on the *Manasaputras*, the fifth hierarchy, which preside over the constellation *Makara*. It is the unique capacity of the exalted beings of this hierarchy to be able to function at the highest metaphysical level while at the same time incarnating on and commanding the terrestrial plane, thus self-consciously bridging the celestial and the terrestrial. H.P. Blavatsky pointed out:

> The Fifth group is a very mysterious one, as it is connected with the Microcosmic Pentagon, the five-pointed star representing man. In India and Egypt these *Dhyanis* were connected with the Crocodile, and their abode is in Capricornus. These are convertible terms in Indian astrology, as this (tenth) sign of the Zodiac is called *Makara*, loosely translated 'crocodile.' The word itself is occultly interpreted in various ways, as will be shown further on. In Egypt the defunct man – whose symbol is the pentagram or the five-pointed star, the points of which represent the limbs of a man – was shown emblematically transformed into a crocodile: *Sebakh* or *Sevekh* 'or seventh,'...showing it as having been the type of intelligence, is a dragon in reality, not a crocodile. He is the 'Dragon of Wisdom' or *Manas*, the 'Human Soul,' Mind, the Intelligent principle, called in our esoteric philosophy the 'Fifth' principle.

> *The Secret Doctrine*, i 219

Egyptian symbolism, which echoes the arcane *Gupta Vidya* and anticipates the Christian notion of resurrection, depicts in the *Book of the Dead* the osirification of the soul. In this account, which has more to do with spiritual birth than physical death, the Manasic soul is represented under the glyph of a crocodile-headed god. This crocodile, or *Manas*, is represented as choosing a life ahead and descending through a ray which is a sacrifice, a self-imprisonment voluntarily chosen. After the death of the physical body, the crocodile is shown sifting out the quintessence of its life, through an impartial, impersonal and mathematically accurate judgement, balancing the soul's inherent claim to self-conscious immortality in the scales of justice against a feather, representing truth. In their higher periods the Egyptians emphasized the extreme precision of the mathematics of karma, which resembles the cosmic computer programme permeating all vestures. In this judgement, which is welcomed by the immortal soul, there is no room for vicarious atonement, gratuitous absolution or any escape into cowardliness, whether occasioned by individual ignorance or pseudo-religious priestcraft.

Whatever the system of symbolic representation, every ancient account of the origin of human self-consciousness points to the mystery of incarnation, the mystery of the descent of the highest beings into terrestrial life, and the retention of spiritual knowledge as spiritual memory in the midst of a world of change, illusion and flux. This is the quintessential characteristic of the fifth hierarchy which could not be fulfilled by either the fourth, the sixth or the seventh group. The relationship between the highest *arupa* hierarchies and the human principles is conveyed in the Japanese system of symbolism in which a kind of celestial anthropogenesis precedes cosmogenesis. In the esoteric wisdom one usually begins with cosmogenesis and comes down through anthropogenesis, in order to grasp the successive connections between the cosmic hierarchies; in the Japanese system, devised as a convenient mode for disseminating the Teachings while preserving the significant connections, purely cosmic principles are represented by personages that are archetypal embodiments of human principles. Thus, terms are used that apply to the human constitution, but not specifically to humanity.

> When all was as yet Chaos (*Kon-ton*) three spiritual Beings appeared on the stage of future creation: (1) *Ame no ani naka nushi no Kami*, 'Divine Monarch of the Central Heaven'; (2) *Taka mi onosubi no*

Kami, 'Exalted, imperial Divine offspring of Heaven and the Earth'; and (3) *Kamu mi musubi no Kami,* 'Offspring of the Gods,' simply. These were without form or substance (our *arupa* triad), as neither the celestial nor the terrestrial substance had yet differentiated, 'nor had the essence of things been formed.'

The Secret Doctrine, i 214

This account may be correlated with a passage from the Commentary on the *Stanzas of Dzyan*:

'The first after the "One" is divine Fire; the second, Fire and Aether; the third is composed of Fire, Aether and Water; the fourth of Fire, Aether, Water, and Air.' The One is not concerned with Man-bearing globes, but with the inner invisible Spheres. 'The "First-Born" are the LIFE, the heart and pulse of the Universe; the Second are its MIND or Consciousness.'

The Secret Doctrine, i 216

Combining the two accounts, there is first the divine Flame, the 'One' which is prior to the sequence, from which are lit the three descending groups or hierarchies. Seen cosmically, the first is Atmic or divine fire. The second group is fire and ether, *Atma-Buddhi,* the light of the *Paramatman* diffused throughout the cosmos as its spiritual soul, *Daiviprakriti,* the Light of the unmanifested *Logos* become in differentiation *Fohat* or the Seven Sons. From these twofold monadic units emanate the threefold composed of fire, ether and water, correlative with the *Atma-Buddhi-Manas,* fusing the three-in-one into a triad that is capable of connecting itself with a quaternary through incarnation. Succeeding these three is the fourth group comprised of fire, ether, water and air, which provides the invisible grounding of the higher three spiritual principles of the cosmos into a diffused kind of aura that permeates and surrounds the whole globe. All these hierarchies have their analogues within the human being, because they represent a separation between the celestial and the terrestrial, but, as the Japanese understood, they do not give the capacity to link the celestial with the terrestrial. This belongs to the fifth hierarchy. Hence the sacredness of *Makara*-Capricorn.

There is a mysterious anagrammatic connection between *Makara* and *Kumara*, the host of virgin ascetics and *yogins* presided over by Shiva-Saturn. The term '*Makara*' itself is a composite of *ma*, meaning 'five', and *kara*, meaning 'hand' or 'side'. Thus, *Makaram* is the same as *Panchakaram*, or the pentagon, the five-pointed star linking heaven and earth through the divine proportion. There is a symmetry and logic to the human body, to man standing straight with his arms and legs stretched out, as in Leonardo da Vinci's drawing of the terrestrial man within the universal man. In the present zodiacal system *Makara* is the tenth sign, connected with the idea of the cosmos as bounded by pentagons, though in the older zodiac *Makara* was the eighth sign, connected with the eight faces bounding space, a reference to the *lokapalas*. The significance of man as a five-pointed star, a microcosmic reflection of the macrocosm, lies in his capacity to realize his solidarity with the fifth host of *Dhyan Chohans*, the *Kumaras*. If, when man stands erect, he is governed by that which enters through the crown of the head from above below, he is a *Manusha*, capable of firm resolve. By raising his spiritual vision, he can at once look heavenward towards the empyrean and enclose the entire cosmos within his creative imagination. At the same time, if he is also full of love for the earth upon which all beings live and move, he can consciously bridge the most celestial with the most terrestrial elements in Nature. It is this profoundly sacrificial privilege that is given to man by the fifth hierarchy, the *Kumaras* or *Agnishwatha Pitris*. The esoteric name of this solar host, the endowers of man with self-consciousness, is *Pranidananath*, Lords of Persevering Ceaseless Devotion, a designation which points to the true meaning of the later Greek term *philosophia* or love of wisdom.

Kamadeva, the Vedic *Logos*, is *Atma-Bhu* – unborn and self-existent – one with Agni, and also *Makara-Ketu* – he who bears the emblem of *Makara* on his banner. The *Kumaras*, sprung from *Kamadeva*, preside through *Makara* over the birth of the spiritual microcosm as well as the dissolution of the physical universe and its passage into the realm of the spiritual. Mysteriously, *Mara*, the mocking demon of illusion and the god of darkness and death, is yet another name for *Kamadeva*, the Vedic *Logos*, and the unconscious quickener of the birth of the spiritual. Rising like a crocodile out of the waters of the sacred river of life to greet the fiery rays of the rising sun, *Makara* and the host of the *Kumaras* are the archetype of nascent intelligent humanity and its infinite capacity for perfectibility. The cosmic glyph of *Makara* is that of the waves, which resembles the letter M and is doubled in the sign of Aquarius. Its geometric emblem is the pentagram, the sign of spiritual and physical health in the Pythagorean School, and a symbol of the divine descent and universal solidarity of humanity.

The full significance of the five-pointed star only emerges when it is inscribed within the six-pointed star, but this cannot be understood unless one has first mastered the five. This is the point at which human beings must begin, for humanity is now in the Fifth Sub-Race of the Fifth Root Race of the Fourth Round. Through incarnation and the lessons of karma, one must come to comprehend all that is implicit in five, as well as in five doubled, which yields ten, the perfect number.

> The fifth group of the celestial Beings is supposed to contain in itself the dual attributes of both the spiritual and physical aspects of the Universe; the two poles, so to say, of *Mahat* the Universal Intelligence, and the dual nature of man, the spiritual and the physical. Hence its number Five, multiplied and made into ten, connecting it with *Makara*, the 10th sign of the Zodiac.
>
> *The Secret Doctrine*, i 221

If man is seen from this standpoint, as a monadic and Manasic being, a bridge between the cosmic and the sub-human, the enormous importance of self-consciously bridging the two poles naturally follows. Aspiration, idealism and resolve may be fused into fidelity to the best and highest that one knows within oneself. Through this fidelity, the most sacred of all virtues, it is possible to use the *antaskarana* bridge. Only thus can one invite the descent of the *Dhyanis*, the overbrooding triad within the temple of the human form. It is, therefore, vital to understand both the nature of human individuality and its difference, conceived in relation to the fifth hierarchy, from any sense of individuality connected with the lower hierarchies. On these lower levels, individuality is the characteristic of the entire hierarchy, and not of its individual units, and hence it has nothing to do with identification with particular units, but only with broader planes. At the higher stages of spiritual initiation, the human being necessarily must dispel the sense of a distinct individuality, but first he must entirely transcend the passions of the personality, as well as the illusory identification with name and form. This itself will occupy several lifetimes and is essential before the full awakening of true individuality.

The deep sense of separateness and the seeming cohesiveness in the personality are due to the diffused Fohatic action of differentiated kama operating within the *kama rupa*. The cosmic potency acting on the differentiated planes has a dual manifestation as *Lakshmi-Kali*, its black and white sides. Long before the pristine electro-spiritual Buddhic force of compassion can be released self-consciously, and the higher powers of the soul unlocked, all attachments to form through inverted desire must be transcended. The more progress one makes in this direction, the more one can at first generate a Manasic identity, a sense of 'I-am-I', a sense of being a ray independent of the *rupa*. Then it is possible through meditation to draw oneself towards the Spiritual Sun and to recognize the unity of all the rays that come out of that One Sun, all the living ones, all the streams projected on the cosmic screen of illusion from the absolute life. Thus one strengthens the spiritual fibres of the *karana sharira*, the causal body. This is the task of discipleship, and it demands effort over successive lives.

The highest beings, who transcend individuality, are quite different from the *Dhyanis* who have no individuality because they function only in terms of the collective. These latter belong, one might say, to a grouping that has a single function. They participate in a kind of higher specialization of cosmic intelligence and they have no separate will. This is not the same as the conscious capacity of the perfected human will to attune itself to that which is the transcendent source of all the *Dhyanis*. If one truly masters the egotistic desires and delusions of the personality, one can become effortlessly capable of non-separateness in consciousness. By pledging oneself to be a true apprentice on the path of daily meditation, one may develop increased continuity of consciousness, and so establish a noble line of life's meditation. Eventually, one may be able to envisage *Dhyana*, true ceaseless contemplation.

The arduous task of transcending and subduing the personality is a preparation for exercising the supreme prerogative of being human.

The immense Logoic potential of human perfection and its virtually unlimited power of benevolence are thus conveyed by H.P. Blavatsky:

> Man being a compound of the essences of all those celestial Hierarchies may succeed in making himself, as such, superior, in one sense, to any hierarchy or class, or even combination of them. 'Man can neither propitiate nor command the *Devas*,' it is said. But, by paralyzing his lower personality, and arriving thereby at the full knowledge of the non-separateness of his higher SELF from the One absolute SELF, man can, even during his terrestrial life, become as 'One of Us.' Thus it is, by eating of the fruit of knowledge which dispels ignorance, that man becomes like one of the *Elohim* or the *Dhyanis*; and once on their plane the Spirit of Solidarity and perfect Harmony, which reigns in every Hierarchy, must extend over him and protect him in every particular.

The Secret Doctrine, i 276

Here the terms 'superior' and 'inferior' are relative to one's perspective.

If by superior one means 'closest to the One', then the highest beings will be the *arupa* forces, the *Ah-Hi*, the first three descending groups. But if by superior one refers to the capacity of perfected human beings operating in the middle realm to bring down the highest vibration and to infuse it into all beings, then, of course, an entirely different perspective emerges. It is in this sense that the Avatar is far superior to the Mahatma, although he is seemingly incarnated. At the level of non-incarnation, such comparisons can hardly apply. The essential capacity to become an active embodiment of universal divine compassion is the mighty prospect of perfectibility for all immortal souls alike. By the power of meditation and devotion, they can all become co-worshippers of the highest in Nature, the highest within their own hearts, and the highest in all beings. Thus they can become able to handle at will all the subcolours of the spectrum through the one light of the Central Spiritual Sun.

Owing to the gift of self-consciousness through the *Kumaras*, every human being has the potent capacity of sacred speech. Each and every human being may meditate upon the *Gayatri*, and through the creative potency of sound evoke the spiritual light of the Invisible

Sun on behalf of all beings. This means that every human soul can, to some degree, attune itself to what Pythagoras called the music of the spheres. Though totally inaudible to the outer human ear, it is a sound so intense, so profound, that it reverberates constantly through the cosmos. Akashic sound and the primordial light of the Central Spiritual Sun are a primordial vibration reflected in the *AUM*, and also mirrored in *bhur*, *bhuvah* and *svah*, the three worlds invoked at the beginning of the *Gayatri*. Ultimately, that light is *Daiviprakriti*, awakened within *Hiranyagarbha* by the first ray of the Divine Darkness in the precosmic dawn. It is this light, quickening the fiery ethereal waters of space, which is greeted by the *Kumaras* as the light of their true selves.

> 'When the ONE becomes two, the three-fold appears': to wit, when the One Eternal drops its reflection into the region of Manifestation, that reflection, 'the Ray,' differentiates the 'Water of Space'; . . . 'Chaos ceases, through the effulgence of the Ray of Primordial light dissipating total darkness by the help of the great magic power of the WORD of the (Central) Sun.' . . . issuing from the DEEP, . . . the divine Universal Soul in its manifested aspect . . . Narayana, the *Purusha*, 'concealed in *Akasa* and present in Ether.'

> *The Secret Doctrine*, i 231

There is, then, a mysterious sound, neither the *AUM* nor the sounds in the *Gayatri*, which is the *Verbum*, the Word of the Central Spiritual Sun dissipating the primordial darkness. Perfected human beings can thus live, move and breathe in and through *Akasha*. These are the true Men of Meditation, self-governed Sages constantly attuned to the vibration of the One Flame. By ceaselessly negating all mayavic manifestation, they affirm its true meaning going back to the precosmic and primordial darkness that is prior to the dawn of manifestation, and even precedes the distinction of Being and Non-Being. Having gone back to that state of undifferentiated oneness, they can penetrate the world of manifestation without illusion. They can bear witness to the hidden essences and meanings, the hidden possibilities and promises, concealed within *Akasha* and partially present in ether.

Exemplifying the sacred existential connection between "Who am I?" and "THAT thou art", they serve as the antaskaranic bridge which, when crossed, makes of man a god, "creating him a Bodhisattva, son of the *Dhyanis*". Masters of all the living elements from the *Atman* to the physical form, they are the bearers of the immutable, indestructible and deathless vibration of Eternal Life that is even present within the great Night of non-manifestation. The heart of universal self-conscious intelligence, the Brotherhood of Bodhisattvas ever remain the invisible allies of every human being aspiring through sacrifice and renunciation to the effective service of the whole of humanity.

> Where is thy individuality, Lanoo, where the Lanoo himself? It is the spark lost in the fire, the drop within the ocean, the ever-present ray become the All and the eternal radiance.And now, Lanoo, thou art the doer and the witness, the radiator and the radiation, Light in the Sound, and the Sound in the Light.

The Voice of the Silence

Hermes, September 1983

METAPHYSICS AND ETHICS

Tat tvam asi

It is natural for us to make a firm distinction between our study and our application of Theosophy, between theory and practice. As a result, we contrast the capacities of the head and the heart, and assume that we seek and secure different kinds of nourishment from *The Secret Doctrine* and *The Voice of the Silence.* At the same time, we also know that Theosophy is essentially the Heart Doctrine, distinct from the head-learning with which our world abounds. What is more, the whole purpose of Theosophical discipline is to blend the head and the heart, to broaden our mental sympathies and to awaken and direct the intelligence of the heart. Does this simply mean that we need for conceptual clarity the dualistic view of the spiritual life as long as we remain as inwardly divided as we are, and that this dichotomy is made only so that it may be destroyed as we become rooted in the holiness that reflects an inner wholeness? It is certainly convenient to regard all conceptual distinctions and classifications as mere scaffoldings and to choose the best available at any particular stage of our growth. But in order to appreciate the distinctive significance of Theosophical classifications, we cannot merely regard them like the maps of early mariners, whose explorations needed as well as corrected their initial cartographical knowledge. We need, in fact, to acquire an entirely new and original view of the relation between true metaphysics and enduring ethics and to appreciate the profound epistemological nature and the peculiar therapeutic value of Theosophical statements as indicated in the First Item of *The Secret Doctrine.*

Metaphysics, as normally understood, is speculative rather than gnostic and is often the product of the propensity to subsume existing knowledge under a complete system, an imposing pattern that is then ascribed to reality with a dogmatism that pretends to a certainty that it cannot possibly possess. It is in accord with cyclic law that this kind of metaphysical system-building is suspect today and has even led to an extremist and naively positivistic reaction among die-hard empiricists. Similarly, ethics, in the everyday sense, consists of injunctions and imperatives that are rarely susceptible of rational enquiry and are either endowed with spurious absoluteness or are regarded as relativist and subjectivist preferences, from which we choose as from a menu. Given the pretentious nature of ordinary metaphysics and conventional ethics, we can understand the insistence of Hume, the sceptical Scot of the eighteenth century, that metaphysical statements are *a priori* assertions that are incapable of verification, that we cannot logically derive any ethical imperatives either from them or from statements of fact, and that our ethical preferences cannot possess certainty or universality or freedom from arbitrariness. The metaphysical assertion that "X is true or must be true" cannot help us to answer the question "Why ought I to do Y?" It is indeed not surprising that the speculations of most metaphysicians do not give us a basis for moral conduct and moral growth, and that the injunctions of many conventional ethical codes do not have their basis in the moral and spiritual order of our law-governed cosmos.

In Theosophical literature, however, every metaphysical statement has an ethical corollary and connotation, and every ethical injunction has a distinct metaphysical basis. It is impossible to grasp the force of any of the seven *paramitas* of *The Voice of the Silence* without a comprehension of the Three Fundamental Propositions regarding God, Nature and Man that underlie the order of reality intimated by the *Stanzas* of the *Book of Dzyan,* on which *The Secret Doctrine* is closely based. Theosophical literature assumes, as shown especially by *Light on the Path,* the truth and validity of the Socratic axiom "Knowledge is virtue." For example, to know, with the heart as well as the head, and to be fully aware that the sin and the shame of the world are verily our own, must totally transform our actions as well as our attitudes in relation to all our fellow men and also to our own sins and lower self. We cannot rely on that which is not real, in an ultimate and philosophical sense. Theosophical ethics teaches the only possible reliance – on the Divine Ground of all Being and beyond – that is available to those who become aware of the degrees of reality in an ever-evolving universe that is itself only a relatively real emanation from the Eternal Reality. Our conduct consists of emanations that cannot but harm us and others if they are not emanated in the creative and impersonal manner and with the conscious control that marks the ceaseless process of cosmic emanations from a single source – Life of our life, Force of our force. Until we are free from the dire heresy of separateness *(attavada)*, we cannot claim to have grasped the doctrine of *samvriti* or of the *nidanas* that teaches us about the origins of delusions and chains of causation. To know is to become, and to become is truly to know.

In an illuminating passage in *The Secret Doctrine* on the "Causes of Existence" and on the Buddhist concept of *nidana* and the Hindu concept of *maya*, H.P. Blavatsky said that science and religion, in trying to trace back the chain of causes and effects, jump to a condition of mental blankness much more quickly than is necessary,

> for they ignore the metaphysical abstractions which are the only conceivable cause of physical concretions. These abstractions become more and more concrete as they approach our plane of existence, until finally they phenomenalise in the form of the material Universe, by a process of conversion of metaphysics into physics.

> *The Secret Doctrine*, i 45

If we consider this even as a logical possibility, then clearly the knowledge of these metaphysical abstractions gained and given by trained Initiates is epistemologically prior to the external order of reality in the material universe. Such metaphysics, the product of intuitive apprehension and capable of patient verification by the extrasensory experiences of independently acting individuals, is different in kind from the speculative metaphysics of the ordinary variety and is more analogous to the methods of investigation of the greatest natural scientists. This is why we are told that

> it is difficult to find a single speculation in Western metaphysics which has not been anticipated by Archaic Eastern philosophy. From Kant to Herbert Spencer, it is all a more or less distorted echo of the *Dwaita, Adwaita,* and Vedantic doctrines generally.

> *Ibid.*, 79

The very nature of Theosophical metaphysics is such that we cannot approach it merely with the head, independently of the heart. The purely ratiocinative and intellectualist approach to ordinary metaphysics is itself the result of "the inadequate distinctions made by the Jews, and now by our Western metaphysicians", so that "the philosophy of psychic, spiritual, and mental relations with man's physical functions is in almost inextricable confusion". Our metaphysical conceptions are clearly conditioned by our own mental development and cannot have the absolute validity that we claim for them. This is especially true of the evolution of the GOD-IDEA. Hence, says Theosophy, for every thinker there will be a "Thus far shalt thou go and no farther", mapped out by his intellectual capacity.

> Outside of initiation, the ideals of contemporary religious thought must always have their wings clipped and remain unable to soar higher; for idealistic as well as realistic thinkers, and even free-thinkers, are but the outcome and the natural product of their respective environments and periods.

Ibid., 326

Not merely does modern metaphysics fall far short of the truth, but even its basic concepts and usages of terms like 'Absolute', 'Nature' and 'matter' are shallower and cruder than their corresponding concepts propounded by the Theosophical Adepts. Initiation into Theosophical metaphysics is more than an intellectual or moral enterprise; it is a continuous spiritual exercise in the development of intuitive and cognitive capacities that are the highest available to men, a process that includes from the first a blending of the head and the heart through the interaction of *viveka* and *vairagya,* discrimination and detachment. Even our initial apprehension of a statement of Theosophical metaphysics involves an ethical as well as mental effort, just as even the smallest application of a Theosophical injunction to our moral life requires some degree of mental control and the deeper awareness, universal and impersonal in nature, that comes from our higher cognitive capacities. Moral growth, for a Theosophist, presupposes "the silent worship of abstract or *noumenal* Nature, the only divine manifestation", that is "the one ennobling religion of Humanity".

Despite its contempt for metaphysics and for ontology, materialistic science is honeycombed with metaphysical and contradictory implications, and even its "atoms" are "entified abstractions". "To make of Science an integral *whole* necessitates, indeed, the study of spiritual and psychic, as well as physical Nature." But although *real* science is inadmissible without metaphysics, and those scientists who trespass on the forbidden grounds of metaphysics, who lift the veil of matter and strain their eyes to see beyond, are "wise in their generation", H.P. Blavatsky declared towards the end of *The Secret Doctrine* that the man of exact science must realize that

> he has no right to trespass on the grounds of metaphysics and psychology. His duty is to verify and to rectify all the facts that *fall under his direct* observation; to profit by the experiences and mistakes of the Past in endeavouring to trace the working of a certain concatenation of cause and effects, which, but only by its constant and unvarying repetition, may be called A LAW. . . . Any sideway path from this royal road becomes *speculation.*

> *Ibid.,* ii 664

It is a sign of advance that scientists today are less given than their predecessors in the latter half of the nineteenth century to "metaphysical flights of fancy". Bad metaphysics is clearly worse than none. On the other hand, as modern psychology becomes less materialistic and as race evolution proceeds, a greater appreciation of the higher intuitive and cognitive capacities will emerge and may enable the most intuitive scientists to venture more effectively into metaphysics.

It is, therefore, necessary for students of Theosophy to see the fundamental difference between what goes by the name of metaphysics and has rightly become suspect today, and the "metaphysics, pure and simple", with which *The Secret Doctrine* is concerned. We cannot, however, grasp the metaphysics given in Theosophical teachings unless we perceive its close and inseparable connection with Theosophical ethics. We are told in *The Secret Doctrine* that the "highly philosophical and metaphysical Aryans" were the authors of "the most perfect philosophical systems of transcendental psychology" and of "a moral code (Buddhism), proclaimed by Max Müller the most perfect on earth". Without a proper understanding of Theosophical psychology and the teachings regarding the nature and constitution of man and the working of karmic law, we cannot appreciate the metaphysical basis of Theosophical ethics or the ethical significance of Theosophical metaphysics. Hence the importance of a careful study and application, from the first, of the Ten Items from *Isis Unveiled* or the Propositions of Oriental Psychology, and of the Aphorisms on Karma by W.Q. Judge. Until this is done, we cannot begin to see the ethical import of the statements in *The Secret Doctrine* or the metaphysical basis of the statements in *The Voice of the Silence* and *Light on the Path*.

We are told explicitly in *The Secret Doctrine* that "to make the workings of Karma, in the periodical renovations of the Universe, more evident and intelligible to the student when he arrives at the origin and evolution of man, he has now to examine with us the esoteric bearing of the Karmic Cycles upon Universal Ethics". Our ethical progress depends on an increasing awareness of the "cycles of matter" and the "cycles of spiritual evolution", and of racial, national and individual cycles. The kernel of Theosophical ethics is contained in the statement that "there are *external and internal conditions* which affect the determination of our will upon our actions, and it is in our power to follow either of the two". This contains a great metaphysical and psychological truth, which is illuminated by the seminal article on "Psychic and Noetic Action", written, late in life, by H.P. Blavatsky, the Magus-Teacher of the 1875 cycle.

Theosophical ethics is in the end no easier to understand properly than Theosophical metaphysics. It can no more be grasped by the mentally lazy than Theosophical metaphysics can be comprehended by the morally obtuse. There is nothing namby-pamby about Theosophical ethics and it is as fundamentally different from conventional ethics as Theosophical metaphysics is from conventional metaphysics. Just as modern metaphysics is a shadowy distortion of archaic metaphysics, modern ethics is a sad vulgarization of the archaic ethics taught by the early religious Teachers of humanity. It is to be welcomed that more and more questioning people today are less and less prepared to accept blindly conventional ethical codes merely because they are traced back to so-called scriptural revelations, just as they have little use for the metaphysical speculations of even the formidable minds of the past. If the ethical nihilism of today is even more repugnant to the Theosophist than sterile positivism, he would do well to regard both as the karmic price we have to pay for the moral and metaphysical dogmatism of the past.

Although we may talk of Theosophical metaphysics and Theosophical ethics, and classify texts broadly under these heads, we must get beyond the conventional distinction between metaphysical and ethical statements and grasp central concepts, such as Dharma and Karma, which are protean in scope and profound in content, and incapable of being regarded as purely metaphysical or exclusively ethical. It is significant that the supposedly anti-metaphysical and superbly moral teaching of the Buddha was centred in the complex concept of Dharma rather than in *Brahman* or *moksha,* in the stern law of moral compensation and universal causality, rather than in a conception of infinite Deity constructed by the finite mind of man or in any notion of salvation or redemption which caters to the spiritual selfishness of the individual.

In the European tradition, a natural reaction to theocentric systems of thought was the Cartesian affirmation of the autonomy of the individual in relation to knowledge and the later Kantian proclamation of the autonomy of the individual in relation to morality. The Theosophist, however, holds to the Pythagorean and ancient Eastern maxim that man is the mirror and microcosm of the macrocosm. It is in this context that he must evolve from egoism to egoity, from personal self-love to individual self-consciousness, which is impossible without a heart-understanding of the Law of Universal Unity and Moral Retribution. The close connection between metaphysics and ethics in Theosophy is ultimately based on the workings of Universal Law, which affects the exact and occult correspondences between the constituents of man and of the cosmos. This ancient doctrine of correspondences has been ignored by modern metaphysicians and moralists, but it was known to modern mystics and poets from Boehme to Swedenborg, Blake to Baudelaire.

Hermes, May 1975

MEDITATION AND SELF-STUDY

Atmanam atmana pasya

Meditation and self-study are of immeasurable importance to every single person. They concern the longest journey of the soul, the divine discontent in human life. The quest for true meditation and the yearning for real self-knowledge are as old as thinking man. Today, more than ever before in recorded history, there is a widespread hunger for teaching and instruction concerning meditation and concentration. Some seek even more, longing for a way of life irradiated by the inward peace and joyous strength of contemplation. Ours is an age of acute, almost obsessive, self-consciousness. Everyone is oppressed by the ego-games endemic to contemporary culture, the thought-forms and speech habits, the paranoid, loveless and competitive modes seemingly required merely to keep body and soul together. We are tempted to think that there is some inescapable necessity to assert ourselves to survive, to protect ourselves from being exploited, engulfed or drowned. At the same time, we look in many directions, to ancient and modern as well as to new-fangled schools of psychological health, hoping to enhance our capacity for self-analysis, mental clarification, and minimum control over our personal lives.

The hunger for authentic knowledge and reliable techniques of meditation, and the poignant concern for self-definition, are paramount needs of our time. They are more fundamental, more lasting and more bewildering than all other clamorous claims. But they appear to move in opposite directions. The impulse toward meditation seems to be towards opting out of the world – the world of illusion – or at least the decaying structure of any society. It suggests liberation, an escape from the great wheel of birth and death and the whole life-process. It involves the desire for an equivalent to the conventional concepts of heaven. Images of eternal, nirvanic and absolute self-transcendence are often analogous to the perpetual and perfect release which men desperately seek and fail to find on the physical plane of the lower *eros.* On the other hand, the entire concern for self-analysis and self-understanding is bound up with the need to improve our relation to our fellow men, our capacity for survival, the abject dependence on acceptance and love. It is so much directed to a re-entry into the world that self-study and meditation seem to represent poles that fly off in opposite directions. And in both cases there are more teachers than disciples. There are so many schools, so many sects, such a vast range of panaceas that there is something absurd and also deeply sad about the ferment on the threshold of the 1975 cycle.

If we think for a moment of another age, a distant time in which men sought for supreme wisdom concerning the immortality of the Self and the ultimate joys of contemplation, we may discern that there were men and women who gave their whole lives to a sustained and desperate search. They consecrated everything they had for the sake of finding some answer by which they could live, and from which they could gain a more fundamental insight, a more permanent solution, not only for themselves, but also in relation to the intense human predicament, the malaise of mankind. Today we certainly do not find anything comparable to the exacting demands and the aristocratic sense in which many are called, few persist, fewer are chosen, and very few succeed. There is a tantalizing statistic in the *Bhagavad Gita* suggesting that one man in a million succeeds in the quest for immortality. When we think of that exalted perspective upon the journey, in an age where there is an almost universal concern, and if we consider it in impersonal terms, for the sake of all and not only for ourselves, we are bound to feel deeply puzzled. Something is going wrong. Yet there must be a legitimacy in what is happening. How can one understand this? Where can one find the true wisdom and teaching? Where are the real teachers? Where are those authentic men of meditation who can by their compassion consecrate the whole endeavour, showing not only discrimination in the choice of deserving disciples, but also a supreme justice befitting the total need of the world as a whole? The more we ask questions of this kind, the more we must retreat, if we are honest, into a cleansing confession of absolute ignorance.

We do not know whether there is in the world any knowledge, of which there are external signs that are absolutely certain, in relation to a sovereign method. The conditions, the requirements and the object of the quest are obscure to us. Viewing the immense need of our age, we are uncertain whether there is anything that could adequately serve the diverse needs of vast numbers of varied kinds of human agony, sickness and pain. We might think we are in the Dark Ages, that the Wise Men have gone, and that there is no longer access to the highest conception of wisdom in relation to meditation or self-knowledge. This answer would come naturally to a humble and honest man in the context of the immemorial tradition of the East. In the West one might be inclined either to argue that having no way of knowing whether the whole thing is a distraction, it is better not to look in any direction, or, to see our plight in terms of the messianic religious traditions of the Piscean Age.

Thus there is a restless intensity to the search for a technique or formula, which is not merely a surefire method of meditation or of self-study, but which is in fact a panacea for salvation. Those who are not only concerned for themselves, but share a sense of awareness of the common needs of men, think less in terms of a mere panacea than of a mandate for universal salvation. They seek what is not only supremely valid, decisive and certain, but what could also be made available to all and is capable of ready use by human beings as they are – with all their fallibilities, limitations and imperfections – whether as apprentices and beginners, or merely for the sake of avoiding the slide into self-destruction. They are looking for what can in fact be widely marketed and made available. Put in another language, the idea of a mandate for salvation becomes more understandable, and can be lent a certain minimal dignity. It is as if one says that one wants, for any ordinary person in the street, not the knowledge he needs for him to become a saint or a sage, or a man of meditation perfected in self-knowledge, but simply the knowledge that would enable him to have what he cannot find in any pill or potion, and cannot get from any physician or psychiatrist.

It is the knowledge that will help him to balance his life and to gain, in a chaotic time, enough calm and sufficient continuity of will-energy, to be able to survive without succumbing to the constant threat and danger of disintegration, ever looming large like a nightmare. What is needed is the ability to avoid the dreadful decline along an inclined slope tending towards an awful abyss of annihilation and nothingness.

On that inclined slope are steps that are very painful and readily recognisable, not only by oneself but by each other. They represent the weakening of the will and the progressive inability to reinforce the will, especially amidst the breakdown of all those collectivised goals of societies and men in terms of which one was once able to generate a kind of extraordinary will-energy. In our Promethean or Faustian culture individuals simply do not have the will-energy required for the most minimal notions of survival. When we put the subject in this agonizing contemporary context, and not in a classical context seemingly removed from our time, we are entitled to ask whether there is any Theosophical text on meditation and self-study worthy of scrutiny and deeply relevant in one's life, which is in principle capable of universalization and could have the widest relevance to our contemporary condition.

Here one may turn to the meticulous and enigmatic wisdom of that immensely compassionate and extraordinary human being whom we know as Helena Petrovna Blavatsky. She chose, though only at the very end of her life, to give to the world and yet dedicate to the few, a translation from unknown Tibetan sources of stanzas, still chanted in monasteries and sanctuaries of initiation, which she called *The Voice of the Silence.* This beautiful book was blessed in her time by the man whose karmic privilege it was to assume the custodianship of all the orders and schools in Tibet, the Dalai Lama of her day. Early in this century it was published in a Peking edition that had a preface from the Panchen Lama. It is a book that has been blessed by the visible representatives of the authentic tradition of Tibet. For those who have read the book and compared it to the *Bhagavad Gita,* and to the classical Indian texts on meditation and the Self, either going back to Patanjali or Shankaracharya or coming down to modern representatives of the old tradition – to those who have done this at even some elementary level, it is clear that the book is extremely difficult but also that it is an invitation and a challenge.

There are those who have actually taken very seriously, on trust, the words of H.P. Blavatsky on the very first page of the book – "Chosen Fragments from the Book of the Golden Precepts, for the Daily Use of Lanoos." Only wishing to become a *lanoo* or a disciple, they aspire to a discipline that is divine but which must be practised every single day. Those who are simple enough, like God's fools, to have this kind of response to the book, and who use it, soon find themselves in the position of asking whether they really understand what is being taught and whether these instructions are living and relevant realities in their lives. No doubt there may be moods in which the text may seem to be empty words, but over a period does it honestly make a difference to one's consciousness, one's daily life, one's capacity for calm self-control and growth in self-knowledge? When a person applies these tests to himself, all that can be said in advance is that people who have so used the book have found it of sufficient help to them to become immeasurably grateful to those responsible for giving the world this version of an old and traditional discipline, which we associate with the Theosophical Movement. Indeed, there must surely be a few for whom the book ultimately ceases to be a book, and for whom the very pathway of ascent through portals becomes a supreme reality in their lives. For them the problem becomes not one of questioning this reality, but one of relating it to the so-called realities of the world in which we live. How do we live this life, not in some secluded and protected spot on earth, but here and now? In crowded cities, among lowly human beings, everything seems to drown and crowd out the message of this book. Anyone who wishes may consider meditation and self-study in the context of the teaching in *The Voice of the Silence.* It seems only appropriate that Theosophical students should avail themselves of the privilege of doing this, not only for their own increasing benefit, but also out of a genuine wish to share with those who may not have had the opportunity to give themselves a chance to use this teaching and this book. Minimally, one could say that this would be no worse than anything else they could think of. But each one must decide on his own.

If we do approach the subject in this context, we might ask how this book, even what one knows of it, helps to link up the contemporary agony with the supreme flights of meditation of the classical past. Astonishingly, both are in the book – at the beginning and at the end. Early in the book we are told about the immense tragedy of the human condition – "Behold the Hosts of Souls. Watch how they hover o'er the stormy sea of human life, and how, exhausted, bleeding, broken-winged, they drop one after other on the swelling waves. Tossed by the fierce winds, chased by the gale, they drift into the eddies and disappear within the first great vortex." The crisis of identity, the psychological terror, the desperate struggle for survival and for a minimum meaning to be attached to one's life – these are all around us. At best we can only imagine the boundless compassion of beings so much greater than ourselves who are capable of comprehending the enormity of the anguish. At the same time, the book tells us what the ideal man of meditation would be like. It gives us a moving and compelling picture, a vibrant image of the man of meditation. It shows how he is mightier than the gods, that he is so strong that he "holdeth life and death in his strong hand." His mind, "like a becalmed and boundless ocean, spreadeth out in shoreless space. So great is the emergence of such a Being, at any time or place hidden in the obscurity of the secret history of mankind, that it is known and recorded and receives a symphonic celebration in all the kingdoms of nature. The whole of nature "thrills with joyous awe and feels subdued."

The text evokes in us memories of a forgotten past, of mythic conceptions, of golden ages that are gone, when men, like children, sat in an atmosphere of trust and peace, with abundant leisure, under the shade of trees. While some came for shelter, some to fall asleep, some to sit and learn, and some to sit and chat about everything ranging from the most metaphysical to the most practical, still others came for the sake of the existential embodiment of the discipline of a life of contemplation. Images of this kind come into our minds, while at the same time we perhaps see that there is a continuity within the agony of mankind throughout history. There is a deeper anguish, a divine discontent at the very core of the human condition, which is as old as man and which is as strikingly pertinent as all the accounts of the needs of our age. Somewhere there is a connection between the tremendous consummation of the Supreme Master of meditation and light – he who has become one with the universe, who has become a living mirror of the glory of the garment of God, of the universe as a whole, of the Self of all creatures – somewhere there is a connection between that Being, if he is a part of the family of man, and all those who are on the verge of disintegration.

There is in every single human being the embryo of this ideal man of meditation, and we can at least imagine what it would be like for such a being to be present somewhere in our midst, if not in ourselves.

We also can recognize that we have our own share in the desperate demand for psychological survival. In this way we restore an integrity to our own quest and are somewhat deserving of that illumination which will take hold in our consciousness in relation to the great and priceless teaching. We might begin to wonder whether perhaps there is a golden chord that connects the golden sphere of a man of meditation and the complex intermediary realms in which he must, by pain and anguish and awakening, by knitting together minute golden moments rescued from a great deal of froth and self-deception, come to know himself. If there were not a fundamental connection between meditation and self-study, something of the uniquely precious wisdom in this great text would be lost to us. When we begin to realize this in our lives, we come to appreciate that, while we may not be in a position to make judgments about teachers and schools in a vast and largely unrecorded history or in our own time, nonetheless we do know that there is something profoundly important in stressing *both* meditation and self-study, in bringing the two together. We must reconcile what looked like a pair of opposites and get beyond despair to something else which allows an existential and dynamic balance between meditation and self-study. This is the quality of compassion. It is in the heart of every human being in his response to human pain, and brings him truly into the fellowship of those Beings of Boundless Compassion.

A man is a Buddha before he seeks to become a Buddha. He is a Buddha potentially. The Buddha at one time must have had a desire to become a Buddha, to understand human pain. The Buddha vow is holy because it is a vow taken on behalf of all. There is in everyone the capacity to want something for the sake of all, and also honestly to want it for oneself. In this there is an authentic mirroring, in every human heart, of the highest, the holiest and the most pregnant of beginnings of the quest. There are many beginnings, many failures, and many seeming endings. The quest itself, since it applies to all beings and not only to any one man, is beginningless and endless. It is universal, since any individual quest in this direction becomes at some point merged into the collective quest. Put in poetical form, or recognized in the simplest feelings, there is something metaphysically important and philosophically fundamental to the connection between meditation or self-transcendence, and the kind of self-study which makes true self-actualization possible. There is a way in which a man can both be out of this world and in this world, can forget himself and yet be more truly himself. These paradoxes of language are difficult to explain at one level and yet we all know them to be the paradoxes of our very lives. In our moments of greatest loneliness we suddenly find a surprising capacity to come closer to beings far removed from us, men of different races and alienated groups in pain. Then we come to feel a brotherhood that is so profound that it could never be secured in any other way. These are part of the everyday experience of mankind.

Here we touch on a crucial emphasis, maintained sedulously by the Gelukpa tradition of Tibet, which affirms that unless you spend sufficient time in refining, studying and purifying your motive, in using compassion as fuel to generate the energy needed to take off and land, you should not begin to rush into meditation. It is a slow school, but it greets the aspirant in the name of all. It scorns powers and the notion of one man becoming a superman in isolation from the quest of other men. Making no promises or claims, it does not insult our intelligence by promising us something to be attained without effort.

Are we not old enough in history to be somewhat apprehensive of schools that promise too much and too soon, when we know that this does not work in any sphere of life? Would we go to some local, loud-talking musician who tells us that he could make us as good as Casals in a week? Would we even take him seriously? We might go to him out of fun or sympathy or curiosity. Why in the most sacred of all realms should we be misled? Is it because of our impatience, our feeling of unworthiness, an advance fear of failure? These questions throw us back upon ourselves. In raising them, in probing our own standpoint at the original moment of the beginning of the quest, we make discoveries about ourselves. They are very profound and important, as they may sum up for us a great deal of the past. They would also be crucial in the future where we may come to sense the supreme relevance all along the way, when it is hard and rough, of what Merlin said to Arthur: "Go back to the original moment." If one could understand the fullness of what is anticipated in that original moment of our quest, one could trace the whole curve of our growth that is likely to emerge, with its ups and downs. Yet it cannot tell all as long as there are unknown depths of potentiality and free will in a human being.

A statement in *The Morning of the Magicians* suggests that as long as men want something for nothing, money without work, knowledge without study, power without knowledge, virtue without some form of asceticism, so long will a thousand pseudo-initiatory societies flourish, imitating the truly secret language of the 'technicians of the sacred.' There must be some reason why the integrity of the quest requires that no false flattery be made to the weaker side in every man. *The Voice of the Silence* tells us early on: "Give up thy life, if thou would'st live." That side of you which is afraid, which wants to be cajoled and flattered and promised, which would like an insurance policy, must go, must die. It is only in that dying that you will discover yourself. We all limit ourselves. We engage in a collective act of daily self-denigration of mankind. We impose, in addition to our tangible problems, imaginary and insurmountable difficulties owing to our dogmatic insistence on the finality of our limitations.

The Wisdom-Religion is transmitted so as to restore in the human being, and collectively in the world, the reality of the perfectibility of man, the assurance that men are gods, that any man is capable of reaching the apex, and that the difference between a Buddha or a Christ and any one of us is a difference of degree and not of kind. At the same time it shows that the slaying of the dragon, the putting of the demon under the foot, the command of the sovereign will of the Adept, "Get thee behind me, Satan," are heroic deeds every one of us could accomplish. Potential gods could also become kings. Every man could be a king in his own republic, but he can only become a king and eventually a god if he first experiences the thrill of affirming what it is to be a man – man *qua* man, one who partakes of the glory, the potentiality, the promise and the excellence of human nature, one who shares points of contact with the mightiest man of meditation. He must understand what the power of his thought can do, and discern a connection between the imagination of children and the disciplined imagination of perfected teachers.

With this exalted view of the individual embodiment of the collective potentialities of man, a person can say, "I'm proud to be a man and man enough to give myself a minimum of dignity. I'm willing to be tried, to be tough, to go through a discipline. I'm willing to become a disciple, and dissipate that portion of myself which is pretentious, but which is also my problem and my burden – like the donkey the man carries on his back in the Japanese fable – instead of making it an ever-lengthening shadow by walking away from the sun. I can make that shadow shrink by walking towards the sun, the *Logos* reflected in the great teachers, which is real and in me and every single living being." This is a great affirmation. To make it is profoundly important. It is to affirm in this day and age that it is meaningful for a man to give up lesser pretensions and engage in what may look like presumption, but is really an assertion in his life that he can appreciate the prerogative of what it is to be a *manushya*, a man, a self-conscious being. That is a great step on the path of progressive steps in meditation and self-study.

So far all that has been said is about beginnings, but this really is an arena where the first step seems to be the most difficult. Also, it is a matter of how you define the first step. An analogy may be made here with our experience in the engineering of flying machines. The designs were there; the diagrams were there; the equations were there; the knowledge of what is involved in maintaining a jet engine at high altitudes was there. The tough part was the take-off and landing problem. We now know more widely, in an age when people turn in desperation to a variety of drugs, that it is very difficult to have control over entry into the higher states of consciousness in a manner that will assure a smooth re-entry into ordinary life. It is because of the take-off and landing problem that we need both to be very clear about our beginnings and also to see the whole quest as a re-sharpening of the integrity of the beginning, in relation to meditation and self-study.

In the Gelukpa schools one would be told to spend a lot of time expanding compassion but also meditating on meditation. What is one going to meditate on? Meditate on meditation itself. Meditate on men of meditation. In other words, the more you try to meditate, the more you realize that meditation is elusive. But this is an insight that protects you from self-deception. Ultimately, the entire universe is an embodiment of collective mind. Meditation in its fullness is that creative power of the Platonic Demiurge, of the Hindu *Visvakarman*, of the *Logos* of the Gnostics, which could initiate a whole world. That initiation or inauguration of a world is a representation of the mighty power of meditation. You can become, says *The Voice of the Silence,* one with the power of All-Thought, but you cannot do so until you have expelled every particular thought from your mind-soul. Here is the philosophical and cosmic basis of meditation in its fullness. All meditations can only be stepping stones towards a larger meditation. What will give us a gauge of the quality, strength and meaningfulness of our power to meditate, and of our particular meditations, is our ability to harvest in the realm of self-knowledge that which can be tested in our knowledge and understanding of all other selves. To put this in another way, if to love one person unconditionally is so difficult for us, how extraordinarily remote from us seems to be the conception of those beings who can unconditionally love *all* living beings. We cannot do it even with one. Now someone might say, "No, but I can do it with one or a few sufficiently to understand in principle what it would be like to do it for all." Someone else might say, "Oh, when I look at my life I find that I don't know what it is fully to love any one, but I do know that somewhere in my loneliness and pain I feel the closeness of anonymous faces, a silent bond of brotherhood between myself and many others."

There are different ways by which we could see in ourselves the embryo of that boundless love and compassion which is the fruit of self-knowledge at its height, where a man becomes self-consciously a universal embodiment of the *Logos*, having no sense of identity except in the very act of mirroring universal light. There must be a tremendous integrity to a teaching and discipline which says that every step counts, that every failure can be used, and that the ashes of your failures will be useful in regrafting and rejuvenating what is like a frail tree that has to be replanted again and again. But the tree one is planting is the tree of immortality. One is trying to bring down into the lesser vehicles of the more differentiated planes of matter the glorious vesture of immortality, which showed more clearly when one was a baby, which one saluted in the first cry of birth, and of which one becomes somewhat aware at the moment of death.

There is a hint at the moments of birth and death, something like an intimation of the hidden glory of man, but during life one is not so awake. This becomes a problem of memory and forgetfulness.

The chain of decline is started. It was classically stated in the second chapter of the *Gita:* "He who attendeth to the inclinations of the senses, in them hath a concern; from this concern is created passion, from passion anger, from anger is produced delusion, from delusion a loss of the memory, from the loss of memory loss of discrimination, and from loss of discrimination loss of all!" Every man is fragmenting himself, spending himself, limiting himself, finitizing himself, localizing himself, to such a degree, with such an intensity and irregularity, and such a frenetic, feverish restlessness, that he is consuming himself. Physiologically we know that we cannot beat the clock time processes of the changes in the physical body. Therefore we cannot expect to find the elixir of immortality on the physical plane. But we all know that by attending to the very process of growth and change, and by awareness of what happens to us in sickness, that we do have some control and can make a difference by our very attitude and acceptance of the process. If you are very ill, by worrying about it you are going to make yourself worse, but there are people who are really quite ill, who by acceptance have gained something of the aroma of well-being.

These are everyday facts having analogues and roots in a causal realm of ideation and creative imagination which gives shape and form to the subtle vehicle, through which a transmission could take place of the immortal, indestructible and inexhaustible light of the *Logos* which is in every man and came into the world with every child. It is the radiance of *Shekinah,* the *nur* of Allah, the light of St. John. It is a light that looks like darkness and is not to be mistaken for those things that have a glamour on the sensory plane. To bring it down or make it transmit through the causal realm and become a living *tejas* or light-energy issuing forth from the fingers and all the windows and apertures of the human body is, of course, asking for a great deal. But what one is asking is meaningful, and we have got to try to understand.

It is so important in this quest to keep asking questions, both about apprenticeship in meditation and the repeated attempts and failures at gaining self-knowledge, that this in itself brings about a great discovery. There is a critical factor or determining role that may be assigned to what *The Voice of the Silence* calls the principle of sifting. " 'Great Sifter' is the name of the 'Heart Doctrine'. " The ratio between meaning and experience, which in Plato's definition of insight is the learning capacity of the human soul, is that which enables one man to learn from one experience what another man will not learn in a lifetime. We see this all around us. We often see ourselves repeating the same mistakes and at other points we are relieved that we finally learnt something sufficiently well. That is the x-factor, the mystery of each human being, the capacity to be a learner when it is tough, to say, "I don't want to kid myself." In this way a man builds a raised platform of confidence that is authentic and stable because the man at the height of the quest is a man of such supreme confidence that it is no longer personal. It is the confidence of the universe, and he embodies it. He becomes a conscious agent of the collective and creative will in the universe. What this means in another sense is spontaneous forgetfulness of self. He is so assured that he doesn't have to claim anything. He can forget name and form. He can totally afford not to think of the small self, the little 'me,' because he has accepted and inherited, come to embody, renounce and enjoy, the entirety of a universe of infinite possibilities. He acquires the psychological capacity to maintain a meaningful relationship between a universe of ontological plenty, analogous to a realm of illimitable light where giving does not deplete, and a universe of scarcity, a region of finite matter where there are hard choices to be made and where to move in one direction is to negate another, to take one thing is to give up something else, and to use time or energy in one way is to deny their use in other ways. Not to see the latter is to be a fool. Not to see the former is to deny oneself the opportunity to enjoy and actualize the potentiality and plenty of the universe in every man.

Instead of being depressed that we cannot really do more than meditate in small ways and that we are liable again and again to get into the cuckoo cloud of fantasy which we have to give up, we must say, "I will persist." What is important in meditation is continuity of consciousness. All attempts at meditation are merely fumbling attempts at building a line of life's meditation. A being who does this fully, like the Buddha, could say when asked whether he was a man or a god, "I am awake." To be fully awake is difficult. We are partly awake and partly asleep. One only fully meditates when one is fully awake and one cannot be fully awake except in relation to the One which is hidden, the supreme reality which has no form, which will never show its face, and yet which can include all faces and assume all forms. One is fully awake only when one can know proportionality, and accurately assign relative reality to everything. One must be able to say, "Yes, that's true. I can understand Eichmann. I know there is that in me which can be the embryo of a Hitler. I also know there is that in me which makes me feel close to Christ." A man can then expand his conception of the Self, so that nothing outside annoys or attracts him of which he cannot see in himself exact and genuine analogues. He can also say, "Somewhere I understand, at the very root of my nature, what it would be like to visualize the Golden Age where all men are consciously and continually bathing in the noon-day glory of the Divine." As Paul Hazard said: "As long as there are children, there will be a Golden Age." All of us can attempt to make mental images of the Golden Age, and to do so is deeply therapeutic, individually and collectively.

The Gelukpa tradition, which seems so demanding, has points of contact for all of us with our daily lives. One could say that to meditate is to remove hindrances to continuity of consciousness caused by the modifications of the mind. We do have to go on doing this again and again. You do it much better when you sit down to it and prepare for it properly, but above all you do it best when you meditate on universal good, as Plato taught. When you sit down to meditate on universal good – which you cannot conceptualize and which includes and transcends all conceptions of welfare and particular goods – you can free yourself from a great deal of tension. But you cannot stay there very long without the danger of falling asleep, of becoming passive, of fantasizing. You have to pull out at the right time. You do not want to dilly-daily, least of all to be anxious and settle for imitations. You want the real thing even if for a moment. The more you do this, the more it becomes like breathing. You do not have control over breathing, but fortunately most of the time your breathing can take care of itself.

What about mental breathing? That is where discipline is needed in regard to meditation. You can do something about the disordered, unregulated mental breathing, the way in which you receive the world of objects and in which you forget that awareness which you do have of the One that is hidden. Unless you can regulate this mental breathing, you cannot authentically laugh at and look at the absurdities and weaknesses of your lower self and make it genuinely meaningful for you to say, "I am more than you think. I am more than anyone else understands. And so is everyone else." Not only that, but this can be extended. One can be convinced in one's darkest hour, like men in concentration camps, that there is something profoundly precious to one's own individual sense of being human. One can be proud of what one somewhere knows one has to give to the world, which can be an authentic gift to the whole of mankind. When one can legitimately be proud of that, and increase the content of that knowledge, it ceases to be a feeling. Then one is not afraid of anything in oneself. Then one can understand and rejoice in the statement in the *Light on the Path*:". . . no man is your enemy: no man is your friend. All alike are your teachers."

Life is a school. There is an eternal learning and at any given time you alone can determine how much improved you are as a learner. One comes to see that while the whole of life is a teacher of concentration, that the whole of life also makes it difficult for you to retain the power needed to become continuous in your consciousness. This means that you are both immortal and mortal. To recover immortality while you are aware that you are mortal is not easy. You can do it at one level in one way at one time. You can feel it at some other time in a certain mood. To really do it, however, you have to know it in the classical sense defined by Plotinus – by reason, by experience, and by illumination, independently and by each. You have only half-knowledge otherwise. Knowing it mentally is not enough, though it is important. Knowing it in terms of a peak experience, though very grand, is not adequate to the demands of life. That we may fail to know independently by an appeal to illumination, reason and experience is to say that we know nothing. Yet, what we seek potentially includes all knowledge. These are paradoxes which become realities, truths about consciousness, because consciousness knows no limitations. The power of identification, the power of projection, the power of making yourself, of self-analyzing reflection or *svasamvedana,* is immense. You can play roles and if you can play every role, you can also play the role of the Christ. You can play the role of the Buddha. But you cannot begin to understand what this means unless you can also recognize what it is to play the role of a

Hitler, and furthermore, what it means to be the *Kutastha,* he who plays no role whatsoever.

There is an integrity to this quest which is coeval with the whole of life. No one can reduce it to a technique. It is a very beautiful teaching. There never could be enough time, nor could there be any meaningfulness in assuming that anyone could ever fully tell anyone else what is involved. In the end each has to plunge into the stream. Every attempt at meditation within the context of universal meditation, and every attempt at self-knowledge within the context of the fullest concept of self-knowledge, is a meaningful stepping-stone. It can be carried forward in a ceaseless process of alchemy. Once we decide not to settle for the easier way out, once we taste the joy of the toughness of the Path, then we also find it is fun. It is enjoyable. One can truly say that he even enjoys knowing his failures. Then one may fall into another trap. One may too much enjoy being aware, but if one does, life will correct. We will suddenly look and find that we are ready to plunge into the abyss again.

All of these are representations of what in reality is a process of building, out of the repeated dyings of our vehicles, that fabric of stable, subtle, radiant matter which can be inhabited by ceaseless ideation and universal contemplation, so that one can be a man of meditation who can live as and for every other being. You are a Bodhisattva. You can become a Buddha. It is not possible for any of us to say this to ourselves except in the context of some genuine understanding. Otherwise it is false. Hence, of course, we need teachers. The best Teachers give us the confidence that we have access, each uniquely but within ourselves, to that triadic sanctuary within, which becomes the gateway to the cosmic triad. We can then say, as did the ancient Aryans, *Atmanam atmana pasya:* "See the universal self through your own immortal self." The issue is one of reaffirmation but it is a reaffirmation we can receive only from those who, as they affirm it, can make us believe. Of this we could never be judges, because we would never know whether the problem was in us or in them. But if we are sufficiently in earnest we will know, even though we will make mistakes. We will say, "This is real. This not only speaks *to* me; this speaks *within* me. I am hearing a voice which is the voice of my own Self." When this becomes real for a man, then indeed he is blessed. He enters that kind of initiation and reaches that threshold beyond which the quest will be extremely challenging, but from which he cannot fall back.

There is such a point. To reach that point is possible. This is the great priceless boon of learning the truth about meditation and the Self that all the great texts give, which was for long periods of time used as the basis of a discipline in secret sanctuaries of initiation, and which we have in *The Voice of the Silence,* the voice of *Brahma Vach.* It is possible for any person to make the wisdom of this book a living power in his life. Then he does not have to be wasting energy and time as to what he thinks of someone else, because that no longer matters, since there is no longer any 'someone else.' He has become the One. The seeker has become the object of his quest. There is no gap between himself as a knower and the known and the knowledge. The three are in one. They are all in one at the beginning, but unconsciously to him. Self-consciously they become one again. Until he reaches that point, or until he makes a proper beginning, let him not waste time running around in circles, expending energy, asking all those kinds of questions which are really the questions of the man who is never going to climb mountains, who is never going to swim, who is never going to walk. The lame cannot be made to walk unless they want to walk upon this path. The sick cannot be healed unless they wish to be healed. Therefore we are profoundly grateful to all those Teachers of *Gupta Vidya* who once again gave us the knowledge and the assurance, the faith and the conviction, that we are the Path, that we can heal ourselves, and that we can become what we may now think is impossible. We can become that, not for our own sake, but for the sake of all and thereby become guides and exemplars to those who need our help.

Toronto
October 9, 1971

Hermes, March 1976

COGNITION, BREATH AND SPEECH

In the 'Book of Hermes', Pymander, the oldest and the most spiritual of the Logoi of the Western Continent, appears to Hermes in the shape of a Fiery Dragon of 'Light, Fire, and Flame'. Pymander, the 'Thought Divine' personified, says: 'The Light is me, I am the Nous (the mind or Manu), I am thy God, and I am far older than the human principle which escapes from the shadow ('Darkness', or the concealed Deity). I am the germ of thought, the resplendent Word, the Son of God. All that thus sees and hears in thee is the Verbum of the Master, it is the Thought (Mahat) which is God, the Father. The celestial Ocean, the Aether...is the Breath of the Father, the life-giving principle, the Mother, the Holy Spirit...for these are not separated, and their union is LIFE.

The Secret Doctrine, i 74-75

In the compelling mystical dialogue between Pymander and Hermes, the personified Thought Divine delivers a magnificent affirmation of the descent of the fiery power of Universal Thought from the Divine Darkness to give light and life to an intelligent and intelligible cosmos. The Divine Pymander speaks as the Dragon of light, fire and flame – the resplendent Word sprung from the primal germ of thought that lies beyond being and non-being alike. Pymander represents the concealed Deity, the ubiquitous presence and vital potency of the Word, the basis of all cognition in the cosmos. Hermes represents the finest aspect of human consciousness, involved in a sublime quest for union with *Atma-Buddhi*. It is that noetic intelligence, inseparable from the Thought Divine, which is capable of resonating in devotion to the vibration of the Word from which it sprang. The sacred dialogue of Pymander and Hermes intimates the mysterious relationship between mind and speech in man and the cosmos, alluding to the significance of their interaction in the mystic path towards fusion with *Atman*. The dialogue also points to an archetypal series of correlations between diverse principles, uniting the Aether-Breath of the Father with the life-giving Holy Spirit of the Mother within the ONE LIFE.

144

In explicating this passage from the "Book of Hermes", H.P. Blavatsky correlated the Thought Divine with *Mahat,* a generic term having different meanings in different contexts. In its highest meaning it conveys the Universal Mind, an ideal and pre-genetic abstraction eluding any formal definition. In *Gupta Vidya* a fundamental distinction divides Universal Mind as the permanent possibility of Thought from universal mind as the mind of a cosmos in manifestation. Ontologically prior to any set of elements that embody it in a cosmos, *Mahat* in its most primary sense is the all-pervading first *Logos.*

> The *Mahat* (Understanding, Universal Mind, Thought, etc.), before it manifests itself as Brahmâ or Siva, appears as Vishnu, says *Sankhya Sara;* hence *Mahat* has several aspects, just as the *logos* has. *Mahat* is called the Lord, in the *Primary* Creation, and is, in this sense, Universal Cognition or *Thought Divine.*

> *The Secret Doctrine,* i 75

Even though one may distinguish between *Mahat* as that which precedes the cosmos and *Mahat* as the cosmic mind, this distinction is essentially one of epistemological convenience. Ultimately, *Mahat* as the cosmic mind is itself only a kind of condensation or emanation, a radiation from the Universal Mind. As such, it is entirely unconnected with the emergence and disappearance of worlds. When Universal Mind is juxtaposed with the idea of thought, as in the conception of the Thought Divine, there is no reference to any discrete or individuated thinker. Rather, the Thought Divine conveys the idea of a purely transcendental Universal Cognition, without implying any linear succession in time. Like an eternal vision of the cosmos that was, is and shall be, the Thought Divine encompasses an entire series of possible creations and stages of the unfoldment of Universal Mind in manifestation. This pure self-reflection of *Mahat* at the highest level is prior to all manifestation. But it represents a plane of reality which is perpetually accessible to those awakened minds that empty themselves through meditation and learn to insert themselves self-consciously into the unmanifest ground of their own being.

The ascent towards this inward realization must begin with the recognition that everything that is manifested is a reflection of that which is invisible, manifest only on subtle planes. One must learn to understand the visible in terms of that which is only perceptible to astral and higher senses. Yet even beyond those invisible planes of subtle manifestation abides that which is beyond all manifestation and prior to it ontologically. This is referred to as Universal Cognition or Thought Divine. Universal Cognition is incapable of having any attribute and, therefore, is incapable of predication. It cannot be the subject of any verb or the referent of any adjective. Nor should it be mistaken for a noun simply because in various mystical texts it occurs as a substantive term. It is the primordial plane of pure consciousness or reality which is fundamentally so different from everything that belongs to the process of becoming that it cannot even be thought of in terms of existence. An intuition of this reality may be glimpsed through contemplation of ideas like Be-ness and pure being, which have built into them an element of self-existence in an abstract universal sense which in no way makes any reference to any process of manifestation. Nor should it be thought of in terms of any specific absence or privation of manifestation in connection with any concretized idea of *pralaya*.

Mahat as universal self-existence is beyond existence and non-existence as a pair of opposites. It is only possible to ascend to such a metaphysical idea through an extremely long and arduous course of deep meditation maintained over lifetimes. Yet if one can grant in principle that there could be such a plane of Universal Cognition, a supernal realm of Universal Ideation which is the plane of the very highest perfected beings, and that there is in this a basis for universal self-existence, then one could conceive how, through a downward reflection into the world of differentiated matter, there could arise a conception of what is called, in the Second Creation, a feeling of self-consciousness or egoism.

> 'That *Mahat* which was first produced is (afterwards) called *Egoism*, when it is born as "I", that is said to be the *second* Creation' (*Anugita*, ch. xxxvi) . . . i.e., 'when *Mahat* develops into the feeling of Self-Consciousness – I – then it assumes the name of Egoism', which, translated into our esoteric phraseology, means when *Mahat* is transformed into the human *Manas* (or even that of the finite gods), and becomes *Aham*-ship.
>
> *The Secret Doctrine*, i 75

The progressive unfoldment of *Mahat* is inconceivable without a parallel and coordinate development of undifferentiated matter or *Mulaprakriti*. Just as there is an essential aspect of *Mahat* that is independent of the alternation of *manvantara* and *pralaya*, there is that eternal root of all substance, the virginal veil of *Parabrahm*. Its first radiation may be conceived of as a super-astral or noumenal light – the mystical Sea of Fire of the *Stanzas of Dzyan*. This sublime ocean of primordial light, akin to *Aether-Akasha*, becomes in turn the realm of differentiated matter, the vesture of evolving *Mahat* in manifestation. The deeper this descent into manifestation, the more distorted and distorting this material medium becomes, until it reaches the stage of gross astral matter – also known as the Fiery Serpent. This transformation in the *upadhi* or basis of the field of manifestation is expressed by Plato in the *Timaeus* in terms of the same and the other. Originally, there is that which is pellucid and homogeneous, inimitable and indivisible. In the descent from the highest plane, it becomes on the lower planes divided and distorted, confused and partaking of otherness. Yet it remains through all things a projection of that which is intrinsically pellucid, intrinsically homogeneous and undifferentiated. There must be a germ within the confusion of the lower astral substance that corresponds to or is consubstantial with the pure parentage of that from which it is ultimately an emanation. Hence, there is an element of illusion in the seeming separation of *Mulaprakriti* and *Daiviprakriti* during the process of manifestation from the seemingly different gross differentiated dregs of the lower planes of material existence. If one penetrates far enough into the essential ground of every point in space, one will eventually reach *Mulaprakriti*, that which is the veil upon *Parabrahm*. This absolute notion of substance has no reference to any modes of motion or forms, but represents root matter which is connected with the primary ground of *Akasha*.

As the teachings of Pymander to Hermes intimate, there is an analogy and a correspondence between these levels of the differentiation of the universal substance-principle and the levels of manifestation of Universal Cognition. There is that at the core of Universal Cognition or *Mahat* which corresponds with primordial root substance or *Mulaprakriti*, that which is beyond all reference to manifestation and which is, therefore, unconscious during the process of manifestation. It is neither a subject nor an object to consciousness or of consciousness.

Yet it can in turn emanate, and this would be represented mystically as Divine Thought condensing into the Word or the *Verbum*. This is the cosmogonic and metaphysical basis of the mysterious relationship between speech and mind. Within the mystical Sea of Fire there is fiery substance affected by fiery ideation. The fiery cognition that is inseparable from fiery substance on the plane of the super-astral Akashic or noumenal light is the ultimate basis of the records in the library of *Akasha* that constitute the great spiritual utterances of humanity. This would be the storehouse of wisdom-consciousness, the *Alayavijnana* of the Buddhists and the supernal realm of the Vedic hymns and all the other sublime utterances that have come down in human life. All these manifestations of sacred speech have their roots in *Akasha*. Whether they are known or not in external form to particular human beings in any given period of history, they have their persisting reverberations. They endlessly reproduce themselves in multitudinous ways, permeating the processes of human evolution throughout manifestation, serving as the intelligent order of Nature sprung from divine ideation.

If an individual has some theoretical appreciation of this dual unfoldment of *Mahat* and *Mulaprakriti,* then it becomes possible to discover within one's own self-consciousness, within one's own egoism, a means and method of drawing towards Universal Mind. Here *egoism* must be clearly distinguished from *egotism.* Egoism is the pure sense of 'I-am-I' consciousness, bound up with the principle of individuation. It is possible to detach the pure sense of 'I' from every object and every kind of concern or conception which is centered upon a differentiated world. Through an interior discipline of concentration, which may be called the *aham* meditation, it is possible to withdraw that sense of 'I-am-I' into itself to such a degree that it can light up a field of higher awareness. This is the ultimate reason for and the basis of the imperative importance of daily and indeed constant meditation.

Perfected human beings are masters of ceaseless contemplation. Whilst they may be recognized as heroic individuals, engaging in courageous deeds, they are essentially men of thought, constantly plunged into deep reflection. By contrast, human beings who do not master the power of thought and the differentiations of matter in their vestures are fragmented in consciousness and at the mercy of external influences. In effect, they are slaves to the desire principle, driven by limited modes of thought towards transitory objects. This is the common plight of vast numbers of human beings, and whilst all have the opportunity in one form or another to deepen their powers of reflection in life, one who postpones the effort will undergo extraordinary difficulty. It is of vital importance that children learn how to sit down, to be quiet, to meditate and concentrate. At any age in life, one must attempt these disciplines. No matter at what level one approaches the problem, one must learn to abstract, to withdraw, to sustain intact a subtler awareness. If one can develop a capacity to enjoy ideas and to penetrate through meditation to a certain level of consciousness, this will eventually become a continuous current in one's life to which one can return again and again.

All of this amounts to a re-ascent in consciousness through the vestures of the mind towards their ultimate ground in that which is beyond manifestation. The same process may be understood in relation to the complex teaching of *Gupta Vidya* concerning the different aspects of breath and their relationship through speech to mind. Like everything else in arcane metaphysics, the concept of breath does not refer merely to something physical. It refers, even at the lowest level, to that which is astral, but which has its analogues all the way up to and including the highest vestures and beyond. When texts like the *Anugita* speak of the discipline of the breath or *pranayama*, they refer not to the crude physical manipulations of the breath that often pass in ignorant circles for a form of *yoga*. These physical practices are often dangerous in the extreme and invariably result from a fatal misunderstanding of the Teachings. Philosophically, the breaths are rhythms and motions in the *karana sharira* or the *anandamaya kosha*, inseparable from *Buddhi*.

> In the *Anugita* a conversation is given (ch. vi, 15) between a *Brahmana* and his wife, on the origin of Speech and its occult properties. The wife asks how Speech came into existence, and which was prior to the other, Speech or Mind. The *Brahmana* tells her that the *Apana (inspirational breath)* becoming lord, changes that intelligence, which does not understand Speech or Words, into the state of *Apana*, and thus opens the mind.

> *The Secret Doctrine*, i 94

Inspirational breathing is important in relation to being able to aspirate properly, to speak clearly, and so to control the power of sound. To control a restless mind, for example, one could try reading aloud some passage from a sacred text, The principal thing is to forget oneself, in the lower sense. Yet this is no easy task, if only because one has spent too much time, too much energy and too much wasted breath over so many lives in lower self-meditation. Even if this is so, one can use the vestures of the lower self on behalf of a higher egoism. Through intoning sacred words, paying attention to the sound of one's own voice and the words being formulated, one may employ the power of speech to govern the restless lower mind. Because one is lending voice to intoning that which is meaningful and powerful, the practice will, after a point, prove helpful. The simplest way of doing this, honoured the world over, is by chanting. Take, for example, a single sound like "*Rama*" and continually chant it. Of course, this must be done with attention. There is a thin line between chanting "*Rama, Rama*" and chanting "*Mara, Mara*", between invoking the *Atman* and intoning 'death'.

When people take advantage of the power of sound through speech in chanting to calm the mind, they are able to gain some relief from its restless activity. But as the *Anugita* teaches, speech which is uttered audibly is capable of affecting only the lower or movable mind. Audible speech cannot affect the immovable mind except in the case of an Adept, who is above both the immovable and movable minds and can use all energies noetically. Thus, the *Anugita* points to the important use of the power of audible speech in reference to the lower *manas,* working through the power of recitation of texts and *mantras* to gain self-control. This is in line with the common-sense recognition that sometimes it is necessary to talk to oneself, disconnecting from one's lower *manas* and giving oneself instructions, or in Buddha's phrase, "dictating terms to the mind". This can be helpful in strengthening the practice of one's resolves, in holding fast during difficult times, and it is also related to the practice of singing and chanting while working in order to maintain a certain rhythm. All of these are legitimate uses of speech. In the use of audible speech to govern the lower mind, that speech must originate in a self-consciousness that is superior and prior to the utterance. It must be inspired, guided by a breath that comes from a region of more subtle and universal substance and intelligence, if it is to have a harmonizing effect upon the physical and lower astral field of the personal mind and the body.

According to the *Anugita,* it is possible through the power of silent or inaudible speech to approach the realm of the immovable mind, enabling one to draw upon its powers of inspiration. Ordinarily, people find it difficult to distinguish between what they call thought and silent speech. This is because ordinary views of the power of thought are extremely vague. Hence the crucial importance of regular efforts to engage in meditation, attempting to hold ideas in the mind, if only by trying to hold sentences or stanzas from sacred texts before the mind. As one does this, one can intone the sentence in the mind, and as one intones it, one can dwell upon it. Gradually becoming one with the Teaching in the mind, one may increasingly learn to think upon it in the true sense of the word 'thought'. In this way, one can begin to apprehend both noiseless speech and the mystical process whereby it nourishes the life of the soul.

Having recounted the Teaching of the *Anugita* regarding the relationship of inaudible and audible speech to the immovable and movable mind, H.P. Blavatsky remarked:

> This allegory is at the root of the Occult law, which prescribes silence upon the knowledge of certain secret and invisible things perceptible only to the spiritual mind (the 6th sense), and which cannot be expressed by 'noisy' or uttered speech. This chapter of *Anugita* explains, says Arjuna Misra, *Pranayama,* or regulation of the breath in Yoga practices.... This story is quoted to show how inseparably connected are, in the metaphysics of old, intelligent beings, or rather 'Intelligences', with every sense or function whether physical or mental. The Occult claim that there are seven senses in man, as in nature, as there are seven states of consciousness, is corroborated in the same work, chapter vii, on *Pratyahara* (the restraint and regulation of the senses, *Pranayama* being that of the 'vital winds' or breath).

> *The Secret Doctrine,* i 95–96

In this passage the *Anugita* affirms that the mind is the lord of the senses. Although in ordinary language one speaks of touch, taste, smell, sight and hearing as independent powers of sensation, all of these are closely interrelated with each other. Furthermore, as the *Anugita* teaches, without the mind, "the senses never shine, like an empty dwelling, or like fires the flames of which are extinct". Only through the mind are the various senses able to apprehend their respective objects. Unlike some epistemological systems which attempt to conceive the full operation of the senses independently of the mind, and then to depict the activity of the mind in relation to the senses as purely inferential, the *Anugita* points to a much more intimate relationship.

Each sense is seen as a differentiation both of the abstract power of thought and the abstract principle of substance on a particular plane. There is no mind-body problem in the philosophy of *Gupta Vidya*. There are, instead, corresponding to different planes of Universal Cognition and *Mulaprakriti* in manifestation, different sets of senses and organs of action. By recognizing the predominance of the mind in relation to the lower astral and physical senses, it is possible through deliberation and thoughtfulness to rise above the compulsive and involuntary processes that operate through the sense-organs of the gross body. Just as audible speech can aid in calming the lower mind, so too physical movements and disciplines can aid in gaining steadiness and control on the physical and even mental plane. This is why physical exercise or, at another level, certain physical postures can aid in clearing the mind and making it more direct. This can help an individual to moderate emotional extremes, to cut through a great deal of the confusion of the lower *manas* caught up in sensory life.

> This, of course, with regard only to *mind on the sensuous plane*. Spiritual mind (the upper portion or aspect of the *impersonal MANAS*) takes no cognisance of the senses in physical man.... The ancients were acquainted with the correlation of forces and all the recently discovered phenomena of mental and physical faculties and functions, with many more mysteries also.

The Secret Doctrine, i 96

The entire capacity to calm the lower mind through the power of audible speech or physical movement depends upon tapping a reflection of the synthesizing principle of *Buddhi. Buddhi* is mirrored in every object, in every sense and sense-organ. Above all, it is mirrored in the higher *Manas* itself. In turn, it is mirrored in the synthesizing power of lower *manas,* considered as the lord of the senses. Higher *Manas* is capable of synthesizing and abstracting from all the senses, including the lower mind, which, though subtler, still exists on a plane of differentiated space, time and substance.

By invoking the power of *Buddhi,* it is possible to transcend everything in this lower realm, while at the same time giving proper value to all that is being transcended. This means recognizing that the entire realm of the lower senses is a dynamic field of minor deities and intelligences. All of these work and have their place in differentiated life, and so it is always meaningful to sanctify and revere everything in reference to the sensory plane. There is also a mirroring – in the integration of these senses and powers, these deities and intelligences – of a higher synthesis to be attained self-consciously through the union of *Manas* and *Buddhi.* As the *Anugita* teaches:

> 'There is one unmoving (life-wind or breath, the "*Yoga inhalation*", so called, which is the breath of the *One* or Higher SELF). That is the (or my) own Self, accumulated in numerous (forms).' This Breath, Voice, Self or 'Wind' (*pneuma?*) is the Synthesis of the Seven Senses, *noumenally* all minor deities and esoterically – the *septenary* and the 'Army of the VOICE'.

> *The Secret Doctrine,* i 96

This mysterious unmoving breath can only be experienced if one has become proficient in deep meditation, capable of remaining abstracted from the astral form for long periods of time. This, in turn, is possible only if one has learnt how to make the astral form coil down and attenuate itself, virtually destroyed at will. These are very high states indeed, but even if unattainable at present, they are well worth thinking about. Just to appreciate these possibilities is helpful in learning to master the outer vestures.

At the root of these mysteries of mind, speech and breath lies the mysterious union, spoken of by Pymander, of the celestial ocean, the Aether, the breath of the Father and the life-giving principle, the Holy Spirit or Mother, which together are LIFE. The Father-Mother-Son are

One, the three-tongued flame that never dies, the immortal spiritual Triad in the cosmos and in man – the *Atma-Buddhi-Manas*. Anyone who carefully contemplates this divine unity, as conveyed by the teachings of Pymander to Hermes, will soon transcend the majority of foolish questions and doubts that arise regarding the ontology of *Gupta Vidya*.

> If the student bears in mind that there is but One Universal Element, which is infinite, unborn, and undying, and that all the rest – as in the world of phenomena – are but so many various differentiated aspects and transformations (correlations, they are now called) of that One, from Cosmical down to micro-cosmical effects, from super-human down to human and sub-human beings, the totality, in short, of objective existence – then the first and chief difficulty will disappear and Occult Cosmology may be mastered.

The Secret Doctrine, i 75

As people typically cannot get rid of separateness, they go on mutilating Divine Wisdom in the name of making distinctions. In reality, the entire cosmos is a series of exact correspondences, like a series of lenses in perfect alignment and continually transmitting prismatic rays of refracted light. Since the cosmos, including human nature, is completely in order, it does not matter at what level one begins one's meditations, so long as one is inwardly attuned to a line of transmission and reflection. The source of this series of reflections and transmissions is what people often loosely call the Higher Self. It is, in reality, the spiritual fire within the human being, the *Atma-Buddhi-Manas* which is overbrooding. This cannot be tapped and its energies cannot be lent merely in providing continuity through the states of consciousness of the lower self. It cannot be drawn upon merely to hold body and soul together. It can only be tapped by a specific means of self-discipline which involves the transformation of the sense of self, the idea of 'I-am-I', from its lower application in terms of name and form to its original meaning connected with *Mahat*. This discipline requires a continual balance between the differentiated aspects of Universal Cognition and those of Universal Root Matter. Whether one thinks of this as ascending a ladder or travelling a path or any other of the symbolic metaphors available to the disciple, it connotes the cognition of synthetic relationships – between *Mahat* and the Mahatmas, between *Atma-Buddhi-Manas* and the *Avatar*, between *Nous, Daiviprakriti* and the *Verbum*. All of these are varied but precise expressions for different levels of reflection of one and the same spiritual energy or spiritual breath and fire. In every case, however expressed, it is the seventh principle in Man and the Kosmos, one with the seventh Cosmic Principle, the highest *Logos*, the *Avalokiteshvara*.

Hermes, December 1984

SPIRITUAL WAKEFULNESS

Paranishpanna, remember, is the summum bonum, the Absolute, hence the same as Paranirvana. Besides being the final state it is that condition of subjectivity which has no relation to anything but the one absolute truth (Paramarthasatya) on its plane. It is that state which leads one to appreciate correctly the full meaning of Non-Being, which, as explained, is absolute Being. Sooner or later, all that now seemingly exists, will be in reality and actually in the state of Paranishpanna. But there is a great difference between conscious and unconscious 'being'. The condition of Paranishpanna, without Paramartha, the Self-analysing consciousness (Svasamvedana), is no bliss, but simply extinction (for Seven Eternities).

The Secret Doctrine, i 53-54

Wakeful consciousness, *Turiya,* in eternal duration is the vital core of authentic participation in *Brahma Vach.* The practical embodiment of potent ideals depends upon the fusion of individual consciousness with boundless duration. The alchemical transformation of life into eternal Life is equivalent to the mystical passage from death to immortality. All self-conscious spiritual growth is a function of continuity and discontinuity of consciousness, associated with the phenomena of birth, death and rebirth. The more sedulously individuals sift through the world's particulars, the more meaningful and enduring are their perceptions, the keener are their differentiations between various levels of reality. Thus, they can also recognize the relative unreality of all things.

The capacity to affirm and negate at the same time rests upon the rootedness of souls in a timeless realm of reality above the phenomenal processes of change, above the shifting dichotomies of subject and object or past and future. With abstracted attention and attained alertness, they may consider life in terms of one great forward push at the cosmic and at the human level. This evolutionary thrust is progressing neither chaotically nor arbitrarily but under the laws of cause, effect and further cause. Life may be viewed as an arrow, directed from the past to the future. It may also be seen from the standpoint of Deity, which is a circle with its centre everywhere and its circumference nowhere. To combine both perspectives is the prerogative of man, who can both expand and contract, diffuse and deepen the range and reach of self-consciousness.

Paradoxically, the more one's consciousness is located beyond the particulars of time, the more attentive one may be to them. Timelessness is neither inertia nor indifference. It is not a blurring of impressions of mortality, but an intense sharpening and heightening of perceptions relevant to learning and living and delivering one's *dharma*. All elemental lives, moving in and through myriad shifting shadowy forms, participate at some level in incipient or higher degrees of abstract subjectivity, the basis for the distinction between the different kingdoms. Each represents the different degrees of power of the matter-moving *Nous*, the animating soul of the universe immanent in every atom, manifested in man, and inseparable from the ONE LIFE, or *Jivatma*, the transcendental and wholly immaterial ground of all design in living nature. This soul of the world, or *Alaya*, has a dual aspect correlative with the alternations of *Maha-Manvantara* and *Maha-Pralaya*.

> *Alaya*, though eternal and changeless in its inner essence on the planes which are unreachable by either men or Cosmic Gods (Dhyani Buddhas), alters during the active life-period with respect to the lower planes, ours included. During that time not only the Dhyani-Buddhas are one with *Alaya* in Soul and Essence, but even the man strong in the Yoga (mystic meditation) 'is able to merge his soul with it.'

> *The Secret Doctrine*, i 48

Furthermore:

> In the *Yogacharya* system of the contemplative Mahayana school, *Maya* is both the Universal Soul (*Anima Mundi*) and the Self of a progressed adept. 'He who is strong in the Yoga can introduce at will his *Maya* by means of meditation into the true Nature of Existence.'

> *The Secret Doctrine*, i 49

In its absolute and eternal aspect, *Alaya* precedes the sevenfold differentiation of *Prakriti*, is the unevolved cause of comprehension of all the diverse manifestations of life in the seven kingdoms. During the period of manifestation it is the vital basis of intelligence distributed by degrees throughout the kingdoms of evolved life. The human capacity to merge through meditation the self-conscious soul – *Alaya* in one aspect – with *Alaya* in its eternal aspect is the basis of conscious immortality and boundless compassion. The more deeply and irreversibly one can do this, the more one can retain wakefulness outside the realm of temporal change and remain consciously rooted in what is called pure Being, which is also pure Non-Being. This ultimate spiritual wakefulness can only be attained by abstraction, by blanking out all impressions and by meditating upon both the ceaseless and cyclical disintegration of worlds. In *Maha-Pralaya* all possible concepts and worlds are reabsorbed into the one primordial material substratum, which, having reabsorbed into itself all the elements, falls into a state of total latency wherein ideation is potentially present but without any urge to manifest. It is then that the *Alaya* of the universe is in *Paramartha*, entirely transcendent comprehension and absolute true Being.

The capacity to void the mind through meditation and to become aware of what seems like non-being whilst one's body is asleep is essential to the realization of true Being and presupposes a fundamental alteration of one's conceptions of life and vitality. To a great extent, mechanistic views of life arise because of a narrowness of perception, together with an action-centered view of vitality. A healthy antidote to societies caught up in the frenetic rush of consumption is to spend leisure time by the ocean listening to its ancient rhythms, or in the mountains silently attentive to nature's sounds. In these ways one can approach a deeper and more undifferentiated field of consciousness that is motion at a subtle level of vibration. To do this self-consciously, to establish within oneself a permanent core of silence, is the task of meditation.

Initially, one must set aside some time daily and blank out everything: one's total sense of identity, one's memories and expectations, all images and all impressions. Doing so, one gradually enters with adoration into the most abstract homogeneous realm accessible. As one gains a progressive kinship with the realm of Divine Darkness, free of the interplay of light and shadow that characterizes the world of relativities, one begins to sense within oneself living depths upon depths in consciousness. Philosophically, this negation of all limited states of consciousness, of all illusory distinctions between spirit, soul and matter, is equivalent to the affirmation of universal life and absolute freedom. Real vitality has its basis in the realm of non-being that is beyond the calculus of sequential causation.

As the *Upanishads* teach, the spiritual path is like the razor's edge. The effort to realize true immortal life in non-being requires the utmost discrimination with regard to motive. At every point, one must keep in mind the archetypal distinction between liberation and renunciation. Everything in the Teachings of the *Gupta Vidya* may be viewed in the context of a search for heightened awareness, or merely as a quest for escape. The desire for extinction is extremely strong throughout nature, whether conceived in terms of *Maha-Pralaya* at the end of an age of Brahmâ, or in terms of *Nitya Pralaya,* ceaseless dissolution. Everything in manifest nature is reabsorbed into the whole. In human beings this force of dissolution may be converted into a desire for extinction because many do not wish to engage spiritually in a world pervaded by shallow values, frozen expressions and limited conceptions. Through the principle of negation, nature balances the over-assertion of the manifested ray with disengagement in sleep or in death. Whilst the human desire for extinction can reflect the final reabsorption of everything into the whole, this desire itself reflects attachment to manifested existence. It betrays a wish for escape, an irresponsible quest for liberation. This is entirely different from the search for self-conscious attunement to universal self-consciousness, the state of those who are awake during the night of non-manifestation.

Without the self-conscious realization of *Alaya,* without *Paramartha,* the *Paranirvana* of the universe is mere extinction. Unless and until the divine essence in oneself, which is one with the essence in the heart of every atom, is made the self-conscious basis of boundless compassion towards all beings, the soul cannot realize the permanent potential of universal and eternal life.

Thus, an iron ball placed under the scorching rays of the sun will get heated through, but will not feel or appreciate the warmth, while a man will. It is only 'with a mind clear and undarkened by personality, and an assimilation of the merit of manifold existences devoted to being in its collectivity (the whole living and sentient Universe)', that one gets rid of personal existence, merging into, becoming one with, the Absolute, and continuing in full possession of *Paramartha*.

The Secret Doctrine, i 54

The fundamental distinction between liberation and renunciation implies that true love is proportional to spiritual wakefulness. The capacity to love all life-atoms depends upon one's understanding of their various orders and functions within the World Soul. Through appropriate arrangement and discipline, they must be given a chance to become apprenticed in discipleship, even at the level of unself-consciousness and incipient consciousness. No mere facility with intellectual constructions or recourse to ritual techniques is going to sustain the tremendous power of attention needed for this learning. This capacity of the soul for wakefulness is dependent upon previous lives of meditation, renunciation and service. Thus, in the meta-psychological perspective of the *Gupta Vidya*, there is no basis for understanding soul powers and the development of magical possibilities, whether in their beneficent or maleficent uses, apart from an understanding of karma and reincarnation.

Every human being has brought into the world some distinctive experience of the immortal soul and its theurgic powers, some indelible marks of past proficiency and past deficiency. Spiritual growth cannot, therefore, be explained by the principle of desire operating in the present. Filtered through the distorting prism of *kama manas*, the ideal principle of aspiration becomes a concretized impression of temporal and temporary desires. Such illusory impressions are merely projections out of *tanha*, the root desire to exist and subsist in a form or body in a world that is limited in space and time. There can be no true wakefulness, no release of the spiritual will, and no moral and mental growth based upon such an obscured and distorted sense of self-existence.

The real person or thing does not consist solely of what is seen at any particular moment, but is composed of the sum of all its various and changing conditions from its appearance in the material form to its disappearance from the earth. It is these 'sum-totals' that exist from eternity in the 'future', and pass by degrees through matter, to exist for eternity in the 'past'.

The Secret Doctrine, i 37

The deeper conception of time which is needed to understand these karmic sum-totals can only arise from an extraordinary detachment. Burdened by individual and collective karma on the one hand, confronted by the necessity of supreme detachment on the other, many find it difficult to retain a vital enthusiasm for the world. They must realize that even the most magnanimous souls cannot give themselves fully to every living being without voiding every element of meretricious attraction to the shadowy self. Detachment from the personal self is necessary for those who wish to view the world without bondage to attachments and illusions. The inner ray of *Alaya* cannot be freed for the exhilaration of universal compassion until it is disengaged in consciousness from its own reflection localized in time and space upon the waves of differentiated matter. This disengagement, equivalent to awakening true continuity of consciousness, proceeds through an undivided process of unfoldment that may be represented by an orderly series of law-governed phases. If these stages are not clearly understood, the nature of detachment may be distorted and its motives debased. Each stage accompanies a growing transcendence of the illusion of time and comprehension of Karma. At the same time, each stage represents a growing awakening to essential degrees of *Alaya* or noetic intelligence. Souls progress from the restraint of the lower self or personality by the divine Self or individuality to the restraint of the Self divine by the Eternal, in which even the latent consciousness of desire and *tanha* is torn out. Thus the soul is merged in self-consciousness with the eternal essence of *Alaya*.

The first problem of withdrawal of consciousness from form may be understood best through the relationship between karmic attachment and memory. So long as karmic attachment operates through personal memories, individuals will experience pleasant and unpleasant reactions. As Shri Shankaracharya taught, "So long as we experience pleasure and pain, karma is still working through us." The more violent these emotional reactions, the stronger is the dead weight of karma. In extreme cases, a terrible and intensely traumatic experience in previous lives, coupled perhaps with a short or non-existent *devachan*, may bring about a tremendous burden on consciousness in the present incarnation. Attracted, under karma, to parents and companions bound by likes and dislikes, one may likewise experience emotional extremism. But, whatever its cause, volatility is invariably symptomatic of a high degree of karmic bondage. Its victims must learn painfully over a lifetime to void a false sense of reality or romance, of security or expectation. The seeming burdens of karma are in direct proportion to the delusions that must be voided. An Initiate, seeing the aura of a human being mired in delusion, knows that at the moment of that being's death one question remains: Has his understanding of the *ABCs* of life improved since his birth? If so, the individual can begin to discharge the debt of karma. Thus, if he is fortunate, the individual will gravitate to environments where there is little attention to likes and dislikes and where the options for the personality are fewer. Through successive incarnations, Karma compassionately reduces opportunities for protracted delusion until the individual is compelled to learn essential lessons.

In terms of the self-conscious pursuit of moral and metaphysical ideals, Karma operates with the same dispassion, progressively narrowing the margins for error. Individuals vary in their degrees of wakefulness in proportion to their *kamic* attachment. They burden consciousness with fragmented memories, which must be distinguished from soul reminiscence, a reflection of universal memory beyond parochial and ephemeral likes and dislikes. As an individual learns to overcome the blurring of attention induced by personal memory, he will receive greater aid through moral allegiance to chosen ideals. Plato and Gandhi wisely recognized that most people in the Age of Zeus, *Kali Yuga*, are burdened by hostile memories and desperately in need of hospitable ideals.

Transmitting ideals to children and pupils through example and through precept is both beneficent and constructive. Their capacity for credible ideals increases with practice, and, as attention is focussed upon the possibilities of the future, it continues to develop. Naturally, ideals recede as they are approached, but they are nonetheless essential; they provide directions, if not destinations, and propel the individual ever forwards. As long as there are ideals, pointing to the imaginative possibilities of the foreseeable future, one can appreciate the salutary lessons of karma without becoming overburdened by collective memories of failure. Ultimately, all potent and transcendental ideals have their origins in divine thought, and their realization cannot be restricted to the solitary pilgrimage of any individual soul. As presented in the portraits of perfect enlightenment in various scriptures, they represent the source and apex of universal spiritual unfoldment. The true mystery of ideals is bound up with that of Avatars and Manus, the exalted incarnations and prototypes guiding and overbrooding manifestation, but rooted in the unmanifest divine thought and the Host of *Anupadaka*.

At the simplest level, the development of a mature consciousness of magnanimous ideals is central to the ethical growth of human beings, individually and collectively. The more potent ideals any living culture can express, the greater the hope it preserves. As a society grows weary, its scintillating ideals evaporate. From the era of Arthurian legends to Victorian dreams, England was characterized by its rich, understated yet resonant ideals. Now, all those souls engaged in this exuberant period of flowering have vanished or incarnated in Africa, Asia and elsewhere. Contemporary Englishmen and women find themselves unable to vitalize the ideals they inherited and succumb to nostalgia. Likewise, the Scandinavians passed through this transformation of ideals into memories long ago and then purged themselves of the corrosive tendency of self-flattery. Such purgation is particularly difficult in America, because to this day, America is the dumping ground of the world's malcontents. Whenever America begins to grow up, it receives a burden of memories dumped by new immigrants from declining or dissipated cultures. Thus, through *kamic* attachment or karmic precipitation, societies become weighted down by memories, and soon they find themselves caught in a downward cycle. Yet, if an individual or a society can become electrically charged by ethical ideals, can rekindle a sense of wonder towards creative possibilities, can look to the future with cool confidence, a life-giving and forward-looking current is released.

The capacity for intense involvement with the beauty of ideals is central to the problems of pessimism and optimism, apathy and initiative, for individuals as for societies. Viewed more metaphysically, the problem of attachment and memory is founded in the illusion of time itself. If one understands the present moment as merely a mathematical line separating those logical constructs called the past and the future, the present amounts to a virtually invisible and illusory division constantly in movement. Thus, everything is constantly absorbed from the past into the future. According to Buddhist metaphysics, however, "The Past time is the Present time, as also the Future, which, though it has not come into existence, still is." From this perspective, both the future and the past exist even now, because everything that has happened to humanity over eighteen million years is summed up here and now within the subtle vestures, whilst everything that will happen in myriad lifetimes to come is already implicit in the programming of our invisible vestures. Coping with this in a meaningful philosophical way, and without costly escapism, requires a meticulous attention to timing.

One must gain sufficient detachment from the past, the present and the future in the ordinary sense, from memories and ideals, to be able to see the abstract open texture of universal possibilities that the present, that imperceptible mathematical line, represents. Albertus Magnus is said to have made a homunculus, which could only come alive if the correct operation were performed at a certain moment. As that moment approached, the homunculus said, "Time will be, Time is, Time was." Because the key was not promptly applied as it said "Time is", it rapidly went on to "Time was". Such is the condition of human beings caught up in the past and the future, oblivious to what is pregnant in the present moment. Here one encounters the paradox of time and wakefulness. The more timeless one's consciousness in the true philosophical sense of expanding self-consciousness, the better one can appreciate the present moment and the sharper one's sense of timing.

The so-called realists, constantly marshalling convenient or frightening facts from the past, are only compensating for their lack of lively awareness in the enigmatic present. Whilst prating of proven realism, they entirely miss the present moment. Through the karmic process of acceleration of contagious delusion, operating on the social plane, those individuals with the most constrained sense of duration and most misplaced sense of realism tend to become the strident spokesmen of declining cultures in a dark age. Under the guise of accredited authority, misusing the channels of the media, they feverishly seek to impress their own confined consciousness upon others, parading the language of fear, pragmatism and survival. As, alas, many souls are susceptible to the pulls of pleasure and pain, this pseudo-realism becomes a dominant thought-form for a generation, and is passed on from parents to children as an insidious cowardice concerning the future. True realists, however, are those who are imaginatively practical with regard to ideals. They evidence no such impotence. Knowing that the negation of form is essential to the realization of ideals, they see the present moment rather as the wise view the moment of death, the great destroyer of illusions. Only when one releases the fragments can one see the picture as a whole, distil the quintessential from every experience, and free oneself from obscuring projections and distortions.

All negations of false continuity of consciousness are vital opportunities to awaken to a deeper continuity in consciousness. It is in this light that one should view the immemorial Teachings of the *Gupta Vidya:* nothing on this earth has real duration, nothing remains for a moment without change. So too Krishna asserts in the *Bhagavad Gita* that he, as the manifested *Logos*, never remains for a moment inactive. The blurring sense of duration that accompanies sensory awareness, like the blurred impression on the retina caused by an electric spark, is due to identification with transitory form. It is impossible to gain a right perception of reality, of the relationship of the immortal soul to its evolving vestures, without withdrawing attention from such nebulous images of personal consciousness.

> No one could say that a bar of metal dropped into the sea came into existence as it left the air, and ceased to exist as it entered the water, and that the bar itself consisted only of that cross-section thereof which at any given moment coincided with the mathematical plane that separates, and, at the same time, joins, the atmosphere and the ocean. Even so of persons and things, which, dropping out of the to-be into the has-been, out of the future into the past – present

momentarily to our senses a cross-section, as it were, of their total
selves, as they pass through time and space (as matter) on their way
from one eternity to another: and these two constitute that 'duration'
in which alone anything has true existence, were our senses but able
to cognize it there.

The Secret Doctrine, i 37

Fundamentally, the illusion of time must be traced to the experience
and expression of ideation through a limiting vesture. Mind, at
every level of manifestation, is equivalent to a summation of states
of consciousness grouped under thought, will and feeling. During
manifestation these mutable aggregates are the basis of capricious
memory; during non-manifestation they fall into complete abeyance.
Thus, when divine thought or universal ideation is unmanifest, the
mental basis of temporal existence has ceased to be.

A noumenon can become a phenomenon on any plane of existence
only by manifesting on that plane through an appropriate basis or
vehicle; and during the long night of rest called *Pralaya,* when all
the existences are dissolved, the 'UNIVERSAL MIND' remains as a
permanent possibility of mental action, or as that abstract absolute
thought, of which mind is the concrete relative manifestation.

The Secret Doctrine, i 38

It is from within this *plenum* of divine thought, eternal duration and
absolute harmony that the deathless Watchers in the Night maintain their
calm and compassionate vigil over the entire spectrum of manifested
life. Viewing *Mahat* and *Manas* from above below, they calculate
the sum-totals of collective human karma and, through benevolent
ideation, ameliorate the agonizing condition of trapped human souls.
This is the predicament of the parrot mind, of the partisan heart, of
the deluded soul enslaved by externals. The temporal confinement
of the projected personal ray has obscured the Buddhi-Manasic Ego
and impeded its active realization of its authentic inheritance as a ray
of Universal Mind. It is essential to strengthen the self-redemptive
conception of the *antaskarana* bridge between the immortal and the
mortal egos. Through meditation upon the higher pole of egoity, it is
possible to withdraw the mind from limitations. This is the basis of

true self-abnegation, self-discipline and clear-sightedness.

As this clarity of vision matures into spiritual wakefulness, one can reverse the polarity of the different centres in the lunar vesture, thereby affecting the desire-nature, sensory states and the deepest feelings. So great is the potential of the pure crystalline ray of *Alaya* that even such a profound change can take place at any time. But the transformation must be thorough and fundamental, with no quarter given to mental laziness or moral cowardice. All dullness of attention is caused by a fear of non-being acting through *tanhaic* attachment to some limited view of life. Human beings are like shadowy creatures, clutching to the trappings of existence because they are terrified of real life, like mountaineers paralyzed by fear, grasping on to precipitous ledges. They must let go their frozen grip on the niches of illusory security, if they wish to regain the freedom to move and to aid each other. They must ever be willing to be thrown back totally upon themselves, relying upon no outward circumstances or props, but only upon invisible and unbreakable cords of compassion linking one with all. Thus, they may approach the *mysterium tremendum,* the noumenal realm of Non-Being, wherein true Being lies, in the bosom of the Eternally Self-Existent. By entering the *Nivritti Marga,* the path of inwardness, one may commence the mystic return to Maha-Shiva.

> Thou hast to saturate thyself with pure *Alaya*, become as one with Nature's Soul-Thought. At one with it thou art invincible; in separation, thou becomest the playground of Samvritti, origin of all the world's delusions. All is impermanent in man except the pure bright essence of *Alaya*. Man is its crystal ray; a beam of light immaculate within, a form of clay material upon the lower surface. That beam is thy life-guide and thy true Self, the Watcher and the silent Thinker, the victim of thy lower Self.

The Voice of the Silence

Hermes, February 1983

REINCARNATION AND SILENCE

Every man's soul has by the law of his birth been a spectator of eternal truth, or it would never have passed into this our mortal frame, yet still it is no easy matter for all to be reminded of their past by their present existence.

Plato

While we may know about the long and complex history of the doctrine of reincarnation, the crisis of our time is such that the response of thinking men and women is and should be, "How does it help me? What difference could it make to my life?" In the *Bhagavad Gita* Lord Krishna, speaking as the *Logos* in the cosmos, but also as the hidden god in every man, makes a supreme, unqualified affirmation. Like similar utterances in the great scriptures of the world, the words of Krishna have a ring of self-certification. He simply affirms for all men that there is an inexhaustible, inconsumable, incorruptible, indestructible, beginningless and endless spirit that is the sovereign ruler within the temple of the human body. Yet the same Krishna, having made this affirmation, ends his speech by asking Arjuna to recognize the honest position of the finite mind of the ordinary man by saying, "The antenatal state of beings is unknown; the middle state is evident; and their state after death is not to be discovered."

Any human being must recognize that, insofar as his mind is a bundle of borrowed conceptions – because he has grown up conditioned and circumscribed by the limiting factors of heredity, family, education and the social environment – he cannot do any more at first than come with pain to the point of declaring with profound honesty, "I really do not know. I do not know about evil. I have no idea of many things that happened to me earlier in this life. I have no idea of what will happen to me tomorrow, next year, let alone after the moment of death." This could give integrity to the quest. At the same time, when a human being begins at the level of categories and concepts, he also knows that there is something unspoken about his particular life – his tears, his thoughts, his deepest feelings, his loves and longings, his failures and frustrations, his invisible, hidden determination to hold fast in times of trial, to triumph over obstacles that seem forbidding. Beyond all of these there is that secret of his own soul which he cannot share with anyone else or even bring to the level of human speech. He knows that there is a depth and dimension to his own experience as a conscious sentient being which can participate in the transcendental wonder of the world, which can be aroused to depths and to heights and to a tremendous breadth of cosmic vision when looking at awesome vistas in nature or when surveying the great epochs of human history. But at the same time this secret cannot be conveyed. It cannot be demonstrated or fitted into the workaday categories and concepts needed to survive in a world of psychological limitation and scarcity.

The problem is one of translation. Seen philosophically, if we assume that there is something prior to be translated into something else that is shareable, it is a problem of self-discovery. It involves integrating the potential, intermittently intimated in our consciousness, with the actual which is a story that could be streamlined and which any Hollywood scriptwriter could convert into a celluloid version, a banal sequence of scenes. There must be something between our inchoate intuition of the inexhaustible and our painful recognition of the factuality of the temporally finite sequence that seems to string these events together. Memories clutter the mind. We look back with regrets or look forward with hopes, with longings that may be vain and ineffectual or may be impossible to share with anyone else.

What is self-validating for a Krishna or for the immortal spirit of man can only become a supreme and total fact for a human being when he has begun to strip away the layers and vestures of consciousness through which he is bound. In a Wordsworthian sense, every child is crowned by the aura of the divine, and has in his eyes some recognition of having lived before, some glint of an ancient wisdom distilled into the very essence of his response to the furniture of the world. Yet every human being, growing out of the child-state, loses those intimations. How are we to recover them compatibly with the integrity and self-consciousness that we must bring to every level and aspect of our human experience? This necessitates further work upon the whole of one's nature. Where we do not know, we may discard the dogmas that claim to know. There are those which insist that man is merely a fortuitous concurrence of atoms – in the name of a science which would be disowned by the greatest, most agnostic and creative scientific thinkers. There is the dogma derived from religion that man is a soul created by an anthropomorphic being at a certain point of time and consigned to eternal hell or heaven, and there are other corruptions of thought such as transmigration into animal form.

When a person discards dogmas and starts with the standpoint of genuine unknowingness, combined with a willingness to learn, he has taken a stand that is truly individual, yet within the context of all mankind. Then, as he works upon himself, he must find out what is unique and gives continuity to himself. At the same time, further growth in this quest will only be possible when he can truly dissolve the sense of separateness between himself and other beings. When the barriers fall away, his love can become almost limitless in scope. He can feel the pain in every human heart and enjoy the world through the eyes of every human being. Clearly, this cannot be done by a person except at some specific level and cannot be done totally within any short-term curve of growth. We would need a number of births to attain that degree of universalization wherein we could merge the universal and the individual and also maintain stasis throughout the different levels on which we have to communicate with widening or narrowing circles of human beings. In that sense, what is self-validating at one level could only become wholly valid and be a fully embodied truth when one's whole life revolves around it.

Many an unlettered man, in the words of the poet, is a mute, inglorious Milton, unknown, unnoticed by other men, and, like Markham's man with a hoe, conveys through his eyes the sad awareness that this is an old story that includes all beings and will persist far into the future. For the pseudo-sophisticated intellectual classes to see as much would be extremely difficult. People for whom there is very little else can sustain the awareness of some fundamental truth. To be able to do this self-consciously within a process of growth is extraordinarily elusive for a man burdened with the mental complexities of contemporary civilization, because he cannot ascend to universal brotherhood except very partially, intermittently and, alas, defensively.

To make reincarnation a vital truth in one's personal life is to treat each day as an incarnation, to greet every person as an immortal soul, inwardly and in silence, and to empathize with every human failure as a limitation – an effect with causes – comparable to all other limitations. It is the ability to see, even in the longing of the person who is almost totally lost, that spark of the Divine which could eventually be fanned into the flame of the cosmic and compassionate fire of wisdom of the Buddhas and Bodhisattvas. It is an old tradition in the East that those who truly know of the immortality of the soul can only say, "Thus have I heard."

Why is there no immortality for what we call the 'personality,' the particular mask that we wear, through which we appear to other people to be someone with a name and a form, a recognizable identity? However glorious the aggrandizement of personal selfhood may seem in a Nietzschean sense, it is still something that limits and is limited, and hence must participate in finitude and mortality. To wish immortality for that which is visibly mortal, for a mind which is like a cobweb of confusing conceptions, is at best a compensatory illusion. Ultimately, it is a sign of weakness. But the Great Teachers did not come to tell man what he already knows – that there are limitations. They came to tell him that beyond these limitations he could be free. The Buddha declared: "Know ye who suffer, ye suffer from yourselves. None else compels that ye are caught in this Wheel of Life." When Jesus spoke of the weakness of the flesh, he also intimated that the spirit is free, that it is the source of will, and that when it is truly willing, it is immortally free.

It is only by reinforcing a weaker side of our own nature that we could project from a limited view of ourselves a confused picture of personal immortality. Despite all the self-advertisements of the age, hardly any man can do full justice to himself. A man who is loudly making the case for himself is all too often belittling himself. Even the finest self-images have some illusion built into them, and to extrapolate them into the future and into the past is to limit oneself unduly. The notion of personal immortality becomes extremely degrading in a universe of law, where everything experienced by consciousness is connected, in the course of time, with everything that follows it. If a person, early or late in life, uses the doctrine of rebirth, or some notion of personal immortality, as a crutch to cling to, physical death may well be succeeded by a dreamy state of illusory happiness after a period of purgatorial separation from all the excrescences of the life just lived. Then he will have to come back, and alas, in so doing, as Plato suggests in the "Myth of Er", he may choose the very opposite of what he seeks. A person who mistakes the external tokens of the good, the true and the beautiful for the transcendental *Agathon* may well find himself drawn, even propelled, into an environment where he is punished by getting what he wants.

What we need is *metanoia,* a fundamental breakthrough in consciousness. Otherwise the notion of immortality avails us naught. Many Theosophists of every sort hold to reincarnation as a dogma rather than as a basis for meditation. It cannot help unless a man can really come to see that it is a fact in nature – a law of life in a universe of cyclic processes – and can live by that law increasingly. He can recognize mistakes, and through repeated self-correction, open new vistas. He may make existential affirmations of perfectibility – which must be on behalf of all if they are to be authentic – and give everyone he meets something of the taste of true optimism in regard to the future. Unless a person can do these things, even if he speaks the language of *impersonal* immortality, still it would be nothing but a projection of a personal conception of immortality.

The teaching of the Mahatmas is utterly uncompromising on such matters. For the personal consciousness there can be no immortality, while for the indwelling soul, for the individual ray of the overbrooding *Atman,* immortality is a fact. For the mediating mind of the middle, immortality has to be won, to be earned, and is neither a gift nor a fact. The mind must progressively detach itself from its external vestures, like a musician who goes beyond worship of his instrument or of his fingers moving on the instrument or of his own self-image, and is merged into something beyond all recorded music, into a reverence for the inaudible music of the spheres. Until a man can do this self-consciously as a soul (and he cannot do it without pain and thoroughness if he is to be honest with himself), immortality for him will be merely a compensatory myth. It will not carry that conviction with which alone he could lighten the loads of others and, through eyes of love, make many lives more meaningful.

If we trace the English term 'soul' to its Greek antecedents and equivalents, we soon find a wide variety of meanings. Even before the time of Socrates, many accretions and materializations had already gathered around the concept. It was compared to the wind. It was also supposed to mean 'that which breathes,' 'that which is alive.' And it was given many other meanings and often couched in metaphorical terms through analogy with sparks and a central fire. It became crucially significant for Plato to enrich the notion of 'soul' and to give it an existentially human meaning to do with the very act of search, the very desire to know the good, the hunger to make distinctions – not only between the good and the bad but between the good and the attractive, not only between the true and the false but between the true and the plausible. The desire to make noetic discriminations becomes the basis for a functional definition of the soul. Plato taught that, metaphysically, the soul may be seen either as perpetual motion or as a self-moving agent. In one passage he refers to a particular kind of motion which is not visible in the material realm but may be properly ascribed to the hidden *Logos*, the invisible deity. Elsewhere, what he identifies as the soul is connected with volition. What would it avail a man who uses the word in a Socratic sense but does not come to terms with his own will-problem, or worse still, becomes identified intellectually with his weak-willed self?

Language is very important here. The prolonged abuse of the term 'soul' in the Middle Ages resulted from a decisive shift in meaning. An active agent was replaced by something passive, something created. In a corruption of the Socratic-Platonic meaning, the 'soul' became merely something acted upon, a passive agent receiving reward or punishment. The term 'soul' almost became unusable, so that in the Renaissance, humanists had to assert the dignity and divinity of man in ways that did not involve them once again in the debased coinage of the terminology of the past. In the twentieth century the term 'self' is coming into wide circulation, recovering some of the dignity of the classical conception of the soul.

A person brought up in a corrupt language system could receive tremendous help by borrowing a term from Sanskrit and trying to recognize its open texture. The compassionate Teachers of the Theosophical Movement chose to introduce from that sacred language terms like *manas* – the root of the word 'man,' from *man*, 'to think' – into the languages of the West. When Emerson eulogizes "man thinking" he is using two English words in a manner that confirms exactly the full glory of the idea of *manas*. Yet we also know that both the words 'man' and 'thinking' can be so degraded in everyday usage that they do not convey the glory of manhood implied by *manas*. The term *manas* in Sanskrit means not only 'to think,' but also 'to ideate,' 'to contemplate.' To contemplate in this classical sense is to create, to sustain a continuous and controlled act of creative imagination enveloping more and more of the whole, while retaining that core of individuality which signifies responsibility for the consequences of all thoughts, all feelings, all words, and all acts. This is a kingly conception.

It is often advantageous for a person to go outside his particular prison-house of debased language and explore classical concepts. As we grow in our awareness, we may make the beautiful discovery that even in the accents of common speech there are echoes of those pristine meanings. The literal meaning of words is less important than the tone of voice in which we use them. It is possible for a man in the street to say to another, "Hi, man" with unconscious contempt, and for a traveller in the Sierras to say, "Hi, man," in a manner that expresses genuine fellow-feeling. Miranda in *The Tempest*, seeing human beings for the first time, exclaims:

> O, wonder!
> How many goodly creatures are there here!
> How beauteous mankind is! O brave new world,
> That has such people in't!

Every word has a depth and beauty of feeling that makes ordinary English words rise like winged skylarks into the universal empyrean – generous, cosmic and free. Beyond all languages and concepts, the very act of articulation is of immense importance.

Perhaps the most beautiful passage on the subject of reincarnation is to be found in *The Human Situation* by Macneile Dixon. This great lover of the literatures of the world, of Plato and Shakespeare, dared to suggest:

What a handful of dust is man to think such thoughts! Or is he, perchance, a prince in misfortune, whose speech at times betrays his birth? I like to think that, if men are machines, they are machines of a celestial pattern, which can rise above themselves, and, to the amazement of the watching gods, acquit themselves as men. I like to think that this singular race of indomitable, philosophising, poetical beings, resolute to carry the banner of Becoming to unimaginable heights, may be as interesting to the gods as they to us, and that they will stoop to admit these creatures of promise into their divine society.

By speech a man can betray his divine birth, and just as this is true of speech in its most sacred and profound sense, it is also true of human gestures. The simple mode of salutation in the immemorial land of Aryavarta is filled with this beauty. When the two hands come together, they greet another human being in the name of that which is above both, which brings the two together, and includes all others. There is something cosmic, something that has built into it a calculation of the infinite in the expedient, even in this gesture.

But what is true of gestures could be even more true of human utterance. The surest proof of the divinity and immortality of man is that through the power of sound he can create something that is truly magical. He can release vibrations that either bless or curse, heal or hinder other beings. This is determined by motivation, intensity of inmost feeling, and the degree of individual and universal self-consciousness, nurtured and strengthened through constant meditation and self-study.

Suppose one were to ask of the gods, "Give me one of two gifts for all men. Give me first that gift which will suddenly enable all men to say that they know about reincarnation and the soul, and that they believe in immortality. Second, give me that gift which enables all men to help babies to grow with a feeling of dignity, deliberation, beauty and sanctity in regard to human speech." The wise would know that the latter gift is much more valuable than the former, because mere beliefs will not save human beings, even though truly philosophical reflection upon alternatives is part of the prerogative of a manasic being, a man in Emerson's sense. These beliefs can only be made to come alive through the exercise of conscious and deliberate speech, with a delicate sensitivity for the existence of other beings, and an immense inner compassion for all that is alive. If human speech were not constantly wasted and made into something so excessive and destructive, so mean and niggardly, we would not find so much of the self-hatred, mutual distrust, pessimism and despair that characterize our lot. We would not find ourselves in a society which is free but where, alas, the loudest voice is the most feared and tends to have the widest impact.

Anyone who can existentially restore the alchemical and healing qualities of sound, speech and silence, to some limited extent, in the smallest contexts – in relations with little children, with all he encounters even in the most trivial situations – does a great deal for the Bodhisattvas. Those Illuminated Men, by their very power of thought and ceaseless ideation, continually benefit humanity by quickening any spark of authentic aspiration in every human soul into the fire which could help others to see. The truth of reincarnation requires much more than a casual scrutiny of our external lives and our spoken language. It must be pondered upon in the very silence of our souls. It is a theme for daily meditation. In the *Bhagavad Gita* Lord Krishna tells Arjuna that true wisdom is a meditation upon birth, death, decay, sickness, and error. To meditate upon each of these and all of these together is to begin to know more about the cosmic and the human significance of the truth of reincarnation.

> 'To others also,' said the voice of the divine one who had thus saved me – 'to others in the like state it has been permitted to see something of their pre-existence. But no one of them ever could endure to look far. Power to see all former births belongs only to those eternally released from the bonds of Self. Such exist outside of illusion – outside of form and name; and pain cannot come nigh them.'
>
> Lafcadio Hearn

Hermes, September 1976

RESONANCE AND RESPONSIBILITY

Sickness does not depart by speaking of medicine unless the medicine be drunk; liberation comes not through speaking of the Eternal without immediate experience of the Eternal.

Shankaracharya

There is a vital relationship between modes of resonance and the potencies of emanations. One can readily see that if resonance and purity of tone have some connection with *Rta* and *Dharma* – cosmic order and moral solidarity – much depends upon the level of conscious awareness with which any sound is uttered. Every human being who emits any sound at any level of awareness releases a chain of consequences for which one is responsible, affecting monads, atoms and gods, all sentient points in nature. *The Voice of the Silence* teaches: "Help Nature and work on with her; and Nature will regard thee as one of her creators and make obeisance." This sacred injunction presupposes a sublime philosophy of Nature. Perfected human beings have trained themselves over myriad lives in the masterful use of everything that Nature provides, including their own vestures. They work for the good of the whole and on the invisible plane, producing reverberations in the visible world. Surely this conception must be based upon a very different view of Nature from that which is found in materialistic science or in conventional religion.

The term 'nature' is derived from the root *nasci*, 'to be born'. All things are born in space and in time. They must grow, decay and die in time and in space. Just as the searing and decaying of a leaf into autumnal yellow suggests a mellowness in Nature, so Nature is meaningful at every level and in all its processes. The vital part of its ceaseless activity is hidden. Even though the invisible side of Nature cannot be seen by the naked eye, nevertheless by watching how Nature works, one can work with Nature and trust in the Law – this is the ancestral wisdom of humanity. If Nature is everything that is born and everything that exists, then even etymologically Nature is a vaster whole than is conveyed merely by visible phenomena. Science has evolved because human minds penetrated the veil of the visible and formulated theories, equations and models that pertain to the invisible mathematics of Nature. In the twentieth century science came to recognize the limitations of traditional mathematics as well as its own limitations in the use of mathematics. In quantum mechanics a shift from mathematical certainty to statistical generalization permits probabilistic explanations that encompass a great deal of what goes on invisibly in Nature and which can be tested under controlled conditions. Experimental science is very young, going back to the seventeenth century and the founding of the Royal Society. Science is growing, evolving, and it has the discipline of its methodology as well as an increasing awareness of its own methodological limitations. It was initially handicapped because it inherited a conception of matter which came from traditional religion, specifically from the narrow theological view of biblical cosmogony which declared that matter is inert. This static conception of matter is associated with the dogma that the world was created out of nothing.

Unlike the ancient Greeks who had a subtle metaphysical concept of Chaos, modern science inherited a view where 'nothing' simply meant the absence of any visible world. This unphilosophical view arose because people took literally a mythic statement in the New Testament and thus missed the mystical power and evocative meaning of the text: "In the beginning was the Word." Whenever a mystical statement is translated into a literal proposition or a dogmatic belief, its inner meaning is lost. Scientific methodology distorted by philosophical crudity reinforced the view of matter as inert, which in theology needs to be acted upon by an external animate being of which there was only one. The problem became ontological in that this animate being – of which there is only one – was held to be everywhere and simultaneously in an anthropomorphic form. This raises the insoluble problem of assigning the authorship of the entire visible world to a superhuman entity with an inscrutable will. This materializes the concept of Godhead and destroys the ethical foundations of nature and man. Even today many people continue to be influenced by facile concepts picked up in casual conversation and especially in the vast array of sensory images. In general, owing to mental laziness and for lack of contemplation, people cannot cut through the chaos, let alone consciously initiate a series of emanations out of deep meditation upon the Soundless Sound.

Given any cogent doctrine of ethical responsibility, we are truly thrown back upon ourselves. Human beings can always make a difference by the power of choice in the use that they make of what they know at any level and by translating what they know into practice. What is it, then, that blocks an individual who knows all of this from putting it into practice? The question could be framed in specific terms: Why is it that when somebody sincerely wants to meditate upon the *OM*, he is repeatedly obstructed? This is due to the accumulated karma of misuse, non-use and incompletion. When a person wants to meditate deeply, the level of consciousness becomes critical. Pure consciousness arises in *manas* and is rooted in the Buddhic light of eternal motion, the universal consciousness of the *Atman*. Filtering down, no doubt slowly, it can be focussed intensively by concentration, and when practised with continuity, it can arouse intuition, the insight and illumination of *Buddhi*. Every human being has all of these available within his own nature, and, therefore, can self-consciously release the spiritual will. A person must initially allocate time not only for meditation but also for deliberate planning and calm contemplation, and also show a continuing care of thought-patterns that emerge and which can be modified by deliberation and discrimination. This can be done with an authentic sense of the sacred in a deepening silence that increasingly controls the use of words.

The greater calm arising through a stronger sense of the sacred helps one to move beyond sound – toward the Soundless Sound – from an initial level of consciousness to higher levels of universal self-consciousness by degrees and by a slow ascent. This persistent process also makes a decisive difference to one's relationship to invisible Nature, to one's appreciation of physical nature, and one's capacity "to help Nature and work on with her". One is everywhere and nowhere in one's deepest Self, and yet one is helpless if one has created a false identity out of ever-moving tendencies. Rather than experiencing the living stasis of universal consciousness, people cling to a false static conception of self because they cannot control the mind and still their thoughts and withdraw into the inmost silence, the sanctuary of which Krishna speaks in the ninth chapter of the *Gita*. How, then, can continuity and steadfastness be discriminated from inflexibility? Such queries point to a more fundamental question: How can one determine what is an adequate idea? If one has an inadequate idea of the Self or an inadequate idea of mind, can one have an adequate idea of anything? Obviously not, for the ordinary mind is not only ontologically limited by finitude but also psychologically limited by lethargy. It is limited by seizing upon tokens of something larger. Here we have the basic distinction between *kama manas* – desire-mind – and pure *manas,* the true principle of creative thought. The ideas that people have are inadequate because the power of thinking is not freed from fixed preconceptions, fleeting sensations and partial perceptions. The great hope of spiritual growth lies in that just as the inexhaustible wealth of manifestation is itself only like a drop in the ocean compared to what is beyond – *TAT* – so, also, for a human being, the whole of a lifetime, the succession of lifetimes, is like a drop in the ocean of the potential power of the *Atman* that is focussed through *Buddhi* in *manas*. Meditation is the perennial source of hope for the whole of humanity.

But what hope is there for a particular individual? There is hope according to the degree to which that individual puts to work such powers as he or she has already developed. Take an idea that is adequate at one level, say, a relatively restricted idea of space, time or self. One may initially think of space in one's room. Then one can go beyond as far as one can, so what seems adequate at first can be replaced by something more adequate. One can keep extending one's concept of space, keep extending one's concept of time, keep extending one's concept of selfhood. There is the danger that one might still remain narcissistic and selfish. One might be deluding oneself, which is one of the hazards of transferring higher knowledge to the lower plane. The whole point of expanding one's view of space and of time is to go beyond the personal self. Inadequacy of ideas is due to the inadequacy of selfhood when rooted in personality, which is synonymous with limitation. Any *persona* is limited, and in fact illusory and ever-changing. How can the personal mind have an adequate idea of Absolute Space or Eternal Duration or Unconditioned Consciousness? Therefore one has to concentrate calmly when one studies, gradually gaining the powers of attention, contemplation and meditation. Though this may require a lifetime to accomplish, one must repeatedly begin at some point where one can forget narrow perspectives and the illusion of false knowledge and be willing to confront the abyss, the Divine Ground, the *Mysterium Tremendum*.

The Law ceaselessly moves towards greater good, deeper harmony and towards ever-widening expansion of the possibilities of consciousness. The wheel of the Good Law moves swiftly on, and as it moves it sifts. Nature is on the side of every human being. Nature mercifully sifts through sleep every night and through death. Since this is taking place already with the help of Nature, one needs only to assist the process. Even though people make a mess of living, the fact they are still alive means that Nature wins. That is the Law, which works on behalf of every monad and of every human being, of every atom and of the entire solar system. It is not supportive of the shadowy ' I ' which does not really exist. It is not on the side of the false identity that is bound up in a changing flux with seeming fixities. Nature cannot do anything for one if one has already decided to be one's own enemy. Some people, alas, made such a decision through soul-perversity in former lives. Perhaps their conception was inflexible to start with; maybe they had an inflexible view of who they are; and maybe they foolishly fixed their minds upon some false image of the goal. They may have tried to do some figuring out on their own, but only on behalf of the shadowy self. They may have thought they were an exception to the laws of nature. That is where the tragedy begins. Once one imagines one is an exception to the laws of nature, one can do oneself a lot of harm and become one's own enemy. All learning will be painful because of the perverse unwillingness to learn. And one reason why one will not learn is because one refuses to be flexible. One mistakes the shadow of truth for the substance, the distorted semblance for the reality, and that makes one inflexible. Trapped by static conceptions, the mind becomes ritualistic, and one is trapped by forms, colours and limitations.

Since this tendency can assert itself in each and every one at any moment, it must be understood properly. Understanding begins with pondering the instruction of Jesus: "Judge not, lest ye be judged." Any attitude which implies judgement upon the human race snares one in inflexibility. The occult law of responsibility suggests that if one harshly judges a human being, one transfers that presumed or actual evil to oneself. Being judgemental makes one inflexible and this makes one's steadfastness rigid, one's conduct ritualistic. One really needs a deeper continuity that is based upon inward contentment, spiritual wakefulness, a readiness for everything, but also a sheer joy in learning. The wise person recognizes that it is educative and edifying to live in a universe under Law. One is fortunate that it does not depend upon votes as to whether there would be sunshine tomorrow. One is fortunate that it does not depend upon the whim of any personal self as to whether there will be night, the night that is needed, the night of non-manifestation that is called sleep. Nature works rhythmically and yet flexibly, for each day and night and every hour of each day or night is not the same as any other. And it can be coloured, given a tone and texture by the way in which one uses it by withdrawing into one's inmost, deepest self. There is flexibility in the very attempt to keep pace with the Law, even though one does not understand it but only senses its direction. If one respects that Law, one can take proper advantage of it and thereby develop a cheerful, creative flexibility. Creative flexibility is meaningful if it is accommodated within a self-chosen discipline. Using what one already has allows magic to take place, but not using it will have its own unnecessary karma, which means one has made oneself unworthy by non-use of what one has. What can be done about this? Nothing in terms of the restless mind. The restless mind is constantly trying to figure out short-cuts and diversionary tactics, which are inefficient because illogical.

One must necessarily return to where it all starts and ends in the realm of manifestation, the problem of the mind. The mind must be stilled. The mind must be subdued by the power of attention that is called concentration, by the power of meditation that is called continuity in contemplation and which results in inner calmness. It is not as difficult to accomplish as it seems, because in some significant degree one has done it before and others are doing it right now. At some level one has to face oneself. One has to take an honest inventory and at the same time purge oneself of the consolidation of the false shadow by turning to the light with the whole of one's being. When this is done, there is no room for separation of oneself from other selves, from the Bodhisattvas, from Nature and its transcendental Source. One can overcome separateness, arising in the mind through false identification with a form, at the very core of being. One has seen wonders done by people; one can do a number of things oneself. But one cannot change everything suddenly overnight by means of a miracle. Any magic that works under laws must not be mistaken for miracles that cannot really happen. Miracles do not even occur in fairy tales except when they are earned by moral and spiritual worthiness.

Real magic can only work through the higher principles for those who meditate by the light of the *Atman* and the love of *Buddhi* and through the lens of *manas*. These must be brought in line with the creative *Logos* in Nature and in man, that which lights up every being and illumines the world. Insight has to be earned by the power of the whole of one's attention over a period of time. If one's concepts of creation and of emanation are philosophically continuous, and if at the same time detachment is psychologically possible without discontinuity, then truly one can work with the ordered harmonies of Nature, the whole of life, and everything generated in and through one's sacred vesture, the temple of the living god within. This is a very beneficent teaching, and as Krishna stated in the second chapter of the *Gita*: "In this system of Yoga no effort is wasted, nor are there any evil consequences, and even a little of this practice delivereth a man from great risk." Krishna also declared, "The duty of another is full of danger", and "a man enjoyeth not freedom from action from the non-commencement of that which he hath to do". Even a little of this wisdom can deliver a man from great risk when it is put to use. One must begin to think in terms of a micro-approach if one wants to make a break with the pseudo-philosophy of a dying culture. The micro-approach applies every day and was known in the beginning of human history. One can find golden opportunities at the present moment. Continuity generated by concentration, fused with a recognition of responsibility in a universe of Law, opens a glorious vista of possibilities before the intuitive individual in becoming a creative artist who merges his or her own sphere into "the mighty magic of *Prakriti*". Such "fortune's favoured soldiers" rejoice in the service of the Brotherhood of Bodhisattvas who self-consciously radiate the harmony which is the root of Nature, the energy of evolution and the resonance of the Soundless Sound.

Hermes, June 1979

GANDHIAN TRUSTEESHIP
IN THEORY AND PRACTICE

The Art of Renunciation

The act of renunciation of everything is not a mere physical renunciation, but represents a second or new birth. It is a deliberate act, not done in ignorance. It is, therefore, a regeneration.

Mahatma Gandhi*

For India, the most critical issue involves the current rethinking of Mahatma Gandhi's philosophy. Gandhi said that soon after his death India would bypass and betray his ideas, but that thirty years later India would be compelled to restore them. Events have begun to validate his prophecy, and the trend will accelerate.... When India fully accepts that it cannot conceivably emulate Japan without harnessing its own indigenous values and providing new motivations, and when out of necessity its leadership recognizes that it can no longer inflate the token symbols of Gandhi or the facile slogans of socialism, she will be forced to ask more fundamental questions. Only then can the real social revolution emerge, which could have a strong radical base and also borrow from ancient traditions as well as modern movements. While it would be difficult to predict the changes themselves, they will require serious reassessment of Gandhi's questions relating to the quantum of goods needed for a meaningful and fulfilling way of life.

Parapolitics–Toward the City of Man

Mahatma Gandhi held that all human beings are implicitly responsible to God, the Family of Man and to themselves for their use and treatment of all goods, gifts and talents that fall within their domain. This is so because Nature and Man are alike upheld, suffused and regenerated by the Divine. There is a luminous spark of divine intelligence in the motion of the atom and in the eyes of every man

---

* M.K. Gandhi, "The Golden Key", *Harijan*, January 30, 1937.

and woman on earth. We incarnate our divinity when we deliberately and joyously nurture our abilities and assets for the sake of the larger good. In this sense, the finest exemplars of trusteeship are those who treat all possessions as though they were sacred or deeply precious beyond any worldly scale of valuation. Thus, it is only through daily moral choice and the meritorious use of resources that we sustain our inherited or acquired entitlements. For this reason, the very idea of ownership is misleading and, at root, a form of violence. It implies rights and privileges over Man and Nature that go beyond the bounds of human need – although not necessarily beyond the limits of human law and social custom. It obscures the generous bounty of Nature, which provides enough for all if each holds in trust only what he needs, without excess or exploitation.

Gandhi sensed that all our resources and possessions, at any level, are not merely fragments of the Divine but are also inherently mortal and mutable. The Divine in its active aspect is ceaselessly creative and ever fluid in form. By analogy, human needs and material circumstances alter even while cultural patterns and social customs purport to maintain temporal continuity through established traditions. Ownership, from this standpoint, is truly a costly and illusory attempt to ensure permanency and succession. It gives birth to unwarranted attachments and insupportable expectations. The selfish grasping for possessions of any kind not only violates the deeper purposes of our human odyssey but eventually breeds possessiveness and greed, exploitation and revenge. This appalling moral malaise leads to inordinate self-assertion and self-projection which can only yield distrust, sorrow and "loss of all". But when we attain the sacred mental posture of the trustee who regards all possessions as held in trust for the good of all, we can progressively approach the high spiritual state of mental renunciation. We can, in the Upanishadic phrase, "renounce and enjoy". It is only when we voluntarily relinquish our unnatural claims and consecrate ourselves to a higher purpose that we can freely enjoy what we have. Thus, self-satisfaction is a natural outcome of a generous perspective and a greater purity of heart. It is truly a function of the harmonious cultivation of our spiritual, mental and material resources. In Gandhian terms, guilt-free enjoyment is inseparable from ethical probity. The real issue, then, is not how much or how little we possess in the way of property or talent, but the reasons and motives behind their allocations and uses.

Gandhi approached the concept of trusteeship at four different levels. First of all, trusteeship, as the sole universalizable means of continuously redistributing wealth, could be seen as a corollary of the principle of non-violence and simultaneously assure the generation and intelligent use of wealth.

> No other theory is compatible with non-violence. In the non-violent method the wrongdoer compasses his own end, if he does not undo the wrong. For, either through Non-violent Non-co-operation he is made to see his error, or he finds himself completely isolated.*

Even if wealth could be coercively redistributed, the resulting greed and inexperience on the part of many and the resentment on the part of the dispossessed would lead to economic instability and rapid decline. More likely than not, it would lead to class war, anomic violence and widespread self-alienation. Trusteeship, however, encourages owners to see themselves as vigilant trustees of their accumulated wealth for the larger community without threatening them.

Secondly, Gandhi's practical psychological intuition allowed him to see that fear would prevent other means of economic distribution from succeeding in the long run. A fundamental change in the concepts of activity and courage is needed to overcome passivity and cowardice. Courage must be detached from violence, and creativity must be dislodged from the self-protective formulations of entrenched elites. This involves rooting new notions of noetic activity which are creative, playful and tolerant, and new notions of moral courage which are heroic, magnanimous and civil, in a search for universal self-transcendence. An individual must feel, both abstractly and concretely, a secure sense of joyous *eros* in fellowship, and a positive sense of solidarity with hapless human beings everywhere. He must feel at one with the victims of incomplete revolutions, with the understandably impatient and occasionally mistaken pioneers of great revolutions, and even more with those willing to defy every presumptuous criterion and form of authority which trespasses upon individuality.

---

* M.K. Gandhi, "Theory of 'Trusteeship'", *Harijan*, December 16, 1939.

The fearful man tyrannizes others: forced redistribution would bring fearful responses from owners, who would see their lives and futures threatened, and fearful masses would deal with excess wealth incompetently. For Gandhi, the ever-present possibility of social change must be approached from a position of truth and courage, whereas fear is weakness which leads to violence. Strength should not be mistaken for the modalities of violence, which are instruments of fear and always lead to varying degrees of self-destruction. Since strength rests on human dignity and respect, workers must approach exploitative capitalists from a position of self-respect based on the capital of labour, for "labour is as much capital as metal". To abolish fear and even failure itself requires a fundamental change in the social structure. The feasibility of this social transformation does not lie in denying the judgements of others, but rather in regarding them as partially relevant though in no sense compelling. Individuals can commit themselves to increasing their own capacity for self-transcendence of external criteria of differentiation, and thereby attain liberation from the self-perpetuating iniquities and horrors of the System.

> Therefore, workers, instead of regarding themselves as enemies of the rich, or regarding the rich as their natural enemies, should hold their labour in trust for those who are in need of it. This they can do only when, instead of feeling so utterly helpless as they do, they realize their importance in human economy and shed their fear or distrust of the rich. Fear and distrust are twin sisters born of weakness. When labour realizes its strength it won't need to use any force against moneyed people. It will simply command their attention and respect.[†]

Gandhi discerned the critical role acceptability plays in legitimating a social order, and distinguished between a people's tacit acceptance and active dislike of an economic regime. So long as any society finds its socio-economic system acceptable, that system will stand even if a militant minority detests it. But should a significant number of individuals find it unacceptable, it is shaken to its foundations, regardless of the complacency of privileged élites.

Thirdly, Gandhi contended that the idea of trusteeship could be put

---

† M.K. Gandhi, "Letter to B. Srirangasayi", *The Hindu*, October 11, 1934.

into practice non-violently, because it could be instituted by degrees. When asked if such 'trustees'–individuals who possessed wealth and yet saw themselves as stewards for society–could be found in India in his day, he rejected the question as strictly irrelevant to the theory, which can only be evaluated by extensive testing over time.

> At this point I may be asked as to how many trustees of this type one can really find. As a matter of fact, such a question should not arise at all. It is not directly related to our theory. There may be just one such trustee or there may be none at all. Why should we worry about it? We should have faith that we can, without violence or with so little violence that it can hardly be called violence, create such a feeling among the rich. We should act in that faith. That is sufficient for us. We should demonstrate through our endeavour that we can end economic disparity with the help of non-violence. Only those who have no faith in non-violence can ask how many trustees of this kind can be found.*

Gandhi knew that he sought the widespread realization of a forgotten ideal, but he repudiated the conventional notion that an experiment is unworthy to be tried simply because it stems from an exacting ideal. Even if one argued that trusteeship was doomed to failure, it ran no greater risk than the conventional social proposals of the day. Committed to principles but flexible in policies, Gandhi saw no reason to neglect ideals and to institute social reforms from a defeatist standpoint. Such an approach only guaranteed that structural faults would be built into the new social order. Rather, he emphasized, it is better to move towards the ideal and make appropriate adjustments necessitated by the specific failures encountered in attempting to reach it. In doing so, principles would remain uncompromised and the possibility of improvement would always remain, whereas in a system which assumes cupidity and corruption in human nature, nothing encourages their eradication.

Gandhi not only had faith that it was possible for human beings to become trustees of their resources for the sake of all, but also that

---

* M.K. Gandhi, "Answers to Questions at Gandhi Seva Sangh Meeting, Brindaban–II", Gandhi Seva Sanghke Panchama Varshik Adhiveshan (Brindaban, Bihar) ka Vivaran, pp. 50–59. Cf. "Gandhi Seva Sangh – IV: More Communings", by M.D., Harijan, June 3, 1939.

many in fact were already and had always been trustees. They are the preservers of culture and tradition, who show their ethical stance through countless daily acts of graciousness and concern for others. To treat man as man requires not so much the acceptance of the equal potentialities of all men, let alone the infinite potentialities of all men, but rather the acceptance of the unknown potentialities of all human beings. Given scarce resources and the limits of productivity and of taxable income, there are definitely limits to what the State can do, but is there any reason why voluntary associations should not be entrusted with the task of extending the avenues of opportunity available to the disinherited? The socialist could argue that by an indefinite extension of opportunities (not always requiring State action) and by changing not only the structure but the entire ethos and moral tone of society, new social values could slowly emerge and usher in an era in which men show mutual respect which is not based on skills and promotions, rank and status.

The minimal goal of basic economic equity is easily stated, yet it is the fundamental first stage for the uplift of the whole.

> Everybody should be able to get sufficient work to make the two ends meet. And, this ideal can be universally realized only if the means of production of elementary necessaries of life remain under the control of the masses. These should be freely available to all as God's air and water are, or ought to be; they should not be made a vehicle of traffic for the exploitation of others. Their monopolization by any country, nation or groups of persons would be unjust. The neglect of this simple principle is the cause of the destitution that we witness to-day, not only in this unhappy land, but other parts of the world, too.†

The principle of trusteeship in its application to the equitable distribution of wealth, as well as to the non-violent socialist reformation it underpins, is practicable because it does not require everyone to undertake it all at once. Unlike most socialists who reason that they must seize the power of the State before instituting effective reforms, Gandhi held that enlightened individuals could initiate the process of divesting themselves of what is unnecessary while becoming true

---

† M.K. Gandhi, "Economic Constitution of India", *Young India*, November 15, 1928.

trustees of their own possessions.

> It is perfectly possible for an individual to adopt this way of life without having to wait for others to do so. And if an individual can observe a certain rule of conduct, it follows that a group of individuals can do likewise. It is necessary for me to emphasize the fact that no one need wait for anyone else in order to adopt a right course. Men generally hesitate to make a beginning, if they feel that the objective cannot be had in its entirety. Such an attitude of mind is in reality a bar to progress.*

Once the barrier in consciousness is broken, the principle of trusteeship can be made to work by letting go of the demand for a mechanically equal distribution, something Gandhi doubted could ever be realized. Instead, he held to the revolutionary ideal of *equitable* distribution, which would not only be possible but necessary in the non-violent socialist State.

Should attempts to encourage the abandonment of exploitation through misappropriation of the means of production fail, trusteeship could be made to work through non-violent non-cooperation, wherein workers realize the capital worth and collective strength of their labour. Should it succeed, ideas which arise out of narrow acquisitive thinking would vanish because they were rooted in unacceptable and illusory assumptions.

> If the trusteeship idea catches, philanthropy, as we know it, will disappear.... A trustee has no heir but the public.†

Gradually, statutory trusteeship could be introduced in which the duties of the trustee and the public could be formalized. The trustee may serve so long as the people find his services beneficial. He may even designate his successor, but the people must confirm it. Should the State become involved, the trustee's power of appointment and the State's power of review will strike a balance in which the welfare of the people will be safeguarded.

Fourthly and finally, Gandhi believed that social conditions were

---

* M.K. Gandhi, "Equal Distribution", *Harijan*, August 25, 1940.

† M.K. Gandhi, "A Question", *Harijan*, April 12, 1942.

ripe for imaginative applications of the principle of trusteeship. The collapse of Western imperialism, the spiritual and social poverty of fascism and totalitarianism, the psychological failure of capitalism, the moral bankruptcy of state socialism and the ideological inflexibility of communism all indicate an ineluctable if gradual movement towards a reconstitution of the social order which will compel some form of redistribution.

The limits to growth make themselves felt through the undermining of social virtues like trust and truthfulness, restraint and mutual acceptance, as well as a sense of fraternal obligation, all of which are essential to individual initiative in a contractual economic system. If such virtues are treated as public goods necessary to universal welfare, then unrestricted individualism faces noticeable limits, lest the social justification and viability of the whole system be destroyed. C.B. MacPherson went so far as to predict that the time will come when it will no longer be feasible to put acquisition ahead of spiritual values, and that national power will become a function not of market power but of moral stature. Although we have to confront scarcity, the emphasis on Hobbesian self-preservation alone is adequate.

> The rich should ponder well as to what is their duty today. They who employ mercenaries to guard their wealth may find those very guardians turning on them. The moneyed classes have got to learn how to fight either with arms or with the weapons of non-violence.... I see coming the day of the rule of the poor, whether that rule be through force of arms or of non-violence.‡

Even though the war against poverty will take a long time to win, it is necessary for the State to adopt various measures to reduce the sharp economic inequalities that undermine the working of mass democracy, and to strengthen the organizing power of peasants, artisans, and industrial and clerical workers. In addition to fiscal and monetary measures to reduce income ceilings, it would be desirable to assist wealthy landlords and industrialists in parting with portions of their wealth, property and earnings as public contributions towards specific local schemes and plans. The more the redistributive process

---

‡ M.K. Gandhi, "Advice to the Rich", *Harijan*, February 1, 1942.

can be extended beyond legal compulsion and political action, the more democracy is strengthened at the social level. The more the State can bring together representatives of richer and poorer groups, stronger and weaker sections of society, in planning local programs, the better it will be for all.

At this point the socialist's faith as well as his integrity are tested, and so are his ultimate premises. Does he believe in perfectibility or in original sin? If, like Condorcet, he believes that the historical process and the progress of humanity involve an increasing equality among nations, equality within nations and the perfectibility of man, how much emphasis does it put on human growth and perfectibility rather than on inherent flaws and weaknesses? If committed socialists are not imbued with atavistic or original sin, if they hold to a truly open view of human nature, then they could adopt a different parapolitical standpoint.* They could say that it is because they believe in the unknown possibilities of every human being that they are concerned to extend the idea of human excellence to a point where external social distinctions do not matter, but where trusteeship is honoured wherever it is witnessed in human beings.

Owing to his unshakeable conviction that violence can never produce permanent results, only Gandhi's modesty prevented him from asserting that his ethical solution would come to be seen as the only feasible alternative to wholesale misery and destruction, if not now, then in the foreseeable future. He deliberately avoided elaborating a complete system of statutory or voluntary trusteeship out of the conviction that structural and organizational details necessarily varied with the social and political context and with the personnel, whilst the essential core of the ideal was universally applicable. Thus he could gain a serious hearing from those who would be most affected by the implementation of his proposals without threatening them.

> I am not ashamed to own that many capitalists are friendly towards
> me and do not fear me. They know that I desire to end capitalism

---

* Raghavan Iyer, *Parapolitics—Toward the City of Man*, Chapter 5, Oxford University Press (New York, 1979). Second edition: Concord Grove Press (Santa Barbara, 1985), p. 89.

almost, if not quite, as much as the most advanced Socialist or even Communist. But our methods differ, our languages differ. My theory of 'trusteeship' is no make-shift, certainly no camouflage. I am confident that it will survive all theories.†

Hermes, July 1985

---

† M.K. Gandhi, "Theory of 'Trusteeship'", *loc. cit.*

GANDHIAN TRUSTEESHIP
IN THEORY AND PRACTICE

Regeneration and Rebirth

Ideals must work in practice, otherwise they are not potent.

Mahatma Gandhi

Looking at Gandhian trusteeship more closely, we might ask what it actually means to be a trustee. A trustee is one who self-consciously assumes responsibility for upholding, protecting and putting to good use whatever he possesses, acquires or earns. For an individual to be a trustee in any meaningful sense implies that he is self-governing and morally sensitive. He is acutely aware of the unmet needs of others and, simultaneously, is capable of controlling and transmuting his own appropriating tendencies. He is deeply committed to cultivating his most generous feelings and altruistic hopes for others while consciously and patiently freeing himself from all recognized exploitative attitudes and relationships. He strives to become self-regulating, reliable and sacrificial. But he must become so in a courageous and intelligent way. He must learn to think and feel altruistically. He must learn by degrees the heart's etiquette – to speak, touch and act with the utmost purity and solicitousness. He must become, by virtue of self-training, very attentive to every resource at his disposal – both inner and outer. It is precisely because he sees his abilities and possessions as belonging to God, mankind or to future generations that he is eager to use them to the maximum. His posture towards his overall resources is therefore not one of a lazy or selfish indifference. He is not concerned with hoarding nor is he fearful of multiplying his gifts, talents and possessions. Like the good servant in the *New Testament*, he wishes to increase his meagre "talents", but not for his own sake, nor merely for his own family.

The best trustee is indeed someone who has attained an inward moral balance. He is serenely detached, magnanimous and imaginative. But his detachment is never cold or narrow. It is an expression of his unshakeable confidence in the ontological plenty of Nature and the inexhaustible resourcefulness of Man. His steadfastness and trustworthiness are principally due to this broader focus of concentration. Likewise, his motive is benevolent and self-sustaining because it is not mixed with the turgid waters of personal aggrandizement. Instead, he expresses a quality of love and appreciation for what he has that enhances its moral and practical value for others. He might even possess little, but his sense of when, where and how to use what he has increases its potential good a hundredfold.

If this conveys the invisible grandeur of the Gandhian trustee, then what steps can we take to become more like such sage-like trustees and less like small-minded appropriators? Gandhi might well suggest that our first steps should be the fruit of honest self-examination. Grandiose gestures about giving up external possessions and impulsive statements about our good intentions have little practical impact on our character. The initial step should be at the level of thought. We should think clearly and deeply about the principles of trust and trusteeship. What does trusteeship mean as an idea and as an ideal? What are its practical implications? And what would we have to give up for it to become a potent *mantra*m in our lives? This form of reflection and self-questioning initiates a period of "mental gestation". It allows us to strengthen our understanding, dispel illusions and light the subtle fire of altruism.

Once we have grasped the principle of trusteeship at a rudimentary level – and recognized its radical implications for our personal lives and impersonal relationships – then we could commit ourselves wholeheartedly to the moral heroism of non-possession. Thus moral commitment would be fused with clarity of thought and psychological honesty. Clarity in relation to the ideal of non-possession is vital, as is firmness of resolve. Mentally, we must see where we are going – even though it be only the next step – and we must be unconditional if we hope to approximate the end in view. Otherwise, we will neither overcome nor transform the possessive attitudes that self-examination reveals. This is a fundamental theme in Gandhian thought. We must be courageous and unflinching in our efforts to fulfil our self-adopted vows. Only an unqualified resolve can generate the curve of growth necessary to negate and transcend our appropriating tendencies.

If wholeheartedness or total renunciation is the ideal, we might ask ourselves, do little renunciations count? Yes, so long as they are unconditional. If, for example, I promise myself to return all that I borrow, then this promise is binding in relation to my children, to people I like, to people I dislike and to those who rarely return what I lend them. This illustrates the principle that non-possession (*aparigraha*) presupposes a change of heart, not merely a change of intellectual viewpoint. To be genuine, the change of heart must come about non-violently through the *tapas* of a self-imposed discipline. This is why Gandhi encourages us to integrate unconditional commitment with both philosophical thought and mature self-honesty.

A second step towards instilling the spirit of trusteeship is taken when we simplify our wants. This is a pivotal point in Gandhi's concept of non-possession. If we want to make the most deliberate and compassionate use of our individual talents, gifts, faculties and skills, then we need to simplify our desires and wants. Gandhi insisted upon this minimal moral asceticism for the trustee because he saw that unrestrained wants waste our internal capital and channel our resources into selfish uses. Inordinate wants obscure perceptions both of basic needs and deeper human aspirations. They diminish our sense of dignity as self-governing agents and corrode our credibility with others. Furthermore, when the multiplication of possessive desires proceeds far enough, it leads to self-destruction. This is compellingly depicted in Tolstoy's short story "How Much Land Does a Man Need?", in which a petty landowner is undone by his unchecked desire for land and wealth. He is initially simple and good, but his wish to improve his lot in life is progressively corrupted by a swelling ambition to own and possess more. In the end, Tolstoy answers the question raised in the story's title by wryly stating that the only land we truly need is a grave six feet long by three feet wide.

We might ask ourselves what it means to simplify our wants or needs in a Gandhian manner. It would seem that we can simplify our lives in at least two primary senses. First of all, we can make a concerted effort to reduce the sheer number of encrusted desires and habit-patterns that vitiate our altruistic impulses and fond dreams for others. We self-consciously check the tendency of the aggressive and expansive self to acquire more at the expense of others. But secondly, we take care to do this discriminatingly. We must, like the smelter and the goldsmith, extract and refine the pure metal from the crude ore. We want not just less possessive desires but more benevolent ones. Furthermore, as we cleanse the energy of desire, we purify our imagination. When we gain control over imagination, we establish mind control and render ourselves capable of using all personal, financial and other resources skilfully. We are more earthed, so to speak. With minds unclouded by vain imaginings, we feel more in charge of ourselves and are more responsive to the needs of fellow human beings. Our feeling for what others may attain is gradually enriched, whilst our fantasies about what we hope to acquire wane. We eventually insert our resources into the expanding circle of human interdependence.

Two other factors contribute crucially to our becoming authentic trustees – the art of silence and the ability to put trust in others. Silence or "speech control" is a precondition for all moral and intellectual growth. A trustee must guard his speech if he is to uphold and extend the good. This is not secretiveness but healthy common sense. A trustee's intentions should be as pellucid as crystal and visible to all. But wisdom is needed in all relationships. Hence, a trustee gradually learns not to speak prematurely or out of turn. He fosters a refreshing candour and reserve in speech which enables him to initiate constructive activity in season. He views wise silence and worthy expression as golden keys to maximizing the appropriate use of resources. No one would entrust us with anything precious or worthwhile if we were known to be garrulous, profligate, promiscuous or indiscreet. Nor could we be credible to ourselves and others if our speech is compulsive.

If the ears are the gates of learning and the eyes the windows of the soul, the tongue is the key to the alchemical transmutation of resources and the freemasonry of benevolence. Thus, a benign and intelligent silence is the precursor of effective, beneficial action. It aids mind control and augments true wealth. For example, parents often discern certain admirable qualities in their own children and those of others. These qualities are frequently at a germinal stage. We notice them intuitively but only partially observe them at an empirical level. By a sage-like silence we can help these virtuous traits to grow and luxuriate, thus becoming serene and sacred trustees of the good. Without drawing premature attention to what we perceive, we are ready to acknowledge or welcome the child's unfolding abilities when it seems helpful or important to do so. This makes every man and woman a custodian of the good in others. This is a high responsibility assumable by the poorest and most destitute as well as by the wealthy. Whenever any one of us treasures the finest qualities and exemplary contributions of another, we add to the store of human good. This commonwealth grows unseen but yields great benefits to all. Its value is especially apparent when we help someone going through difficult times. To remind someone gently of the best in himself is to remind him of what is most salutary and what is relevant to the moment of death.

Finally, we strengthen our desire to act as trustees for the good when we imaginatively extend our trust and the sacred responsibility for our riches in relation to others. This is integral to Mahatma Gandhi's idea of trusteeship. But what is the obstacle? According to him, the root of the problem lies in a fearful refusal to relinquish attachments. We often fail to confer equal trust on others or fail to share responsibilities with others because we will not distance ourselves from our suspicions and mental images of them. This is noticeably true with respect to parents faced with granting their own and other children a wider circumference of choice. It seems that a detached love is the only cure because there is no growth unless we expand the circle of opportunity continually and appropriately. This is not always easy, and good results are certainly not automatic. To confer upon the untried or inexperienced that which we have so judiciously cultivated is no simple task. To retire, like the court musicians of Akbar, from the limelight at the right time is a sign of self-mastery, while avoiding the sorry humiliation of hanging on to offices and honours. Such renunciation calls for a great deal of thought and a definite degree of risk-taking, but at least the risks are on the side of the potential good in others.

If every man or woman has some innate recognition of the true and the good, enriched by active participation in a theatre of political interaction, then a collectivity of citizens is a mature moral community.

It necessarily rests upon and reinforces social sympathy born of self-awareness and a shared consciousness of "the species nature", the common humanity and essential similarity, of individuals in diverse roles, situations and circumstances. With this wider perspective, it is possible to derive a viable conception of the common good or public welfare from the individual's pursuit of the good in the privileged company of other men and women. This humane pursuit requires a reasoned reflection upon oneself in relation to others and an imaginative empathy with an expanding circle of human fellowship. The germs of noetic change – hidden within the depths of human beings – can become the basis of communities, communes, conceptions of community, at several levels and in concentric circles, in a novel and more intentional sense than any known in recorded history. They serve as the seeds of a rich variety of modes of participation in the politics of perfectibility. An ideal community is as utopian as the ideal man or the ideal relationship. But every human being is constantly involved in some kind of correction from his external environment, so that he engages in criticism of others (often his own way of criticizing and defining himself). Everyone can see through formal laws and coercive sanctions and recognize constructive alternatives among true friendships for an easier, more natural, trustful context in which one can free oneself and grow.

If this is what is involved in becoming better and abler trustees, then what concrete implications could trusteeship have in relation to day-to-day matters? In other words, if we wish to embody the quintessential principle of trusteeship more fully, how might it affect our attitude and response towards (i) property, (ii) money, (iii) time, and (iv) skills?

Several points should be kept in mind when considering trusteeship and property. In the first place, most of us do not own property, but we all occupy, use and share it. As trustees we should make every effort to look upon all private and communal property with gratitude. We should be grateful for what we have and treat it with respect – whether it be our bodies, our books or the flowers in public parks and private gardens. This mental posture helps us to divest ourselves of the false modern expectation that there is always more, that everything is replaceable, and that there is always someone else available to tend, fix or clean our material possessions – whether a gardener or a doctor.

When we treat all matter with respect, we develop an immense appreciation for those who willingly help in the physical upkeep of our homes and grounds. Those who perform this specialized familial and communal service are thereby less likely to fall prey to an often unarticulated resentment when they see our authentic gratitude and the meticulous care we take with all our possessions and resources.

What could it mean for us to be scrupulous trustees of our money? What attitude and conduct are compatible with the living ideal of trusteeship? Money is a means of meeting certain basic needs, and not an end in itself. It must be handled with the same degree of care that we exercise in relation to electricity. We should plan for its proper use so that it fits into the overall purpose and rhythm of our individual and collective lives. It works best when it is in its proper place, and it can be put to noble, mundane and ignoble uses. Balance is required and so are balance sheets. If we specify suitable uses for our funds – from donations to necessities – they can aid private and collective endeavours. Often our bad habits make it seem as though we lack money, and we seek to earn or grab more. This merely creates an unnatural strain. If, however, we study our spending patterns, tracing them back to their roots, we will frequently find the existence of an unacknowledged trait or hidden desire that needs to be transmuted. As we simplify our wants, establish good patterns and set clear priorities, we generate opportunities to build capital for a higher use. Wealth is not itself the source of vice. Its moral meaning depends entirely upon why we seek it, how we acquire it, and how we use or pollute it.

Custodianship of time can confront needlessly possessive and demanding attitudes in relation to time. This appears to be especially true in relation to 'open time' or non-compulsory time. It is undoubtedly true of obligatory time as well. When we are at work or performing necessary responsibilities at home, how conscientiously do we use our time? Is it well thought out? Is it properly coordinated? Are we cheerfully open to unexpected needs? Do we somehow manage to dissipate time through several 'chat sessions' a day? More significantly, how high is our precise level of constant attentiveness? How often does someone have to repeat the same points to us? Time is, to some degree, a function of conscious attention to duty. The more attentive we are, the more we learn and the more helpful we are to others with our time.

This is because, paradoxically, the more concerned we are to do our best with and for others, the more we forget ourselves. Our troubles and trials are largely forgotten when we shift our focus of awareness to a higher and more considerate level of human involvement.

How possessive are we about our leisure – limited though it may be? Do we insist that this 'free' time is 'my' time because well earned? We may be quite entitled to what we term our 'private time'. Private time is an elementary human need (although not to the *yogin*, for whom time is a continuous inward state called 'living in the eternal'). But, whilst we are entitled to leisure time, we must, as ethical trustees, be willing to utilize it well. Furthermore, our chaste or corrupt visualization and use of free time often tells us something about the colour and direction of our spiritual will. If, for example, we use our leisure time constructively, then, in fact, time is a friend and not an enemy – either to us or to others. We work with the critical points within time – called cyclic recurrences – to regenerate ourselves within the spacious transcendental realm of the timeless. If we are wholly unable to use voluntary time well, then we sadly diminish ourselves and rapidly subtract from our opportunities to add to the sum of good. *Adharma* inevitably invites destructive Karma, "for whatsoever a man soweth, that shall he also reap".

When we turn to individual skills, we can appreciate the full significance of trusteeship – its subtle power of reconciliation and its ineffable moral beauty. In what sense, we might ask, are our individual skills to be held in sacred trust for others? In what sense can we badly abuse our skills and even use them to exploit others? The litmus test as to whether or not we are true trustees of our skills lies in our expectations of return for using them. Our motivation and our expectations are generally interwoven. In the modern West, and increasingly in the modernizing East, skills and specialized knowledge are felt to be convertible into personal success and personal status. We might suppose that we are too mature to fall for the 'lure of filthy lucre', the cancer of greed, the canker of soulless competition. However, we are often all too susceptible to self-deception in this regard. We are subject to the satanic temptation that our hard-earned skills should purchase some intangible reward – from spiritual salvation to public praise. If we receive no external acknowledgements, then we are almost certain to be insidiously tempted to retreat into the tortured world of self-pity and self-approbation. This is because the tenuous exercise of borrowed knowledge and routinized skills is inescapably bound up with a fragile and fugitive self-image. Our frail sense of self-regard is disastrously opposed to the Aquarian spirit of effortless renunciation and intelligent sacrifice.

In practice, our daily approximation to distant ideals will depend upon the extent to which a substantial number of individuals balance their timid concern with individual claims to freedom against a calm willingness to consider the moral claims of the larger community of mankind. Can even the most ingenious organization of industry be dynamized by the innate desire to serve, not merely the desire to be served, the readiness to hold in trust and not the urge to appropriate? Psychologically, the spontaneous commitment to serve a community selflessly may be a self-conscious development, but the primary impulse to serve others is as much rooted in the universal desire for self-expression as the familiar instinct of self-preservation. The noble impulse to serve others, first displayed in the family, could progressively develop into the Bodhisattvic vow to serve the community of souls. This rests upon the compelling assumption that as citizens mature into creative individuals, the very process of individuation requires the growing recognition of the just claims of other individuals and of concentric communities, as well as a deepening concern with self-transcendence and the pilgrimage of humanity.

There is indeed no external cure for egotism or pride in what we have accomplished – especially when we strive and hope to see that it has truly benefited others. It is only through pain and patience that we learn to enjoy giving freely without expectation. However, if we readily recognize that trusteeship is a form of sacrificial action (*yajna*) natural to man, then it can truly help us to release the exhilarating sense of soul-satisfaction and soul-emancipation taught by the *Ishopanishad* and exemplified by Mahatma Gandhi. Our daily sacrifices merge into the mighty stream of *Adhiyajna* or cosmic sacrifice. Such ungrudging contributions cannot be measured and meted out in the meagre coinage of thank yous and material rewards. Voluntary sacrifice (*tapas*) releases its own incomparable spiritual elixir. The sacramental yearning to use everything wisely for the greater welfare of our Teachers and for all

Humanity could progressively dissolve the noxious sense of 'mine' and 'thine'. The raging fires of rampant greed, insatiable craving, and demonic possessiveness could gradually subside because there would be less and less fuel to sustain them. There would then arise, Phoenix-like, the incandescent spirit of love and longing for *Lokasangraha*, universal welfare, the ceaseless celebration of excellence and promise. Meanwhile, courageous pioneers could light up all over the globe the sacred fires of creativity, altruism and universal fellowship in the common cause of *Lokasangraha*, human solidarity and welfare, enlightenment and emancipation.

Hermes, August 1985

TRUTH AND NON-VIOLENCE

The ethical potency of Gandhian thought was grounded in moral clarity and metaphysical simplicity. Without succumbing to either the illusion of infallibility or the delusion of indispensability, Gandhi sought to achieve a balance of intellect and intuition, warning his followers against both rationalization of weakness and erratic emotionalism. Again and again he found that the powerful combination of faith and experience, pure reason and daily application, was both self-transforming and infectious, and he felt that his own life vindicated its strength. Spurning all Manichaean tendencies as snares, he deepened his conviction that God is formless and utterly beyond formulation. Individual integration and self-transcendence, he thought, can be achieved through considering and consolidating the close connection between truth and non-violence, *satya* and *ahimsa*. His unassailable belief that the conceptual foundation of his ethics was strong and sound – though he would refine his insights whenever his daily experience required him to do so – enabled him to find flexibility amid constancy.

Gandhi was a practical idealist. Untrammelled by the dead weight of convention, he was equally unconcerned with formal consistency. As a *karma yogin*, he had neither the time nor the aptitude for constructing a systematic philosophy. Instead, he discerned archetypal patterns and eternal possibilities for growth in the shifting conditions of human interaction. "Men are good," he wrote, "but they are poor victims making themselves miserable under the false belief that they are doing good." * To overcome the false basis of thought and action, human beings must learn to question themselves and others, for, said

---

* M.K. Gandhi, "Letter to A.H. West", *The Collected Works of Mahatma Gandhi*, K. Swaminathan, ed., Navajivan (Ahmedabad, 1958–1984), vol. 10, p. 127 (hereafter cited as *CWMG*); reprinted in *The Moral and Political Writings of Mahatma Gandhi*, Raghavan Iyer, ed., Clarendon (Oxford, 1986–1987), vol. 2, p.16 (hereafter cited as *MPWMG*).

Gandhi, "we are all bound to do what we feel is right". In translating his metaphysical assumptions into ethical principles, Gandhi always pointed to the basic impulses that underlie all action. Holding that there is a universal human nature which mirrors the Divine and may best be characterized as pure potential, he found it natural to use his own life as a crucible in which to test his principles and precepts. He felt that the extreme burden of expectation which the masses thrust upon him expressed the yearning of men and women for a freedom and self-reliance they could sense but seldom experienced. Conscious of his own limitations, he in turn drew strength from the latent goodness of the untutored peasants he sought to help.

Gandhi held that intelligent submission to the laws of cosmic interdependence and natural harmony would result in enduring fulfilment of one's true being. "Has an ocean drop an individuality of its own as apart from the ocean? Then a liberated soul has an individuality of its own." For Gandhi, this hoary metaphor enshrined the key to the metaphysical problem of the individual and the whole, and to what Plato formulated as the problem of the One and the many: "I do believe that complete annihilation of one's self-individuality, sensuality, personality – whatever you call it, is an absolute condition of perfect joy and peace." † However bestial in origin, man is human because he is potentially and essentially divine. Any pattern of thought, direction of energy or line of action hostile to that primordial unity leads eventually to frustration and misery; those acts in tune with it will initiate a happy, if sometimes unanticipated, outcome. Thus the individual who would be truly human must reduce himself to a zero in the eyes of the world. Then he can mirror infinitude in his heart and in his life.

Any feasible conception of human nature, Gandhi felt, must allow for the heights as well as the depths of human attainment and longing. *Satya* and *ahimsa*, truth and non-violence, were the two ultimate and universal principles he used to clarify the chaos of sense-impressions and conflicting desires. Human beings are, at heart, amenable to moral persuasion. Any compelling moral appeal must, therefore, be addressed to the human soul, not to the assemblage of habits and traits

---

† M.K. Gandhi, A Letter, *CWMG*, vol. 29, pp. 397–398; *MPWMG*, vol. 2, p. 20.

that make up the separative personality. A constant awareness of the primacy and supremacy of Truth *(sat)* frees one from needless over-assertion or violent appropriation of any partial or particular truths. "My *anekantavada* [belief in the manyness of reality] is the result of the twin doctrine of *satya* and *ahimsa*." *

Gandhi castigated much in modern civilization because it withers human dignity and impedes moral growth. It establishes a social structure based on the law of the jungle, a tense and competitive rat race relieved only by spasms of furtive self-indulgence. If the salty drop cannot exist without the ocean, the ocean itself has no existence independent of its myriad drops. Using another metaphor, Gandhi wrote that "we are all sparks of the divine and, therefore, partake of its nature, and since there can be no such thing as self-indulgence with the divine, it must of necessity be foreign to human nature". † The process of igniting the spark must, therefore, begin within individual consciousness, then spread among the masses, before ultimately transforming the entire social order. To effect such a change, the questions which the mentally lazy and morally cowardly set aside as irrelevant must be honestly confronted. Inverted notions must be corrected. And fundamental issues – the scope of self-consciousness, the purpose of life, the role of the individual – must be considered and reconsidered.

For Gandhi, one central truth becomes the starting-point for all such enquiries. "The purpose of life is undoubtedly to know oneself. We cannot do it unless we learn to identify ourselves with all that lives. The sum total of that life is God." ‡ Though individual perfection may be distant, human perfectibility is omnipresent. "To say that perfection is not attainable on this earth is to deny God.... Life to me would lose all its interest if I felt that I *could* not attain perfect love on earth." §
The permanent possibility of perfection can be translated into a

---

* M.K. Gandhi, "Three Vital Questions", *Young India,* Jan. 21, 1926; *MPWMG,* vol. 2, p. 23.

† M.K. Gandhi, A Letter, *CWMG,* vol. 69, p. 231; *MPWMG,* vol. 2, pp. 27–28.

‡ M.K. Gandhi, A Letter, *CWMG,* vol. 50, p. 80; *MPWMG,* vol. 2, p. 28.

§ M.K. Gandhi, "Letter to Esther Faering", *CWMG,* vol.14, p. 176; *MPWMG,* vol. 2, p. 36.

continuous expansion of love and truth as embodied in selfless service. Nonetheless, the gap between the elusive ideal and an existing reality will inevitably distort one's understanding of individual perfection. Each individual must constantly rethink and renew his sense of the relation between ideal and reality. He must contemplate these matters with a faith that is beyond knowledge, but not incompatible with reason. "Faith is not a thing to grasp, it is a state to grow to",¶ and "the fact is that perfection is attained through service".** Firm faith prompts selfless service, as selfless service preserves firm faith. Such is the time-honoured pathway to individual perfection and universal enlightenment.

Faith is not itself to blame if some who profess religious faith prove corrupt. In men of great intellect, mental agility can sometimes obscure the intuitions of the heart. Only when the intellect is in harmony with the heart can it be rescued from the tyranny of egotism and enlisted in the service of humanity. But the process of purification is arduous indeed. For even if self-centeredness and hostility are transcended, irrational fears and doubts, tensions and pressures, may remain.

The moral culture of man must begin, then, not with an external improvement of morals, but with a basic transformation of the mind, a systematic training of the will. Only sustained *tapas* – self-suffering – is permanently purifying. Prolonged suffering is therapeutic only when undertaken for the sake of all and for Truth. "Progress is to be measured by the amount of suffering undergone by the sufferer."†† Suffering for the truth facilitates self-knowledge; in addition, it may subtly heal the individual and those around him. Whilst Gandhi saw no reason to assume a linear historical process of collective ascent, his view of *tapas* as a foreshadowing of *moksha* or emancipation, and his conviction that the human spirit is one with the divine, fortified his optimism. "Only an atheist can be a pessimist."‡‡ By optimism, he

---

¶ M.K. Gandhi, A Letter, *CWMG*, Vol. 61, p. 28; *MPWMG*, Vol. 2, p. 34.

** M.K. Gandhi, "Letter to K. Santanam", *CWMG*, vol. 30, p.180; *MPWMG*, vol. 2, p. 38.

†† M.K. Gandhi, "The Law of Suffering", *Young India*, June 16, 1920; *MPWMG*, vol. 2, p. 41.

‡‡ M.K. Gandhi, "Optimism", *Navajivan*, Oct. 23, 1921; *MPWMG*, vol. 2, p. 45.

meant not that everything will invariably augment the happiness of every person, but that all moral strivings will ultimately find their fruition.

Since individuals can intuit ethical principles when the veil of forgetfulness and fear is lifted, and since the patient application of principles is strengthened by self-correction, no one needs to be taught what is right. Nor does anyone need to be shown the practice of self-examination. Instead, everyone must be encouraged to exemplify what he or she knows to be right. True religion is identified by moral vigour and contagious example, not by theological sophistry or hortatory skill. Gandhi constantly shattered the hypnotic spell cast by sanctimonious beliefs in collusion with hypocritical practices. He knew that mere moralism cannot redeem a materialistic social structure estranged from the rhythms of Nature or an economic framework which fosters greed and exploitation. "Is it not most tragic", Gandhi lamented, "that things of the spirit, eternal verities, should be regarded as utopian by our youth, and transitory makeshifts alone appeal to them as practical?" * The penetrating clarity of W.M. Salter's *Ethical Religion* spoke to Gandhi's heart, and he paraphrased eight of its chapters in Gujarati. He strongly endorsed Salter's reasoned conviction that an ethical idea is useless unless put into practice, even though right action may not always be recognized or repaid. Fidelity to conscience, however, needs no public approval; it is its own reward.

However strong the moral impulse in men and women, living in the world seems to demand intolerable yet inescapable compromises. In response, Gandhi advised all social reformers to assume responsibilities willingly, accept the limitations they involve, and trust in Truth, which is God. "As the sea makes no distinction between good rivers and bad, but purifies all, so one person, whose heart is purified and enlarged with non-violence and truth, can contain everything in that heart and it will not overflow or lose its serenity." † Divine discontent and a natural longing for *moksha* or emancipation should not be distorted

---

* M.K. Gandhi, "Academic v. Practical", *Young India*, Nov. 14, 1929; *MPWMG*, vol. 2, p. 25.

† M.K. Gandhi, "Letter to Gangabehn Vaidya", *CWMG*, vol. 35, p. 220; *MPWMG*, vol. 2, p. 71.

into selfish salvationism or crafty escapism. Liberation from the bonds of conditioned existence admits of no short-cut or escape-route, but comes unsought from assiduous perseverance in *dharma,* the path of duty. For Gandhi, *dharma* has no more to do with ritual or convention than true religion has to do with church-going or temple-worship. *Dharma* is nothing less than progressive concern for *lokasangraha,* the welfare of the world. Just as self-realization depends upon self-conquest, so both must be cherished in terms of their contribution to the common good. *Dharma* is to be ceaselessly discovered. Its avenues are self-chosen.

Gandhi drew a firm distinction between ultimate values, which must be impervious to concessions or compromises, and concrete applications, which derive from patient efforts to discern meaning and truth within the flux of events. "You may have faith in the principles which I lay down," he wrote, "but the conclusions which I draw from certain facts cannot be a matter of faith." ‡ This elusive ideal is interpreted differently by each individual. But it is always true that *dharma* lies, not in securing uniformity of conception, but in striving for the ideal without allowing its remoteness to tempt one into shrinking or twisting it. Under all circumstances, "the striving should be conscious, deliberate and hard." § Self-discipline is not a matter of technique; it must become a way of life. Moreover, the temptation to compromise grows stronger as it becomes subtler. "Man's ideal grows from day to day and that is why it ever recedes from him." ¶ Since true knowledge and free action consist in conformity with an order which is prior to human action, Gandhi felt that man's moral stature depended on a constant readiness to hold certain values as sacred and absolute. At first, one must relinquish everything that distracts one from the universally valid ethical order. One must free oneself from passion and prejudice, from whatever bears the stamp of the conditioned personality and the circumscribed environment. To think

---

‡ M.K. Gandhi, "Letter to Mathuradas", *CWMG,* vol. 38, pp. 216–217; *MPWMG,* vol. 2, p. 87.

§ M.K. Gandhi, "Discussion with Teachers", *Harijan,* Sept. 5, 1936; *MPWMG,* vol. 2, p. 91.

¶ M.K. Gandhi, "Letter to Gangabehn Vaidya", *CWMG,* vol. 63, p. 451; *MPWMG,* vol. 2, p. 88.

and live universally – the height of true individuation – necessitates a purificatory discipline. Such discipline, at any level, can best be undertaken with the help of a binding oath.

Such a vow is not merely a promise to oneself to do the best one can, for any conditionality betrays a lack of self-confidence as well as a shallow conception of human potential. "If we resolve to do a thing, and are ready to sacrifice our lives in the process," wrote Gandhi, "we are said to have taken a vow." * The assumption of unconditional vows acknowledges lapses, but provides criteria and incentives for growth. It is far better to fail and to learn, Gandhi thought, than to live with so much moral ambiguity that growth becomes impossible. "A life without vows is like a ship without anchor or like an edifice that is built on slip-sand instead of a solid rock." † With the aid of vows, *tapas* becomes more catalytic than mere suffering. It is transformed into creative self-restraint and therapeutic self-sacrifice; it purifies consciousness and clarifies vision. Vows can help to induce self-knowledge and enhance self-transcendence. They can spur one to refine *dharma*, to discharge one's duties with skill and timeliness, and to hold true to a programme of progressive self-reform.

For Gandhi, the English term 'vow' carried with it all the meanings of the original Sanskrit terms *vrata* (a solemn resolve or a spiritual decision) and *yama* (a spiritual exercise or a self-imposed restraint). In its oldest meaning, *vrata* refers to a divine will or command, which establishes and preserves the order of the universe. Since this divine nature is inseparable from essential human nature, individuals can, through their vows, reflect cosmic order by deliberate and vigilant performance of *dharma*. Gandhi did not set limits to the degree of moral development and spiritual resolve of which any person is capable. Taking vows beyond one's capacity betrays thoughtlessness and lack of balance; the essential value of a vow lies in a calm determination to hold to it regardless of all difficulties. By holding the vow intact within one's heart, the energies of the soul may be released, transforming one's nature.

---

* M.K. Gandhi, "Importance of Vows", *Indian Opinion*, Oct. 8, 1913; *MPWMG*, vol. 2, p. 92.

† M.K. Gandhi, "The Efficacy of Vows", *Young India*, Aug. 22, 1929; *MPWMG*, vol. 2, p. 102.

Conscience remains a potential force in every human being, but in all too many it remains half asleep. "Conscience has to be awakened"‡ through the power of a vow. Emotions which are stimulated by unconscious social and environmental pressures cannot count as conscience. Indeed, a person who has not consciously sought to strengthen and sharpen conscience cannot be said to possess one. "Youngsters as a rule must not pretend to have conscience. It is a quality or state acquired by laborious training. Wilfulness is not conscience.... Conscience can reside only in a delicately tuned breast."§ Conscience is, moreover, the single strongest force against the degradation of human dignity; once man is stripped of conscience and reduced to a mechanical aggregate of perfunctory acts, he becomes an object rather than a subject, a passive instrument rather than an intrinsic end. By casting the cultivation of conscience in terms of vows, Gandhi sought to socialize the individual conscience rather than internalize the social conscience. At once compelling and self-validating, the awakened conscience is an inner voice, the voice of God or Truth. The veracity of such an inner voice can be confirmed only by direct experience resulting from training in *tapas;* indirect evidence, however, can be seen in the inner consistency and transparent integrity of a Socrates or Gandhi. A well-nurtured conscience results in heroism, humility and high saintliness. Such virtues are the ripe fruit of *tapascharya* a consecrated life of austere yet unanxious commitment.

Heroism is a quality of the heart, free of every trace of fear and anger, determined to exact instant atonement for every breach of honour. More than any rule-governed morality, heroism can enable a person to stand alone in times of trial and isolation. It can also establish a deep concord between like-minded men and women loyal to their conscience. But for Gandhi, the greatest obstacle to the incarnation of the heroic ideal in society is, paradoxically, the absence of humility. When human beings do not adequately recognize their fallibility, they will not make sufficient effort to arouse individual conscience. Foundering in a delusive sense of security, they are caught in a 'mobocratic' state of

---

‡ M.K. Gandhi, "Note to Gope Gurbuxani", *CWMG*, vol. 79, p. 206; *MPWMG*, vol. 2, p. 128.

§ M.K. Gandhi, "Under Conscience's Cover", *Young India*, Aug. 21, 1924; *MPWMG*, vol. 2, p. 125.

collective helplessness. Only after the heart is touched by the enormity of divine truth will the distance between the ideal and reality become painfully evident. And only then will genuine humility flow forth. Whilst heroism is cultivated skill in action *(karma yoga)*, humility is the virtue of effortlessness *(buddhi yoga)*.

> Humility cannot be an observance by itself. For it does not lend itself to being deliberately practised. It is, however, an indispensable test of *ahimsa*. In one who has *ahimsa* in him it becomes a part of his very nature.... Truth can be cultivated as well as love. But to cultivate humility is tantamount to cultivating hypocrisy.*

Gandhi's conception of human nature, social solidarity and historical promise compelled him to rethink constantly his ultimate principles. Throughout his life, he was convinced that God is Truth. But if *sat* or Truth is the essence of Deity, every relative truth is a reflection of God from some particular angle. Since every standpoint or perspective contains some kernel of truth, God is everywhere. In 1929 Gandhi subtly altered the emphasis by declaring not that "God is Truth", but that "Truth is God." This simple juxtaposition of equivalencies radically changed the questions Gandhi felt he had to ask and answer. One can always ask if a certain proposition is true, but one need not strain to prove the reality and pervasiveness of Truth. That one can ask the question, or even breathe, is proof enough. Further, Gandhi's formulation curbs the itch to anthropomorphize. It also clarifies the close relation between truth and love. If truth is corrupted, it ceases to be truth, even though corrupt love may still be love. When one obtains the assurance of truth, one's love is purged of consoling illusions. In metaphysical priority, one must say "Truth is God", then add "God is Love", and yet "the nearest approach to Truth is through love." † Like Plato, Gandhi here distinguished between how one knows and how one learns. Fifteen years later he wrote: "I do not believe in a personal deity, but I believe in the Eternal Law of Truth and Love which I have translated as non-violence. This Law is not a dead thing like the law of

---

* M.K. Gandhi, "Letter to Narandas Gandhi", *CWMG*, vol. 44, p. 203; *MPWMG*, vol. 2, pp. 145–146.

† M.K. Gandhi, "Speech at Meeting in Lausanne", *CWMG*, vol. 48, p. 404; *MPWMG*, vol. 2, p. 165.

a king. It's a living thing – the Law and the Law-giver are one."‡

Gandhi saw no sense in the claim that one must know all truths to adhere to Truth. One need merely follow the truth one knows, little or partial though it may be. The individual who would be faithful to what he knows and who aspires to greater wisdom will work to reduce himself to a cipher in his quest. For Gandhi, there can be no beauty and no art apart from truth. When one finds truth beautiful, one discovers true art. When one loves Truth, one expresses a true and unconditional love. The seeker must only be honest with himself and truthful to others. Where he cannot speak the truth without doing great harm, he may be silent, but Gandhi, like Kant, insisted he must never lie. The truth-seeker cannot be so concerned with his own safety or comfort that he abdicates from his larger duties. "He alone is a lover of truth who follows it in all conditions of life." § The virtues stressed by most religious and philosophical traditions cannot be dismissed by the genuine seeker of truth as alien or beyond his concern. He must, rather, synthesize these virtues in *ahimsa* or non-violence, the moving image and decisive test of truth. If all existence is a mirror of the divine, violence in any form is a blasphemous repudiation of Deity itself; if all souls are sparks of the divine, rooted in the transcendental Truth, all violence is a species of deicide.

Just as humility is the natural accompaniment of true heroism, *ahimsa* is the necessary correlate of fearlessness. In Gandhi's vision, the maintenance of moral stature and spiritual dignity must be based upon the practice of *ahimsa*. He conceived of *ahimsa* as an integral part of *yajna* or sacrifice, a concept rooted in the Indian conception of a beneficent cosmic order and a humane discipline requiring self-purification and self-examination. The moral force generated by *ahimsa* or non-violence was therefore held by Gandhi to be infinitely greater than any force founded upon selfishness. The essential power of non-violence was viewed alternatively by Gandhi as being 'soul-force' and 'truth-force'. The two terms are fundamentally equivalent, and differ only in their psychological or ontological emphasis. For Gandhi, *ahimsa* represented

---

‡ M.K. Gandhi, "Letter to Roy Walker", *CWMG*, vol. 77, p. 390; *MPWMG*, vol. 2, pp. 192–193.

§ M.K. Gandhi, A Letter, *CWMG*, vol. 50, p. 76; *MPWMG*, vol. 2, p. 204.

not a denial of power but a renunciation of all forms of coercion and compulsion. He held in fact that *ahimsa* had a strength which no earthly power could continue to resist. Although Gandhi was noted for his advocacy of *ahimsa* in social and political arenas, its most fundamental and intimate use lay for him in the moral persuasion of free souls.

Just as Gandhi sometimes inflated the word *ahimsa* to encompass all virtues, he equally broadened the notion of *himsa* or violence to include all forms of deceit and injustice. *Himsa* proceeds from fear, which is the shadow of ignorant egotism. Its expulsion from the heart requires an act of faith which transcends the scope of analysis. Gandhi held, however, that just as intellect plays a large part in the worldly use of violence, so it plays an even larger part in the field of non-violence. The mind, guided by the heart, must purge all elements of egotism before it can embody *ahimsa*. Gandhi postulated that the willingness to kill exists in human beings in inverse proportion to their willingness to die. This must be understood in terms of *tanha* – the will to live – which is present to some degree in every human being and reinforces the concept of the separative ego. As that ego is illusory and transitory in nature, it has a necessary tendency to fear for its own future, and with that an inevitable propensity towards violence. Gandhi held that *ahimsa* could be taught and inculcated only by example, and never by force. Coercion, indeed, would itself contradict *ahimsa*. The roots of violence and *himsa* lie in the mind and heart, and therefore mere external restraint or abstention from violence cannot be considered true *ahimsa*. Gandhi chose the term *ahimsa* because *himsa* or violence is never wholly avoidable; the word *ahimsa* stresses that which is to be overcome. Whilst acknowledging that some violence can be found in every being, Gandhi could never concede that such violence was irreparable or irreducible. He held that those who begin by justifying force become addicted to it, while those who seek the practical reduction of *himsa* in their lives should be engaged in constant self-purification.

Ahimsa, in the widest sense, means a willingness to treat all beings as oneself. Thus *ahimsa* is the basis of *anasakti,* selfless action. It is equivalent to the realization of absolute Truth, and it is the goal towards which all true human beings move naturally, though unconsciously. *Ahimsa* cannot be realized alone; it has meaning only in the context of universal human interaction and uplift. Like truth, *ahimsa,* when genuine, carries conviction in every sphere. Unlike many forms of love, however, *ahimsa* is embodied by a truth-seeker not out of longing or lack, but out of a sense of universal obligation. It is only when one takes the vow of *ahimsa* that one has the capacity to assess apparent failures in terms of one's own moral inadequacies. *Ahimsa* means, at the very least, a refusal to do harm. "In its positive form, *ahimsa* means the largest love, the greatest charity." * Gandhi's refusal to set different standards for saints and ordinary men, combined with his concern to give *ahimsa* a practical social function rather than a purely mystical use, led him to extend and employ the word in novel ways. The political strength which *ahimsa* can summon is greater and profounder than the impact of violence precisely because *ahimsa* is consubstantial with the immortal soul. Any programme of social or political reform, including civil disobedience, must, therefore, begin with the heroic individual, for only when such pioneers radiate the lustre of *ahimsa* will all humanity be uplifted.

Anyone may practise non-violence in the absence of support and even in the face of hostility. Indeed, *ahimsa* in the midst of adversity becomes the sovereign means of self-purification and the truest road to self-knowledge. *Ahimsa* is the anti-entropic force in Nature and the indefeasible law of the human species. Just as unconditional commitment to Truth can lead to limited truth in action, so too the universal creed of *ahimsa* may yield an appropriate policy of non-violence. As a policy, non-violence is a mode of constructive political and social action, just as truth-seeking is the active aspect of Truth. Truth and non-violence are the integrated aspects of immutable soul-force. "Non-violence and truth together form, as it were, the right angle of all religions."†

One must be sure, however, not to believe conveniently in *ahimsa* as a policy, whilst doubting the creed.‡ Whether or not any specific policy

---

* M.K. Gandhi, "On Ahimsa", *Modern Review*, Oct. 1916; *MPWMG*, vol. 2, p. 212.

† M.K. Gandhi, "Problems of Non-Violence", *Navajivan*, Aug. 9 1925; *MPWMG*, vol. 2, p. 218.

‡ See Raghavan Iyer, *The Moral and Political Thought of Mahatma Gandhi*, Oxford University Press (New York, 1973, 1978); second edition: Concord Grove Press (Santa Barbara, 1983), ch. 8.

is demonstrably effective, it is imperative to hold true to the creed. Gandhi distinguished, moreover, between policy and mere tactics. Some successful tactics might at times be inappropriate, but the policy itself continues to be apt. Gandhi marvelled at those who, conceding that his non-violent programme worked in the case of the British, insisted that it must inevitably fail against a Hitler or Mussolini. Such a view romanticized the benevolence of the British and altogether denied that tyrants are a part of the human species. Gandhi's own experience had shown him that the British could be utterly ruthless or devious, even though his firm faith forbade him from excluding anyone from the possibility of growth, change of heart and recognition of necessity. Something more reasonable than subtle racism would be required to challenge the universal relevance of *ahimsa*.

It is in the application of *ahimsa* to the issues of war and peace, however, that Gandhi's teachings can be seen to be uncompromising. Non-violence does not signify the unwillingness to fight against an enemy. But, he argued, the enemy is always ignorance and the evil which men do: it is not in human beings themselves. Even though he loathed war and violence in all its forms, Gandhi could not be classified as an orthodox pacifist. Indeed, he held that the courage and heroism often displayed by war-struck individuals reflected well upon their moral character, even if war itself was a dark moral blot on those who encouraged or allowed it to happen. For himself, he rejected indirect participation in war, and refused to let others fight his battles for him. "If I have only a choice between paying for the army of soldiers to kill my neighbours or to be a soldier myself, I would, as I must, consistently with my creed, enlist as a soldier in the hope of controlling the forces of violence and even of converting my comrades." *

Training for war demoralized and brutalized people, Gandhi believed, and its after-effects brought nations down to abysmal levels of dissolution and discontent. He therefore strove to show how non-violence was the cleanest weapon against terrorism and torture. He asserted that the man who holds to a high sense of dignity and brotherhood, even to the point of death, confounds aggression and may

---

* M.K. Gandhi, "Difficulty of Practice", *Young India*, Jan. 30, 1930; *MPWMG*, vol. 2, p. 394.

even shame his attackers. Whilst insisting that non-violence was the only means for bringing to an end the familiar vicious cycles of revenge, he recognized that this required expert timing. Poor timing could lead through foolhardiness to a form of suicide or martyrdom, and Gandhi held that there was a higher truth in living for non-violence than in inadvertently dying in its name. Witnessing the course of warfare from the Boer War through the Second World War, he only strengthened his conviction in regard to the basic creed of non-violence. Indeed, when he heard of the bombing of Hiroshima, he declared, "Unless now the world adopts non-violence, it will spell certain suicide for mankind." †
In a non-violent state, it should finally be possible to raise a non-violent army, which could resist armed invasion without recourse to arms. However distant such a prospect, Gandhi refused to relinquish it, for he knew that violent triumphs guarantee nothing but the brutalization of human beings and the perpetuation of further violence.

The individual who would strive to be fully human – to embody *satya* and *ahimsa* to the fullest possible extent – should not rely on others to display a moral courage which is the mature product of an inward transformation. Nonetheless, like-minded seekers and strivers can offer each other moral support and mutual encouragement. If the political life of any nation is to be spiritualized, the process must begin in intentional communities. Gandhi's *ashrams* were such pioneering attempts – small communities committed to embodying the principles they upheld. Chief amongst these principles were the vows of *satya* and *ahimsa*. Self-restraint and purification involved mental, verbal and physical continence, control of the palate, and the vows of non-possession and fearlessness. Also essential were non-thieving, in the broadest sense of the concept, and the vow of *swadeshi*, self-reliance. The strength of the *ashram* lay not so much in the establishment of detailed rules for living as in the conscious effort to exemplify a shared perspective and to conduct "experiments with truth".

The *ashram* may be seen as a sphere of fellowship in which one can test oneself, taking truth one step beyond oneself. *Anasakti* could be nurtured, errors corrected, solutions tried, *tapas* magnified.

---

† M.K. Gandhi, "Talk with an English Journalist", *Harijan,* Sept. 29, 1946; *MPWMG,*
   vol. 2, p. 455.

The fortunate could discover that "the secret of happy life lies in renunciation".* For Gandhi, the *ashram* was a microcosm which might come to mirror the full potential of the macrocosm, a minute drop that reflects the shimmering sea. The progressive renunciation of puny selfhood could, he felt, open minds and hearts to the Self of all humanity. Embracing the globe, Gandhi's hopes were addressed not only to his own generation but also to all posterity.

> It remains for those therefore who like myself hold this view of renunciation to discover for themselves how far the principle of *ahimsa* is compatible with life in the body and how it can be applied to acts of everyday life. The very virtue of a *dharma* is that it is universal, that its practice is not the monopoly of the few, but must be the privilege of all. And it is my firm belief that the scope of truth and *ahimsa* is world-wide. That is why I find an ineffable joy in dedicating my life to researches in truth and *ahimsa* and I invite others to share it with me by doing likewise.†

Hermes, March 1988

---

* M.K. Gandhi, "Living up to 125", *Harijan*, Feb. 24, 1946; *MPWMG*, vol. 2, p. 637.

† M.K. Gandhi, "Jain Ahimsa", *Young India*, Oct. 25, 1928; *MPWMG*, vol. 2, p. 224.

KARMA AND TRANSMUTATION

According to esoteric teaching there are seven primary and seven secondary 'creations'; the former being the Forces self-evolving from the one causeless FORCE; the latter showing the manifested Universe emanating from the already differentiated divine elements.

Esoterically, as well as exoterically, all the enumerated Creations stand for the (7) periods of Evolution, whether after an 'Age' or a 'Day' of Brahmâ. This is the teaching par excellence of Occult Philosophy, which, however, never uses the term 'creation' nor even that of 'evolution' with regard to primary "Creation", but calls all such forces 'the aspects of the Causeless Force'.

The Secret Doctrine, i 446

Each individual is an essential if unequal participant in the fourteen phases of evolution indicated in the Puranic Teachings concerning the seven creations. All human beings share in the most subtle and sublime spiritual resources of the universe as well as in its more manifest and mundane features. From the standpoint of mental growth and moral learning, the foremost element of human self-existence is its partial participation in the Mahatic self-transcendence of the *Kumaras*. Through the fiery spark of universal self-consciousness, every human being is sacrificially endowed with the priceless gift of learning truth, the right perception of existing things, and the capacity for Bodhisattvic action. Existing as the latent seed of divine self-consciousness, it is an inseparable portion of the impartite field of primordial Wisdom – *Dzyan* – which supports and pervades the differentiated universe.

Divine Wisdom is at once the luminous awareness of its origins lost in the ineffable Darkness and Silence as well as the directing intelligence of the noumenal cosmos. As *Brahmâ-Mahat* it is the architectonic wisdom of Karma mirrored in the Buddhic faculty in man. As *Brahmâ-Rudra* it is one with the hosts of *Manasa-Dhyanis*, endowing human beings with the immense potential of its transcendental wisdom. In the devotional heart of every human being it is *Ishwara*, the *Ishtaguru*, the prototype and preceptor, the living light of the lost Word guiding the pilgrim-soul along the Path.

The awakening of wisdom is not the exclusive concern of human beings as distinguished from the other kingdoms of nature. Rather, it is the common current carrying every centre of life forward through evolutionary cycles of transformation. Governed from within by the universal law of harmony and compassion, each phase of evolution and each kingdom of nature elaborates and defines one of a series of indispensable stages of growth. Each affords its own array of opportunities and each is circumscribed by its own limiting laws. Poised between transcendental unity and mayavic differentiation, consciousness experiences a series of states distinguished by permutations of space, motion and duration. Through birth and death, through involvement and withdrawal, through affirmation and negation, the appropriate soil is prepared and the seeds of self-consciousness quickened so that they might germinate and flower into the fullness of *svasamvedana*.

Viewed in this light, the present phase of human evolution may be seen as a period of mature awakening to universal responsibility. To the extent that human beings realize their inmost identity with the *Kumaras* and Bodhisattvas, they may perceive the solidarity of their being with all other souls and hence the universality of their obligation of compassion. To the extent that they are illuminated and energized by the transcendental wisdom of the *Kumaras*, they will find within themselves the skill and strength needed to meet the just demands of a life of joyous service to other beings. As the active awareness of the bond of Being hidden in Non-Being, Karma is the basis of a philosophic fusion of the concepts of human nature, obligation, potentiality and destiny. Encompassing all from *Brahmâ-Mahat* to the tiniest atom, Karma is inseparable from the world-wielding spirit of Wisdom which creates, sustains and regenerates manifestation out of non-manifestation.

Karma is thus one of the most mysterious and at the same time one of the most practical themes. In the present cycle it is the sacred responsibility of those who have been fortunate to receive the teaching of karma to use the doctrine intelligently and patiently, so as to be able to communicate by example – which is the school of mankind – as well as by precept – which is the mode of service to one's fellow beings – those insights into karma which they have been privileged to garner. Buddhic intuition with regard to the operation of karma is indispensable to human beings who wish to gain noetic control over their lives and instruments so that they may remain attuned to the potent vibration of the New Cycle. As the karmic station of humanity demands the integration of Buddhic awareness and Manasic deliberation, the cultivation of mindfulness through daily exercises in meditation is an essential starting-point in gaining insight into karma. The practical art of mindfulness can begin with attentiveness to extremely simple and elementary points of existence. For example, in a variety of Buddhist schools aspirants are encouraged to observe their mode of breathing. By counting breaths over a period of time and by observing the rhythms of outbreathing and inbreathing, one can become aware of the pauses involved in breathing – before an outbreath, after an outbreath, before an inbreath, and after an inbreath. Such attention to breathing is not, however, equivalent to mindfulness, but must be linked through contemplation to an understanding of inward processes in consciousness. Inbreathing is important in relation to the powers of assimilation, preservation and absorption. Outbreathing is important in discharging one's debts to the seven kingdoms of nature and to all human beings, seen and unseen, with whom one interacts. Each opportunity to breathe outwards is an opportunity to either bless or curse life-atoms.

Every human being is a receptacle of life-atoms from billions of other beings, immersed in a constant circulation that passes in and out of every astral form. In and through these *shariras* or vestures there is a ceaseless movement in the ocean of life of classes of life-atoms, which themselves belong to the hebdomadic kingdoms and sub-kingdoms of nature. Each entering and exiting life-atom experiences and retains the impress of the thought and feeling of the human being presiding over the ephemeral vesture. All of these kingdoms and classes of elementals have had an archetypal function in the history of cosmic and human evolution. By combining a firm if rudimentary grasp of the metaphysics of the *Gupta Vidya* concerning the seven creations with a persistent attention to the elementary processes of life, one can acquire through mindfulness a minimal insight into the magical process of breathing, thinking, feeling and willing. Minimally, one can begin to see that crude empirical notions like good luck and bad luck, being accident-prone or fortunate, are inadequate to an understanding of the exactitude and precision of karma. Similarly, one may come to see that neither wishful or dreamy thinking nor mechanistic or reductionist assumptions can be adequate to comprehend or cope with the challenges of life.

The awakening of the divine creative potential within human nature through an apprehension of karma requires a blending of a macro-perspective with a micro-application. Human beings in the Aquarian Age are the cultural inheritors of a vast vision of the physical universe constituted out of billions upon billions of galaxies. Whilst they may have few opportunities to observe the galaxies, they have many opportunities to hear and read about them. The reality of galactic space is much more alive for modern man than it was for the masses of people living before the present century. Through planetariums, through books and through the mass media, millions of people have been able to gain a glimpse of the awesome reality of myriad stars. Through the excitement of mental and physical voyages of discovery, many children of the present century have gained some inkling of the place of the earth amidst the starry heavens. Through this macro-perspective, which is the heritage of contemporary humanity, individuals everywhere have gained access to the vast purifying powers of space. At the same time, the capacity to make use of such knowledge in daily life requires a micro-approach, something of that sort of attention stressed with great integrity in the Buddhist tradition. Beginning with Gautama's enigmatic Flower Sermon, there is a subtle emphasis placed upon the mystery of the individual flower, the beauty of the particular petal, the intimations of the individual moment.

Something of the same spirit was exemplified in the long life of Albert Schweitzer, who, out of his enormous compassion and sacrifice, laboured from small beginnings until his dying day, serving the needs of the ailing and the distressed. Schweitzer thought that the central problem of modern civilization came down to its lack of a sense of the sacred, its lack of "reverence for life". Through this great *mantram*, his therapeutic legacy to humanity, Schweitzer drew attention to the need for compassion, intelligence and humility in every interaction with nature or other human beings. Through reverence for the smallest things and empty spaces in life, reverence in human relationships and for the potentials in all human beings, the sense of the sacred can be restored. As Schweitzer said, "Truth has no special time of its own. Its hour is now – always." This is the micro-approach, through which in every single hour one can make a significant difference. If only one would see clearly, every moment can make a decisive contribution to the current of ideation that is the surest sovereign protection of each and every human soul.

There is an essential relationship between the degree of one's reverence for life and the degree of one's apprehension of the mystery of life itself. Understood causally, *it is the rate of vibration of one's ideational current which determines the degree of integration between one's macro-perspective and micro-approach to life.* Some understanding of this principle may be seen in contemporary science, which seeks to connect the laws governing the life and death of galaxies and stars with the laws of micro-physics governing the vibratory properties of particles and energy. The same tendency in modern thought is seen in attempts to connect even the somewhat mechanistic theories regarding brainwaves and neurological phenomena with the still rather crude notion of mental vibrations affecting feelings and behaviour. The awakening of Divine Wisdom and the establishment of true continuity of consciousness depend upon a clear insight into the relationship between ideation and the involvement of life in form. The *Gupta Vidya* teaches that life precedes the first atom of form, and that its manifestation on the seven planes must be traced to the active Dhyani-energies on the plane of *Mahat*.

Beginning with the primordial self-evolution of *Mahat*, Divine Mind or the Spirit of the Universal Soul, from the One Causeless Force, the series of seven primary 'creations' traces out the differentiation of the divine elements of invisible Nature. From the aggregate of spiritual intelligences, the *Dhyanis* and *Manus* constituting the primordial *Logos*, the first manifested and creative power, issue the influences stirring the first breath of differentiation of the pre-cosmic elements in primordial *Akasha*. This is the passage from the chaotic pre-nebular period of cosmogony to the first stages of cosmic life, the fire-mist period, wherein atoms emerge from *laya*. Here the second hierarchy of *Manus* and *Dhyanis* arises, those who in turn will originate the realm of form or *rupa*. Thus, in the sevenfold primary creation, as well as in the sevenfold secondary or material and terrestrial creation, the differentiation of the primordial germ of life precedes the evolution of life and form. The laws governing the manifestation of life on the terrestrial globe mirror the laws governing the agitation of undifferentiated cosmic matter by *Mahat* or Divine Intelligence. Through a purely transcendental process, witnessed solely by the supra-divine intelligence of the *Rudra-Kumaras*,

> The Supreme Soul, the *all permeant* (*Sarvag*a) Substance of the World, having entered *(been drawn)* into matter (*prakriti*) and Spirit (*purusha*), *agitated* the *mutable and the immutable principles*, the season of Creation (*manvantara*) having arrived.

> *The Secret Doctrine*, i 451

Pointing to the pervasive and profound mystery of the relationship between ideation, life and form, H.P. Blavatsky intimates something of the connection between breath and vibration, and speaks hopefully of the approach of modern thought to the ancient mystery.

> . . . the *absolutely eternal* universal motion, or vibration, that which is called in Esoteric language 'the GREAT BREATH,' differentiates in the primordial, first manifested ATOM. More and more, as chemical and physical sciences progress, does this occult axiom find its corroboration in the world of knowledge: the scientific hypothesis, that even the simplest elements of matter are identical in nature and differ from each other only owing to the variety of the distributions of *atoms* in the molecule or speck of substance, or by the modes of its *atomic vibration*, gains every day more ground.

> *The Secret Doctrine*, i 455

The ability to sustain a current of ideation, or vibration, through mindfulness in the blending of a macro-perspective and micro-application is the mature fruit of meditation and self-correction nurtured over lifetimes. Continuity of consciousness is the result of continuity of striving rooted in knowledge of the laws of Karma. For the ordinary human being who does not remember much of the past ten years of the present life, speculative pseudo-knowledge and supposed information regarding past lives is neither reliable nor helpful. All genuine knowledge is self-knowledge and derives from the soul-powers of deliberation, discrimination and detachment. It requires the ability to look at the world of objects in relation to the subjectivity of the ray of light that comes from a single universal and transcendent source. Gradually, through self-devised efforts checked by Karma, one must deepen devotional reverence for life, progressively purifying the inner vestures and the mind through the negation of all identification with form. Entering the void, one must seek the archetypal perspective of the Rishis who witness the eternal dawn of manifestation with the words,

> 'There was neither day nor night, nor sky nor earth, nor darkness nor light, nor any other thing save only ONE, unapprehensible by intellect, or THAT which is *Brahma* and *Pumis* (Spirit) and *Pradhana* (crude matter)' *(Veda: 'Vishnu Purana Commentary')*; or literally: 'One Pradhanika Brahma Spirit: THAT was.' The 'Pradhanika Brahma Spirit' is *Mulaprakriti* and *Parabrahmam.*

The Secret Doctrine, i 445

Mulaprakriti is the veil of primordial matter, or pre-cosmic chaos, upon *TAT*, the unthinkable and the unspeakable. This ever exists, whether there are manifestations of myriads upon myriads of galaxies and stars, or whether there is nothing in the Divine Darkness in boundless space and eternal duration in which the ceaseless motion of the potential breathing of the One breathes breathless. When the mind is raised to the apex of contemplation of non-manifestation, one voids the entire cosmos. When this is done again and again, then, like those who get used to the rarefied air of higher altitudes by climbing mountains, one's mental breathing changes. It becomes possible to return to the daily sphere of obligations with a freshness, sweetness, and an *afflatus* of supernal light. The more one experiences this, the more the mystery deepens and the more one is grateful for breathing, and grateful for learning and living. To learn truth and to see life rightly are the prerogatives earned by those who under karma become *srotapattis,* entering the stream of search for Divine Wisdom.

Every aspirant at the portal of the Path should know that it is possible by meditation to go beyond the galaxies, to reawaken the lost Eye and to restore the lost Word. No human being should ever hesitate to dare – spiritual life demands daring and courage, the *virya* of authentic striving. In that sense, every human being should reach for the sky, and indeed go beyond the sky, and having done so should come down to the tip of the nose. Of the five ordinary senses, the sense of sight is the most extraordinary in that the horizon of vision is much greater than the parameters of the other four senses. For example, it is possible for any person of average eyesight to see the tip of the nose, but at the same time to see the sun ninety-three million miles away. Even the most rudimentary reflection upon the power of vision reveals the immense privilege that human beings enjoy in their power of sight. In many meditative exercises it is useful to start by bringing together both eyes in a focus at the tip of the nose. There will be some initial eye strain for those unaccustomed to the practice, and it should not be forced. Nor should one engage in this practice of focussing the organs of vision upon the organ of breath merely upon the physical plane without thinking of that which is beyond oneself and also within the heart.

Ultimately, the quest for the awakening of wisdom through meditation is the quest for the realization of *TAT* – That which is the boundless space beyond the cosmos and also present in every atom. It is in the eyes and at the ends of one's fingers, and also at the tip of the nose. It is everywhere and nowhere, transcending mind and the categories of thought. It is the ONE that is neither first nor last, but ALL. As H.P. Blavatsky suggested,

> It is on the right comprehension of this tenet in the *Brahmanas* and *Puranas* that hangs, we believe, the apple of discord between the three Vedantin Sects: the *Advaita, Dwaita,* and the *Visishtadvaitas.* The first arguing rightly that *Parabrahmam,* having no relation, as the absolute *all,* to the manifested world – the Infinite having no connection with the finite – can neither *will* nor *create;* that, therefore, *Brahmâ, Mahat, Iswara,* or whatever name the creative power may be known by, creative gods and all, are simply an illusive aspect of *Parabrahmam* in the conception of the conceivers; while the other sects identify the impersonal Cause with the Creator, or *Iswara.*

> *Mahat* (or *Maha-Buddhi*) is, with the *Vaishnavas*, however, divine
> mind *in active operation,* or, as Anaxagoras has it, 'an ordering and
> disposing mind, which was the cause of all things'.

> *The Secret Doctrine,* i 451

Sometimes the Absolute has been characterized as the supremely
passive unconscious, but this is merely an expression because, strictly
speaking, it is neither conscious nor unconscious. *It ever is.* Brahmâ,
Mahat and *Ishwara* are all references to the creative principle in the
cosmos. They afford different ways in which to understand the non-
relationality of the absolute abstract *Parabrahm.* At the same time,
however, if they are not anthropomorphized or concretized, they can
provide a ladder of ideas for use in meditation for those who wish to
bridge the gap between the knower and the known, and between the
unknown and the Unknowable.

For the human being who adopts the spiritual discipline of
meditation in earnest, it becomes enjoyable to undertake repeated
exercises in spiritual training, in mind-control and in mindfulness.
Through unwavering resolve and unremitting attention to details,
the *srotapatti* enters upon the arduous path of self-evolution which
leads ultimately to the unfoldment of the Third Eye. Under the ever-
watchful eye of Karma, which must be mirrored in the disciple's own
vigilance, the mysteries of the seven primary and seven secondary
creations must be unlocked from within. These 'creations' correspond
with periods of cosmic and human evolution, as well as with various
modes of differentiation in the *rupa* and *arupa* worlds, and the
respective hierarchies of solar and lunar *Dhyanis* which constitute the
inner nature of man. This process of awakening to the fourteen colours
of the rainbow is referred to in the *Puranas* as the Eighth Creation,
concerning which H.P. Blavatsky stated:

> The 'eighth creation' mentioned is no *Creation* at all; it is a *blind* again,
> for it refers to a purely mental process: the cognition of the 'ninth'
> creation, which, in its turn, is an effect, manifesting in the *secondary*
> of that which was a 'Creation' in the *Primary (Prakrita)* Creation. The
> *Eighth,* then, called *Anugraha* (the *Pratyayasarga* or the *intellectual*
> creation of the *Sankhyas,* explained in *Karika,* v. 46, p. 146), is 'that
> creation of which *we have a perception*' – in its esoteric aspect – and 'to

which we give intellectual assent (*Anugraha*) in contradistinction to *organic creation*'.

The Secret Doctrine, i 456

A relevant and accessible example of this process of voluntary Manasic self-evolution can be found in the practice of taking daily *mantrams* or seed-thoughts for meditation and application. In this practice depth will follow upon continuity and continuity will follow upon resolve. The aim is to employ potent ideas in order to blow away mental misconceptions which are bound up with the limitations of the lunar astral form. Human beings are liable to limit themselves through sense-perception, acquiring a foreshortened and angular view of who they are. Through the progressive negation of false limitations, it is possible to regenerate awareness of the sphere of light that surrounds every human being, and to sense the intimate and close connection between that sphere and the sphere of light that surrounds every animal, every object, even every globe and planet, ultimately even the sun and the entire starry universe.

To remove the scales from one's eyes, to dissolve the encrustations and petrification that block the inner currents of vision, is a matter of careful concentration, wherein one focusses upon the core, the mathematical central point, in metaphysical space. Metaphysical space is a homogeneous medium in which there are none of the relations between parts that are found in the differentiated world of ordinary sense-perception. There are regions wherein the familiar divisions of time have no meaning, and light-energy flows instantaneously. To learn to inhabit these regions self-consciously, one must develop conceptions of energy-fields very different from those encountered when, for example, one pushes a cart through the aisles of a supermarket. But if one cannot do the latter calmly and patiently, one cannot learn to do the former.

One must learn to go at a speed which is governed by the needs of many other beings, but also amidst the clutter of objects and the narrow corridors through which one must move with patience and humility, stopping at each counter until one finds what it is that can be used to feed one's child and family. Again, it is the micro-approach to daily obligations which is the basis for deepening the powers of concentration and meditation. Owing to the enormous elasticity of the mind, it is capable of tremendous expansion as well as intense focus, but its wings will be clipped if it is weak in the embodiment of *dharma*. To understand in any degree the ubiquity of *TAT* is simultaneously to realize one's obligation to every point of life and to find within oneself the resources required to fulfil one's *dharma*. Broadly considered, the Eighth Creation spoken of in the *Puranas* is the transmutation through meditation, devotion and action of the responsibilities of human existence.

> It is the correct perception of our relations to the whole range of 'gods' and especially of those we bear to the *Kumaras* – the so-called 'Ninth Creation' – which is in reality an aspect of or reflection of the sixth in our *manvantara* (the *Vaivasvata*). 'There is a *ninth,* the Kumara Creation, which is both primary and secondary', says *Vishnu Purana,* the oldest of such texts. 'The *Kumaras*', explains an *esoteric* text, 'are the *Dhyanis*, derived immediately from the supreme Principle, who reappear in the *Vaivasvata Manu* periods for the progress of mankind.'

The Secret Doctrine, i 456

Behind the screen of what seems to be material objects there are myriads of *devas* and elementals, gods and demi-gods, but to see them requires the eye of Buddhic intuition. One has to break down the false screen which is imposed upon objects and creates the illusion of the furniture of the world, with all its tables and chairs, cabbages and kings. Behind all of these are whirling centres of energy revolving in ceaseless motion at tremendous and different rates, and some of them are fundamental particles connected with what is called anti-matter. They are capable of instantaneously affecting fields extending over millions of miles. To penetrate the false screen of the visual world of objects, which is false because entirely relative to sense-perception, it is necessary to seal up the eyes and the mouth, as was the tradition in the Mysteries. By closing the mouth, one shuts out the desire to manifest, and with that the perceptual screen. One is liable initially to experience a dizzy buzzing in the brain, the bees of scattered thoughts, but they can be wiped off as one would wipe a slate clean with an eraser. The mental screen can be cleaned by thinking of the Divine Dark. One must banish all thoughts, voiding the sense of self, voiding the illusion of objects, voiding the sense of time, of yesterday, today and tomorrow. One must void all the six points of perception – north, south, east, west, above and below – but this is difficult because one has to start from below and to reach above, and it then takes time to destroy the distinction between the above and the below. To do this one must travel so far within that what is within is without, and what is without is within.

As the discipline of mental renunciation matures, a vast range of possibilities will unfold before the eye of the soul. One will become extremely aware of 'gods', which are millions upon millions of *devas* and *devatas* called elementals and belonging to the different kingdoms of nature – sylphs and salamanders, gnomes and undines – all of which are invisible to the physical eye but cluster and move together in extremely disciplined arrays. Many people have some vague sense of this, through their relationship to machines and to animals, but when one becomes directly aware of this invisible world, then it becomes possible to raise one's sights cosmically to the magnificent perspective wherefrom one can broadly view human karma over eighteen million years. This is a vast period of time, far beyond the conception of many of the greatest minds of the age, but it is the privileged perspective of the human being who sees himself or herself as an immortal soul and wants to enact this truth in daily life. It is a perspective based upon meditation and the conviction that every being is an immortal soul. It is tested through one's ability to perceive others as rays of one source of light, enacting the reality of the immortal soul in all the vicissitudes of life.

As this conviction deepens and ripens, one will begin to sense the privilege of breathing on earth and will recognize the gift of the *Kumaras*, the *Dhyanis* who lit up the spark of self-consciousness in every human being. In Puranic tradition the *Kumaras* are Sages who live as long as Brahmâ, being created by him in the first *kalpa*. Esoterically, they are the progenitors of the true spiritual SELF, the hierarchy of the higher *Prajapati* under the guardianship of and headed by Rudra-Nilalohita, and *derived immediately from the supreme Principle*. Meditation upon the *Kumaras* is both potent and benedictory, and once truly touched, it will leave one silently absorbed in deep rapture for a significant period of time. But then one will recall the teaching about mindfulness, and go forth into the world combining refined karmic precision with authentic creativity in the performance of duty out of love and compassion. Practising balance, one will both reach with extreme humility to the highest conceivable meditation, and at the same time act in the world with the inner confidence that one can genuinely help other human beings. Maintaining mindfulness, one can transmute work and home into sacred arenas for the elevation of life-atoms, and can discover in every circumstance of life the golden opportunity to render true service.

Long before one can honour the true presence of the *Kumaras* within, and regain the lost Word and the lost Light, one must come to see that there is no karmic meaning in meditation apart from the desire to render service to all that lives. Long before one can gain any direct sense of the ways in which nature is the ally, pupil and servant of the perfected human will, one must quicken through meditation gratitude and deep inner humility for the privilege of being able, as a human being, to do something constructive each and every day. However intermittent the effort, one can create a noetic current which extends through the seasons until the point is reached where one wins true self-respect for the first time by staying with something that one starts. Authentic self-respect comes from binding oneself to do something noble and worthwhile for the sake of the human race. It is the karmic consequence of mindfulness. Once established, it will gradually bring about a change in the tropism of the life-atoms of the vestures. Meanwhile, under karma, one will encounter the hosts of angry elementals impressed by one's own past errors, delusions and incompletions, which are now neglected and want to be indulged but should be ignored. If one holds fast to the heart-vibration and the central current of ideation, then these will go away, and one will become like a child living in a magical world.

Whispering to the *Ishtaguru* within, who is felt but not yet seen, and listening to the whispers of *Buddhi* to *Manas*, but without speaking about these matters to anyone else, one may begin to recover the child-state. There is a holy simplicity in being like a little child, and a tremendous protection from interference with one's inner life by ignoramuses in the world. In time, under karma, as one becomes wedded to a life of meditation, service and consecration, one will become prepared for the linking of the Eighth to the Ninth Creation, the union of *Manas* and *Buddhi* in the presence of the *Paramatman*.

> Learn now that there is no cure for desire, no cure for the love of reward, no cure for the misery of longing, save in the fixing of the sight and hearing upon that which is invisible and soundless. Begin even now to practise it, and so a thousand serpents will be kept from your path.
>
> Live in the eternal.
>
> The operations of the actual laws of Karma are not to be studied until the disciple has reached the point at which they no longer affect himself. The initiate has a right to demand the secrets of nature and to know the rules which govern human life. He obtains this right by having escaped from the limits of nature and by having freed himself from the rules which govern human life. He has become a recognized portion of the divine element, and is no longer affected by that which is temporary. He then obtains a knowledge of the laws which govern temporary conditions. Therefore you who desire to understand the laws of Karma, attempt first to free yourself from these laws; and this can only be done by fixing your attention on that which is unaffected by those laws.
>
> *Light on the Path*

Hermes, August 1982

SELF-MAGNETIZATION

Thus proceed the cycles of the septenary evolution, in Septennial nature; the Spiritual or divine; the psychic or semi-divine; the intellectual; the passional; the instinctual, or cognitional; the semi-corporeal; and the purely material or physical natures. All these evolve and progress cyclically, passing from one into another, in a double, centrifugal and centripetal way, one in their ultimate essence, seven in their aspects.... Thus far, for individual, human, sentient, animal and vegetable life, each the microcosm of its higher macrocosm. The same for the Universe, which manifests periodically, for purposes of the collective progress of the countless lives, the outbreathings of the One Life; in order that through the Ever-Becoming, every cosmic atom in this infinite Universe, passing from the formless and the intangible, through the mixed natures of the semi-terrestrial, down to matter in full generation, and then back again, reascending at each new period higher and nearer the final goal; that each atom, we say, may reach through individual merits and efforts that plane where it re-becomes the one unconditioned ALL.

The Secret Doctrine, i 267–268

Throughout manifested nature and in all beings – human, animal, vegetable, mineral and elemental – there is a universally diffused magnetic field in which one common vital principle circulates that may be controlled by the perfected human will. Beyond the illusion of time produced by the succession of finite states of consciousness, every present moment of manifest life is both a summation of a series of moments that goes back into the night of time and the dawn of cosmic manifestation, and also an emanation from a single stream of consciousness, an immortal ray of Light that travels through a long journey over eighteen million years and stretches into future time. The emergence from past time and the entry into the future are illusory in so far as these alterations in awareness or modifications of mind only affect the elemental vestures. Made up of changing combinations of sentient lives, these enveloping vestures are involved in an ever-revolving motion under a universal law, which balances every outgoing and ingoing – the Great Breath. In every human soul there is an innate tropism, a natural propensity towards the Good at some level of self-persistence. Not a living being on earth lacks a germ of good, a spark of truth and a ray of supernal light. Nothing could survive in the realm of form apart from this essential element of universal light-energy which makes cohesion possible. But this same law of balance also decrees the dispersion of life-atoms, providing for decay and death as well as for birth and growth, and hence permits not only rebirth but also regeneration or retrogression.

The path leading to conscious immortality, to freedom from the grip of all-devouring Time, must necessarily involve a spiritual process of progressive self-regeneration; it is founded upon detachment from form, veneration of the universal sacrifice of life, and serene meditation upon the One Light beyond all manifestation. The Buddhas of Contemplation are constantly established in the pristine unmodified state of cosmic meditation. Krishna, the *Logos* incarnate, instructs Arjuna: "Out of a single portion of myself I create this entire universe and remain apart." This is the highest standpoint conceivable in cosmic evolution. It is a supreme state of freedom which is accessible only at the summit of enlightenment, attained by those Bodhisattvas who have become illumined beings in the fullest sense, capable of mastering all the vestures of incarnation and remaining in effortless attunement to the Great Breath, the Soundless Sound. Acting in time but abiding outside time, moving in space yet resting beyond all visible space, they remain in an Atmic state of eternal motion which is motionless in comparison with all modes of motion recognizable on the external planes of matter. This is the ultimate object of mystic meditation and continuous contemplation by the developing disciple who sits ready for *Dubjed* (Initiation). After a long period of preparatory discipline, the neophyte reaches repose wherein it is meaningful to ask whether, and in what sense, there is any essential difference between such fundamental conceptions as space, causality, time and motion. Are they merely conceptually interdependent facets of a single reality, or are they ontologically separate? To the ordinary mind they would seem to be separate because the familiar framework of cognition identifies a spatio-temporal context or sphere in which one is firmly focussed upon a single point of concentration. The mind would persistently seek to focus upon a seed-idea as the germ or cause of a new train of self-reproductive thought which might take root in the Tree of Life, and in successive lives of spiritual discipline the seed may sprout into the Tree of Immortality.

The disciplined mind could also become intensely aware of the rates and phases of breathing and soon discover that it is impossible to go from the in-breath to the out-breath, or from the out-breath to the in-breath, without a minimal pause or interval, some sort of *laya* point. Many a monk seeks to prolong the interval of stillness between inbreathing and outbreathing, or between outbreathing and inbreathing. At this stage the discursive mind notices that there are distinct differences of time intervals in varying contexts. With steadfast persistence in such a simple exercise, these differences become less important, especially when there is a decisive shift of attention from physical to mental breathing. A heightened concentration of awareness is possible when one can smoothly dissolve the seemingly discrete intervals between breathing in and breathing out. This can arouse the power of noetic discernment, giving a finer sense of the particularity of each moment, and sharpening the intensity of awareness. This will help in time to attain an assured sense of what is essential in every momentary experience, of the hidden core meaning in a humdrum day of familiar events and responses. There is that which is truly valuable in every context of human interaction, but the discerning soul can only learn from each day by rendering gentle service to all that lives. Within a limited sphere of duty – on a single day for a particular period of time while meeting other beings – one must pierce the veil of unconscious collective processes, which otherwise leave one a victim, more acted upon than acting, mentally passive rather than spiritually awake.

Buddhic insights are best understood in terms of the attempt to transcend all divisions, to go beyond every sense of separateness. It may be initially difficult to avoid the feeling that one is oneself, that one has a neighbour, that one is passing other human beings, that one meets *A* and *B* and *C* while at work. This is an illusion which is needed at a certain stage of differentiation but which must be transcended on the Path. The goal is first to see only rays of light in those who masquerade under different names and diverse forms, and then to go further: not only to see no differences but also to see oneself in each and every other person one encounters. This means projecting not one's lower self (that merely inverts the process), but one's truest Self. The aim is to see the best one knows in each and every human being, and also to recognize the best in each and every human being as present in oneself. This psychological process takes years of sustained self-training and self-correction, with concrete tests applied to the reflected ray which is involved in the many pairs of opposites – heat and cold, loss and gain, growth and decay, fame and ignominy, creation and destruction, and so on. These are all part of the ethical burden of incarnation, while one is alive and awake, and while one is moving in and through a world of many minds and hearts, lives and souls, each of whom is on a solitary pilgrimage. It is the longest journey for each and every human being, dateless and deathless: no landmarks are on the visible plane, but all are eternally enshrined within the tablets of the astral light and upon the records of *Akasha,* the fiery mist out of which the Golden Egg encircling the universe is constituted. Consubstantial with the universal *Hiranyagarbha,* there is that which is like a minute portion of it, and provides protection for each and every human being. It is largely potential, but may be activated during deep meditation, when one has abstracted from the physical body with its senses and organs, and from the reflected ray of the lower mind with its likes and dislikes, fears and hopes, hates and suspicions, its pride, conceit, delusion and illusion. All of these, endemic to the assemblage of lower lives, can be let go and the mind may be withdrawn to that still, motionless centre unmodified by colour, by limitation, by form, by change, by seeming movements of succession in time or coadunition in space. All of these could be transcended because one could bring consciousness to a still centre in the place between the eyes where the eternal motion of *Alaya-Akasha* becomes the alchemical elixir of life.

> Whatsoever quits the Laya State, becomes active life; it is drawn into the vortex of MOTION (the alchemical solvent of Life); Spirit and Matter are the two States of the ONE, which is neither Spirit nor Matter, both being the absolute life, latent.... Spirit is the first differentiation of (and in) SPACE; and Matter the first differentiation of Spirit. That, which is neither Spirit nor matter – that is IT – the Causeless CAUSE of Spirit and Matter, which are the Cause of Kosmos. And THAT we call the ONE LIFE or the Intra-Cosmic Breath.
>
> *The Secret Doctrine,* i 258

What is true of the phases and pauses of breathing is also true of the cycles and seasons of Nature, as well as the divisions of lifetimes. At every level of organization of the countless lives mirroring the One Life, unseen creators and destroyers are constantly engaged in a sort of combat. At the molecular level this may be seen in reference to the microbes and life-atoms which make up the vestures, and in their aggregate action give rise to the four phases of human life, comparable, according to Pythagoras, with the four seasons. Attentive observation of Nature reveals a function in her economy for each and every thing. There is a function for the sere and yellow leaf of autumn which must die when the chlorophyll has so saturated the leaf that the green has become a yellow-brown. It is a breaking-up – a function of Shiva – which allows its restoration to the mud of the earth so that all of those lives are released. They go into the non-manifest only to re-enter in new arrangements the realm of the manifest. The ceaseless activity in Nature is at all times constructive, requiring the disintegration and rebuilding of structures, expressing a distinct beauty in every one of the seasons. If one can experience through meditation the continuous process of construction, destruction and regeneration that persists throughout human life, one becomes much more willing to accept these different phases and their distinct characteristics in terms of the total economy of human life. Through the incarnation of the projected ray there is an impingement of the subtler vestures upon the astral and the physical. By the power of thought one can enable what is in the higher vestures to act magnetically upon the lower vestures. By mere reaction and emotion, one may intensify the obscuring reaction of the lower vestures upon the higher vestures.

This is the choice life continually affords to a human being. Either one chooses to become more deliberate and ideative by the magnetizing power of thought, functioning in terms of manifold cycles rather than the overall cycle of the gross astral, and so, by the power of higher thought, discovering and giving significance, beauty and meaning to life-atoms at each stage. Or one can merely be emotional, using language and thought to rationalize emotion, building up an ego and defending it, corroding the channels of connection between the higher and the lesser vestures till there is an atrophy of creative centres. After a point, the more one does this, the harder it is to gain the power of attention, to hold an idea, to become completely absorbed in a therapeutic teaching. Instead, through self-examination and meditation, one ought to learn to take advantage of the properties and powers of the higher which do not belong to the same cycles that work upon the lower vestures. So, to achieve a total renovation of the lower vestures from the standpoint of the immortal individuality will take many years. One must be willing to look back at seven, fourteen, twenty-one years of life and courageously acknowledge the chaotic patterns of so-called thinking and feeling which mauled, weakened and atrophied the constructive, creative and consecrating powers of the correlative faculty of *Manas* reflected in all these vestures. Without either being irresponsibly fatalistic, or delusively emotional, one must acknowledge that a thorough renewal requires many years of courageous effort. Damage done over a long time can have no instant solution. To succumb to the flattery that suggests otherwise is to deny oneself the opportunity to learn properly the alchemical art of self-regeneration.

Rather, one must resolve to spend a number of years establishing and strengthening countervailing tendencies, recognizing old tendencies when they come, and counteracting them with deft precision. Robert Crosbie suggested that as soon as one discerns a mood or tendency which is deleterious, one should immediately think of the opposite. Ineffectually thinking of the opposite, and being unable to do anything when the challenge has already come to full flower, is like refusing to treat a disease when its initial symptoms appear. It is precisely when a tendency from the past first registers in awareness that one must act calmly. Like wise soldiers in times of great crisis, one must become especially cool and exceptionally slow. One must find the correct countervailing mood; and until one ties the ailment and remedy together, it is hard to break up a mood. But if one makes the effort with total trust in the law of cycles, and does this sufficiently often, it will begin to happen naturally. Then it will wear away the old tendencies until they fall away, and a refreshed class of life-atoms will become a permanent component of one's vestures.

The metaphysical basis of this theurgic work of self-regeneration lies in the ultimate identity of all life, both in the physical realms studied by chemistry and physiology, and in the invisible realm of life-atoms:

The Occult doctrine is far more explicit. It says: Not only the chemical compounds are the same, but the same infinitesimal *invisible lives* compose the atoms of the bodies of the mountain and the daisy, of man and the ant, of the elephant, and of the tree which shelters him from the sun. Each particle – whether you call it organic or inorganic – *is a life*. Every atom and molecule in the Universe is both *life-giving* and *death-giving* to that form, inasmuch as it builds by aggregation universes and the ephemeral vehicles ready to receive the transmigrating soul, and as eternally destroys and changes the *forms* and expels those souls from their temporary abodes. It creates and kills; it is self-generating and self-destroying; it brings into being, and annihilates, that mystery of mysteries – the *living body* of man, animal, or plant, every second in time and space; and it generates equally life and death, beauty and ugliness, good and bad, and even the agreeable and disagreeable, the beneficent and maleficent sensations. It is that mysterious LIFE, represented collectively by countless myriads of lives, that follows in its own sporadic way, the hitherto incomprehensible law of Atavism.

The Secret Doctrine, i 261

There is an atavistic return to psychic tendencies of the past, as well as elements of physical heredity, and they go back over many lives, connecting with patterns over many generations. All of these are in the astral light, permeating the lower vestures so that any attempt to assign a single extraneous cause, or to blame them on other individuals in this life, would be unphilosophical. There are so many life-atoms involved in the vestures that every day through thought, breath and speech, one charges enough life-atoms to affect many lives. It is absurd to try, on the basis of some narrow span of illusory time, to blame all one's ills upon a single lifetime. One must, at some point, penetrate to the causal level, and mentally cleanse one's sense-perceptions. To understand how Manasic concentration of *Buddhi-Akasha* can purge and purify the lower vestures, one must grasp the correlative action of thought upon the fiery lives of the lower vestures as they alternate in their function of building and destroying:

The 'fiery lives' are the seventh and highest sub-division of the plane of matter, and correspond in the individual with the One Life of the Universe, though only on that plane. The microbes of science are the first and lowest sub-division on the second plane – that of material *prana* (or life). The physical body of man undergoes a complete change of structure every seven years, and its destruction and preservation are due to the alternate function of the fiery lives as 'destroyers' and 'builders'. They are 'builders' by sacrificing themselves in the form of vitality to restrain the destructive influence of the microbes, and, by supplying the microbes with what is necessary, they compel them under that restraint to build up the material body and its cells. They are 'destroyers' also when that restraint is removed and the microbes, unsupplied with vital constructive energy, are left to run riot as destructive *agents.* Thus, during the first half of a man's life (the first jive periods of seven years each) the 'fiery lives' are indirectly engaged in the process of building up man's material body; life is on the ascending scale, and the force is used in construction and increase.

The Secret Doctrine, i 262–263

Any individual who is magnetized through great ideas and benevolent currents of thought and feeling during that period should be so grateful that he cannot awaken on any single day without feeling this gratitude intensely. The ideal *chela* who is going to gain the elixir of life, wakes up daily with a virtually inexpressible awareness of the privilege to be able to breathe, when he has already contacted the Teachers of *Brahma Vach.* A person who experienced this gratitude in any significant degree in those early years is extremely fortunate; through constant gratitude one gives enormous strength to the subtler vesture of ideation. One is therefore ready in the subsequent period to put to proper use all that has been evolved. "After this period is passed the age of retrogression commences, and, the work of the 'fiery lives' exhausting their strength, the work of destruction and decrease also commences." On the physical plane, this is a reflection of what occurs on all planes and involves the subtlest energies. The subtler the energies, the more they are affected by whether the will, motive and impulse of thought and feeling are benevolent or malevolent, selfless or selfish. That is ultimately the only issue. Because people in general cannot handle this, metaphysically and mathematically, through meditation and ideation, they require a system of external ethics that puts a brake upon their selfish misuse of life-atoms. Because the body was given a certain name, because others acknowledged that there was a separate being, they were misled into thinking that one owns everything. In truth, one owns nothing.

It is an abnormal notion in human evolution that one owns anything at all. Not only is everything held in trust, but one is a Manasically individuated being chiefly for the sake of expressing gratitude. There is no higher reason. The sole purpose of human sound and speech is to be able to resonate with gratitude to the cosmic sound, *Nada Brahman.* By using the measure of gratitude, which is appropriate to the symmetrical ways of life of the civilization of the future, one can see the abnormality of a great deal of contemporary existence. One can also see how difficult it is to reverse these tendencies because people constantly contaminate the few grains of rice they receive from the Wisdom Religion with the muck and the mire of the shallow culture that surrounds them and suffocates their innate intuitions. Nonetheless, if they develop a genuine capacity to use the Teaching on a day-to-day basis, and if they are also willing to be patient and to work in terms of seven-year cycles, they can decisively amend their own patterns, structures and cycles, replacing former tendencies by new powers and new levels of creativity, continuity and choice. They can begin to benefit from painful construction (which takes place through lower destruction), endured with a selfless attitude of sacrifice, renunciation and detachment.

> When the 'Devourers' (in whom the men of science are invited to see, with some show of reason, atoms of the Fire-Mist, if they will, as the Occultist will offer no objection to this); when the 'Devourers,' we say, have differentiated 'the fire-atoms' by a peculiar process of segmentation, the latter become life-germs, which aggregate according to the laws of cohesion and affinity. Then the life-germs produce lives of another kind, which work on the structure of our globes.

> *The Secret Doctrine,* i 259

At the foundation of all the seven subdivisions, and corresponding to *Manas,* is *Akasha,* the fifth cosmic principle which is fiery, but not like fire on the physical plane. It is also watery, airy, but it is none of these as they are known in terms of ordinary conceptions of fire, water and air. *Akasha* is the very essence of higher *Manas,* hence of ideation and thought. Ideation is a sacred word, not to be confused with what people call thinking, which is really the mind chattering away. To ideate is to blend the energy of ideation and a universal truth. It is to moisten, to vivify, a universal truth by calmly and repeatedly dwelling upon that idea so that it becomes an abstract image or a matrix that can act upon the will through *Akasha*. Through abstract meditation the perfected will can guide the material correlates of *Akasha*, following a series which corresponds to the successive differentiations of the proto-elements underlying the various globes of the earth chain. Beginning with Fire and the fire-atoms in the First Round, these proceed through Air, Water and Earth in the succeeding Rounds. Since each of these elements is the source of the diverse properties of the subtler vestures behind the physical, all the globes and all the Rounds have their connections with different aspects of the human being. According to the ancient Commentaries on the *Stanzas of Dzyan: "It is through and from the radiations of the seven bodies of the seven orders of Dhyanis, that the seven discrete quantities (Elements), whose motion and harmonious Union produce the manifested Universe of Matter, are born."* H.P. Blavatsky points to the necessary nexus between these substantial elements and spiritual consciousness:

> Our physical light is the manifestation on our plane and the reflected radiance of the *Divine* Light emanating from the collective body of those who are called the 'LIGHTS' and the 'FLAMES.'

> *The Secret Doctrine*, i 259

A person who truly begins to understand the possibility of the process of alchemical transmutation inherent in incarnated life will set apart both time and space every day, as well as appropriate symbols and magnetic centres of association, with a continuous stream of creative ideation. This is difficult in the course of a crowded day in the presence of others; but one can sit alone at night and propel these divine ideas to act as living forces. If one adopts the proper mental posture – one of great reverence, gratitude and obeisance to all Divine Hierarchies – these forces will act infallibly. But the process is hard, unless one is genuinely grown up. Unless one has been taught gratitude as a child, seeing it practised by others, one will not understand the sacred idea of intelligent obedience. Knowing nothing about truly free will, and therefore living compulsively in terms of wants, a shadowy life becomes established which makes it difficult to summon pure mental images. One must assail the root of false identity, expose it as a lie, and let it all go. One must break it apart. It is especially important not to cooperate with those types of language that contaminate, corrupt and misuse spiritual truths, including mindless appeals to experience "for its own sake" and vain assertions of illusory free will that are merely popular forms of lunar game-playing. At some point, these will take their inevitable toll, and will weaken the capacity of the mind to focus Buddhic Light, blocking opportunities for self-regeneration.

Instead of consigning oneself to the captivity of psychological delusions and temporal illusions through moribund attachment to fleeting forms, one must renounce separative and self-limiting life. Then one can enjoy the pulse of universal life. When each day becomes a constant "thank you" to the entire human race, one takes one's true place in the human family. One recognizes that the human family, in some mysterious, unthanked, but also unobtrusive manner, has made it possible to breathe and to eat, to live and to sleep, to walk on this good earth. Meditation is a kind of thankfulness; and when it is thankful it is cool, like the "cold brightness" of the fire-atoms of the First Round, for it is freed altogether from the lie and lust of self. It is freed from any care for the shadow and from any attachment to the mask. By voiding altogether the personal self, by making it a zero, one enjoys living in and through all beings. Meditation becomes a "thank you", which lightens one's load, increases the light in the eyes, deepens the power of silence and changes the tone of one's voice. One acquires a cool appreciation of the human condition, of its poignancy and its pain, but also of its silent grandeur, its inward dignity, and its unscrutinized meaning.

Then one begins to recognize that manifested life is merely a participation in formation, preservation and destruction, the three aspects of the *OM*, the three *hypostases* of the manifesting spirit of the Supreme Spirit by which title Prithivi, the earth, greets Vishnu, the *Logos*. The earth as a whole engages in a daily greeting of Narayana, and this celebration of life is expressed in the endless re-enactment of the triune activity: firstly of formation, germination, creation, the giving of birth; secondly of preservation, support, stability and survival; and thirdly of destruction, dissolution, rearrangement, regeneration. Thus, at the hidden core of life is that which does not perish with manifested forms, *Achyuta,* the abstract Triad. When meditation has reached a certain point within the ever-expanding sphere of higher awareness, there is a recognition and reverence of the cosmic Triad which is incarnated in those who are enlightened. Then, there is an irreversible increase in the light of awareness of the invisible guardians of the human race. Humanity is an orphan; but there are those who guide and guard its destiny. As one becomes profoundly moved by the Great Sacrifice, one is able to make each day count more as a contribution in a life-count well lived. At the moment of death one will recognize that one has brought a golden thread of gratitude from the first moment of birth to a state that resembles death, but merely is a prelude to rebirth, a preface to the reassumption of one's true vesture wherein, self-consciously, one can return to the world to serve on behalf of all that breathes.

Hermes, March 1981

THE SEVEN DEADLY SINS

III. Non-Violence and Regeneration*

The seven deadly sins can be viewed independently of their historical and theological interpretations. They may be seen as an open-textured set of human actions, attitudes and dispositions related to each other through their common participation in an underlying spiritual condition of the soul. In particular, in a Gandhian perspective they may be seen as complex instances and ramifications of violence deriving from untruth. One may leave open the question whether all forms of violence are comprehended within the moral connotations of the seven deadly sins. Certainly, a broad and important range of ethically problematic action does arise through what we understand as pride, avarice, lust, anger, gluttony, envy and sloth. Each of these terms has a rich penumbra of meanings, and each at the core represents the obscuration of an essential aspect of human strength (or virtue, in the classical sense of the word). In a Spinozist analysis they are passions, passive reactions of the human being informed by inadequate ideas — a lack of fullness of spiritual vision of the wholeness of Nature, the wholeness of Man and the wholeness of God. In a Kantian sense they are all fallings off from the ideal of a purely good will. They are forms of moral self-contradiction, inherently non-universalizable, and therefore constituting corruptions of the soul's faculty of reason. In a Pauline sense they are failures of love, of charity and of sympathy. They display the lifelessness, coldness and cruelty that are inescapable so long as the soul lies bound in the coils of mortality and is unable to ascend through an intimate adoration of the divine — that in which we live, move and have our collective being.

All three of these themes — blinded vision, corruption of will and erosion of sympathy — are crucial to an understanding of contemporary

* Parts I and II – The Historical Context (I) and Sin and Violence (II) – can be found online at http://www.theosophytrust.org/rni_articles.php.

moral, psychological, spiritual and social violence, whether one considers the small circle of friends and family, the wider circle of the city and nation, or the great circle of the globe. These three tendencies are like powerful vectors flowing from the centre of one's nature and forming a kind of inverted constellation of force. Where there ought to be vision, strength and love, there is instead blindness, weakness and hatred — a sort of dwarfed and perverted caricature of human nature, a tragic realization of a Hobbesian view of man.

This condition is no doubt pervasive in modern civilization, which Gandhi compared to the South American *upas* tree, a maleficent tree that emanates noxious vapours, choking out life for miles around. But the crucial question is whether this is the natural and inevitable condition of humanity, or whether it is, as Spinoza, Kant, St. Paul and Shankaracharya would affirm, a superimposition upon underlying powers of wisdom, courage and love. The latter view, like its opposite, is unverifiable and therefore also unfalsifiable. Neither optimism nor pessimism about human nature can be given an unexceptionable warrant on narrowly empirical grounds. Yet as Plato observed in the *Republic,* it makes all the difference in the world whether we tell small children that Nature is inherently consistent with human good and also non-deceptive, or the reverse. We either encourage the child's sense of responsibility and natural capacity to learn, or we cripple them. Where there is a firm optimism about Humanity, Nature and History, there will be a lifelong inclination to learning and self-correction. No man or woman would willingly harbour in the heart an untruth, a falsehood, a lie about the most important things, since this would subvert at the core all one's attempts to realize any good in life. Paradoxically, the worst falsehood one could clutch to one's bosom would be the pessimistic doctrine that evil and ignorance are the inevitable moral condition of man. No matter how ugly the moral visage of humanity may seem in an age obsessed with murder, rapine and deceit, and terrified of mass self-annihilation through foolish or self-righteous misadventure — nevertheless, despair and doubt are the most disabling dangers. Perhaps this is why faith and hope are mentioned before charity, even though charity is greatest of all.

In a similar manner Gandhi displayed a marked reluctance to begin with an affirmation of the power of love and then to derive from it all other modes of human strength and goodness. Instead, he began like Plato with an affirmation of the centrality of the vision of truth in one's life and the necessity of unwavering adherence to the truth as one knows it in one's heart. Without this devotion to truth, one's life is worth nothing. It is like a vessel with no compass. It cannot lead one to any fair haven. Yet the Gandhian idea of truth is much more than any merely cognitive state of mind. It is first and foremost an ontological precondition. In Indian thought, *Sat* is absolute reality, beyond the realm of genesis and corruption. It is the ineffable ground of all truth and existence, the source both of differentiated subjectivity and objectivity. The *satya* in a human being is his or her relative and partial realization of the abstract ideal of Truth, what one might call the tap-root of one's true being. According to many cognate metaphors, the life of true Nature is stifled and choked out by a secondary and sporadic growth. In the *Bhagavad Gita* this is powerfully expressed in terms of the great *Ashwatha* tree of the world, growing downwards from its roots in heaven and branching out to fill all space with its mayavic or illusionary foliage. To reach wisdom, one must hew down this tree with the sharpened blade of discrimination. In Chaucer's *Parson's Tale* the whole assemblage of the seven deadly sins is seen as the trunk of a great tree from which ramify all the hosts of sinful acts. In either case, what is necessary is to cut this false growth at the root so that the true individual may flourish. The vision, strength and compassion needed to do this are themselves aspects of the higher life of humanity, and their awakening is the obverse of the extinction of spiritual ignorance, impotence and malice.

Like Gautama Buddha, Gandhi held that "Hatred ceaseth not by hatred but by love", and like Jesus Christ he held that the direct measure of one's love, and therefore truth, was in one's daily conduct in relation to others. One treats everyone with whom one comes in contact either with violence, or *himsa*, arising out of one's own untruth or *asatya*, or with *ahimsa*, non-violence, arising out of one's realization of truth or *satya*. There is no intermediate course, according to Gandhi, and thus human nature either sinks or soars at every moment. There is an earnestness to human life, a moral significance that is either sensed and seized through self-discipline, or allowed to slip away through the insidious influence of the elements of untruth in oneself.

This is an especially dynamic view of moral life, and whilst perhaps explaining in part the amazing intensity of Gandhi's own life, it also draws attention to the volatility of the various vices and virtues with which moral self-discipline is concerned. Every situation brings with it fresh opportunities for learning and new tests and trials in one's grasp of truth. What one may have understood yesterday is valuable but insufficient to meet the challenge of today. Gandhi, therefore, readily recognized that "sufficient unto the day is the evil thereof", and he often recited the invocation in Cardinal Newman's hymn, "Lead, kindly Light, one step enough for me."

This willingness to take an incremental view of moral growth while holding to the exacting universality of truth and non-violence as twin moral absolutes is the Gandhian key to progressive self-transformation rooted in self-transcendence. In this way, one avoids the Scylla of self-righteousness and the Charybdis of despair. No attainment can exhaust the potentiality of truth and non-violence. Hence, every realized good must point beyond itself. No failing can divest truth and non-violence of their vital relevance to the future. Hence, every misdeed must also point beyond itself. By holding to the possibility of progressive growth, and thereby recognizing the possibility of moral regression, one can avoid the static smugness of those who are too confident of their salvation, as well as the stagnant inertia of those who are too assured of their damnation. Either extreme extinguishes initiative. Unlike any conception of a fixed or homeostatic mean between two extremes, Gandhi sought a dialectical balance between theory and practice, ideal and act, which could release the energies of the soul and of truth itself. No doubt this vision of life is both exacting and elusive. But it holds the promise of the amelioration of human misery, transmitting hope and human dignity to the civilization of the future.

If the ontological core of *ahimsa* or non-violence is *satya* or truth, then the various forms of violence must be seen as varieties of untruth manifesting with differing degrees of intensity. Just as one can adopt the ideals of truth and non-violence at a minimal or mundane level and also at a maximal or mystical level, one will find that the moral afflictions of human nature have their grosser and subtler forms. One might exemplify truth and non-violence in certain limited contexts and in one's relations, while at the same time one may have far to go inwardly. This is perhaps what Gandhi meant by saying, when asked whether he had no vices, that he had no *visible* ones. Whilst anyone could overcome one or another of the seven deadly sins outwardly, this would be but a preparation for a more intensive internal struggle. This is only common sense, and it is also the essential teaching of every great tradition of spiritual training, such as that of Gautama Buddha and John of the Cross. Both warn against the subtle recrudescence of the sins awaiting the spiritual seeker. One is never safe until the diseases of the soul are removed at the root. It would clearly represent a tremendous improvement in human affairs to remove physical violence, especially rape, murder and warfare. But this advance means little if it is purchased at the price of a psychological reign of terror and the spiritual murder of souls. It is not so much that the contemporary theory of repression is wrong about human nature, which it is, but rather the reason that it is wrong: it is simply another case of treating the symptoms and not the disease. The roots of ignorance, egotism and attachment must be cut if the poisonous tree of deadly sins is to die and the tree of life is to spring up in its place.

Classically, pride signifies spiritual blindness, overweening self-concern, and arrogant disregard of others in the pursuit of one's own supposed good. Spinoza called pride a species of madness, thereby suggesting that it springs from a fundamentally delusive conception of one's own existence. The image of the tower as the isolated haunt of pride points to its divorce from reality. Pride is the opposite of the sagely posture portrayed in the *Bhagavad Gita,* wherein the wise man is said to be content in the Self through the Self — the universal *Atman.* Instead of this divine sufficiency and transcendent unity, the proud man is restlessness incarnate, holding forth against the world but also hopelessly entangled in snares of his own making. The story of Alexander and the Gordian knot is a parable of pride, and so too is Milton's study of *Samson Agonistes,* doomed to toil "eyeless in Gaza". In both cases, pride seizes upon seeming strength to undo the soul. Even the tragic grandeur of such failures has a magnetic attraction for the proud, a higher self-destructiveness or violence of the soul towards itself. According to John of the Cross, spiritual neophytes take pride in their fervour and diligence, taking on a new layer of false identity directly from their sincerest endeavours. This is known in Buddhist practice as the shadow of oneself outside the Path. To become fascinated by it is fatal to inner growth, since it involves turning away from the source of one's being — the metaphorical and noumenal inner light — towards the image cast by oneself on the field of one's awareness. As Patanjali stressed, the underlying ignorance or *avidya* gives rise to the false idea that the ephemeral non-self is the enduring Self. This false sense of identity is subject to myriad vicissitudes, lifted up and cast down by turns through attraction and aversion. Because of this involuted posture, the capacity of the will is subverted and the power of sympathy for others is blocked. What begins in a form of violence towards one's true Self results in an obsessive self-regard which sees others merely as means to one's own selfish ends. As a form of madness, pride is the root of self-destruction.

All the other deadly sins may be seen as arrayed around the core of pride, some related to its subjective and some to its objective manifestations, obscuring the powers of vision, strength and sympathy. Thus, one may think of avarice, anger and envy as a turning outwards of pride into the objective field. Avarice represents the ignorant attempt to compensate for the felt insufficiency of the false self through external goods. Anger represents the impotent assertion of the unregulated centrifugal force of desire turned outward by the ego into the hall of mirrors of the phenomenal world. Envy represents the loveless striving, contention and opposition of the separative personal will against the seeming otherness of other wills in the world. On the other side, lust, gluttony and sloth may be thought of as manifestations of pride turned inward upon the subjective field of awareness. Lust seeks to fill up the void in the centre of one's being that is due to the ignorance of the joy of awareness of supernal unity with a riot of subjective fantasies of pleasure. Gluttony represents the imbalanced operation of the centripetal force of desire turned inward into an all-consuming vortex. Sloth is the careless indifference of will even to one's own well-being, a perverse inattention to the health and purity of the soul, and a sick lovelessness towards oneself that is rooted in the corruption of the will through despair. In practice, of course, any such systematic conceptualization should function as an aid to reflection and a guide to thought. Nonetheless, it would be useful to trace out the specific relations of the deadly sins to non-violence according to this schema.

Ignorance of the true nature of things, for Plato and Jesus, for Spinoza and Gandhi, is the source of all the futile attempts to fill up life with one or another form of compensatory activity. When these pursuits focus upon external outlets, they involve the acquisition of objective possessions from a deceptive realm wherein to divide is definitely to take away. This striving after external goods is insatiable, since it is a pointless persistence in seeking spiritual fulfilment through material means. Thus, avarice inevitably draws the individual into recurrent conflicts with others. Socrates remarked, after depicting the origin of the luxurious society, that herein lay the cause of expropriation and warfare. Proudhon simply defined property as theft. Gandhi elaborated a similar conception by extolling the virtues of *asteya,* non-stealing, and *aparigraha,* non-possession, as essential to the votary of non-violence. His own individual stance towards personal possessions is well known, but he also put forth a subtle theory of trusteeship for all external goods as an ethically superior alternative to the violence of aggressive capitalism as well as militant communism. When this ontological and psychological sense of deficiency is internalized, there is a futile effort to compensate for it through subjective claims and ideological propaganda. This quest for gross or subtle pleasures is, as contemporary psychology has discovered, extremely malleable and elusive, and is able to adjust itself internally to virtually any external conditions.

Pleasure and pain are not simple terms with stable referents, but amount to a pair of concepts convertible in denotation, depending upon circumstances. In all cases, however, whether one is caught in the attractive or repulsive side of the effort to compensate for a sense of non-being, the direction of attention is away from the centre and towards the elusive focus of desire. For Gandhi, the letting go of all these lustings and longings involved the practice of *brahmacharya,* a term that certainly includes chastity in the ordinary sense, but also means the pursuit of *Brahman,* identical with *Sat,* with one's whole being. True inward chastity is full devotion to the truth, and therefore essential if one is to release the active energy or force of truth through *ahimsa.* According to Patanjali, true *brahmacharya* releases *virya,* inward strength, the strength needed to persevere in one's pursuit of the truth. This strength is vital in the face of the innumerable distractions and snares that trap the ego, annoying and disheartening it. Typically, anger and gluttony are seen as failures of self-control in the face of provocation from without or seduction from within. We sometimes speak of them as connected with sore spots and weak spots in our nature, certain points of vulnerability. They are like apertures through which energies violently rush out or rush in.

For Gandhi, anger and gluttony, *krodha* and *lobha,* are manifestations of a deceptive reliance upon that which is false. They are essentially opposed to true sovereignty and freedom of the will, *swaraj,* and also true self-reliance, *swadeshi.* Where there is reliance upon the truth, it is possible to release the non-violence of the brave and fearless. Where there is true freedom, there is joyous self-mastery. In their absence one will be beset by anger towards those who seem to threaten one's weakness or by a gluttonous craving for whatever seems to veil it from one's view. The oscillation between these two can itself be quite violent and extreme. As John of the Cross noted, anger at others, owing to their perceived virtues, is the reverse of an impatient ambition to see oneself as a saint. When anything happens to challenge the seductive image of one's own goodness that one has swallowed, this is quickly vented in indignation against the merits of others. At a grosser level, everyone is familiar with the infantile and impotent attitude which says, "If I cannot have it, none else can have it." Whether this is said of a plate of cookies or the entire world, the interplay of anger and gluttony is the same, though the degree and scope of violence involved may differ. Essentially, the forces of violent striking and grasping are substituted for the continuous and harmonious noetic energies of the spiritual will.

The strength of the will cannot be separated from the spiritual and moral texture of one's conception of oneself as an ego or individuality in the world. For Gandhi, the question of the ego resolved itself into two complementary ideals. The first involves the reduction of oneself to a zero or cipher. The second involves training oneself as a champion of truth in the world, an exemplar of heroic non-violence, a *satyagrahi.* Gandhi's conception of beatitude is not a state of exile or stoic aloofness, but rather of incessant striving on behalf of universal welfare, *sarvodaya.* At every point, there are unexpected opportunities for service to others and for relieving their spiritual distress. It is through humility, tolerance, and a willingness to work for the welfare of others that the constructive force of *ahimsa,* or love, is released. To abolish the separative ego is like removing an obscuring disc in front of the sun, allowing its beneficent light to stream forth. The absence of obscuration is not anything to be reified in and of itself, in contrast to the reality of the light released. But from the standpoint of the soul seeking to individuate and realize its true relation to the rest of humanity, the removal of this disc blocking the aperture of the inner light is the crucial task. Every thought of envy towards the light of others, and every trace of slothful indifference to the obscuration of the light within oneself, does violence to the life of the soul. It is perverse, as well as loveless, to deny the light of others. It is suicidal to deny one's own light or, what is the same, to insist that it be kept apart from that of others in the name of the separative ego. True individuation involves the universalization of the heart and the mind in what Spinoza called *amor Dei intellectualis,* the intellectual love of God, and what Jesus called the love of God with all one's soul, heart and mind. This is the existential prerequisite to realization of the concrete ability to love one's neighbour as oneself, as well as the Pauline apotheosis of the finest and fullest love.

Clearly, it is not possible categorically to compartmentalize all the vices, sins and misdeeds that arise out of ignorance and to sharply separate them from their effects upon one's strength of will and one's ability to sympathize with the lives of others. This is part of what is meant by saying that all the seven deadly sins arise through proud ignorance manifesting as egotistic violence. The root of the *Ashwatha* tree is not to be understood through any set of analytic terms derived from the phenomenal world. It can be known only by rising in consciousness to the noetic realm of pure ideation, sublime tranquillity and universal benevolence that is hidden deep within the heart of every man and woman alike. Then, descending again into the field of moral action *(Dharmakshetra),* one may use conceptual tools and categories, not for their own sake or for intellectual sport, but rather as practical tools in the tending, refining and purifying of one's habitual nature. One may see oneself as agitated by many modes and manifestations of violence, arrayed in terms of the seven deadly sins. But all of this, like the physician's diagnosis, is only for the sake of applying curative powers to the soul. Bringing forth all violent tendencies into the light of self-awareness is itself a great therapeutic.

In no case, however, should one allow oneself to become hypnotized by the essentially banal and boring assemblage of one's sins and vices. It is like the story Gautama Buddha told of the man wounded by a poisoned arrow. Instead of pulling it out, he succumbed while asking many questions about the arrow maker, the material of the shaft, the type of poison and the feathers with which the arrow was fletched. In thinking of the seven deadly sins in relation to non-violence, the emphasis should be upon the ability to awaken spiritual vision, to recover the lost virtues of the soul, and to release a current of healing sympathy and love towards all other human beings. This was always the focus and intent of Gandhi's life, and the basis of his indomitable goodwill to all. Rather than make one's failings, however portrayed, the immutable centre of one's metaphysical and psychological perspective, one should instead meditate upon the potential of the good, in oneself, in others and in Nature. Then, even if one cannot at once go forth to sin no more, one can at least go forth to sin less and less.

For Gandhi, however, non-violence or *ahimsa* is an infallible and immediately available means to the arduous task of cutting down the ever-expanding tree of sinfulness with the axe of selflessness in word and act, as well as in thought and feeling. *Ahimsa* becomes no less than the gateway towards *moksha* or emancipation from man-made illusion and delusion. Gandhi regarded the aim of human life as *moksha*, liberation from impure thought, and the total elimination of impure thought is possible only as a result of much *tapasya*. The utter extinction of egoism is *moksha* and he who has achieved this will be the very image of Truth or God. "Government over self is the truest *swaraj* (freedom); it is synonymous with *moksha* or salvation." He also said that "*ahimsa* means *moksha* and *moksha* is the realization of Truth". "The test of love is *tapasya* and *tapasya* means self-suffering. Self-realization is impossible without service of, and identification with, the poorest. The quest of Truth involves *tapas* — self-suffering, sometimes even unto death. *Satya* then requires the *tapas* of *ahimsa* and this means self-suffering and self-sacrifice in the midst of society . . . ."

Gandhi's interpretation of *moksha* as the full realization of Truth and his justification of *ahimsa* as an exercise in *tapas*, the self-suffering and service needed for the attainment of *satya*, gave traditional values a new meaning and a fresh relevance to politics and to society. In deriving *satya* and *ahimsa* from what were essentially religious notions he not only gave spiritual values a social significance but also infused into his political vocabulary an other-worldly flavor. His emphasis on suffering as an intrinsic good needed to secure the *summum bonum* is somewhat reminiscent of Kierkegaard's assertion of the concreteness of suffering men against the concept of man as an *animal rationale.* Kierkegaard held that as gold is purified in fire, so is the soul in suffering. Unlike passive and impotent suffering, active and meaningful anguish takes away the impure elements in human nature. It is always man himself that stands in his own way, who is too closely attached to the world, to the environment, to circumstances, to external relationships, so that he is not able to come to himself, come to rest, to have hope, "he is constantly too much turned outward, instead of being turned inward, hence everything he says is true only as an illusion of the senses". If a man has love beyond all measure, he has thereby been laboring for all. All the time he was laboring for his own sake to acquire love, he has been laboring for all others. "It is required of the sufferer that he call a halt to his erring thought, that he reflect what the goal is, that is to say, it is required of him to turn himself about . . . . The difference between man and man is whether they succeed or not in attaining it." *

Hermes, January 1986

---

* *The Moral and Political Thought of Mahatma Gandhi*, pp. 237-239.

SPIRITUAL WILL

The vital interrelationship of nature and of man, as well as the complex process of evolution and of history, is essentially the manifestation of unity in diversity. Man is a compact kingdom with manifold centres of energy that are microcosmic foci connected with macrocosmic influences. There is a fundamental logic to the vast unfolding from One Source through rays of light in myriad directions into numerous centres that are all held together by a single Fohatic force, an ordering principle of energy. The logic of emanation is the same for the cosmos and for man. The arcane teaching of the divine Hierarchies, of Dhyani Buddhas, of the three sets of Builders and of the mysterious *Lipika* conveys intimations of invisible, ever-present, noumenal patterns that underlie this immense universe of which every human being is an integral part. The ordered movement of the vast whole is also mirrored in the small, in all the atoms, and is paradigmatically present in the symmetries and asymmetries of the human form with its differentiated and specialized organs of perception and of action.

Modern man, burdened by irrelevant and chaotic cerebration, often fails to ask the critical, central questions: What does it mean to have a human form? Why does the face have seven orifices? What does it mean to have a hand with five fingers? Why is one finger called the index finger and what is the purpose of pointing in human life? What is the significance of the thumb and what is its connection with will and determination, which must be both strong and flexible? Can flexibility and fluidity be combined in human life in ways analogous to what is exemplified in the physical world by all the lunar hierarchies impressed with the intelligence that comes from higher planes? What is the function of the little finger, which is associated with Mercury? What is the connection between speech and this seemingly unimportant digit which is important for those who have skill in the use of hands, whether in instrumental music or in craftsmanship? When one is ready to ask questions of this kind, taking nothing for granted, then one can look at statues of the Buddha and of various gods in many traditions, where the placement of the hand is extraordinarily significant: whether it is pointing above, pointing below, whether it is extended outwards, whether it is in the form of an oblation or receiving an offering, or in the familiar *mudra* of the hand that blesses. What is the meaning of joining the thumb and the central finger, which is given great importance in ancient mystical texts?

The moment one begins to raise such innocent questions about the most evident aspects of human existence, it immediately becomes clear that pseudo-sophisticated people are prisoners of the false idea that they already know. And yet self-reliance and spontaneous trust are so scarce in the world of the half-educated. Many people are so lacking in elementary self-knowledge that when a person meets another, instead of a natural response of receptivity and trust, there is an entrenched bias engendered by fear and suspicion. This has been consolidated through the establishment of a Nietzschean conceptual framework in which all human relationships are viewed simply in terms of domination and being dominated. This obsessive standpoint drains human relationships of deeper content, of spiritual meaning and moral consciousness. All moral categories and considerations become irrelevant when one entirely focusses upon an ethically neutral and colourless conception of the will. To assume and act as if everything turns upon the master-slave relation is a major block to the development of self-consciousness, as Hegel recognized. Humanity has left behind its feverish preoccupation with false dominance in formal structures. The seventeenth and eighteenth centuries witnessed the emergence of a higher plateau of individual and collective self-consciousness. All men and women are the inheritors of the Enlightenment, with its unequivocal affirmation of the inalienable dignity of the individual, who can creatively relate to other human beings in meaningful dialogue and constructive cooperation.

Rooted in a simplistic but assertive mentality, dissolving all moral issues, the language of confrontation and of submission is irrelevant to the universal human condition and to the hierarchical complexity of nature. Any person with a modicum of thought who begins to ask questions about the marvellous intricacy and dynamic interrelationships of nature – questions about the sun and the stars, the trees and forests, the rivers and oceans, and above all about human growth – will readily recognize that no real understanding of the organic processes of nature can be properly expressed in terms of such jejune categories as dominance and submission. Nor can any meaningful truths about the archetypal relations between teachers and disciples, parents and children, friends and companions, be apprehended through the truncated notion of an amoral will. Human life is poetic, musical and poignant. It has an open texture, with recurrent rhythms, and it continuously participates in concurrent cycles. To know this is to recognize, when viewing the frail fabric of modern societies, that human evolution has not abrogated the primordial principles of mutuality and interdependence, but indeed abnormal human beings and societies have become alienated from their inner resources of true strength and warmth, trust and reciprocity. The Golden Rule remains universal in scope and significance. There is not a culture or portion of the human race, not an epoch in history, in which the Golden Rule was not understood. Without this awareness there would be no social survival, let alone its translation into the language of roles and obligations and into the logic of markets. Reciprocity is intrinsic to the human condition.

By rethinking fundamentally what it means to confer the potency of ideation upon primal facts such as the conscious use of the human hand, one can discard much muddled thinking which is the prolific parent of a vast progeny of distrustful, fearful, weak and wayward thoughts that are constantly tending in a downward direction. Spiritual will can be strengthened when a person meditates upon the cosmic activity which is partly conveyed through creation myths, and may be grasped metaphysically in terms of the abstract becoming more and more, yet only incompletely, concrete. There must be a firm recognition of the necessary gap – inherently unbridgeable – between the unconditioned and the conditioned, between noumenal light and its phenomenal reflections. For those who begin to sense this in the ever-changing world, it can help to initiate a revolution in their everyday relationships. The true occultist starts at the simple level of constant thoughtfulness and moves to a mode of awareness whereby he can effortlessly put himself into the position of another human being. It is the hallmark of spiritual maturity that one has no sense of psychological distance from another, that one can not only salute but also share the unspoken subjectivity of another human being. When a thoughtful person begins to look at others in this way, the need for involuntary karma and mere extensions to superficial human contact will be replaced by the inward capacity, through every opportunity that comes naturally, to discover the universal meaning of human evolution, the potential richness and actual limitations of human nature, and the shared *pathos* of the spiritual pilgrimage of humanity. As depth of awareness is gained, it is possible to educate one's perceptions and one's responses to the world, cleansing the mind and the heart, and releasing the spiritual will. One can cultivate a real taste for the rarefied altitudes of Himalayan heights whereupon sublime truths are experienced as noumenal realities.

The awakening of intuitive insight is an essential prerequisite to authentic participation in human life. Noetic awakening presupposes that one learns to take nothing for granted, and repeatedly re-creates a sense of wonder and openness. It is necessary to increase silence in relation to speech, contemplation in relation to action, and deliberation in relation to impetuous response. Living from within, each day becomes charged with rich significance and is a vital link in a continuous thread of creative ideation. So immense are the potentials of human consciousness that for a true *yogin* a single day is like an entire incarnation. When individuals truly kindle the spark of *Buddhi-Manas,* they can rapidly move away from the nether region of dark distrust and abject dependence, and actively think in terms of the high prerogatives and vast possibilities of human life. Through calm contemplation they can come closer to the highest energies in the cosmos. Through proper alignment with what is above and within, they readily perceive the world as a shadowy reflection of reality, and also see beyond fleeting images to the hidden core of what gives vitality and continuity to the stream of consciousness. The restoration of Buddhic perception gives a preliminary understanding of what it is like to become constitutionally incapable of distrust, delusion, cowardice and craving. The mental portrait of the self-governed Sage, who ever remains in effortless attunement to the parentless Source, becomes a transforming reality in daily life. One no longer inhabits the terrestrial region of time and space in which linger many deluded souls for whom one feels true compassion, but one ascends to the empyrean of divine ideation.

Noble resolves and self-binding commitments are accessible to the spiritual will that is allied with the active aspect of *Buddhi*, which is *Kundalini*. In the manifest world *Fohat* is cosmic electricity, which vitalizes everything and is the intelligent guiding force behind all combinations, permutations and separations which occur throughout all the kingdoms of nature. But in the unmanifest realm *Fohat* is pure consciousness, the energy of potential ideation. This plane of spiritual unity and volition cannot be approached except by intensely developing the power of abstraction. Suppose that a person starts simply with the difficult but necessary meditation upon the corpse. Every human being knows that one day the body will be stiff like a log of wood, and whether it is burnt or buried it will have already begun to disintegrate from what is arbitrarily called the moment of death, about which there is much uncertainty. When is that moment of death? Is it when the heart ceases to beat and the breathing stops, or is it when electrical activity in the brain subsides? Theosophically, there are further critical questions about the progressive withdrawal of the immortal monad from its different vestures. The astral that is bound up with the physical body must go with the disintegrating body because even for disintegration there must be an invisible basis of intelligence, provided by the gross astral. But there are other aspects of the astral that are connected with the departing principles. Profound meditation upon one's corpse and the moment of death can result in a critical distance and increasing freedom from personal anticipations about the coming weeks, months and years. If a person finds anything morbid in this meditation, it is because consciousness has become escapist, delusive and pleasure-oriented. But if one is ardently concerned with meaning and significance, with ethical considerations of right and wrong, with obligation and responsibility, then one may calmly and detachedly see the moment of death as the completion of a cycle of fulfilment of earthly duties and spiritual exercises.

It is necessary to move in thought far beyond this initial meditation upon death. One must think of oneself as having lived through and relinquished a wide range of mortal bodies, as having been through innumerable sets of experiences in many different contexts, enacting myriad roles. For the immortal soul the only significant question is whether one learnt anything deeply meaningful about the world and from any opportunities for the elevation of consciousness that it offered.

How many times was one able to come into contact with spiritual teachers, and in how many lives was one able to intuit something of the meaning of initiation? As one persists in such questions, one begins to live in and through other people, experiencing an intense interest in the human condition as a whole. Seeing the world through many eyes, one identifies with the standpoint of myriad souls. One begins to discover the secret of the *yogin* and the Adept: that the more one withdraws within, the more one can universalize one's own concern for the human race. By giving up the false idea that what is visible is necessarily more real than what is invisible, that one has more pressing obligations to those one sees than to those one does not see, one realizes that human evolution could not have continued, that people would not have planted trees for their descendants, without some awareness of the hidden basis of human solidarity. When one has attained some appreciation of this vital fact, it would be of great benefit to meditate upon the sacred Catechism in *The Secret Doctrine:*

> The Master is made to ask the pupil:
> 'Lift thy head, oh Lanoo; dost thou see one, or countless lights above thee, burning in the dark midnight sky?'
> 'I sense one Flame, oh Gurudeva, I see countless undetached sparks shining in it.'
> 'Thou sayest well. And now look around and into thyself. That light which burns inside thee, dost thou feel it different in anywise from the light that shines in thy Brother-men?'
> 'It is in no way different, though the prisoner is held in bondage by Karma, and though its outer garments delude the ignorant into saying, "Thy Soul and My Soul".'

> *The Secret Doctrine,* i 120

Any person who begins such meditations and persists in them will experience a tremendous cleansing preparatory to the re-education of the powers of perception and action. Eventually, one no more sees the world as the world sees itself, in terms of separation and contrast, dominance and distrust, dependence and change. Instead one learns to see the world in terms of the continuity behind the change, in terms of that which is deathless within that which is ever dying. One begins to sense the noumenal reality of divine ideation behind the flux of fleeting phenomena. When a person starts to think, feel and respond in the light of this transformed way of looking at the world, deliberately choosing ideas, lines of thought, self-reliant acts of service, feelings of compassion, benevolence and trust, then one's whole conception of reality is altered. Even the sense of being bound down by the *persona* begins to loosen up gradually.

Through this regenerative experience one comes to recognize that the motion that is visible is only a surface phenomenon and that the highest energy resides only where all external forces are gathered and withdrawn to a still centre. By the mystic power of ideation one has supersensuous insight and a much sharper sense of the universe as unitary. Until there is Buddhic awareness of the omnipresence and radical unity of unmanifest *Fohat*, there can be no truly free will and self-reliance, but only compulsive restlessness and passive reaction. Free will in the spiritual sense only begins when one enters into a realm of pure freedom from form, flux and change, and from the temporal succession of states of consciousness. This can be readily tested. If one feels that the first moment that one contacted the Divine Wisdom is *now*, then one is free, but if it seems years ago, then one is enslaved by the past. If one feels that one's moment of death is *now*, one is free, but if it seems to lurk in the future, one is mesmerized by change. When one can burst the artificial boundaries of past and future within the present moment, then one begins to experience the spiritual will that is free, powerful and beneficent, and which, because it is unbounded, can lend enormous courage and confidence to the deliberate choice of thoughts and the continuous direction of attention.

Where the attention or the eye of the Adept falls there is a tremendous intensification of noetic life-currents. There is an intimate relation between the Fohatic energies of ideation and attention focussed in the Eye of Shiva and the Kriyashaktic power of quickening spiritual and material life. In their self-training all disciples must progressively learn to master the power of attention preparatory to any real initiation. First, one has to learn to withhold attention, and one has to do it many times over until it becomes a totally natural process. Lowering one's eyes when going out into the world, holding one's tongue when in company, restraining one's hands from grasping at objects, the disciple learns by withdrawing and withholding attention how it is possible to choose a great idea out of the voidness and how to choose by acceptance what comes under karma in the world. There is nothing personal in this because through heightened awareness one sees that what is chosen at any given time is but one out of myriad possibilities. In this way one is not caught in the delusions resulting from a sensationalist fuss about events. Events do not have any such exaggerated meaning because one always sees that about which Gurudeva speaks – the one undivided Flame. One hears all the time that which is inaudible, like that which is in the fathomless depths of the ocean and in the farthest reaches of space, "the VOICE unbroken, that resounds throughout eternities, exempt from change, from sin exempt, the Seven Sounds in one, THE VOICE OF THE SILENCE".

Once one becomes a witness to the incredible ordering of life-atoms and a Buddhic perceiver of the immense possibilities they represent, they truly become one's pupils, friends and servants in the great work of universal evolution. Ultimately, one can even overcome the contrast between subjectivity and objectivity, between spirit and matter. Because people do not do this voluntarily, *Fohat* at one level makes incarnation possible, binding *Atma-Buddhi* to *Manas*. When *Manas* manifests as a man of mighty meditation, it becomes one with *Atman*, and *Buddhi* generates that subtle breath of silent Fohatic energy whereby one withdraws from all reflections of light into the empyrean of Divine Truth. The less one is caught up in the agitations of manifested *Fohat*, the more one feels the intensity of strength of the field of inaudible, unexpressed feeling-energy of *Atma-Buddhi* radiating from the eternal realm of *Sat*.

> This 'World of Truth' can be described only in the words of the Commentary as 'A bright star dropped from the heart of Eternity; the beacon of hope on whose Seven Rays hang the Seven Worlds of Being.' Truly so; since those are the Seven Lights whose reflections are the human immortal Monads – the *Atma*, or the irradiating Spirit of every creature of the human family.

> *The Secret Doctrine*, i 120

Hermes, July 1980

AQUARIAN SPIRITUALITY

*It is argued that the Universal Evolution, otherwise, the gradual
development of species in all the kingdoms of nature, works by uniform
laws. This is admitted, and the law enforced far more strictly in Esoteric
than in modern Science. But we are told also, that it is equally a law that
'development works from the less to the more perfect, and from the simpler
to the more complicated, by incessant changes, small in themselves, but
constantly accumulating in the required direction.' . . . Esoteric Science
agrees with it, but adds that this law applies only to what is known to it as
the Primary Creation – the evolution of worlds from primordial atoms, and
the pre-primordial ATOM, at the first differentiation of the former; and that
during the period of cyclic evolution in space and time, this law is limited
and works only in the lower kingdoms . . . . As the Hindu philosophy very
justly teaches, the 'Aniyamsam Aniyasam,' can be known only through false
notions. It is the 'many' that proceed from the ONE – the living spiritual
germs or centres of forces – each in a septenary form, which first generate,
and then give the PRIMARY IMPULSE to the law of evolution and gradual
slow development.*

The Secret Doctrine, ii 731-732

Viewed from the impersonal standpoint of collective Karma and
cyclic evolution, Nature suffers fools not unkindly but with compassion.
Nature will not indefinitely indulge or underwrite human folly, for
as Cicero observed, time destroys the speculations of man whilst it
confirms the judgement of Nature. Through cyclic opportunities,
Nature actually affords individuals innumerable occasions for the
clarification and purification of perception and intention. If human
judgement and design are to have adequate leverage on Nature, they
must have as their stable fulcrum an intuitive apprehension of law.
At the most fundamental level, human judgement and natural law
alike stand upon a common ground, a single transcendental source of
Being. It is only by rejecting all dualisms, mediaeval or modern, and
by refusing to absolutize polarities that the designs of men and the
differentiations of Nature may be brought into self-conscious harmony.

In the *Gupta Vidya,* the sacred and secret science, there is no cleavage between the aim of Self-knowledge *(Atma Vidya)* and the practical ideal of helping Nature and working on with her *(Ahimsa Yagna).* To the perfected will of the *yogin* of Time's circle *(Kalachakra),* Nature is the ally, pupil and servant. Fully comprehending that man is the key to the lock of Nature, the wise *yogin* finds no intrinsic tension between obeisance to the judgement of Nature in Time and obedience to Shiva, the good gardener of Nature in Eternity.

This philosophic fusion of science and religion, of *vidya* and *dharma,* is essential to the structure of the Aquarian civilization of the future and enshrined in the axiom that there is no religion higher than Truth. In accordance with this evolutionary programme and in tune with the Avataric vibration of the age, the Brotherhood of Bodhisattvas has actively sought to dispel the delusive dichotomy between science and religion. Krishna conveyed the beautiful synthesis of *jnana* and *bhakti* in his classic portrait of the Self-governed Sage in the *Bhagavad Gita.* Spiritual teachers have repeatedly warned against the degrading effects upon the mind-principle of ahankaric greed and atavistic fear working through materialism and superstition. From the therapeutic standpoint of the ancient Rishis, the murky ferment of the twentieth century is not to be viewed as a creative tension between two viable cultures – the one religious and traditional, the other modern and scientific. Rather, it is to be seen as the ignorant and schizophrenic clash of two largely moribund inversions of authentic culture. Neither secular religion, with its crude demonolatry and selfish salvationism, nor materialistic science, with its cowardly conformity and slavish hedonism, still less the mutual recriminations and denunciations of one by the other, can offer human beings an assured basis for fulfilment and growth. Just as two wrongs do not make a right, no compound of these costly inversions can rectify the malaise of modern civilization. Neither fight nor flight nor unholy alliance can correct the deficiencies of two warring schemes of thought that do little justice to Man or Nature.

In order to participate freely in the regenerative, not the destructive, tendencies of the Aquarian Age, one must recognize that true religion and science do not need to be rescued from contemporary chaos by messianic crusaders. On the contrary, creative individuals must learn to cultivate moral courage and cool magnanimity so that they may plumb the depths of pure science and true religion within themselves. This cannot be done without assuming some degree of responsibility for the intense karmic precipitations during the present period of rapid transition. Without self-confidence based upon inviolable integrity, the bewildered individual will regrettably fall prey to the contagion of despairing diagnoses, sanctimonious effusions and evasive rationalizations offered by self-appointed pundits and critics alike. No shallow conceit, cynical or complacent, can substitute for the mental discernment and spiritual strength required of pathfinders in the Aquarian Age. Rather than sitting in idle judgement upon contemporary history and humanity, much less the Avatar, wise individuals will seek to insert themselves into the tremendous rethinking initiated by scattered pioneers in regard to the essential core of Man and Nature and the vital relationship between them. If through earnestness, simplicity and *dianoia* one can radically revise one's conception of Nature and Man, then one may powerfully assist that silent revolution and subtle healing taking place today behind the clutter of competing slogans and chaotic events.

As individuals increasingly recognize that the faults which bedevil them lie in themselves and not in the stars, they will progressively discern the Aquarian design woven in the heavens. Through the religion of renunciation of the personal self and the science of Buddhic correlation, one can begin the difficult ascent in consciousness towards comprehension of the mysteries of heaven and earth.

> As above, so below. Sidereal phenomena, and the behaviour of the celestial bodies in the heavens, were taken as a model, and the plan was carried out below, on earth. Thus, space, in its abstract sense, was called 'the realm of divine knowledge,' and by the *Chaldees* or Initiates *Ab Soo*, the habitat...of knowledge, because it is in space that dwell the intelligent Powers which *invisibly* rule the Universe.
>
> *The Secret Doctrine*, ii 502

Conceptions of space have varied significantly over the centuries, depending largely upon cognate conceptions of time, matter and energy. The arcane conception of space as at once an infinite void and an invisible *plenum*, replete with intelligence, offers a profound challenge not only to post-Einsteinian science but also to post-Gandhian religion. It demands an entirely fresh view of causality and consciousness, of activity and time. From the standpoint of contemporary physics, any object, including the human form, is almost entirely empty space devoid of anything that might be considered matter. Even without studying particle physics, perceptive individuals are prepared to accept that if they could visualize what an X-ray would show, they would find that only about one quadrillionth of any object is constituted of a few particles and that all the rest is seemingly empty space. Similarly, if they could visualize what various detectors operating over the visible and invisible spectrum reveal, they would find that every point in space is the intersection of myriad vibrating fields of energy. Again, if one were prepared to penetrate beneath the surface of personal and collective habits and institutions, through the discerning power of the disciplined conscience and awakened intuition, one would find an array of Monadic individuals suspended like stars in the boundless void of the unmanifest. To the resonant heart, this immense void would reveal itself as alive at every point with the vibration of the Great Breath in its complex rhythmic differentiations. Through such reflection one may recognize that the seeming solidity of things is mayavic. Their surfaces and contours as they appear to the physical senses and the perception of the psyche are enormously deceptive and strangely confining. By using the mind's eye one can come to see that what is seemingly full is void and that what is seemingly void is extremely full of Atma-Buddhi-Manasic or noumenal aspects of invisible atoms.

The term 'atom' itself conveys a wide range of meanings in ancient philosophy, including that connotation which has indelibly impressed itself upon the consciousness of the twentieth century. The Greek root of the term 'atom' literally means 'uncuttable', 'indivisible' or 'individual' and corresponds to the Sanskrit term *anu*. In its most metaphysical sense *anu* is the *Aniyamsam Aniyasam*, the smallest of the small, which is also the greatest of the great, equivalent to SPACE and a pointer to *Parabrahm*. In another sense, *anu* is the absolute Motion or eternal vibration of the Great Breath differentiated in the primordial manifested ATOM, equivalent to Brahmâ. Neither in the pregenetic or primogenetic states is *anu* subject to multiplication or division. The first plurality of atoms arose with the pristine differentiation of the sevenfold Dhyani-energies in the *Mahatattwa* creation, which was in turn followed by further hierarchies of atoms in the succeeding two creations. The meanings of the term 'atoms' as applied to the first three creations refer to spiritual and formless realities, including the use of the term to designate Atma-Buddhic Monads. Beginning with the fourth, or *mukhya,* creation, sometimes called the *primary creation* because it is the first of a series of four creations connected with material form, the term 'atom' has a new series of meanings pertaining to the germinal centres of the elemental, mineral, plant and animal kingdoms. The term 'atom' used in the customary physical sense applies to the extreme degree of differentiation in this series. Just as the infinite points of differentiated spaces are inseparable from the One Point that is the indivisible sum total of boundless Space, the living atoms of every plane are indivisible from *anu* – the ONE LIFE – and all resound to the fiery vibration of its eternal Motion.

To grasp the noetic significance of the existence of atoms, it is helpful to compare the atom with the molecule. The term 'molecule' literally means 'that which is ponderable or massive', and refers in chemistry to the smallest unit of a substance displaying fixed chemical properties. Typically, molecules are complex compound entities produced and altered through processes of action and reaction. From the standpoint of meta-chemistry, atomic energies derive from the indivisible unity of the One Life, whilst molecular actions stem from the interplay of vital though secondary emanations. The same facts viewed from the standpoint of meta-psychology lead to the distinction between the noetic action of *Buddhi-Manas,* which draws upon the light of the one indivisible *Atman,* and the psychic action of the lower *Manas,* which is inherently restricted by the polarities of the *kama* principle to residual effects upon the composite mortal vestures. In essence, the difference between atoms and molecules, between noetic and psychic action, is the difference between seeing from within without and seeing only from outside. Hence, people often come closest to the core of things when they shut their sense-organs, which is where concentration and meditation begin.

By withdrawing, closing the eyes, closing the mouth, shutting the ears, by turning off the tumult of the mayavic kaleidoscope of the phenomenal world, one can draw within and enter into what initially seems like chaotic darkness. By persisting, one becomes more familiar with what may be called the photosphere surrounding every human being, the field of light-energies that operates beneath the visible world of form. As one becomes more sensitive to these indwelling energies, one can begin to apprehend that there are vast arrays of intelligent powers which invisibly rule the universe. What people ordinarily call intelligence is only the most superficial and limited aspect of a single distributed intelligence, working through cosmic hierarchies, and originating in a common transcendental source.

Something of the sacred potency and designing power of divine intelligence was broadly familiar to people in the nineteenth century, though in a distorted form due to the inversions of sectarian religion. Given that the impersonal nature of that intelligence can only be comprehended through the noetic faculties consubstantial with that intelligence, it is scarcely surprising that H.P. Blavatsky took such care to provide accounts of cosmogenesis and anthropogenesis free from any taint of the notion of a personal god or creator. It is also suggestive, given the transcendental and *arupa* nature of the intelligence within cyclic evolution, that she so firmly repudiated the materialist conception of a blind, chemically-driven evolution. What was perhaps not so clear in the nineteenth century was her profound reason for pointing to the essential distinction between the atomic and molecular character of noetic and psychic action.

Humanity now finds itself at a fortunate moment; much of what is happening in the sciences is reminiscent of what was once called occultism. If one reads any first-rate book on the frontiers of science, one is at times encountering the threshold of occultism. As H.P. Blavatsky prophesied, physics and chemistry have begun to penetrate the realm of atomic vibrations underlying the gross physical design of objects, and have partially revealed the complex matrix of differentiations of the ATOM, as they apply to the lowest planes. Whilst these sciences have not yet moved closer towards the metaphysically indivisible ATOM, they have clearly demonstrated that all physical structure is the superficial derivative of more fundamental differentiations. Although much of the systematic elaboration of these scientific insights has taken place since the commencement of the Aquarian Age in 1902, the critical moves were already made between 1895 and 1902, when there was a crucial intersection of cycles involving the close of the first five thousand years of *Kali Yuga* and the six-hundred-year cycle inaugurated by Tsong-Kha-Pa, as well as the zodiacal transition.

Towards the close of the nineteenth century, chemistry and physics found themselves up against myriad dead ends. Drawing upon Dalton's hypothesis of units of chemical type distinguishable by weight called atoms (1803), and Avogadro's hypothesis that standard volumes of gases of different compounds contain equal numbers of molecules (1811), chemistry was engaged in filling in the periodic table of the elements proposed by Mendeleev (1869). Having mastered the arts of ballistics and bridge-building, physics was winding down the practical elaboration of Oersted's discovery of the relation between electricity and magnetism (1819), and its elegant mathematical formulation in the electromagnetic field theory of light-waves developed by Maxwell (1861). Late in the century a noted lecturer even assured the British Association that physics was a closed and completed field, and that young men ought to go elsewhere to find challenging careers. All of this changed abruptly in 1895, when Röntgen discovered an entirely unaccountable type of radiant energy, the enigmatic X-rays. In 1896 Becquerel was able to localize this internal fire of matter to the substance uranium, which was then called 'radioactive'. Following some researches of Crookes, Thomson discovered the 'electron' in 1897, the unit charge of electricity, a genuine Fohatic entity on the physical plane. In 1898, the same year that the Curies discovered the existence and radioactivity of radium, Rutherford was able to identify two of the Fohatic messengers of radioactivity – alpha particles and beta particles – the latter turning out to be identical with Thomson's electrons. In 1899 the Curies made the fateful discovery that radioactivity could be artificially induced. Pursuing quite different lines of thought, Planck proposed in 1900 that all physical change takes place via discrete units or quanta of action. In 1902 Rutherford and Soddy developed the modern alchemical hypothesis that radioactivity was both the result and the cause of the transmutation of atoms from one chemical element to another.

Drawing upon these critical discoveries and insights, the entire face of the sciences has been transformed in the first decades of the Aquarian

Age, and the new alchemists have had more than a little impact upon society. In 1905 an unknown Swiss patent clerk wrote a series of articles synthesizing the discoveries of the time with such remarkable breadth, clarity and force that his name has become virtually synonymous with the atomic age. Within twelve months Albert Einstein demonstrated several revolutionary propositions.

First of all, he showed that all electromagnetic radiations, including light, were composed of packets or quanta of energy, or 'photons', thus resolving the nineteenth century wave-particle debate about the nature of light. This proposal corresponds to the principle that *Buddhi*, the light of the *Atman*, is both indiscrete in relation to the eternal motion of the Great Breath and discrete in relation to the mayavic field of vibratory Monadic emanations.

Secondly, he showed that physical energy and mass are mutually equivalent and interconvertible through a parametric matrix defined by the velocity of physical light. This corresponds to the occult axiom that spirit and matter constitute a double stream starting from the neutral centre of Being as *Daiviprakriti*, the Light of the *Logos*.

Thirdly, he showed that all physical measurements of distance, speed and time undertaken by observers moving relative to each other are transformed through a parametric conversion matrix defined by the velocity of physical light when passing from the frame of reference of one observer to that of another. This proposal, which put to rest the search for a crude material aether by joining light to the metric foundations of all physical phenomena, has its occult correspondence in the triadic unity of pre-cosmic Space, Motion and Duration on the plane of *Aether-Akasha*, mirrored in all relations and phenomena on the lower planes.

Fourthly, he showed the equivalence of the long-observed Brownian motion of small particles with a set of statistical laws of motion of molecules and atoms he derived from thermodynamics, thus developing the basis of the first empirical confirmation of the physical existence of atoms and molecules. This proposal, ending the nineteenth century career of atoms and molecules as merely rationalistic entified abstractions, has occult correspondences to the principles of distributive and collective Karma.

Since 1905 there has been a virtual explosion in the sciences, as successive dimensions and orders of microcosmic and macrocosmic nature have been explored. In 1911 Rutherford discovered the nuclear structure of physical atoms; in 1913 Bohr proposed the quantum theory governing that structure; and in 1913 and 1914, respectively, Soddy and Moseley rewrote the periodic table of the elements in terms of modern atomic theory, thus resuscitating the entire field of chemistry. In 1915 Einstein himself proposed an as yet controversial, and only partially elaborated or confirmed, theoretical synthesis of space, duration, motion and force. This line of enquiry, if perfected, would correspond to the occult correlation of the differentiations of *Fohat* as it "scatters the Atoms" on the plane of *Alaya-Akasha*. In 1927 Heisenberg formulated the 'uncertainty principle' concerning the limits of observation of location and motion, a principle which is gradually compelling scientists to include consciousness in their theories of atomic and subatomic physical nature. By 1953 the labours of many biochemists culminated in the work of Crick and Watson, revealing the double helix of DNA, thus joining atomic and molecular theory to the design of living forms.

Whilst the dawn of the Aquarian Age is as yet far from witnessing the emergence of a complete scientific theory integrating the One Life and the primordial ATOM with myriad lives and atoms on seven planes, it has certainly relinquished the stolid, compartmentalized conceptions of the late Piscean Age. People have now become far more aware that the invisible universe is an extremely intelligent universe; someone well trained in contemporary science is much more aware of the spiritual than those caught up in sectarian religion. Sectarians are often weak in theory owing to their weak wills in practice, and often are merely in search of alibis. But those who deeply ponder upon the cosmos with the aid of physics, biology and chemistry, and who show some philosophical or metaphysical imagination, can readily accommodate the idea that behind the sloganistic term 'vibes' is an exact knowledge governed by precise laws. Given this holistic standpoint, what is the necessary connection between directing these forces and that true obedience to Nature envisaged by the *Gupta Vidya?* This question became ominous and acute for human society on January 22, 1939, because on that day the uranium atom was split by Hahn and

Strassman. Significantly, on the same day in 1561 Francis Bacon, one of the forefathers of modern science, was born.

Bacon's vital insight that "Knowledge is power" echoed the ancient Eastern view that knowledge can liberate men. This perspective made possible the enormous adventure of modern science and the correlative spread of universal education. Before Bacon, despite Renaissance affirmations of the dignity of man, few people were able to read or write. Even the Bible was a closed book to human beings who lacked sufficient knowledge of the language to appreciate religious texts. In the Elizabethan Age, at the turn of the sixteenth century, people had to look to Nature for learning; hence the Shakespearean affirmation that there are "books in the running brooks, sermons in stones", and hence, too, his reference to the "book and volume of my brain". Like the Renaissance, Shakespeare recognized the old Pythagorean and Hermetic conception of man as a microcosm of the macrocosm. If one studies the Elizabethan world, especially in E.M. Tillyard's enthralling book, one finds an extraordinary collection of reincarnated Pythagoreans inhabiting and regenerating a society in which it was the most natural thing to draw from the many great metaphors of the Mahatmic Sage of Samos.

Troilus and Cressida, in one of the noblest passages Shakespeare ever penned, portrays the Pythagorean conception of cosmic hierarchies and their continual relevance to human society. Speaking of the precise degree and placement of everything in Nature, Ulysses affirms that each thing has a function, which stands in relation to that which is above it, that which is beyond it, that which is below it, and that which is beside it.

> The heavens themselves, the planets, and this centre
> Observe degree, priority, and place,
> Insisture, course, proportion, season, form,
> Office, and custom, in all line of order;
> And therefore is the glorious planet Sol
> In noble eminence enthron'd and spher'd
> Amidst the other; whose med'cinable eye
> Corrects the ill aspects of planets evil,
> And posts, like the commandment of a king,
> Sans check to good and bad. But when the planets

In evil mixture to disorder wander,
What plagues and what portents, what mutiny!
What raging of the sea, shaking of earth!
Commotion in the winds! frights, changes, horrors,
Divert and crack, rend and deracinate
The unity and married calm of states
Quite from their fixture! O, when degree is shak'd,
Which is the ladder of all high designs,
The enterprise is sick. How could communities,
Degrees in schools, and brotherhoods in cities,
Peaceful commerce from dividable shores,
The primogenitive and due of birth,
Prerogative of age, crowns, sceptres, laurels,
But by degree, stand in authentic place?

Troilus and Cressida, Act I, Scene iii

This was also the time of the great seafaring adventurers of Europe, with rich memories of Marco Polo's fascinating stories about customs and cultures prevalent in different parts of the Eastern world. It was truly a period of considerable excitement and curiosity about the cultures of humanity and the vast unknown potential and mystery of Nature itself. By the seventeenth century the alchemical and Rosicrucian traditions of mysticism and magic had laid the basis for what is now called modern technology, with its manifold implications in the social, economic and political arenas. The leading scientists of the nineteenth century showed a keen interest in patterns in Nature, and in the connections between them. For it is only by making connections between otherwise isolated and disparate events, and by discerning patterns, that synthesized conceptions of natural order may be developed. Creative individuals tend to think in terms of wholes, in terms of integrated and patterned arrangements of parts. Such holistic thinking is important to painters and poets and spontaneous amongst little children. But it is also central to the acquisition of that knowledge of Nature which, Bacon declared, is equivalent to power. Because the capacity to discern the patterns of Nature is the prerequisite for enlisting the forces of Nature on behalf of human designs, there is an inevitable moral component in every acquisition and use of knowledge.

Bacon, a mysterious man, acknowledged this when he said, "We cannot command Nature except by obeying her."

In effect he showed a concern that there was already a certain presumption towards Nature which would later turn out to be exceedingly costly. Men were seeing Nature in terms of the outmoded conceptions of the Christian church, going back to Augustine and Aquinas, as something dead, inert and wholly apart from the soul. By the eighteenth century, many associated Nature with the chaotic wilderness, and displayed a cultural preference for horticultural hybrids, hothouse growths and elaborate gardens designed by man. It is true that there can be a great beauty in gardens, particularly those of Chinese and Japanese design, wherein beauty and tranquillity are created by the simplest arrangement of stones and plants. Yet, this need not involve despising Nature. And if people in the eighteenth century came to dislike the wilderness because they were frightened by the ghosts and goblins they encountered on the Yorkshire moors, this can hardly excuse the terrible exploitation and desecration of Nature in the nineteenth and twentieth centuries in support of industrialism and technology. This is precisely the hubris of Thrasymachus, in the *Republic* of Plato, criticized by Socrates as showing an inferior intelligence and character, a missing sense of proportion, and an ultimately self-divisive and self-destructive vanity. This Atlantean obsession with the will to dominate completely inverts the principles of proportion, degree and design that govern the evolution of the organic vestures which human beings presently inhabit.

If human beings would prove themselves worthy of the divine apprehension and intelligence within themselves, they must learn to design not merely gardens, but societies and cultures which observe and obey divine proportion and degree. They must learn to awaken and apply the noetic intuitive faculty to the arrangement and rearrangement of communities considering the relationships of individuals not only with each other, but also with empty space. By synthesizing their awakening Buddhic intelligence with the universal intelligence of the One Life, they must learn to cherish the intimations of infinite possibilities contained within the minutest elements of space. Following the Pythagorean conception of the ether as some sort of fluidic substance involved in vortical motion and filled with whirling bubble-like spheres equivalent to atoms, they must come to see that the mathematical laws governing the arrangement of atoms in living forms are the expression of Divine Thought mirroring unmanifest Harmony or *Rta*.

It is not possible to perceive a seemingly opaque world of form as a transparent and luminous manifestation of the One Life without arousing the noetic faculty. Furthermore, it is not possible to awaken the noetic faculty without learning to command the elements of the kingdoms below the fourth plane and without gaining joyous obedience to the Divine Will. It is this combination of self-command and self-obedience which Socrates characterized as *sophrosyne*, the self-government of the soul by its superior element coupled with the consent of the inferior element. It is also the basis of preparation for discipleship and entry into the Path leading towards Initiation. It is also equivalent to the Gandhian conception of *swaraj* or self-rule based upon *swadeshi* or self-reliance, which is sought by the devotee of *satya* in his experiments with truth on behalf of universal welfare or *Lokasangraha*.

If only because human beings have now learnt that there is enough physical energy present in a toothpick to produce twenty-five million kilowatt-hours of electricity, they have reached a point in evolution where they must gain *swaraj* through experiments in the use of soul-force and moral power if they are not to forfeit the divine estate of being truly human. Gandhi's soul-force is equivalent to the atomic noetic force of *Buddhi,* and his idea of moral power is equivalent to the psychic or molecular force of *prana,* moral perception and vital energy. Gandhi demonstrated and taught the possibility of noetic force using psychic force on behalf of human brotherhood and universal welfare. As more and more people come to see that selfishness, invariably rooted in the dissociation of human vital energy from its origins in the Great Breath, is inevitably suicidal, they also begin to recognize that it is only through noetic self-command that there can be genuine self-respect. If they are perceptive, they will readily recognize that the perils and crises of the atomic age are a physical parable of a meta-psychological crisis. As the current of the Aquarian Age compels people to turn inward, the idea is spreading that it is not merely by changing the external environment, or by protesting what other people are doing, that a genuine improvement can be gained in collective human life. As Gandhi taught, the peril of our time arises from the abuse, misuse and neglect of soul-force. In Pythagorean terms, the evolutionary degree, and hence the authentic basis of self-respect, for each soul is to be found in the totality of its intentional relations with the entirety of Nature, both manifest and unmanifest.

The science of spirituality and the religion of responsibility are rooted in the metaphysics of the universe, and therefore have the complete support of cosmic will and design. Hence *The Voice of the Silence* instructs all those who would set themselves upon a secure foundation: "Give up thy life, if thou would'st live." Without a total renunciation of what one hitherto called living – which is really drifting in some sort of psychic daydream – one cannot cultivate the heightened spiritual attention and awareness needed for adequate participation in the Aquarian civilization of the future. The *Gupta Vidya* affirms that it is possible for human beings to cooperate with the invisible world self-consciously and to find meaning and dignity through obedience to the Law of Karma, obedience to the Will of the Spirit, obeisance to the Divine Order, obedience to the *Logos* in the cosmos and the God in man. The test of integrity in this inward search is effortless lightness and joyous control.

In the Aquarian communities and secular monastic ashrams of the future, it will be possible by design to have both free play and also continuous recognition of the evolving patterns and possibilities of Nature. Emancipation from the tyranny of habit and the conscious insertion of spiritual will into one's life will enable men and women to take full advantage of the invisible elements within space, within their own rooms, their brains, their hearts, but also throughout the entire *plenum* of Nature. As they gain a sense of themselves as trustees of a mysterious set of living vestures composed of visible and invisible atoms and nourished by Nature's generous gift of the life-giving waters of Space, then, through gratitude, individuals will become more humane, and more worthy of the Aquarian design of *Civitas Humanum*, the City of Man.

Hermes, October 1982

AQUARIAN THERAPY

To suffer woes which Hope thinks infinite;
To forgive wrongs darker than death or night;
To defy Power, which seems omnipotent;
To love, and hear; to hope till Hope creates
From its own wreck the thing it contemplates;
Neither to change, nor falter, nor repent;
This, like thy glory, Titan, is to be
Good, great and joyous, beautiful and free;
This is alone Life, Joy, Empire, and Victory.

Percy Bysshe Shelley

In the Aquarian Age the mental fire of devotion and sacrifice means purgation, and no substitute will serve. Human beings may seek authentic confidence in their own divine destiny – out of pain through experience, by sifting, by meditation, by mistakes and learning from them. In time they can therapeutically release within themselves that mental breath and spiritual fire where they always feel benevolent towards all, but where that benevolence is backed by depth of thought directed by a precise, luminous intelligence. This great challenge is partly what W.Q. Judge meant when he prophesied that the time will come when powers will be needed and pretensions will go for naught. It is a strange advantage that now there are so many swamis, lamas and gurus of every kind, on almost every street corner, because once and for all people will have to go behind and beyond labels, externals, forms, names, claims and containers of all kinds. They will have to discover the life-giving stream of wisdom that becomes a self-sustaining current, fertilizing the soil of the mind, and giving birth to creative ideas and beneficent impulses. They will have to learn to direct the power to act in new ways, with willing cooperation in a context larger than themselves, and on behalf of a vision that is only dimly sensed. This is what Shelley suggested by pointing to the star,

The loftiest star of unascended heaven,
Pinnacled dim in the intense inane.

'Inane' in ordinary language means "foolish," "idiotic," "chaotic," "meaningless," and "incoherent," but 'inane' in the archaic language of spiritual alchemy refers to something beyond primordial chaos. It is the original ground of creativity in the whole of nature, latent in the unmanifest realm. It is also specifically called a liquid fire, the word *aqua* being an alchemical term. Therefore, the idea of Aquarius the Water-Bringer, even at the simplest level – bringing water to a parched soil, to thirsty human beings, and connected with rain coming down from heaven – has timeless beauty to it. Everyone knows how sweet the earth smells after a generous shower of rain. Each can appreciate that it is universal and innate to feel a natural gratitude when one's thirst is slaked by a glass of water extended by a brother. But these are mere reflections on the physical plane of something metaphysically quintessential. The ancient Egyptians depicted Aquarius as a serpent coiled in a spiral around a jar containing liquid fire. This image has reference to those who can tap the highest sources of primordial energy in invisible nature, and channel it, bring it down and apply it, as in the restoration of sap in a piece of dessicated wood by applying resin from a pine tree. They are able to do as much revitalizing as is allowed by forms that are, alas, nearly dead.

The sacred metaphor of fire is profound, whether applied to the fire of enthusiasm, the fire of devotion, the fire of intelligence, the fire of creativity, the fire that warms, the fire that glows, or to the fire that makes one see beyond to That – *TAT*. Anybody who has sat by a log fire and watched it for a long time has seen something extraordinary. Behind the leaping flames there is an invisible colour. What is seen on the outside is golden yellow but inside there is actually an electric blue. Through such analogies one begins to get more and more to the core of the hidden source of creativity in human beings. More significantly, the Great Teachers of *Gupta Vidya* hint that the noumenon of the Three-in-One – the inmost invisible Triad in every human being and the source of all thought, will and feeling – itself has an invisible central point in Akasa, the noumenon which is the very essence of spiritual fire.

If one is going to learn to kindle this fire, one has to make a beginning somewhere. Consider a person who is fortunate not to have much to unlearn and whose mind was not contaminated, either because the person did not take seriously pseudo-education, or sifted it all and started to think originally. Such a person does not need to make claims to know, but can get excited about a great idea, and can incarnate it by continually dwelling upon it. The idea of aspiration, the idea of harmony, the idea of solidarity in its deepest sense – any of the ideas that are the living germs of Aquarian therapeutics – can be put to use and made to light a fire. By intensely dwelling upon such an idea, a person can actually ignite a small spark which will be sustained by regular return to the thought, looking at it in different ways – from north, south, east and west, above and below, at least from six points of view – without becoming entranced by any false crystallization or rigid formulation. Through returning again and again to the main idea, a person can, in time, light up a radiant centre in the human constitution which may serve as a hooking point from which the person can go deeper and come closer to the noumenal. This can also be done in the realm of action. Sometimes one experiences an immense exhilaration from doing one thing crisply and cleanly, even if it be only taking a bath or sitting down to perform something very simple. To do it crisply, honestly and noetically brings about a perceptible release of silent self-respect.

Spiritual will has to do with true self-esteem, moral firmness and continuity of consciousness. If a person begins without self-esteem – because the person is mauled, extremely weak-willed, or is weighted down by the recurrent karma of incompletion and passively expects it to continue throughout life – the person will complete nothing. Everything seems fraught with failure. But suppose such a person is truly honest and still says, "There is some one thing on the basis of which I can respect myself. I can do it. It is the best I know." Such a person, as Kierkegaard showed in *Purity of Heart*, can one-pointedly will the good. Through the very attempt – not the planning, the anticipation, the calculation, and the anxiety, but just in the simple release of the will in the single act – the person can also come in time to light up the spark of self-confidence by acting in the name of something greater than the shrunken self.

The ideal way and the greatest mode of doing this, going back to the Golden Age of infant humanity in the presence of Divine Teachers, is devotion. This is the Gem of *Bodhi,* the hidden flame in the heart. When the mind is polluted, when the will is perverted, there is still somewhere a small spark of decency in the human heart. If its inaudible vibration were totally destroyed, the person would perish. Months before a person dies this silent sound ceases, the constant pulsation of the spiritual heart known in Sanskrit as the *Anahata,* the indestructible centre. There is a deathless core to the heart of every human being. There is a ceaseless if unheeded hope. Therefore anyone can respond to Shelley's vision in *Prometheus Unbound.* Despite all the most negative evidence, one can still go on. This is why even a tormented person who is about to take his life one day can still get up and make another effort, even if it seems wholly futile.

Instead of merely showing devotion fitfully and fearfully, which is like running away from the divine temple, one must seek it positively, nurturing the finest, the truest, the most valid feelings in one's own heart. One must not make devotion conditional, saying, "I will only give where I can be sure that the other person is going to give back." One should not even think in this way. One must experience the thrill of giving so much that it is impossible to expect anyone else to give anything like the same in return. The outpouring of love and joy cannot be manifest on the external plane, for when it is real it is as constant as breathing. Such is the inaudible hum, the unspoken *mantra*m of the indestructible heart. A person who constantly cherishes this with true humility can effortlessly adopt the mental posture of unostentatious prostration. One of the most beautiful postures that the human body can ever assume is bending low and prostrating on the floor. It is also extremely relaxing and regenerative, in the teaching of Raja Yoga. A person who can assume this as a mental posture in relation to a vast ideal that is relevant to the whole of humanity can begin to perfect mental devotion to what is at the heart of the human heritage – devotion to all the Mahatmas, Bodhisattvas, Krishnas, Buddhas and Christs that ever existed in millions of years, exceeding the possibility of reckoning or measure, beyond the shifting boundaries of recorded history.

If a person can light up that deep devotion and focus it in one direction, serving one's *Ishtaguru* or chosen Teacher, and can totally concentrate with undivided, unbroken, uninterrupted love, loyalty and obedience, there is then the absolute assurance of fanning the flame in the heart. However dark the world appears to be, however heavy one's suffering seems, however confusing the karma of the times, the secret flame ever strengthens itself. Ever reaching upward, it helps *Manas* to salute the *Atman* and to become one-pointed in seeking the *Atman* without expectation. Then as surely as there is a law of periodicity that cannot be confined to the trivial timetable of the ignorant personal self which does not know the vaster cycles or the previous lives of its indwelling monad or what is at the very core of its own being, invariably and infallibly the strength of that impulse will prepare one for that perfectly right moment when the *Atman* through *Buddhi* can initiate and instruct. The *Atma-Buddhi* is the Guru. It speaks to the soul as the inner voice of the *daimon*, the voice of the Master, who is the invisible escort. That is the sovereign experience of true initiation. A constant flame, enabling one to come to ever-higher levels of purification, the ceaseless self-purgation that is a prelude to total self-transformation, can be lit from small beginnings. Such endeavours must be sifted, honed down to a fine authenticity, and not even whispered to a single living person. But at the same time the line of life's meditation must not be forgotten by oneself. That is difficult. Maintained steadily and with continuity of consciousness, sincere efforts will lead from what, at one level, is the spark of simple devotion to an unknown object, to that deeper fire of inward devotion of the whole of one's sense of being in a manifest form, and then to the invisible prototype that is the Guru. This is signified by the higher line in the symbol of Aquarius. It is the vibration of universal consciousness, *Mahabuddhi*, which is always capable of being mirrored in the fleeting moment. It is also capable of dissolving the inverted and perverted image of itself formed in the waters of astral chaos out of conflicting feelings, ideas and wills. These can all be displaced and transcended by the deathless vibration of supreme devotion in the indestructible heart.

There is always that in a human being which says, "If I can only find that one real thing, it can cut through a great deal of the froth and darkness in my life." Even though people say this, do they really mean it? Are they in earnest? Or do they merely say it at one moment and forget it the next? To mean it, to maintain it in the mind and to make it the driving purpose of one's entire life is, doubtless, a daunting task. Just as individuals begin by self-definition to know that they can create this fire and sustain it through the darkness of minor *pralayas*, all human beings will have to admit that they must themselves start again, admitting that they do not know, but can still learn humbly, how to put two sticks together and light a fire. No one need be driven mad by the jackal voices of the jungle which is the crematorium of the psychic corpses of the sad failures in human evolution.

To start again means one must cure the fundamental alienation of the self so pervasive in urban society. When the mind is misused and mutilated, the whole of one's being cannot cooperate with that treacherous mind, and devotion seems to be impossible. When the mind is further alienated by constant association with a crippling self-image, one's condition is terrible. One is trapped by a sense not only of past failure but of permanent failure; a sense not only of how one once erred, but also of how one is irredeemably unworthy of one's innate destiny. In this condition one never really knows whether one was not up to it because of not giving oneself a chance in that mathematics class when one was a child of ten, or because of troubles at home, or because of that gossip next door who was interfering so much. One really does not know. But the fear that one can never accomplish anything real is too tragic. People even fear that they could never for the rest of this life put their minds to concentrate on a simple primer of geometry. Human beings fall prey to these fears because of the pressing pace of change and inexorable karmic precipitation, because of the tremendous sorting out that is going on, involving the collective karma of those who have failed spiritually as well as the karma of those who have misused and perverted the mind in the name of great ideas. They have done it in the name of the Church with the horrors of the Inquisition. They have done it in the name of the State with wars involving the innocent and unborn. They have done it in the pursuit of knowledge. When the karma of misuse is so heavy that there is an ever-growing fear, many neither know what is the root-cause nor sense the possibility of any cure.

This alienation of the mind is very real. It is most poignant in industrial society at this time. But even now there are people in many other parts of the world who are grateful to have the opportunity to sit by an electric light and enjoy the use of a tattered pamphlet. They are thrilled, when living far out in the wilds, to borrow a book or to have somebody send one to them, and to read it, enjoy it, and use it. There are awakened masses all over the globe. In Russia and Japan today, there is a greater *per capita* enjoyment of books than ever before in recorded history. This is happening all over the world. If it is not the same story everywhere, it is because of the changing karmic balances of peoples. Wherever there is a terrible mutilation of the mind, and a consequent anger, a crippling sense of self-alienation, there is the rush of the lemmings, as well as the desperate desire for a simple solution, a fervent wish to cop out altogether from their responsibilities.

When the mind is stretched only by bribe and threat (and more by threat than by bribe), and merely on behalf of restrictive and narrow ideas, then all the most insecure and frustrated souls, all the preachers without pulpits, the self-tormented teachers from past lives and all parts of the globe, grasp every chance to show pretension and fake wisdom in *Kali Yuga*, as the ancient *Vishnu Purana* prophesied. Even when such pseudo-teachers get their pulpit and their opportunity, they do not really believe in anything or in themselves. As this gets worse, year by year, they are constrained to concede to themselves that they do not really have anything to teach or exemplify, though they perfect the art of outward pretense. Thus all the vicious circles of antagonistic counterclaims multiply between the different sects of those who do not believe in themselves. Shelley wrote with poignant and powerful imagery about what happens to the mind when it is so totally immobilized, so wholly corrupted, so vampirical, that it becomes poisonous unto itself as well as to others. Why is such self-destructive manipulation doomed to disappear? The reason is that one cannot take an immortal soul that has journeyed much longer than is dreamt of by the boldest genealogists of the age of man, and expect such a being to swallow the rubbish of reductionism of every sort. The garbage festers, but humanity is too old to be forever victimized by tiny coteries of nihilists.

Human beings need ideas large enough to accommodate their sense of readiness for the future. This means that the only way to overcome self-alienation is by attunement to the Universal Mind through the contemplation of universal ideas. Because the personal mind has become flaccid, especially when it considers noble ideas enshrined in the platitudes of the past, it is liable to cling to mere externals. It must penetrate behind the visible forms to the formless ideas. Then it is meaningful to say, "I do not know," because each idea presupposes a larger idea which in turn ontologically presupposes one which is still more profound. There is an expanding transcendence of existing conceptions of space, time, motion and identity. The more one realizes this, the more genuine is the recognition that one does not know and the greater the possibility of developing the desire to persist, to function freely within a realm of pure anti-entropic thought which is completely potential, for which contemporary languages do not have any words. Sometimes from a Sanskrit root, a Greek term, or even an English word, one can extract a deeper meaning that was lost in the course of time. This is true of the word 'devotion.' It is true of most terms when traced back to their origin. There is a beautiful core to the word 'devotion,' from *de votum*, 'to dedicate by a vow.' As with any important word that has been used for a very long time, it has acquired accretions of meaning and limitations of usage. One has to take a stand somewhere in reference to the inbred tendency to identify the meanings of words ostensively or by rigid definitions, to become fixated on the conventional trappings of language. To start using the mind constructively and freeing it from habitual grooves is going to be difficult and at times extremely painful. It requires at least the level of minimal attention needed for training the lower mind, but which one did not give because it was demanded at too high a price by institutional reward and penalty.

All of this points to the unavoidable suffering caused by persisting errors through repeated mis-identification. Imagine persons who misused the gift of walking by kicking other beings. They might well have several lives without the use of legs. The terrible need and desire to walk and move is there, but they are crippled and bewildered. They need to wear out the karmic causes of their condition through that suffering, which is incomprehensible to *kama-manas*. Understanding such causes in terms of possible past misuse can bring them to a point where they will, when they regain the power of locomotion, never misuse it again. They will not use it to hurt mother earth. They will not dream of using it to kick another human being. They will not use it carelessly and impulsively. What is true in reference to legs is also true in regard to the eyes and to every human organ. Above all, it is true in reference to the mind, which is an invisible organ corresponding to the tongue, to the divine prerogative of speech, and to the power of conceptualization. When imagination is polluted, the mind goes awry. When imagination becomes sterile, the mind becomes paralyzed, and all it can do is to adapt and be imitative. Reductionists, puzzled by any glimmerings of something more to the power of the mind, try to freeze the situation by stating a restrictive theory, holding that the mind can only be adaptive, thereby engendering imitativeness.

The human mind, however, is original. It is self-reproductive. Patanjali says it is capable of two lines of self-reproductive thought. One of these is bound up with memory images, associations, and with likes and dislikes. It is possible to halt this compulsive self-reproductive chain of mere reactive thinking and get to a condition of balance – *nirodha* – if one persists in trying always to bring the mind back to one idea, holding oneself steady, exactly as people would do if they had partially lost the use of their legs and had to re-educate their muscles in a therapeutic ward. This must be done with the brain and the thinking faculties. Then a stage can come where another kind of self-reproductive power begins to be exercised by the mind, where it can maintain in a self-sustaining manner a level of thinking that is more universal and constructive, which is capable of a great deal of diversification, fertilization and replication. Then, when this flow is itself brought to a smooth and controlled pace, it is possible to move to a further stage where one can see oneself from outside, and remain disengaged from the uninterrupted steady flow of higher mental awareness.

Even though it must eventually come to a halt and meanwhile be diagnosed correctly at this point of history, the misuse of the mind is very old. It goes back many lives, to the time when the mind was enormously powerful and was employed on behalf of personal status and power. Every time one hears some person say, "I want to do this because I want to be famous," it is a sign that he is burdened by a fear of failure from the past. If such a person comes into contact with *Theosophia* and still thinks in these ways, the resultant condition is tragic. There is an incredible misplacement and displacement of human energy. What a price to pay when one is young to over-compensate for little hurts and petty slights to the personal self, which needs to be refined into an invulnerable if imperfect instrument for the immortal individuality. People nonetheless get into false and exaggerated attitudes when they want to use the mind, with its limited powers, for some ignoble purpose that involves the illusory security of the personal self. History has now come to a point where, with the abuse of print and the enormity of empty pontification, Nature is insisting that there be a halt to wastage and misuse. People can go on cutting trees to make paper. Society can go on mass-producing people who think they have something to teach, but the game of deception is speedily coming to an end. Frustrated and overwrought teachers do not have credibility with themselves. They do not know how to win the trust of their students, even amongst captive audiences. They are exhausted by their mutual rivalry and they will feel increasingly alienated and miserable. This is the cumulative precipitation of a long process of religious and secular exploitation.

The mind is a glorious gift. In its true function as a means of reflective self-conscious thought, *svasamvedana*, it is the greatest gift of the human being. Plato warned his hearers never to be so naive as to think that any pleasure can ever have any meaning to the heart if the mind and imagination are not involved. To recover the true power of self-consciousness requires a tougher discipline and a larger perspective than can be encompassed by the personal self. It requires *dianoia* based upon Aquarian axioms and involves, above all, a new posture of humility. It is crucial to train human beings in contemporary culture to say, and to enjoy saying, "I do not know." This had become easy for many people at other times and in other places. In a highly competitive society, however, people are encouraged to claim to know when they do not. To acknowledge ignorance is very painful, but that pain is necessary for the restoration of psychological health. It is one of the tasks of the present time to give people the release and strength of saying, "I do not know, but I wish to know." First they have to say, "I do not know," and then they have to learn to practise it, however painful it is, until they burst through the pseudo-image of false knowledge. Then they have to say, "I do not know, but I want to know. I really want to know." They have to hunger for knowledge. This is required for the readjustment of the *psyche* and the awakening of *nous*.

They have to want to know out of devotion to some great purpose for its own sake, which is very difficult to understand in the context of corrupt instrumentalism. They have to want to know for the sake of some larger good, and hence they must think of a larger good in the context of which they have no position of privileged access. This is the ultimate Aquarian paradox. One does not really know what the larger good is, yet one is asked to think about it. This is superb discipline for the human soul. Keep thinking about the good of others, the good of all. One may not know what it is, but keep thinking, practising *dianoia*. Above all, in the process of doing so, one must totally negate any concern for oneself in the future. Through this practice or *abhyasa*, the lower line of the Aquarian glyph, the serpent of self that has got coiled in the wrong way, is being stretched and brought back to a condition where it can be subdued. Paradoxically, when one has totally forgotten any concern for one's own future, then one's true purpose as a soul, one's deeper destiny, will speak as the voice of the spiritual heart. It is the destiny of the divine prototype of every human being who has become alienated, like the estranged face in *The Hound of Heaven* of Francis Thompson. Self-alienation is caused by the wearing of the false mask of which Shelley speaks – the loathsome mask of the personal self. The divine prototype will not reveal the hidden purpose of this incarnation until the loathsome mask is seen for what it is and stripped away, layer by layer.

The purgation of self-crucifixion is painful and protracted until one can fully prepare the ground and find the true self amidst the darkness and agony of not knowing whether one's life has any point. But each will know in time, in a way that is unique and inimitable, and through myriad intimations. Existentially, in the very act of doing something for others, one learns to say readily and simply, "I do not know what is going on in the world. I do not know the future course of history. Above all, I certainly do not know what is unfolding in the Aquarian Age. This means that whenever I hear otherwise, I will turn a deaf ear, without being rude to the individuals concerned." This is hard. Those who can go through such self-chosen mental asceticism will come to a point where they will be able to serve others in simple ways, sharing a vision that is grander than ever could be told to them. They could find themselves sufficiently to know at that beautiful moment when death comes as a deliverer and a friend, "My life had meaning and purpose. I have not lived in vain."

Those who sense the significance of being on the threshold of a New Age will cherish the practice of meditation, of self-study, of listening, learning, and preparing themselves cheerfully and ceaselessly. They must be willing to test themselves, out of self-respect, by prescribing their own daily discipline to follow for a week. Even reduced to this short period, it is very tough for too many. But if even a few persons can follow through for a week, there is a chance that they will do something worthwhile in their lives. Typically, given the widespread fragmentation of consciousness, most people are not going to be able to do this for seven days, much less for successive weeks and months between the solstices and the equinoxes. But they have to keep trying, week by week, testing themselves. "Can I take one thought and can I maintain it as a vibration in my mind and heart for a week?" This is a strain. It will not be immediately possible. The worst will be that one will not even know that one has forgotten. But, giving oneself a chance week after week, a point comes where one must succeed. There can be no respect for oneself if it cannot be cultivated when one's faculties are relatively healthy and when one has received so much from the teachings of the Mahatmas and the abundance of Nature. The very thing that is difficult has to be attempted. Where the entire educational system in a hedonistic culture is encouraging the weak to take what is easy and avoid what is hard, courageous souls should take the hardest test – to maintain one essential idea every day throughout the week.

If a person can really do this, then that person can carry something into the next week, can work with the cycles of the seasons, the solstices, the equinoxes. But, above all, that person will so significantly change the ratios in the astral vehicle that the result will show itself on the physical plane to those who know. Every true aspirant will be recognized and receive unseen help. Who are those who know? Simply those who have mastered this very practice. Anyone who does not even understand the nature of what has to be done is certainly hoping for something which is impossible – some sort of vicarious atonement, some kind of messianic salvation. The latest form of it is the collectivization of the whole of human consciousness, put in terms of evolutionary progress, which is automatically going to become enlightened. Human consciousness is going to do nothing automatically and never has done anything automatically or suddenly in millions of years. In this way the central problem is fudged. It is foolish to imagine that somehow automatically enlightenment will descend in a secular or spiritual garb. All of this is of the past, a ghost of the Piscean Age. Enlightenment can only be reached by thought and effort based upon a sense of individual and personal insignificance. It requires withholding judgment while cheerfully persisting, trying to get to the very core of meaning in every situation and thinking through one's sense of self until it really hurts. It is like squeezing an orange until the pips squeak. Think until the brain is ready to burst. Feel until the heart cries out. Do not stop short. Get to the root. Persist and come out of it a stronger person, regenerated through *tapas*. Then follow the great injunction of the *Upanishad*: "Awake, arise, seek the Great Ones." The Rishis assumed that unless you did all of these you could not begin to understand the meaning of the Law. "Awake, arise, seek the Great Ones, *and learn*."

Spiritual life is the paradigm of learning. Its reflections are all the other forms of learning, but these reflections no longer reflect. To recover the primordial sense of learning that is coeval with breathing requires a total break with existing thought-forms and habits of speech. They are the modes of the past. The one thing that many people rightly sense is that they may be left out of the current and the cycle of the future. But this cannot be safeguarded against by any external means. The only way to enter into that fast-moving and invisible stream, which will become a mighty river in the future, is by becoming capable, through voluntary self-training, of activating the unmanifest potency of the universe – the liquid fire that springs from deep devotion to universal good, and by reaching out to the whole of the human race, including the unborn who are always far more numerous than those who are presently incarnated.

This is a formidable task. But any person, by self-training in the art of using Aquarian axioms, can enter the evolutionary stream which will eventually produce minds as pellucid as crystal and hearts which are wisely benevolent. Luminous with the intelligence of the universe, they shall have done with the pseudo-dramas of the past. They will recognize the beauty and dignity of being like a grain of sand at birth and death, assigning no false valuation to the pseudo-entity called the personality, which is merely a logical construction. Recognizing links at all levels between the atomic and the infinite, they will dispense with the fairy story of name and form, which was born at a certain time, died at a certain time, and achieved this and did not achieve that. Completely wiping it out is a mark of maturity. The currency of thought and language will radically have to change. Individuals will have to stand apart from many of the patterns which have become raucously agitated precisely because they are obsolete. The personality becomes most active when it is threatened. Something like this has happened collectively. This is inescapable and irreversible, and wholly to be welcomed from the mature standpoint of soul-evolution. "Are not our beards grown?" wrote a Mahatma to a prospective pupil.

The most significant hope for the future may well be that people have no authentic way of celebrating festivals, no credible thoughts about the destiny of the world, no clear ideas about what they are going to do this year or next year. The voiding of all shallow expectations is extremely therapeutic. When people practise this sufficiently, they will learn to flow with the current of the whole. What can be seen in terms of law or of many levels of consciousness can also be seen quite simply as flowing like a small stream that must of necessity empty itself into the ocean. One may flow with the vaster forces of history, of humanity, and of the cosmos. When individuals forget themselves, then, paradoxically, they discover themselves. When they consider themselves as irrelevant, they become relevant. When they see themselves as unimportant, they become important. This is the mode of self-definition and the pedigree of the twice-born on the threshold of the epoch of Universal Enlightenment, the Aquarian Age, which has entered its second degree and moves steadily towards its millennial culmination.

Hermes, March 1977

LIGHT, LOVE AND HOPE

Light is the first begotten, and the first emanation of the Supreme, and Light is Life, says the Evangelist and the Kabalist. Both are electricity – the life principle, the anima mundi, *pervading the universe, the electric vivifier of all things. Light is the great Protean magician, and under the divine will of the architect, or rather the architects, the 'Builders' (called One collectively), its multifarious, omnipotent waves gave birth to every form as well as to every living being. From its swelling electric bosom, spring matter and spirit. Within its beams lie the beginnings of all physical and chemical action, and of all cosmic and spiritual phenomena; it vitalizes and disorganizes; it gives life and produces death, and from its primordial point gradually emerged into existence the myriads of worlds, visible and invisible celestial bodies.*

The Secret Doctrine, i 579

The metaphysical *mantram*, "Light is Life and both are electricity", intimates a profound insight that is realized only at the highest levels of meditation. Empty the mind of all objects and subjects, all contrasts and contours, in a world of names and forms and colours, and one can plunge into absolute Divine Darkness. Once in this realm of pure potential, one may apprehend the hidden noumenon of matter, that ultimate substance or primordial substratum which is the sum-total of all possible objects of perception by all possible beings. At the same time, one may apprehend Spirit as the totality of all the possible expressions, manifestations and radiations of one central divine energy or Light. In that Divine Darkness, the realm of boundless potential where no one thing exists, love is like the Light that is hidden in the Darkness. That Light is the origin of all that is latent, of all that will ever emerge and persist, all that will depart from form and yet remain as immaculate rays.

This primordial realm of potential Light and potential Life is also the realm of potential energy. In this pregenetic realm, wherein there is no manifestation, one may apprehend a wholly potential energy which does not produce any interaction between the latent Spirit and noumenal matter. This is not electricity in any manifest sense, nor any force that can be construed in terms of ordinary language or common sense-perception; it is a primordial current. Even the most abstract conceptions of pure science cannot reach this realm, wherein there is a cosmic electrical vibration so fundamental and all-pervasive that it cannot be localized or characterized in any particular way. Out of this Divine Darkness – out of this potential Light, latent Life and hidden energy – there is a coming into manifestation. There is a process of radiation and emanation in which myriad sparks fly. There is a coalescence of the initial primordial ray of light-energy and the latent life-currents which releases pulsations, radiations and currents that flow forth in every direction.

At this stage of the incipient cosmos, *Gupta Vidya* affirms the presence of great beings, great minds and hearts, great souls perfected in prior periods of evolution. Remaining awake during the long night of non-manifestation – yet having no particular object of reference and no particular conception in the state of *Mahapralaya* – they abided in a state of vigilant, ceaseless, harmonious contemplation of all that was potential. These beings emerge with the burgeoning of primordial Light and Life, the primal reverberation of divine energy throughout the glassy essence of space. They become the focussing instrument in what then comes to be known as Universal Mind or *Mahat.* They become the living lens through which all that is latent within the night of non-manifestation is stirred into active life. These perfected beings, who are later mythified in all the religions of the world as Dhyani Buddhas, Archangels, Lords of Light, become self-conscious agents for the direction and focussing into an emerging world of primary particularizations of an essence that is otherwise universal, purely potential and entirely homogeneous. For the sake of meditation, they may be thought of as shooting out rays of colour and emitting sounds within transcendental musical scales. One may then, in turn, think of them as belonging to seven classes, each corresponding to a subliminal note or a colour. Each of them corresponds to a particular number or degree of differentiation, and they all work in unison. They may be imagined as having their own differentiated notes, colours and numbers but also as uniting and synthesizing the multiple potencies of the manifested *Logos*. In that ontogenetically prior state, just before manifestation, there is a tremendous subtle field, a pre-cosmic electrical energy that is sometimes called *Daiviprakriti* – the noumenal Light of the *Logos*.

In the world of visible manifestation, the phenomena which are identified as electricity and magnetism, light and heat, are observable effects of this primary Logoic radiation. Gigantic and titanic as they are, they are nonetheless nothing but shadows of supersensuous matter in motion on a noumenal plane prior to the realm of phenomena. The study of light-energy in manifestation involves complex curves and relationships and requires the use of many categories and instruments. This is the realm of diffraction and diffusion, of reflection and refraction, wherein there are complex possibilities owing to the interference and overlapping of waves upon waves of light-energy. It is simultaneously the realm of photons, particles of light-energy travelling at an incredible speed, such that light from the moon arrives at the earth within a second. The notion of light as a complex, though virtually instantaneous, agency having an impact at every level of the cosmos stirs the heart long before it can be truly grasped by the mind. The heart understands the vital significance of life because it resonates to that which is primordial, all-pervasive and instantaneous. Within every human heart there burns a fire of light-wisdom and love-compassion, *Prajna* and *Mahakaruna*. This spark of the One Fire flickers fitfully in the neophyte at first, but it can be stoked into a powerful flame which burns vigorously, steadily and ceaselessly. In its fullness it directs and guides individuals in the expansive and wise application of the boundless energy flowing from the fathomless love-compassion and light-wisdom within the spiritual heart. The monadic heart of every human being is an exact mirror of the heart of the cosmos, that swelling electric bosom from which the dual stream of spirit-matter emerges.

> The Sixth principle in Man (*Buddhi*, the Divine Soul) though a mere breath, in our conceptions, is still something material when compared with divine 'Spirit' (*Atma*) of which it is the carrier or vehicle. *Fohat*, in his capacity of DIVINE LOVE (*Eros*), the electric Power of affinity and sympathy, is shown allegorically as trying to bring the pure Spirit, the Ray inseparable from the ONE absolute, into union with the Soul,

the two constituting in Man the **MONAD,** and in Nature the first link between the ever unconditioned and the manifested.

The Secret Doctrine, i 119

The presence of this divine Light, Fire and Flame within the secret heart means that every human being is capable of seeing and illuminating a much vaster sphere of existence than he or she is typically prepared to inhabit self-consciously. Similarly, every single human being has a much richer and more profound capacity for effortless love than he or she imagines, love that is spontaneous and selfless, asking nothing and willing to give freely, graciously and generously to all. Yet little of that immense love and light-energy has a chance to come forth in a world of masks and shadows, a world of lies and fears and personal loneliness. Such is the predicament of humanity. Yet this same orphaned humanity, which has barely begun to draw upon a minute fraction of its fathomless boundless potential, can do so if it seeks to sustain a conception of existence that goes beyond all habitual divisions and dichotomies. One must transcend distinctions such as youth and old age, social roles and external labels. Even though the mind has become blunted and the heart tainted, one must unlearn all stifling habits and become able to withdraw the mind and heart from false and fleeting allegiances. Only so can one restore plasticity and resilience to the mind and heart.

In diverse societies at different times in recorded history, seekers have tried to meet this challenge by undertaking systematic monastic discipline. They have tried to be helpful to each other and to bind themselves by self-chosen and inexorable rules, vows and pledges. Through a repeated reinforcement of those fundamental resolves, they have sought to develop a way of life aimed at spiritual self-regeneration. Yet in spite of this, again and again in history these monastic institutions, having flourished for a time, invariably degenerated. The vital impulse went out of them and people came to be caught up merely in imitation, in game-playing and in ritual, hollow mimetics. The lesson of this repetitive pattern is that no amount of regimentation on the outside can work unless it is matched by sufficient concentration and continuity of ideation through meditation from within. One cannot force another human being to become a man or woman of meditation. A human being has to sustain a desire to do this which is sufficiently strong to permit him or her to see through the masquerade of that which is false and deceptive in this world.

Each human being must individually come to a deep reflection upon the meaning of death and its connection with the moment of birth. And each must make for himself or herself a decision which enables one to undertake a freely chosen set of spiritual practices. These self-chosen exercises will, now and again, prove extremely taxing, and they can be sustained only by the momentum of a tremendous motivation. As all the greatest benefactors of humanity have taught, we must be ready to give up everything for the sake of the whole. Unless one releases a motivation which is universal, rooted in a love for all humanity, one cannot keep oneself upon the spiritual Path. It is fatal to rush into any pretence that one loves all humanity. Instead, though it will take time, one should dwell again and again upon the sublime and extraordinary nature of that fundamental and all-embracing motivation which is represented by the Kwan-Yin Pledge and the Bodhisattva Vow. Only through that motivation, authentically released and maintained intact, can there be an awakening of the spark of *bodhichitta*.

The redemptive love of the part for the whole springs from the immortal soul. It is deathless in origin and is the individual's share in what is universal and immortal. Behind all the modifications and manifestations of *prakriti* there is *Purusha* – the single indivisible universal Spirit known by many names. It is indestructible, beginningless and endless. It is itself a pristine reflection of the very essence of the Divine Darkness. The spark or ray of that Spirit within every human soul is the power of love. It can illuminate the mind and enlighten the heart so long as one is ready to give up all, willing to be alone and whole-hearted, single-minded and one-pointed. Then that love becomes a form of wisdom, a ray of light, assuring one in the hour of need and seeming gloom and doom that there is hope. It tells one where to go and what to do, it advises whether one should stand and wait. It gives one immense patience whereby one may recognize those tendencies that come in the way of releasing that spiritual energy. There is that in the lower nature which wants to grab and seize, which also at the same time is insecure and fickle, uncertain of itself and desirous of something from outside. One must learn to wait, to relinquish and wear down that side of oneself which is the weaker, if one is to release the stronger.

Meanwhile, before one is able to release the true strength of the heart, and while one is still in the grip of that which is weaker, one can learn. One can discover the patterns, the instabilities and the vulnerabilities of one's nature. This process of diagnostic learning cannot, however, come to fruition unless it is balanced by a deep adoration of those Dhyani Buddhas who sustain the cosmos. One must deliberately place the mind and the heart within the magnetic field of attraction of the ideal, the mighty Host of *Dhyanis* and Bodhisattvas. One can think of them as galaxies of enlightened beings who are cosmic forces, living facts in invisible Nature, and at the same time shining exemplars to humanity in the visible world. Through hearing about them and through studying the sacred texts and noble traditions that have preserved their Teachings, one may begin to assimilate the way of life exemplified by such beings. Thus one can learn to live in a state of learning and letting go – learning joyously and vigorously while at the same time letting go slowly of the fickle, fearful and furtive self. After a point, one cannot even conceive of living in any other way. One finds a profound satisfaction in this way of life, and as a result one is able to look upon the world not as a receiver but as a giver. In the solitude of one's own contemplation, one will naturally think of hungry hearts and neglected souls to whom one may try to reach out through an ardent longing of the heart and through intense thought.

Breathing on behalf of the world's disinherited, one can become a messenger of hope to others. Everyone has had the experience, in dark periods of doubt and despair, of receiving a sudden bright flash of inspiration and hope. Gratitude for this light mysteriously received can become the basis of a faith and confidence that one may give light to others. If one persists in one's solitude in thinking of all those beings who are disinherited, yet worthy of one's compassion, one can reach to them in their deep sleep and in their dreams. Through the strength of what George William Russell called the "Hero in Man", one can give to them that hope or saving grace that will sustain them, whatever their condition. Thus one forms invisible magnetic bonds with other human beings, channels of transmission that can move in every direction. To do this is to go beyond any conception of individual salvation or progress based upon a personalized and localized notion of love or light. One learns how to move towards the sun so that one's shadow declines, and one begins to understand what it is to stand directly under the sun and cast no shadow. By freeing oneself from self-concern, one becomes truly confident in one s capacity to reach out and help human beings no matter at what distance. Letting go of all external labels, tokens and pseudo-proofs of love and light, one is prepared to bask, so to speak, in the supernal light and truth, the boundless wisdom and compassion, of the Spiritual Sun.

The entry into this light is to be understood not only in terms of a mystical metaphor. It is also linked up to the presence of actual beings who have become Bodhisattvas of Compassion, rays flowing from a cosmic energy such as *Avalokiteshvara*. As the lord who looks down from on high, *Avalokiteshvara* may be envisaged as seated in total contemplation and calmness, wrapped in an extraordinary golden halo of perfect purity and love. He holds within the gaze of his overseeing eye all humanity. To meditate upon this paradigm of all the Tathagatas and Predecessors, Buddhas and Bodhisattvas, is to restore one's sense of the ontological plenty of the spiritual realm. Thus one may transcend confining conceptions of the evolutionary history of humanity or the false notion that human spirituality is entirely dependent upon localized events in the past. Rather, one will come to know humanity as extremely old, extending over millions upon millions of years and sustained throughout in myriads of ways by countless saviours and helpers and teachers. Many of them were humble wanderers in villages who had no external marks, bore no labels and made no claims. Nonetheless, they helped and uplifted the human heart, giving hope to others, and then moving on. Their lives are an uninterrupted and living testimony to the ubiquitous force and presence on earth of the Tribe of Sacred Heroes.

To raise one's sights to this extraordinarily universal perspective is to begin to see that many questions which once were bothersome are no longer difficult. As soon as one thinks of love separatively or in terms of bilateral contexts, one thinks in terms of particularized intentions and externalized concepts of the will. This concretized will is bound up with proving something, showing determination in a context, mostly through verbalizing and acting out. Whereas, if one thinks in terms of vast collective hosts of beings, uniting all humanity through invisible ties, one is drawing closer to an idea of will as a universal and impersonal force. By inserting oneself within the invisible brotherhood of true helpers of humanity, one can learn to do what one can, according to the measure, degree and depth of one's knowledge and feeling, without engendering any false conception of the will.

In whatever one does and in whatever way one releases the higher will, one is merely drawing a certain portion from an inexhaustible and universal source. If one understands this, one will not ask to draw more from it than one in fact can use, or more than one can properly sustain. In other words, one will begin to see through the tricks played by the human mind, which is the great deceiver and the adversary in man, when it tries to escape from what can be done by demanding more. When the mind insists that it must know whether its share of love and light is adequate in relation to its aim or self-conception, it becomes the great deceiver and obscurer of the light and love that are latent in every human soul. Many supposedly philosophical questions and spiritual concerns are really nothing but what the Buddhists call *attavada,* the dire heresy of separateness. They reflect the philosophic error of assuming that all one's tendencies, desires and thoughts make up some kind of entity which is cohesive and persistent and, above all, cut off from the rest of humanity. This is an illusion. There is no such entity. No true sense of selfhood can be located in this aggregate of ever-changing, and second-hand, chaotic tendencies.

Instead, this aggregate of the *skandhas* represents one's karmic share in the collective accumulations of tendencies of all humanity. All human beings, one might say, have contributed to the growing of weeds, and every human being has got his or her share of the world's weeds to take in hand and to cut down. At the same time, every human being has got to find and sow the seeds of wisdom and compassion. This can be done only through cultivating patience and the power of waiting, rooted in the willingness to work with the cycles of Nature. As the prophet teaches in *Ecclesiastes,* there are different seasons, times for sowing and times for reaping, times for living and times for dying. That is true with regard to all the manifestations of love, and the wisest know that the deepest love is beyond manifestation. As Maeterlinck wrote, there are in love silences with so profound a depth that the unexpressed flows with uninterrupted continuity across the barriers of time and space. This deeper love is often forfeited because of a concern with what can be demonstrated, what can be increased, mitigated or compared. To recover the lost potential of the soul, one must rethink what is real. On the one side, there is that which is universal and includes all that is potential. On the other, there is the entire collection of particular, episodic, finite expressions and manifestations. Vast though they are, they are in the end limited in relation to the inexhaustible content of love and light within the immortal soul of every human being and at the heart of the whole cosmos.

By learning to think in this way, one can begin to discern immense beauty in the idea that every human being is, in the simple act of breathing, both living and loving. Most of this is unconscious or unrelated to any particular desires or demands. But in the case of the wisest beings, the most enlightened masters of compassion, this breathing is self-consciously benevolent and universal. Having become conscious of the enormous potential energy within the heart of the cosmos, they are able skilfully to direct and channel that energy to vast numbers of souls. They have learnt how to help particular persons at particular times only through lifetimes of trial and error. They have recognized the proliferating consequences of doing too much or not doing enough. Through practice, over millions of years and myriads of lives, Bodhisattvas become intelligent and skilful in the application of wisdom and compassion, light and love.

To be able even to understand such possibilities in such beings, much less to be able to move in that direction, one must shake off conventional divisions between the head and the heart. Often it is assumed that it is a great thing for the mind to become sharper, smarter and more intelligent. It is also conventional to think of the heart as sentimental. Both these notions are based upon misconceptions. In the subtle vestures of human beings, in what is called the spiritual heart, lies the basis of the highest intelligence, ideation and creativity. Therefore, from the spiritual point of view, one cannot activate any of the higher centres in the brain unless one has first aroused a spark of fire in the spiritual heart. Many human beings are able, sporadically, to release extraordinary powers, skills and flashes of genius. These intermittent abilities represent an unbalanced condition that is a reflection of excess and deficiency in previous lives. They are accompanied by a karmic frustration at not being able to tap and recover knowledge self-consciously, and such individuals have got hard lessons to learn before they can create new and better balances within themselves.

Hence the importance, especially with children, of withdrawing undue emphasis upon the mind and developing instead a sense of the heart. Instead of fostering an obsessive inclination to grade the mind, one should encourage an evolving conception of excellence in relation to the heart. This does not happen automatically; unless one becomes fearless and courageous, one cannot release the potency and spiritual strength in the heart. One must educate the heart in the best truth that one knows. This truth includes the mortality of one's body, the immortality of the soul, and the means of making that immortal soul function within a mortal body. It is crucial to give children some of the fundamental truths of the Divine Wisdom, and in particular to teach them not merely to look at things in terms of today and tomorrow, but rather in terms of their finest impulses and most generous urges. Over a lifetime of learning, these can provide the basis of authentic fearlessness and true universality in compassion and love. One must include in one's heart people whom one does not see. To do this requires an active imagination, ultimately a capacity to visualize the whole of humanity. This involves a dynamic balance between one's contemplation of all the beings that exist on this earth and one's relationships with those who are nearby.

In practice, this requires simplification and a development of precision, which is at the origin of all etiquette and manners. One must learn not to overdo with people who are immediately around oneself. To do less is to do more. Thus one will have a great opportunity to keep oneself intact, without getting into syndromes of excessive expectation and rapid disillusionment. While maintaining a greater steadiness in relationships to those around oneself, one will, at the same time, see beyond them. One will develop a concern to take one's place in the family of man and to become what is called in the Buddhist tradition a son of the Buddha family. Like the Bodhisattvas and Buddhas, one becomes willing to think in terms of serving all beings on earth. This is not something that one can contemplate or emulate in a short time.

Instead, it will require a repeated renewal. It will have some impact at the moment of death and also a distinct effect upon the kind of birth one will have in the next life. Not immediately, but eventually, it will change the current and tropism, the tonality and colouring, of one's varied relationships to the vestures and their use.

By gaining this precision, one will become more free, and at the same time the better able to help other human beings. One's mind becomes more willing, vibrant and versatile by becoming an obedient servant of a heart that has found deep peace within itself. Once the heart has discovered within itself its own secret fire, it can, through various forms of daily meditation and oblation, activate that fire. Whether one calls this the fire of devotion, of *tapas*, of wisdom or truth, these are only different aspects of that which is ultimately the fire of the Mysteries. It is the fire that represents the immortal self-subsisting sovereignty of the individual human soul. It is capable in principle of becoming a self-conscious mirror of the whole cosmos. Therefore it is also capable of reaching out from within the inmost sanctuary and affecting, learning from, teaching and helping everything that exists. This requires deliberate and systematic training because of the diverse kinds, speeds and levels of communication between beings based upon the vibrations of the heart realm. The more skilful one becomes in using karmic opportunities to participate in the partial modes of love and learning of this world, the more one learns how to shed a little light for a few human beings upon a few things, while at the same time ceaselessly looking beyond one's horizon towards the limitless potential within all.

Eventually, one can reach a point where one has the great privilege of seeing no more evil and limitation because they have lost their fascination. They are really nothing more than a grotesque representation of muddle, error and delusion, ultimately based upon captivity to illusion. They are futile and short-sighted, they are short-lived. But so long as there are elements in so many beings that are caught up in short-term considerations, evil and limitation are compounded. While at first they may look like an awesome all-potent monster, one later sees that this is not true. This is a form of protection for those who are on the Path and concerned with the real work of the human race. That work is continuous, though hidden by a stream of invisibility, because most people are simply caught up in the external sights and sounds of reality. They are captives to exaggerations of form, limitation and evil. Hence the importance, at the individual level, for each human being to say, like Jesus, "Get thee behind me, Satan." One cannot say this for others; one must do it for oneself.

As long as there is light, there will be shadow. Yet every human being can at any moment turn his face away from the shadow and towards the light of the sun. Whenever one is with other souls, one can ask oneself, "Do I love others more than myself? Do I take less and give more to others? Do I actually reach out within myself, within my mind and heart, and also in my acts, towards other human beings? In the way I look at other human beings, can I salute the Divine within them? Can I shed light and also be grateful for the light that I daily receive from others?" By asking questions of this kind, one will find that all increments of change become significant. Life becomes not only worth living, but worth consecrating. The mind and the heart recapture the immanence of the ideal of boundless Love and Light.

Hermes, March 1985

THE HEALING OF ELEMENTALS

"How did you come here, O King, on foot or in a chariot?"

"I did not come, sir, on foot. I came in a chariot. "

*"If you came in a chariot, explain to me what that is. Is it the pole
that is the chariot?"*

"Certainly not."

*"Is it the wheels, or the frame, or the ropes, or the yoke, or the spokes
or the goad that is the chariot?"*

To all of these King Milinda still answered no.

"Then is it all these parts that is the chariot?"

"No, Nagasena."

"But is there anything outside them that is the chariot?"

And still he answered no.

*"Then, ask as I may, I can discover no chariot. 'Chariot' is a mere
empty sound. What, then, is this 'chariot' you say you came in?
Your Majesty has spoken a falsehood, an untruth! There is no such
thing as a 'chariot'! You are king over all India, a mighty monarch.
Of whom, then, are you afraid that you speak untruth?"*

Questions of King Milinda

Human beings commonly conceive of themselves as privileged
subjects active in an outer world of objects, and acted upon by a host of
forces and pressures. Though they assign a stable reality to themselves
as subjects and to these objects, they are generally confused about the
dynamic connection between the two. Typically, they picture objects
as having a sort of mechanistic persistence and variability, markedly
different from the kind of vital energy they ascribe to themselves. No
such sharp distinction can succeed, however, in accounting for the
essential facts of human life. Much that is deemed to be subjective
displays the same inveterate and stark routinization held to characterize
the so-called external world of mechanical objects. And supposedly
inert objects often reveal dynamic qualities ranging from the perverse
to the poetic. The nexus or network of this perplexing condition is

centred in the human body itself, which is continually affected alike by seemingly subjective and objective forces.

The arcane mystery surrounding embodied consciousness has been the fertile source of much philosophical speculation, largely bound up with Cartesian dualism and the so-called "mind-body problem". Having severed form and consciousness from each other at a fundamental level, most thinkers, like "all the king's horses and all the king's men", have been unable to put them back together again. Nor does radical objective materialism or extreme subjective idealism yield a consistent resolution of the problem. This philosophical quandary reflects a broader malaise in human understanding and self-consciousness, with vital implications in arenas such as medicine and health, education and therapy, and the crucial connection of individual moral choices with the collective social and political order. Notions like 'psychosomatic illness', 'ego-transference' and 'political charisma' point to lacunae in our basic categories, and provide more heat than light, with few, if any, clues to responsible action. As a result, the well intentioned find themselves unable to instantiate their ideals, and it is small compensation that the perverse and malicious are also rather impotent in imposing on the world their malign schemes for universal degradation.

From the standpoint of *Gupta Vidya,* this entire dualistic approach is rooted in a fundamental philosophical error. Instead of viewing differentiated form and consciousness as two radically separate modes of being, it sees them only as manifesting aspects of a single undifferentiated substance-principle. That rootless root is pre-cosmic ideation as well as pre-cosmic matter, both absolute consciousness and absolute unconsciousness, it being impossible to attribute any finite or formal character to this primordial, pre-genetic Ground. Thus the common-sense distinctions between mind and matter, between body and soul, are merely relative and conceptual, helpful in characterizing different functions and faculties within living beings, but systematically misleading if taken as suggesting any strict dichotomy in the ontological bases of these diverse powers and principles. Further, this singular and sole origin of all consciousness and form implies that there is no unbridgeable gap between modes of manifestation of form and consciousness in various kingdoms of Nature, ranging from the least and lowest to the most metaphysically exalted. All alike are ensouled by one universal and ramifying divine Intelligence, and all are equally embodiments of one supreme and homogeneous light-essence.

These two aspects – *mahat* and *daiviprakriti* – unfold and enfold all the possibilities of differentiated existence throughout the complex realms of visible and invisible Nature, from the highest radiations of Logoic or cosmic intelligence to the subphysical species of elementals – the salamanders, sylphs, undines and gnomes of alchemical and popular folklore. At every successive level, grosser emanations mirror the specific modes of activity and intelligence of their more subtle "parents" but with diminishing ranges of action on every descending plane of existence, until finally the extreme limit of differentiation in a particular cycle of manifestation is reached. The entire web of Nature vibrates and resonates with the pulsations of the Logoic heart, expressing the One Life in myriad modes of manifest sensitivity and action. Throughout, the law of universal harmony reigns unbroken, continually adjusting the relations of all the parts within the impartite sovereign presence and provenance of the One. Its intelligence is behind their intelligence, and as they are drawn together or driven apart in successive communities and aggregations, as they suffer various transformations and transmutations of capability, all this is directly and immediately an expression of the infinite potential inherent in the Logoic root.

Seen in this light, embodied human existence is no different from any other mode of existence, subhuman or superhuman. Indeed, the worlds of *devas*, men and gods are alike guided by one identical Law. Yet each type in Nature carries the potency of its specific divine antetype, one of the seven primal Dhyan Chohanic radiations that make up the living body of the *Logos*. Each ray represents a fundamental note in the scale of specialized possibilities in Nature. From a certain perspective, it could be said that the human kingdom is specifically connected with the ray that expresses itself in man as the creative and synthesizing power of *manas* or self-consciousness. At the same time, all the seven rays have their scintillating expressions in all the kingdoms of Nature above, below and in man. Furthermore, within the human family there are complex cycles of evolutionary development wherein all the seven rays and their subdivisions predominate for periods of illusory "time" in the manvantaric pilgrimage. Consequently, human life is continually immersed in a vast ocean of life populated by hosts of greater and lesser beings, all of whom share the same archetypal set of potentialities, though clearly exhibiting very different actualized potencies.

Every human activity, each breath and thought, affects and is affected by this universal kinship. The energies of man *qua* man may be manasic in essence, but they are as subject to the laws of universal harmony as any other energies, both in origin and in their effect. Depending upon the quality of man's inspiration, motive and aspiration, his noetic and psychic activities draw to a greater or lesser degree upon the pure divine Intelligence of his *Manasa* ancestors. In the same proportion, all his conscious and semi-conscious activity exerts influence for good or ill on every aggregate of subhuman lives that comes within the scope and influence of human action, individual and collective.

The ceaseless interaction of man with subhuman Nature is ordinarily understood only at the level of gross interaction with animal and vegetable life, but even at this mundane level man clearly carries a sacred responsibility for the preservation and extinction of the hosts of species cohabiting the earth with him. Yet, partly because human beings fail to comprehend the nature of their own noetic individuality as manasic beings – and thus tend to ascribe a spurious pseudo-individuality to animals and plants – human beings are largely unaware of their far more intimate and decisive relationship to the hosts of the submineral elemental kingdoms. If lack of self-knowledge blinds human perception to the ubiquitous presence of these denizens of the fourfold elements, this itself is only a consequence of past misuse and abuse of human energies. Affecting the elemental make-up of the astral and physical body, this blindness and deafness to Nature's invisible sprites is the inevitable karmic compensation for past failures to treat these lesser modes of evolving life with the compassion and respect they deserve.

Whether man is aware of it or not, nonetheless every exertion of his *psyche*, every thought, feeling, word or breath, attracts and repels specific classes of elementals, charging and magnetizing them with an unerring exactitude on an incredible scale. One may compare this to the action of a magnet upon iron filings, though the number of elementals polarized and impressed by even seemingly trivial thoughts is surprisingly vast. Once these congeries of elementals have been impressed, they either lodge in one's vestures or move on. They themselves are really moving under certain infallible laws of attraction and repulsion. These laws are integral aspects of the universal forces of attraction and repulsion, ultimately the most fundamental laws of all evolution and existence.

'Attraction' and 'repulsion' should not be thought of perfunctorily here, either in a narrow Newtonian sense or in an anthropomorphic and romantically indulgent manner. 'Positive' and 'negative' are meant in senses that far transcend the myriad examples one could freely take from the external world. These laws are so basic to the cosmic process that there is no way the Seven Sons of the Flame could, by a progressive descent through a second class of mind-born sons and a third class of Builders, give rise to the whole cosmos without becoming both agents as well as victims of the process of differentiation, which subsequently acquires an inexorable logic of its own. Through centripetal and centrifugal patterns and by polar movements, it breathes in and out, swelling from within without and from without within, back and forth ceaselessly forever, until the time comes for the great sleep of the whole cosmos – the *pralaya* that succeeds each *manvantara*.

Until that awesome moment is reached, nothing can still or sway the process or prevent it from going on "without let or hindrance". This is the metaphysical sense in which karma is supreme as to cause but not as to effect. From this it follows that there can be no quick remedy or simple panacea to the long-standing problems of human life and spiritual evolution. Certainly, all pseudo-doctrines of vicarious atonement, instant *satori* or deathbed *moksha* – deceiving the docile and fearful into thinking they could be saved by proxy or by doing nothing – were costly death-traps for human beings over thousands of years. Equally, modern notions of self-reliance and the self-made man are disastrous evasions, deluding people into thinking that the entire globe is here merely to be exploited for private pleasure or personal profit. The hollow pretensions of the typical self-made man are all too evident to his spouse, children and parents, and the same could be said for the self-made woman. It is truly sad that so many are caught up to such an extent in clutching the costly illusion that one has "done it all myself". This standpoint simply will not wash, any more than a desperate immersion in the Ganges, and it is too late in human evolution for souls to be so apathetically forgetful of the time-honoured laws of continuity and transmission, much less the primordial facts of origin and cessation as taught by Buddha.

Anything which takes attention away from these primary facts and the primary obligations they entail is a disastrous mistake. No human being can incarnate on earth without complex, inexorable chains of causation requiring myriads of lives over millions of years to work out. To think that one can mix up fantasy with fact, day-dreaming with spiritual mountain climbing, just because one has received pristine Teachings from those at the summit of evolution, is fatal. That is why there will be recurring as well as instantaneous ethical examinations in the Aquarian Age into which all humanity is entering. No more fooling and kidding will be allowed. Even if one were to screen a collection of people, carefully selecting those who do not have these simian tendencies, chaos would result if one were to put them in a room.

This happens everywhere in contemporary society – in all institutions, offices, committees and classrooms – unless one can keep people quiet. The Quakers tried this in America, but they largely gave up about twenty-five years ago, not because they did not believe in their sovereign method of silence, but because they were not finding enough patient practitioners in America who were willing to come and sit quietly for three hours. What worked in England for the Quakers could not work in contemporary America, but this is only a minor incident in a global malaise caused by Dostoievskian hyper-consciousness which is going to take a radical Tolstoyan shift before it is resolved. That is why the Avatar is pioneering, among small groups of responsive and courageous souls, the creation of a new modulus of the ancient *sanghas* so that, within a hundred years, it will actually be safe for three human beings to be in the same room – safe for them to sit quietly, be wide awake and say something meaningful. This is going to take some time, and long beforehand it will be necessary to handle a number of hard cases in the seats of pseudo-government and the dens of pseudo-revolution, severely traumatised by inane ideologies, ethnic terrorism, ersatz religion, pseudo-psychiatry and behaviouristic nonsense.

The immense difficulty of bringing about such seemingly simple reforms points to the enormity of the gap between disintegrating societies and the ageless Teachings of Divine Wisdom. Yet, if any Aquarian pioneer wishes to begin to learn how to exercise a calming, controlling influence over masses of disturbed elementals – while eating, sleeping and going about the daily round – the first thing to focus upon is silence. A simple rule would be to talk little, if at all, during meals. Whether or not one mutters words of grace, it is most important to eat food calmly and gratefully without words. That would be a definite step forward for most people. Indeed, most health problems arise not because of what people eat, but because of the way they eat it. Whether people pick trash from bins, like homeless tramps or pseudo-hippies, or are given the finest foods on outrageous expense accounts, they are often the worst enemies of their own health so long as they chatter and character-assassinate during meals. To recommend silence at meals may seem a hard measure, but without silence there will be no gratitude, no thinking of the forgotten persons who planted the seeds and took trouble to raise the food, much less any thought of sun and soil, winds or rain. Long before one can sanctify eating, there must be silence during meals.

Similarly, silence as preparation for sleep is important, and so too is silence upon awakening. This must be internal, not merely external, silence. Most people have great difficulty in winding down at the end of the day. They have got to find a way to stop it, whether by music, by yogurt, by telling a nursery tale, by humming or by listening to white noise. One has to find a way to calm down so that one can enter into sleep cheerfully and calmly. One must enter sleep as if one is ready to commune with the divine, to seek true refreshment and the richest spiritual privacy. One should go into sleep as if it were a very great privilege, and then come out of it with as much gratitude and quiet alertness as possible.

It is precisely such simple moves that will do the most good. Telling people to sanctify breathing and eating is too much too soon, especially in an age in which one grows up thoughtlessly, misuses every object, and is totally utilitarian, whilst fudging ethical and even economic accounting. This goes on everywhere all the time, and the massacre of elementals is horrendous, shaming even the Herods of our time. People use all sorts of aids and gadgets in their work and jobs, and when they are finished and do not need these tools any more, they discard them or leave them lying about. This is cruelty and carelessness to the elementals involved, and it negates whatever good intentions one might have had and whatever value and dignity there might have been in one's labours.

It is better to spend half an hour clearing up, and then three hours working, than to spend eight hours working and not one second clearing up. That way, one shows no gratitude to the elementals which have made it possible to accomplish anything. But most people leave messes after themselves and do not even thank those who come along and clean up later. Nobody ever taught them to be grateful, and now it is too late to learn because the habits are too entrenched. Thus, people constantly undo the good they do, since it never occurs to them that they themselves are largely collections of elementals, surrounded by oceans of elementals, for which they are trustees and which they must treat gently. To toss a simple paper clip aside is to incur the wrath of Nature. It is better to have human beings arrayed against one in a court of law than to confront the fury of a cast-off paper clip.

The wisest people in any community are often those who collect the garbage. They are the overlooked toilers who pick up the stuff contemptuously thrown away by others. Cheerful and wise, they help in Nature's work. Incredible though it may be from a middle-class perspective, high beings may well come into this society in the future by entering the families of these people and taking jobs gathering garbage. This is the best protection for high beings because it gives one quiet, privacy and the chance to assist Nature. But what of the people who thoughtlessly create the garbage? Their future is too awful to contemplate. Some are rebellious souls who have lived as the most inconsiderately uncouth beings in villages and towns all over the world for scores of lives, but that is no excuse for an incurably discontented life, coupled with an ingrained contempt for what they use.

Clearly, this Teaching is too difficult for such people, who have good reasons for believing in only one life (as the ads proclaim), and it is definitely not given for their own sake. True Spiritual Teachers do not make such mistakes. It is given for the sake of the millions of elementals which are constantly passing through such people. The more restless they are, the more elementals are affected. They come and go like grey storm clouds, symbolic of the breakdown in society, amidst the dark purple of the night and soft light of dawn. Once impressed, one can count on them to go on doing their irresistible magic, not just once, but again and again. Repetition is the law of life for all classes of elementals, ranging from nature spirits to the presiding constituents of the four elements, as well as the whole host of three hundred and thirty million *devas* and *devatas,* the "nerves of Nature", whose impresses are indelibly recorded upon "Nature's infinite negative". Once they are graciously given that which will benefit them, they will endlessly give it back, such is the richness and generosity of Nature. But once one violates the laws of gratitude and misuses elementals, no amount of hocus-pocus will prevent one from getting retributive karma life after life.

That is why Buddha came to teach the Law, which is meta-mathematical and inexorable. The greatest beings are those who work with and appreciate that Law. They are fearful of nothing, because they know that there is nothing stronger on earth than the power of concentrated benevolence. There is nothing more beautiful than a man who casts no shadow and leaves no footprints. Above all, they know the sacred mark of the twice-born, the truly initiated exemplars and helpers of all humanity. Therefore, they are constantly hoping that human beings will emerge out of the great mass who can procreate with great reverence, humility and gratitude – using a sacred pair of temples and making them one even if for a few moments – for the purpose of aiding these high beings to come into this world. Even if hiding as garbage collectors, they can start to take over the earth and spell out the ethics of the new Aquarian Age, which will be an age of sacred speech, quiet and honest work, effortless cooperation and spontaneous solidarity.

That will mark a tremendously different time from the present, and in this raucous transition one cannot expect one's home to become what it really should be – a centre of light, warmth and love. In fact, one is more in danger at home than one will ever be in the outside world. One must rid oneself of the illusion that hiding behind a set of walls is the same as being alone. On the contrary, that is exactly when one is closest to all the invisible residents of the invisible world. When one is out at the office and working, by contrast, one has more protection, because one is among a lot of human beings who are keeping busy. The privacy of one's own home – be it an apartment, condominium or family residence – is an illusion.

It is perfectly true that the abode of the authentic homeless wanderer, the *sannyasin,* is the sphere of light around him. But one can emulate this only if one can find the true centre of one's consciousness in the divine ray that is prior to the prism. Within that sphere, one will have a home without walls and there will be no problem of separation. This home is open on every side to every entity and elemental. The moment anything comes closer to it, it behaves like the marvellous dogs found outside Tibetan monasteries which, even today after all the horrors of what has happened there, behave as calmly as monks, if not more so. Such animals most easily reflect and mirror what is real in the states of consciousness of cheerfully self-disciplined human beings around them. In the presence of the divine Teachings, even a cat may come forward to receive them, feeling he or she deserves them more than many of the human beings present. At that level, Nature never fails.

If individuals who are faced with numerous stresses and are affected by the surrounding atmosphere of breakdown, gloom and doom would begin to reflect deeply upon these Teachings, they would soon see that there is no trick they can use to avoid depression. No drug or pill, potion or panacea, will help. Instead, they must come to see the central meaning of the Zero Principle (online at http://www. theosophytrust.org/rni_articles.php, or see *The Dawning of Wisdom*) for their lives; everything they need already exists in abundance within their own sphere of light, and no external aids are needed. There is nothing which one does not already have, if one can centre oneself. Thus the moment one grasps an adventitious aid, one is running away from the problem. External aids may work temporarily as a palliative, but they will not, as the best doctors and psychologists know, effect a cure. Instead, one must look calmly at what one is depressed about, and consider the plight of beings worse off than oneself. One should think through what one proposes to do about the problem – and the less one passes it on to others, the better.

Depressed elementals that have come into one's vestures must be welcomed and treated with compassion. They must be told that they are taking themselves too seriously. They should not be ridiculed, but should be put in place and sent off, cleansed, out into the world. This can be done by sitting calmly in a chair and facing the problem honestly. Anything that prevents one from taking responsibility will never get one out of the woods, but will only plunge one much more deeply into difficulty after death. Anyone who sees this clearly will want to take responsibility promptly, without depending upon external aids. This is not to say that one cannot use common sense. If one has a lot of bad habits, one can improve them or replace them with better ones. If one has eaten a lot of junk, one can find an herb shop and get some good herbs. In the end, however, one must not depend upon what is outside. Even if one takes a healing herb, one's mental relation to it, one's faith in it and one's love and gratitude towards it make all the difference in the world. Unless one breathes these subjectively from within without into the herb, it will not release its healing essence.

Nothing, in fact, works automatically or mechanically in living Nature. At most, as in Christian Science, certain semi-occult techniques can work on the physical plane to push problems onto the astral plane, where they will get back at one much more viciously in the future. Rather than ensuring that one's problems bear such compound interest, it is much better to come to terms with them, catching them the moment they start. If one was kept quiet as a child and not encouraged to move one's hands around, and if one has been loved, not so much as a mutable object, but as an immortal soul, one will find it easier to quieten one's elementals. But even if one has become nervous and insecure, and is stuck with a persistent restlessness, one does not want to pass this along to one's elementals all the time. If one does, there will be no place to hide. As an adolescent, one may have gotten away from one's parents, but there is no way one will ever get away from one's elementals.

As the camel insinuated its nose under the edge of the Arab's tent before claiming sole ownership, one will discover, rather unexpectedly, that one's whole vesture is taken over. One will even, alas, become so soulless that no amount of make-up or posturing will hide the fact that the soul is gone. There will merely be one more mediumistic victim for the evil magicians of this earth, caught in the holocaust they instigate. Tragically, there has never been a better time for them to do this, because there are so many people compulsively repudiating the ABCs of living. Too few are willing, when they have enough to eat and enough to live on, to insert themselves into Nature and proceed quietly from middle age to death. In the name of pseudo-democracy, everyone has started using his tongue endlessly in the cause of ego aggrandizement.

The inevitable massacre of innocents has been horrendous. Universal unhappiness, ubiquitous rudeness and pervasive misanthropy, universal ill health, widespread pollution and collective depression have been engendered to a degree that passes beyond belief and all understanding. The elementals are having their riot of rapacious vengeance. They will continue to do so, and be welcome to do so, until the balance of Nature is restored. Indeed, like wise physicians who recognize that a disease must reach and pass through a crisis before there can be healing, those who truly care for the future of humanity look forward to the worsening symptoms with secretly cherished and consecrated hope. On the other hand, those courageous souls who are willing to forget themselves even a little bit, insert themselves into the whole a little bit, and begin to develop the powers of listening and silence will flourish.

There are many fine souls in our society and throughout the world who still know what it is to live quietly, humbly and responsibly. They may be unimportant, but they have learnt how to live in accordance with Nature. Nor are they purchasing the notion that they are useless because they did not go to college and did not study pseudo-psychology or an ethnically and sexually biased mixture of sociology and anthropology. Though many such people exist, others, despite their miseducation and their misanthropy, must go back to the basics (the eternal verities) and learn to speak the language of responsibility and practise the etiquette of silence and reverence. Ultimately, the soul must learn the sacred language of cosmic and theurgic sacrifice, which is the basis of all spiritual alchemy and noetic magic in Nature. In essence and at the root, nothing else exists but intelligent or involuntary participation in *universal cosmic sacrifice*. This is the Teaching of *adhiyajna*, the secret and sovereign remedy hidden, as if inside a series of Chinese boxes, within the words of the *Bhagavad Gita*. It is the noblest teaching, and the most difficult. There is no way to jump to it from the realm of moral and mental chaos, for there are many necessary steps in between.

That is why *Light on the Path* says that one must first learn to observe sensation, and learn from it the true laws of life. Then one can set one's foot on the first rung of the ladder. The moment a person goes back to the ABCs, to the fundamentals of the perennial philosophy of *Gupta Vidya,* and learns what it is to set one's foot on the first step of the ladder, one will attract cheerful, learning elementals. There are plenty of them, actually, millions more than the perverse and malicious elementals, but they will not be attracted unless one is childlike, grateful and wide-eyed. If one does not mean what one says, or does not do what one says one will do, they will be repelled. They are characterized by utter fidelity, and are so chaste, virginal and faithful that they can never be attracted to someone who is unfaithful, fickle or anxious. There is no getting away from the basics – from fidelity, honesty with oneself, internal credibility, chastity of thought, chastity of feeling and conduct, boundless compassion, unconditional love, impeccable integrity and inextinguishable courage. So long as these are present, vast numbers of learning elementals will be attracted, especially during the still hours of the night and at sunrise and sunset.

Sadly, the very times which are most auspicious for the arrival and congregation of these elementals are also the times when people make the most raucous noise, pretending to go to work or come home. To reverse all this radically requires extraordinary patience and mountainous firmness, because one must invite and invoke enough elementals responsive to the basics of the divine art of being human to counter the perverse elementals. It is to be hoped, hoping against all hope, that they will come as a wondrous host, under the same laws of attraction and repulsion, when one is sufficiently armed with the good elementals to engage in the healing of all tortured elementals. Typically, the way people live, they become wide open to the raucous bad elementals, and they create mental walls and barriers before the good pixie-like elementals, either in the name of pseudo-sophistication or some other pretentious nonsense that is altogether against Nature and life. This actually creates walls between them and the Avataric light, between them and the Mahatmas, as well as between them and their companions. Self-immured, they finally become virtual zombies succumbing before the astral light and its noxious pollution.

If one is tough enough to attempt a decisive change in the tonality and tangible quality of one's way of living, one must appreciate the wisdom of considering the arcane and accredited Teachings about elementals. In them one will find the seeds needed for planting fresh resolves in clean soil. Fundamentally, one must learn to see the universal and undivided diffusion of life in all of cosmic Nature, invisible and visible. This means understanding that there is nothing more powerful on earth than the *paramatman*, the Highest Self, and its perpetual *buddhic* radiance, the Holy Ghost, the light of *daiviprakriti*, the voice of *Brahma Vach*. The Father-*Atman*, the Mother-*Buddhi*, and the Son-*Manas* in man, as in the cosmos, are omnipotent. No demon, no illness, no malicious entity, no paranoid ism or ideology, can touch the man or woman who truly lives in the *Atman*. Many lazy, shallow and worldly neo-Vedantins thought that they could skip the ladder of growth by saying "I am *brahman*", but they were only fooling themselves so vainly that Gautama Buddha came and told them to be quiet, to become monks and to observe rules of gentleness and honesty. This is an old story, and it is happening all over again.

What needs to be done can be done, but it will only be done when one feels that it is the single most important thing in one's life. High seriousness immediately arouses and attracts the higher classes of elementals. When one is serious and concentrated – what Emerson termed "man thinking" – and in earnest, one attracts refined grades of elementals. When one is vacillating, loquacious, weak-willed or contradictory, the worst elementals are inexorably drawn to one. Put simply, one must clean out one's house and temple. Turn to the God within and lock the doors to the demons without. Open your eyes to the stars, your ears to the music of the divine spheres, and your heart to the pulse-beat of humanity. Then, very quietly, walk alone in a new direction.

Hermes, December 1987

THE LIFE-GIVING STREAM

The Secret Doctrine is the accumulated Wisdom of the Ages, and its cosmogony alone is the most stupendous and elaborate system: e.g., even in the exotericism of the Puranas. But such is the mysterious power of occult symbolism, that the facts which have actually occupied countless generations of initiated seers and prophets to marshal, to set down and explain, in the bewildering series of evolutionary progress, are all recorded on a few pages of geometrical signs and glyphs. The flashing gaze of those seers has penetrated into the very kernel of matter, and recorded the soul of things there, where an ordinary profane, however learned, would have perceived but the external work of form.

The Secret Doctrine, i 272

The Secret Doctrine is directed to those who are devoutly seeking to bring about a fundamental transformation in embodied consciousness. Early in the book H.P. Blavatsky states: " *'When* Buddhi *absorbs our EGO-tism (destroys it) with all its* Vikaras, Avalokiteshvara *becomes manifested to us, and* Nirvana, *or* Mukti, *is reached,' 'Mukti' being the same as* Nirvana, *i.e., freedom from the trammels of Maya' or* illusion. *'Bodhi' is likewise the name of a particular state of trance condition, called* Samadhi, *during which the subject reaches the culmination of spiritual knowledge."* If *samadhi* and *nirvana* are exalted states of consciousness, evidently the Brotherhood of Bodhisattvas, the Society of Sages, the Lodge of Mahatmas continuously resides on this cosmic plane of supreme cognition. These self-luminous beings are everywhere and nowhere, with three main sanctuaries on this globe: one beyond the Himalayas, which has existed from the most ancient times; another in the Near East, which also goes back far beyond recorded history; and the third in South America. Yet, while there are these secret centres of initiation, access to the Brotherhood has nothing to do with physical nearness or distance. Mahatmas are essentially beings who ceaselessly function on unseen planes of ideation mirroring universal states of consciousness. Any individual anywhere who is universal in spirit, non-sectarian in attitude, free from fixation upon place or time, who is truly devoted

318

to universal good and human welfare, may come into the radius of influence of the Brotherhood of Bodhisattvas and their accredited agents in the world.

The Dedication of *The Secret Doctrine* strikes the self-validating keynote of universality:

> This Work I dedicate to all True Theosophists, in every Country, and
> of every Race, for they called it forth, and for them it was recorded.

In the Preface, the same keynote of universality is strongly stressed. The teachings of Theosophy are not confined to the ancient tetrad comprised by the Hindu, the Zoroastrian, the Chaldean and the Egyptian religions. Nor is it the exclusive possession of the more recent Buddhist, Islamic, Judaic and Christian faiths. The Secret Doctrine is the essence of all these. "Sprung from it in their origins, the various religious schemes are now made to merge back into their original element, out of which every mystery and dogma has grown, developed, and become materialised." Owing to the fall of all religions through false claims and creedal dogmas, true seekers everywhere today are longing to find the pristine source of Divine Wisdom, pure and unsullied. Naturally, even among such earnest seekers there is the ever-present danger of materialization. This can be minimized through close attention to the critical distinction made in the *Bhagavad Gita* between the external attributes and the immaterial essence of the Self-Governed Sage. Those who have eyes will always be able to see and will also be able to know how to come closer to the Trans-Himalayan Brotherhood, which is not to be found by external means. It has monasteries and schools and systems of initiation in secret sanctuaries which cannot be readily discovered by travel and exploration. Even the individual seeker who is able, by undertaking a pilgrimage, to come closer to the Brotherhood, is led on by the intuition of the heart, by inner guidance, and not by maps or any adventitious aids.

H.P. Blavatsky once stated that a single journey to the East undertaken in the proper spirit will do more than all the books in the world. She herself conducted such a journey but she was intensely concerned with fundamental questions: Who, where, and what is God? How can man's spirit prove God's spirit? These were the burning questions in her heart to which she devoted years of thought and enquiry. Having already had the vision of her Guru, asking these questions, she, as a great Teacher, re-enacted for the sake of the entire human race the archetypal quest for enlightenment. This is part of the ever-renewed sacrifice of every Rishi or Mahatma. Inquirers who have sought the Brotherhood of Bodhisattvas through external means are easily misled. In the Aquarian Age, especially, no encouragement can be given to people who want some kind of external and verifiable means of speeding their own growth. True spiritual growth is wholly internal, and only its efflorescence may illumine the external world through wisdom in thought, word and deed. This is the fruition of continuous meditation, and therefore one must realize, as many an ancient seeker knew, that the sacred places of pilgrimage correspond to secret centres in the human constitution. For example, *Prayag*, the meeting-place of rivers, corresponds to a spiritual centre in every human being. The symbolism of a sacred pilgrimage conveys clues to the inner meaning of the teaching, intimating the inward ascent through which a human being comes closer to planes of consciousness involving higher centres within the human vestures. It is possible, through deep meditation, to enter the inmost sanctuary within the tabernacle of Isis, Shekinah, Sarasvati, Kwan Yin, *Brahma Vach*. An indispensable prerequisite is true devotion to the *Ishtaguru*.

The word *Theosophia* goes back to Ammonius Saccas and earlier, and there has continued an unbroken line of shining witnesses in every part of the world – even where the mystery-fires were snuffed out long ago. This line may be discerned in a few Church Fathers like Origen and Clement of Alexandria, as well as in St. Augustine. It is clearly to be seen in the neo-Platonic thinkers, as in Pythagoras and Plato, and also among the pre-Socratics. From further back than Krishna and Buddha, the ancient Egyptians and Chaldeans, and continuing all the way through recorded history, it comes down again through the last seven centuries, starting with the First Impulsion of the modern Theosophical Movement given in the fourteenth century by Tsong-Kha-Pa, who came to resuscitate the Divine Wisdom. Every century thereafter a special effort was made by the Lodge of Mahatmas to awaken human awareness of the accessibility as well as the enduring existence of the Wisdom Religion. Thus, as it is stated in the archetypal affirmation of the Declaration of the United Lodge of Theosophists, *"The true Theosophist belongs to no cult or sect, yet belongs to each and all."* *The Secret Doctrine* of H.P. Blavatsky is an encyclopaedic and talismanic guide to that which is hidden in nature, to the sacred scriptures of the world and to the ancient source of arcane knowledge. It points to the great range of diverse cultures of the recorded and unrecorded past, providing keys to many language systems, mythic maps, code languages in mystical texts, alchemical works and ancient catechisms, some of them orally transmitted or only partly transcribed and some dependent upon further commentaries that are not readily available. The two volumes encompass such a vast and varied range of material that if one were to spend one's entire life trying to follow up on every term and concept, on every school and system, one would find at the end of a lifetime that one would have to start all over again in future lives. This is truly a Himalayan pilgrimage.

Speaking of the great Transmitters of the Wisdom Religion, H.P. Blavatsky states:

> They were the authors of new forms and interpretations, while the truths upon which the latter were based were as old as mankind. Selecting one or more of those grand verities, actualities visible only to the eye of the real Sage and Seer – out of the many orally revealed to man in the beginning, preserved and perpetuated in the *adyta* of the temples through initiation, during the MYSTERIES and by personal transmission – they revealed these truths to the masses. Thus every nation received in its turn some of the said truths, under the veil of its own local and special symbolism; which, as time went on, developed into a more or less philosophical *cultus*, a Pantheon in mythical disguise.
>
> *The Secret Doctrine*, i xxxvi

In the process of transmission there is an inevitable dilution of the life-giving stream of the eternal Wisdom. Every sincere seeker must make an earnest effort to grasp what it would mean for these truths to be actualities visible only to the eye of the Sage and the Seer. For example, many Theosophists are vaguely familiar with the Sanskrit term *Mulaprakriti*, root-matter, which is also known by the English phrase 'primordial root-substance'. If one were to probe deeply into what is currently thought about matter, one would discern that already in contemporary physics the concept of matter is so subtle and recondite, so much an abstraction, that it has nothing to do with crude sensory conceptions of matter. If, through meditation upon the very idea of root-matter, one were to go even further, using several sections of *The Secret Doctrine* which throw light upon the philosophical problems connected with matter and forces, one could begin to comprehend what is meant by pure, noumenal matter. By experiencing even at a preliminary level that which would make the word *Mulaprakriti* sacred, one could become increasingly conscious of the ever-present cosmic sacrifice of which Shri Krishna spoke to Arjuna.

If the seeker is not living out of any concern with individual salvation, but only out of a deep desire for universal progress, then one can become a true devotee of Krishna. The Guru is depicted in the abstract portrait of the Self-Governed Sage given by Krishna. Persisting in true devotion to such a Guru, who will always be both an ideal and a fact, a veil and a presence, a person may experience subtle mutations in his vestures. The physical body changes considerably every seven years. The skin is completely renewed every seven years, and the lines on the hand change more slowly but surely. Micro-changes take place continually, affecting the blood and its circulation. The entire system renews itself so continuously that one is constantly involved in these alterations and changes. They apply not only to the gross astral that is called the physical body, but involve processes which are witnessed by and are relevant to the immortal soul. The way in which the soul sees and apprehends these processes can make a decisive difference to the whole of one's life. The common saying that "You are as young as you feel" is the mirroring of a profound truth when 'feel' is understood in terms of how one thinks and breathes. Spiritual rates of metabolic transmutation, change and transformation can be affected by the Guru who can see into the very essence of things, and deals directly with a facet of *Mulaprakriti* which is the substratum of *Akasa*. If one genuinely tries to work through correspondences, then although one may not directly understand the process, one can at some level appreciate it by analogy to the sense of lightening and refining of the physical instrument that comes with bathing. All human souls have some glimmer of awareness of noumenal states of matter, but to be able to put that knowledge to work needs meditation, continuity of consciousness and continuous concern. Typically this quality of concentration and continuity will not be forthcoming except among those few who have such an overwhelming love for the human race, profound compassion for human suffering and pure joy in the presence of Divine Wisdom, that they would really wish to commit themselves totally and continuously to progressive self-refinement for the sake of all.

With deep concentration there is a distinct change in the quality of perception. The left eye and the right eye focus differently, not only on the physical plane, but also in ways that involve centres behind the eyes suggested in phrases like 'the mind's eye', 'the soul's eye' and what Krishna calls "the place between thine eyes". The eyes are the windows of the soul, and it is possible to unfold spiritual perception slowly, intermittently, but recognizably. The perception which unfolds is similar in kind, even though distant in degree, to the eye of the Sage and Seer. That is an eye for which there is no veil, an eye which can see into past, present and future though it does not see them as such but only an eternal Now. What is day to the Sage is night to the ordinary man, and what is day to the ordinary man is night, the night of ignorance, to the Sage. There is a radical difference in the perception of light and darkness, abstract and concrete, real and unreal, day and night, between the Sage or Seer and the seeker who is still fumbling and stumbling with sensory perceptions, with worldly desires, with carnal limitations, with a narrow sense of identity and personality, but who still wishes to go beyond. There is evidently a radical difference between the spiritual wisdom come alive in those who breathe it, and those who merely have it on hearsay. This is the oldest distinction in the world. In Shankara it is the distinction between *aparavidya* and *paravidya, parokshavidya* and *aparokshavidya,* indirect knowledge and direct awareness.

This is hinted at in the Preface, where the word 'revelation' is used, and in different places in the book where the idea of spiritual revelation or spiritual seership is elucidated. In the beginning we are told that:

> . . . the secret portions of the *'Dan'* or *'Jan-na'* (*'Dhyan'*) of Gautama's metaphysics – grand as they appear to one unacquainted with the tenets of the Wisdom Religion of antiquity – are but a very small portion

of the whole. The Hindu Reformer limited his public teachings to the purely moral and physiological aspect of the Wisdom-Religion, to Ethics and MAN alone. Things 'unseen and incorporeal,' the mystery of Being outside our terrestrial sphere, the great Teacher left entirely untouched in his public lectures, reserving the hidden Truths for a select circle of his Arhats. The latter received their Initiation at the famous Saptaparna cave (the *Sattapanni* of Mahavansa) near Mount Baibhar.

The Secret Doctrine, i xx

And then we are told on the next page:

How the purity of these grand revelations was dealt with may be seen in studying some of the so-called 'esoteric' Buddhist schools of antiquity in their modern garb, not only in China and other Buddhist countries in general, but even in not a few schools in Thibet, left to the care of uninitiated Lamas and Mongolian innovators.

The Secret Doctrine, i xxi

In India, in China and Japan, in Siam and Burma, in Egypt and Greece, in Chaldea and Mesopotamia, later in Rome and in the Arab world and among the Jews, and in the modern age in Europe and the United States of America, also in the last hundred years in the Theosophical Movement, it is the same story of partial understanding leading to misunderstanding, concretization resulting in desecration. That is the karma of the transmission of Divine Wisdom, because the uninitiated will, in the sense in which Jesus spoke of casting pearls before swine, drag down the solar teaching into the murky realm of lunar consciousness polluted by profane sense-perceptions. This is profanation, but at the same time, the immortal soul in those individuals may gain some food for *sushupti* and for *devachan* if they still have some link with the higher Triad. There would also be those who can get their mental luggage ready for another life. One may never really know how the process goes on from the outside, but one can understand why something always had to be kept secret from every person who is self-excluded from the sacred circle of initiates and ascetics. There will always be such a sacred circle, just as there will always be only a few who actually have climbed Himalayan peaks. But there will be very,

very many who are fascinated by the enterprise.

Those courageous souls who are truly drawn to spiritual mountain climbing will be struck by the *Stanzas of Dzyan,* the *sutratman* of the *Gupta Vidya,* which forms the basis of the volumes of *The Secret Doctrine.* These *Stanzas* are also included as an appendix to *The Voice of the Silence,* which is derived from the same ancient source. Through their help, it is possible "to reform one's self by meditation and knowledge", but for this to happen, everything depends upon the state of mind and consciousness in which one approaches them. Those who have found them helpful take the *Stanzas* and read them silently again and again. On the whole, reading them aloud would be unwise because one may activate lower psychical forces much faster than one has gained the ability to govern them. This is a hazard with many people because of the ratios of the noetic to psychic in their lives. It is always a good practice to read quietly and absorb ideas with the mind's eye so that one receives the teaching on deeper planes than merely through the astral senses. Because in the Aquarian Age the mind is very crucial, without some understanding no such activity could be truly helpful ,and it may even degenerate into quasi-religious pseudo-ritual. This one does not want to encourage, and there is a constant danger that people will be pulled back through their *skandhas* into one or another form of ritualistic salvationism. The whole of *The Secret Doctrine* is a partial commentary on certain fragments of a few of many *Stanzas,* most of which are not given. If one understands all of these at some level, and tries to take a particular *Stanza,* making correlations between the *Transactions* and *The Secret Doctrine,* reading a paragraph and making a few notes, thinking deeply about it and meditating upon it, and then rereads the original *Stanza,* it would help. Clearly this is an exercise involving attention, effort, patience and calm. Anyone who has been so privileged as to have entered into the current of Divine Wisdom will have sensed that the *Stanzas of Dzyan* may be correctly intoned as the basis of noetic magic. This can only be done by initiates, a *mantra*mic activity that is not publicized. Nevertheless, it is extremely potent and has a profound effect upon the entire globe and is solely undertaken for the benefit of all living beings.

If a person is very far from these Himalayan prospects, and has in fact gone wrong for a period of time, for a year, for three years, for ten years, for ten lives, yet would wish to begin again on the Path of *Anasakti*, selfless action, and seeks to reform his or her self by meditation and spiritual knowledge, and even hopes for a second birth, this is indeed possible. Not only is it possible, it is verily the true purpose in transmitting *The Voice of the Silence* and *The Secret Doctrine*. The sacred teaching is for those who seek to become *dwijas*, twice-born, those who wish to be born again as in the Nazarene gospel, those who ardently aspire to be spiritually regenerated. But this must be the product of a patient, persistent and yet relatively unanxious reform of the self. Knowledge only becomes wisdom through meditation acting as the basis of realization. The more one meditates, the more one's knowledge becomes real. The more it becomes real, the more it acts upon one's life-atoms and the spiritual will, transforming the sense-organs and the body, altering and elevating one's whole life. It becomes the current of a living power made free in a human being, and is highly potent. *The Secret Doctrine* is for those who devoutly seek to become Men of Meditation. As a preparation, it is helpful to gain even a little spiritual knowledge, by Buddhic intuition, of the universal, hidden, archetypal, regenerating current of spiritual life-energy referred to as the living stream of wisdom. If one can get into the current, it is bound to make a change that will work slowly but infallibly. The proper use of *The Secret Doctrine* and *The Voice of the Silence* could be like unto the study of the *Vedas* or of the Gospels according to John or Thomas. Even if taken in small doses but on a regular basis, the way Nature does all things, much benefit can accrue. This is really the problem: Can people learn to grow as they have seen trees grow? A little bit done regularly is of inestimably more value than doing a lot one day and nothing for weeks.

Just because the study of *The Secret Doctrine* is so vast, it does not mean that one cannot gain some benefit even from taking a single phrase or a sentence from almost anywhere in the book. One can, as sincere effort will surely demonstrate. Sometimes people suppose that they cannot come any closer to *The Secret Doctrine* because they are unworthy, but this is a great mistake and a defamation of human dignity. Some people are always making an assumption that they "belong" to themselves. This is philosophically baseless, since the mere fact that they can formulate such a claim does not in the least imply that either the body or mind is a possession of theirs. Of what is any person claiming to be the owner in this 'private ownership theory' of the vestures? It is an absurd form of ignorance. One must put oneself in a learning mood or posture, and one must forget about worthiness and unworthiness. Instead, one should thrill to enter the perennial stream of supernal knowledge rendered into a living current of spiritual cleansing of the mind and purification of the heart, acting as a solvent to the lower will, and releasing the higher energies, potencies and faculties of the human being. That is what is truly intended, and those who have intuited the intention from the Preface, perhaps even from its very first words – "The Author – the writer, rather..." – will enter the stream in such a way that their lives will never be the same again. It is indeed a great shame that the golden opportunity is not taken by many more people. The reason usually is about the same, whatever the external excuses and explanations. It is a superficial entering of the stream that blocks a real entering of the stream. On the other hand, one who is afraid to enter the stream wastes this incarnation. Both of these are pointed out in *The Voice of the Silence*. Fear kills the will, leaving one paralyzed. Nothing may happen, but one will not get the golden karma, maybe for many lives, of coming any closer to such exalted teaching. Others, on the other hand, forget that the sacred teaching is for the whole of humanity, that it necessarily involves ascending planes of consciousness. Because of salvationist tendencies in previous lives, they take a Fundamentalist attitude towards *The Secret Doctrine*, supposing that through mere ritual repetition they will gain insight and find redemption. A person must, rather, choose a sentence for meditation, take a paragraph for reflection, select a page for reading as a preparation for reflection and meditation. If one has more time, and the energy and will are summoned after one's duties are done by nature and by man, one may read more for the sake of making a deep study in order to strengthen the quality of one's daily reflection and meditation.

One's whole attitude to what one can do every week is crucial. People are of differing capacities and temperaments and also have different ways of ordering their lives or of remaining disordered. It would be helpful if a person altogether avoided the 'hundred per cent *or* nothing' approach, which is Atlantean and adolescent blackmail, saying, "Either

I do it all or I do nothing", a sure sign of spiritual failure through pride and perversity. Just as *chelas* can recognize Adepts, it is only logical that Adepts can recognize failed *chelas*. Rather than become trapped in such foolish pride, one might cheerfully listen to the words of the Buddha: "Drop by drop a jar of water is filled." Choose a sentence, take a paragraph, but use it during the week to prepare for the next week. The real point is to gain greater continuity of consciousness. The Secret Doctrine is the unbroken, uninterrupted Wisdom of Those with unbroken, uninterrupted consciousness for over eighteen million years. They are the *Manushis* who became the Sons of Yoga, and those Sons of Yoga became the Sons of Wisdom. They teach under the same rule that was central to all the ancient systems of Spiritual Teaching: If you take one step in the direction of the Teaching and the Teacher, the Teacher will take one step in your direction and help you to become more capable, through meditation and practice, of spiritual regeneration, maybe even a second birth leading to further changes in lives to come.

> He who would hear the voice of Nada, the 'Soundless Sound', and comprehend it, he has to learn the nature of Dharana.

Hermes, January 1980

TO BE AND NOT TO BE

Guarding the nest beneath through the life-breath, the Spirit of man rises immortal above the nest.

Brihadaranyaka Upanishad

In earlier eras death and regeneration were often no more than remote subjects of philosophical curiosity or idle speculation. In contemporary history, however, this is increasingly the burning issue in the daily lives of innumerable individuals. Many people are afraid to formulate the central concern, but somehow they sadly acknowledge to themselves that Hamlet's question – "To be or not to be" – no longer has for them the literary flavour of a formal soliloquy. It is an anguished question so acutely pertinent at any moment that many people approaching the moment of death, as well as half-alive hosts of young men and women, are anxiously asking what is the meaning of modern life, and the possibilities of sustaining a clear, firm hope for the future. At a time of critical transition from obsolete formulae and shallow answers to a stark future without familiar guarantees, the very idea of survival takes on a strange and awesome meaning. In the early nineteenth century, when Prince Talleyrand was asked what he did during the French Revolution, he simply replied, "I survived." This is poignantly true of millions of people today. The mere fact of existing through one day from morning to evening, one week, one month, seems like a singular achievement. Is this because, as some rashly assert, a malign historical fate in the form of some tyrannical and frightening monster or ever-resourceful and vindictive scapegoat is responsible? Or does the explanation lie hidden in a new intensity of psychological pain of vast numbers of people nurtured by an inexplicable convergence of individual insights? People sense something about each other because of what they partly know about themselves. They recognize that many of the illusions that made modern life a spectacular caravan of glittering progress have become insupportable. These illusions are seen to be either deliberately manufactured lies or pathetically ineffectual forms of perception.

A person who really does believe that "God's in his heaven, all's right with the world", may either have had an inexplicable stroke of good fortune or some apparent reason for smug satisfaction in personal or professional life measured in terms of status or achievement. Even if such a person senses the grandeur of the world, he can no longer expect other men and women to concur with him. If they are tolerant and good-humoured in the way so many young people were for a golden moment in 1967, they might concede, "If it makes you feel good, go ahead." But such indulgence is now a luxury that few people apparently can afford. A person dare not admit to himself that he is enjoying himself. To do so seems somehow to hurl a blasphemous curse upon the social scene. Is this really because the sufferings of men are visible tokens of physical torment, or rather because there is a profound and pervasive soul-frustration? Behind the restlessness of vast ill-directed energy are haunting questions. Human beings do not find time for thought or contemplation. They do not sit down and calmly question where they are going, who they are, why they are doing what they are doing, why they share with many other human beings a seeming paralysis of will. Those who have been fortunate, owing to their early upbringing in easier times, to build up an infrastructure of habits which enable them to get up early and to greet the dawn, or to smile after breakfast and to have a sense that they had planned the day, at least have a sense of being able to cope at some level with life. But their sense of coping with it is wholly parasitic upon the acceptance of an excessive valuation placed upon something which is sacred only so long as no one questions it. The same people, late in the evening or around the time of twilight, or over the dulling effect of mixed drinks, suddenly only too readily admit the emptiness of their day. They willingly plunge in the opposite direction into a malaise which they dare not acknowledge during the day.

The rare opportunity at this moment lies in an increasing recognition by many that the time is past for diagnosis, patter and endless stating of the obvious. It is time to find out what one can do to make a difference in one's own life. The difference is, at heart, between the living and the dead. One might deliberately assume a critical distance from the contemporary scene and ask why the original impulse behind the technological culture with its staggering vitality – unprecedented in recorded history – seems to have run down. One might ask even more fundamental questions in terms of essential categories of apprehension that transcend history as a chronicle of events. That history is a tedious catalogue of sins, crimes and misfortunes is no new discovery. Gibbon came to this conclusion when examining the Roman Empire. Hegel held that the only lesson learnt from history is that nothing is learnt. Far more is needed than a feeble explanation of the contemporary hiatus with its anomie in terms of any rationalist philosophy of history. The relationship between propositions about collectivities and their fate and the individual's inability to give credible meaning to his own life is difficult to establish. Psychologically, the problem manifests as the apparent need for constant reinforcement. This has taken such an acute psycho-physiological form that most human beings today manage to cope with the enormous flux of sensory stimuli only by attenuating or toning down the impact of external stimuli. If they attempted the opposite, magnifying auditory and visual responses, intensifying sense-perceptions in general, they would be utterly lost. They would be smoked out amidst the blazing chaos of the surrounding world. So they take the opposite path – though seldom choosing it consciously – and it consolidates into a habitual pattern. They tone down, turn off, maintain a seemingly safe standpoint of passivity in relation to the world. They purchase magazines they do not read, see pictures they cannot grasp, greet people they do not truly notice. They deal with seemingly diverse objects of interest with minimal involvement. In a short time, this inevitably becomes self-defeating.

The more one reduces the impact of external stimuli upon one's sensorium, the more one needs more intense inputs of the same kind to sustain any residual capacity for assimilation. Therefore, it is not just metaphorically true that the U.S.A. is now a nation in which vast numbers of people suffer from spiritual hypoglycemia, an inability to distil the essence of experience into a form that could meaningfully channel energy, nurture creativity and sustain commitments. It is deeply threatening to many on the Pacific Coast that the sun shines, suspended like a blazing jewel over the ocean. Nature's abundant intimations may remind some of Athens, Alexandria and Knossos, of places far apart in historical time but where seminal impulses from a tempestuous intellectual and psychic ferment led in time to a tidal wave of creative energy, a renaissance of the human spirit. Though many may have a dim awareness that something like this seems to be imminent, they cannot in any meaningful manner connect themselves with what they see around them. The sense of the emptiness of all, the voidness of one's life, the meaninglessness of everything into which one is tempted to throw oneself with a false intensity, is intensifying so rapidly that all words seem irrelevant mutterings. Promises of golden citadels in the future resemble the unsecured promissory notes of a defunct company. Vision has no point of contact with anything in daily experience which all can use, to feel that they are truly affecting the world. It provides no basis for growth, no stimulus to the acceptance of pain, denial and death. The physical body, owing to its homeostatic metabolism and the involuntary processes of nature, functions as a system which can continually restore equilibrium. This is hard to achieve on the psychological plane in relation to the arbitrary fabrication of *namarupa,* name and form.

Brahma Vach speaks directly to any human being willing to get to the root of his own self-questioning. One has to ask fundamental questions. Is one willing to grant that this vast universe is a macrocosm, a single system, beyond comprehension and cataloguing, dateless yet with a future history which is unknown? If Nature exhibits processes that seem to move in opposing directions – expansion and contraction, withdrawal and involvement, separation and integration, aggregation and disintegration – can these be seen as the warp and woof of a single texture, interdependent aspects of an intelligent life-force? If this is true, why is it that human life has become so detached from the ordering principle in the cosmos? Why is the hazy conception of organic growth in nature, man-made conceptions, human lives and plans and notions of success and failure, satisfaction and misery, so inadequate to resolve fundamental questions about wholeness and disease? Is the individual prepared to concede that the physical body is fighting a constant and futile battle against inevitable disintegration, without which the organism could not even maintain itself? It surely seems like a losing battle. One is dying every moment. But is a person psychologically prepared to welcome this inescapable truth? Is one prepared to create for oneself, at least as an abstraction, a viable sense of identity that has no relationship to heredity and environment, to past events and future hopes, anticipations and regrets, fears, muddles and neuroses? Is one willing to see oneself not as a static sum of psycho-social conditions but as a dynamic series of states of mind over which one has little control, especially over their unavoidable shadows?

Could a person place his or her sense of selfhood beyond the proscenium of the theatre in which there are disordered scenes, a chaotic flux of deranged events with no inner connection? Is it perhaps meaningful for a person to say that to be a human being lies in the very act of seeking connections? If so, in discovering connections between events, past, present and future, between different elements in oneself, between elements in oneself and in others, why is it that one is such a cocksure coward? Why is one so willing to edit perceptions and memories to a degree that shuts out intermediary facts? Why is it that one will refuse to face what is readily confirmable by statistics concerning the untoward consequences of certain lines of activity? Human beings have become clever at avoiding the cancelling of their illusions to a point where they could not live. They have become adroit in avoiding those extreme conclusions that in concentration camps, in arenas of acute suffering, individuals in our own time have been forced to consider. The stark language of existentialism can be purchased so easily that anyone may quote Sartre or discourse in romantic terms about the Promethean agony and the burden of living. It is too easy to entertain the deceptive feeling of sharing in the poignant experience of Camus' *The Stranger* or of some piteous character in Sartre's *No Exit*.

In a deep sense human beings are afraid that neither the past nor the present contains clues to the future, collectively, historically or individually. The recognition that the restless intensity of men and women in pursuit of so-called progress was achieved only by making a Faustian deal with the devil, with some illicit external authority, is sufficient to show that the deal can no longer be made. Human beings cannot go back in the same direction; least of all can they do this if they inherit more opportunities for choice and greater psychological and social mobility than has ever been available to so many. All the games are over. Suddenly people are discovering the full implications of what it is to live in a society without moorings, charts or maps. Many are not even concerned to destroy the pathetic delusions of others because they feel that merely by ignoring them, these illusions are shown to be the more brittle. If a person consults the wisdom of the ancients, he will come to recognize that there is something true of nature as a whole which is also fundamentally significant to the human psyche.

Two contraries are simultaneously true of every person. First of all, at all times and in all contexts, any person can only live by making some unchallenged assumptions – that he is the centre of the world, that the world exists for his benefit, that his parents lived to bring him into the world, his teachers laboured to help him to get on in the world, his friends exist to support him in the world, that the vast panorama of visible nature exists for his enjoyment. Evil exists for his own moral education; he can recognize his assured detachment from evil by readily condemning it. The whole world for every man is seemingly a spectacle of which he is the central actor, the hero in a drama which, though private, can extend in every direction and become coterminous with as much of the social scene, of contemporary history and of the cosmos as he chooses to make it. At the same time, however, the contrary proposition is also true: the universe is indifferent to him. He is a very small affair in relation not only to the whole universe, to humanity or his nation, but even in relation to his immediate neighbourhood. For a man to feel fully conscious of both propositions at the same time is extraordinarily difficult – like telling a man who pleads, "To be or not to be, that is the question", that the unavoidable answer is "To be and not to be". This has little meaning unless one begins to ask what it means to say that one is or one is not. What is the very basis, the cash value, the logical foundation, the *raison d'etre,* the psychological significance of existing in a world unless one can understand what it is to exist in a world, to be anything at all? Why do men and women assume that because their categories, utterances and theories limit human consciousness, any difference is made to the vast energy-fields in the universe?

Consciousness is prior to form. Consciousness defies categorization. Consciousness is indefinable. All states of mind are only arbitrarily connected with an apparent succession of moments in time. Time is only an illusion produced by the succession of our states of consciousness as we travel through eternal duration. It does not exist where no consciousness exists in which the illusion can be produced. There could not be a world of objects perceived by human beings unless it were a kaleidoscope of forms which had the illusion of stasis. Yet this is a universe of perpetual motion in which the appearance of stasis in form is a psychological trap resulting from an optical illusion. This persistent illusion becomes inescapable because one has a magnified sense of one's own existence. One's ego-sickness thus becomes a form of health. The excess of exaggerated valuation becomes normal because it can neither be contradicted nor falsified. When a boy first meets a girl and says he loves her, thinking that his love for her is infinite and inexhaustible, that she is infinitely worth loving and his love is the greatest thing on earth, this is really a truth about himself. If he believes in it, he is the only one who can verify or falsify that belief. No one else can deny it to him, and no one can confirm it. If a person gets into the habit of excessive valuation of seemingly separate objects which are apparently static in a universe of motion, he must do this as a conscious participant or as an unconscious agent in the illusion. He could do so as a conscious negator who has to use the language of stasis in the discourse of daily life and in the ritual responses of everyday human encounter. He has to be many selves. But at any given time, only that self is alive and relevant to him which he can actualize and maintain in a collective context. This means that the self which engenders his deepest thoughts and feelings, woven from the fabric of his private meditation and secret heart, that self which has no assignable name or date, which has no reference to events, is a self that simply cannot be rendered in language. Only by a systematic and deliberate process of inverting the naming game can a person become self-conscious of that which is fundamental to life itself – the ceaseless motion at the very core of life which cannot be subsumed under any pair of opposites, even life and death.

At this point, mythic images and archetypal analogies are more helpful than the tortured language of discursive reason. The greatest living image of antiquity is the cosmic dance of Shiva. Brahmâ – from *brih*, "to expand" – is the creative expansive force that nurtures the universe of differentiated life. Vishnu is the preserving and sustaining continuity in the field of consciousness which enables a world to maintain itself. Death and regeneration may summon that supremely enigmatic god Shiva, engaged in a spectacular cosmic dance which effortlessly negates all ephemeral expectations. Shiva's magically fluidic movement in the sublime cosmic dance *(Tandava Nritya)* re-enacts the continual victory of immortality over death, of consciousness over form, of the ever-existent over the necessarily limited and evanescent. And yet Shiva has the appearance of being immobile. It is an overwhelming image. Anyone who has seen a statue of Shiva Nataraja could recognize that it is full of a burgeoning potential energy, immeasurable yet motionless. It is a glorious presentment in a divinely human form of the universe as a whole – a rhythmic, harmonious, ceaseless motion. While there are sporadic staccato movements, while there are dense shadows and great empty spaces in contrast to the dramatic intensity of movement, at the same time it is like a blank screen. From one standpoint one sees form and nothingness, lights and shadows; from another point of view one senses something deeper which relativates light and shadow and makes both equally unreal in relation to primordial, ever-existent darkness pregnant with infinite possibility. There is inconceivably more light than could ever be shown by visual contrast with darkness. Metaphysically, a profound and purifying theme for deep meditation is the Void or Darkness, the *Mysterium Tremendum*, beyond all light and darkness.

As an aid to understanding, one might think of the mystical analogy of the midnight sun. Most human beings under the sun cannot transcend the awareness of what the sun does for all, beyond complimenting the sun by saying that it is gorgeous or great. To be able to visualize the reality of the sun without form or visible representation is an act of philosophical re-creation, metaphysically and magically enshrined in the great myth of Shiva. There is the glorious prospect of self-conscious godhood in man which accepts, enjoys and celebrates; of continuity of consciousness which looks forward to recurrent psychological death as a necessary step in a subtle process of invisible growth; of cancellation and negation, voluntarily chosen or compelled by nature, which makes possible endless re-creation. There is only one ultimate choice for the human being. He must *either* void his puny plans, his absurdly narrow impositions upon the world and the great fluid process of life, *or* it will be done for him in a universe of constant interaction and total interdependence. There is a tremendous difference between taking the standpoint of a being who is unconditioned, who sees beyond form, who stands behind the veil of appearance and yet participates in the flux and thereby cooperates with the negations of his own externalizations, and the personal stance of someone who lives as if he dare not know what other people think of him. He sadly dwells in a protected cocoon of self-spun illusion from which he will never emerge, hiding from everything which threatens the false stasis and equilibrium derived from a premature cohesion that he imposes, preserves and reinforces in his plausible identifications. In the words of Plotinus:

> The Soul is bound to the body by a conversion to the corporeal passions; and is again liberated by becoming impassive to the body. That which Nature binds, Nature also dissolves; and that which the Soul binds, the Soul likewise dissolves. Nature, indeed, bound the body to the Soul; but the Soul binds herself to the body. Nature, therefore, liberates the body from the Soul; but the Soul must liberate herself from the body. Hence there is a two-fold death; the one, indeed, universally known, in which the body is liberated from the Soul; but the other, peculiar to philosophers, in which the Soul liberates herself from the body. Nor does the one entirely follow the other.

Although this esoteric doctrine is far-reaching and fundamental, it is meaningless for a person who does not seriously use it in daily life in alert "care of the soul", as Plato taught. This is also true of the whole of *Brahma Vidya*. The Buddha taught the doctrine of *anatta*, 'non-self', and Buddhist monks insisted on the idea that there is no personal entity or separate existence. One finds similar utterances by Krishna, Shankaracharya and Christ, and by all true Teachers, showing the supreme need for self-transcendence and second birth. Being alive in a world where the common denominator of illusions constantly throws a shadow upon the screen of time compels even those who know better to drink the muddy waters of collective delusion. Everyone has ample experience of this dross. One may generate a sense of what one is going to do this week, of premeditation and deliberation, allowing quiet spaces between moments and events, being alone, determining what one wants to do, deciding how much value to put upon each engagement in the week. Taking mental stock in advance of every week is a talismanic act of courage, and it must be repeatedly tested. How else will one know that one is aligned with any realistic thinking about the future, about the coming season or decade? Having resolved to live one's own life as well as possible for an entire week, one enters into one or another institution replete with the drugged – doped on alcohol, amphetamines, or one or another illusion – wandering around like psychic automata, heavy with fatigue, uttering words without meaning and making gestures without faith. One is going to fall prey to the collective psychic *turba* and one is going to forget. According to the Buddhist texts on meditation, if a person truly meditates upon *Tathata*, he soon comes to comprehend the wheel of births and deaths. He will begin to see why people cling to those few oases in their spiritually desolate lives where they enjoy a sense of the timeless, states of mind unconcerned with the succession of events, where they can appreciate a natural flow. These periods have become rare, and so that which takes place unconsciously during sleep or in the trance state cannot be made relevant to the conscious self. A person must put these aside and accept the fact that life is one tedious thing after another. Being able to live from within, meaningfully and creatively, to live without illusion by negating without suspicion and distrust, is extraordinarily difficult to understand. Yet it is this mystical paradox which is the secret of immortality represented by the ceaseless outpouring of life and light from the sun. There is a rhythmic solar breathing in and breathing out, recapitulated for each human being in the heartbeat – the systole and diastole, the contraction and expansion that maintains in continuity a living process that sustains itself. The process is not wholly self-generating because there is no such thing in the realm of differentiated gross matter; nonetheless, even in the realm of matter, the process of life assumes a certain rhythm of self-replenishment.

Great spiritual teachers know that the only way to overcome time is through the untapped wisdom of the soul, which is immutable and immortal in relation to all its vehicles. By returning to the very root of consciousness, it is possible on the plane of thought or ideation to create around oneself a self-sustaining field, at a certain critical distance from form, out of a living awareness which is always deeper than that needed to maintain and sustain activity in existence. Self-consciousness at its very beginning is like the 1 that commences the arithmetical series. Form at its root is geometrical and assumes the primary geometrical expression – that of a sphere. Thus, every human being must think of the Self as the One that is pre-existent to all the manifestations of one's own personal self, one's own states of mind and emotion, one's ties through time to the past and the future through memory, anticipation and regret, through destructive and wasteful re-enactment of what has gone, reliving in advance what cannot therefore be truly experienced. For a person to do all this is continually to restore the full awareness that, as the *Katha Upanishad* teaches, "Higher than the impulses, higher than the bodily powers and the emotions is the soul, and higher still is the Self. Higher than this is the unmanifest and higher than the unmanifest is the Spirit." This is the hidden SELF. It is prior to all manifestation. What is unmanifested in that SELF is ontologically prior to and psychologically more potent than all that is manifested. To use a simple analogy, a truly creative architect is absorbed in the intrinsic activity of creation out of the alembic of his imagination, against the plastic and fluidic energy of the materials with which he works. For him to visit a building that he has planned and built is really to see something with which he has very little concern. He does not involve himself in that which shows itself, for it is lost in the limbo of the past. There are human beings in life who can relate in this way to other human beings, situations and events by self-consciously managing minimal involvement sufficiently well to make the involvement meaningful for others. This requires a conscious training of the ' I ', an increasing ability to invoke that which is beyond all the actors present. Every good actor knows what is meant by the famous utterance, "The play's the thing." So with every walk of life.

Reflective human beings find that there is something that maintains and sustains systems, industries and institutions, something impersonal, unaffected by who comes and goes, arising out of collective need, articulation and incarnation, maintained in existence and given life by collective wills, minds and imaginations. When a person asks himself what in him is dying and relinquishes what is already passing, he releases a golden opportunity to re-create himself. *When a person balances out in one's own daily equations what is dying against what is opening out from within, one becomes a free human being who existentially discovers in time the secret of immortality.* One also discerns that the secret of immortality is merely a puzzling phrase in ordinary language. But where a person gains self-awareness through intensive self-knowledge of all the variables and sub-sets that constitute one's emotional and psychic natures, one's mind-being and one's own sense of physical and mental selfhood, one may become a magician. By abstracting oneself away from all that in which one had contained one's sense of self, one can attain an amazing capacity to see an expansive Self that has no relationship to events, persons or places, to yesterday and tomorrow, to bits and pieces of oneself emotionally, psychically or mentally. One begins to live with a new awareness actuated from deep within one's consciousness. One begins to activate the Buddha-body of the Buddhist tradition, the light-body of mystical texts, the resurrection-body in Christian mysticism. This subtlest of all vestures is gestated by the primordial root causes which are ontologically prior to all the constellations of secondary and superficial causes. One's critical decisions arise out of basic desires, ultimately rooted in a fundamental willingness to endorse a limited sense of reality.

Between the unmanifested world and the SELF we find the truly "real". What is real is prior both to what is latent and to what is active, and yet it is posterior to SELF. That SELF has nothing to do with what is usually called the self, collective or individual, wholly parasitic upon the process of manifestation. Everyone knows the differences among human beings arising from how they see themselves. To flee every intimation of one's deeper Self out of fear for the manifesting and ever-dying self is not to live at all. This is the toughest aspect of the immemorial teaching of *Theosophia* – the ever-present beginning. The Theosophical Movement since 1875 seems to have made a relatively small difference to the scene of recorded history in modern civilization, and it even appears at times as if Krishna, Buddha, Shankara, Pythagoras, Plato and Christ came in vain. There is an essential sense in which they all came in vain in the midst of unregenerate humanity. The first step of initial detachment is the most difficult and threatening for disciples. It is a detachment in which a person is willing to put one's entire sense of self upon the dissecting table and to renounce it while doing this with no promise, no guarantee, nothing to comfort one in relation to the great venture, a dark and unknown journey. It is a deeply private journey, and it is a journey where the first step is the most difficult. In recent years many people have been playing an intolerable game of talking ignorantly about this sacred journey, but suddenly they discover something painful about each other – that there is a new breed of cowards who lack the will of those with older illusions who put their frothy energies to practical use. These are weak-willed men and women wanting to be saved, dramatically and messianically, and they unconsciously engender a nefarious vampirism, stealing energy from those more vulnerable and susceptible. It is a ghoulish game of those who cannot go back to the old illusions and yet do not have the courage to commence the spiritual path in earnest.

Brahma Vidya is exacting because it instructs the individual who is truly serious about apprehending the meaning of death and discovering the secret of immortality – "Give up thy life, if thou would'st live." Give up everything associated with so-called living. See it for what it is. Only after a sufficient period of courageous persistence can one begin to live. This painful recognition might well have the dignity and the power of a vow. It could summon a fresh release of creative energy from the inexhaustible, indescribable Self within, which has been repeatedly denied but which is relentlessly chasing one like the Hound of Heaven. It is oneself, one's only friend, one's best ally and invisible escort, one's own priest and authentic prophet, the guru and the guide, the radiant *Christos* within. To hold firmly to this sovereign truth is to make a new beginning and a radical change in consciousness. A person cannot move from the first part of the injunction, "Give up thy life", to the second, "if thou would'st live", on individualistic and separative terms, because no personal life means anything to the passionless and ever-revolving universe. New life may be found only by those who can find some meaning in the lives of others, can throw themselves into a vaster vision of life which is universifiable, in which others can share and participate. It is elementary wisdom and commonsense that makes a human being recognize that the larger circle must prevail. Each and every person must go along with the ever-expanding circle or be left behind in the great pilgrimage of humanity. Many men and women cling to their own contracting circles of confining allegiances, limiting ideas, base and petty plans, prating about absurd delusions of self-importance – all because they are terrified of the uncharted Void which is the creative abyss from which tomorrow must spring. And for such people necessarily there is a *Gotterdammerung*: they are doomed through avoidable selfishness, and there is no providential or accidental escape. But when, from the very intensity of one's own concern with the *Gotterdammerung,* a human being really begins to extend out the radius of selfhood, then one suddenly begins to find that one lives in a radically new sense. In such a totally different way of life, one is apparently wholly involved, but only because one is always laughing, always voiding, always seeing through, without hurting the feelings of others, without denying to oneself the unsought opportunity of participating in the play.

One gradually becomes a person for whom it is true that in giving up life, one begins to live. One has learned that it is possible to be and not to be – to be in space-time and yet not to be in space-time. This is to live infinitely, eternally, and immortally. It is to live the sovereign life of the king with the inward light of indissoluble consciousness focussed through a continuous golden thread of mystic meditation, upon which could be strung, like so many beads, everything that is meaningful within the great reservoir of experience. This tremendous vista restores to life its fundamentally joyous optimism, its core of creativity. They are wise who say, even at the level of a slogan, that the person of tomorrow is mature in some sense that was not true of the people of the past. It requires a new kind of adult hope, a new kind of maturity, to live coolly in this new dimension in a manner that transcends past societies. To live is to maintain that kind of coolness which is sustained by an ever-expanding, living warmth for all beings on earth. One can only inherit the kingdom by claiming it. Hence the Biblical saying that the kingdom of God must be taken by force – the force of courage. This is the courage to be alone, to be a *raja* within one's own realm, and to re-establish order among the insurgents that masquerade as unavoidable drives, basic necessities and necessary patterns. To restore order in the kingdom of one's life is to attain the sovereignty of a truly free human being who is at once determining the value to put upon things and voiding them as well. One is living and not living, dying and not dying. One is constantly reclaiming the virgin nature of a boundless consciousness that flows through one in a stream, reclaiming it from the necessary process of disintegration that must characterize all forms and finitude.

One finds out for oneself that immortality can have no meaning except in reference to a recognition and acceptance of mortality. Though the language is paradoxical, the experience is possible. Alas, many men and women fail to come closer to experiencing it because they are excessively afraid to die. Ascribing mortality to parts, one can consciously do what Nature does with organisms, thereby maintaining one's individuality in the whole. Through letting go of particular things, one keeps the core of one's identity beyond time and space, beyond flux and cessation, beyond form, colour and limitation. A person who attains to this point moves naturally in embodied consciousness into a condition of something like serenity, obeisance and discipleship. Such an individual is sufficiently on the threshold to want the full incarnation of the Triad that is above him, to seek it with the whole of his being. One makes room for it (because Nature abhors a vacuum) by expelling all lesser energies and persisting in silent mental obeisance to the god within. The Triad has begun to mirror itself. It has not yet fully incarnated in the disciple, but the Triad overbroods and its mirroring shows in the calm of one's nature. The peace that passeth all understanding is like the calm of the depths of an infinite ocean. It is beyond description, but once experienced or realized, it can never be confounded with what the self-deluded call pleasure. There can be no ego-satisfaction, for this calm involves self-forgetfulness. It is a calm where there is no awareness of being calm. It is a flow that is not aware of itself as separate in the great process of life. The Triad can incarnate gradually. Every time it enters the soul there will be a kickback in the shadowy self. When it fully descends, it can maintain itself only by a self-conscious union with the Brahmâ-Vishnu-Shiva Triad – pure creativity, patient preservation of the essential and meaningful, and passionless elimination of the redundant and irrelevant. When this is attained, it becomes a rhythmic process coeval with the whole of one's life. Then it becomes as natural as breathing. As the *Brihadaranyaka* intimates:

> Then the point of the heart grows luminous, and when it has grown luminous, it lights the soul upon its way: from the head or from the eye or from other parts of the body. And as the soul rises upwards the life-breath rises upwards with it; and as the life-breath rises upwards with it, the powers rise up with the life-breath. The soul becomes conscious and enters into Consciousness.
>
> Then his wisdom and works take him by the hand, and the knowledge gained of old. Then as a caterpillar when it comes to the

end of a leaf, reaching forth to another foothold, draws itself over to it, so the soul, leaving the body, and putting off unwisdom, reaching another foothold there, draws itself over to it.

As a worker in gold, taking an ornament, moulds it to another form newer and fairer; so in truth the soul, leaving the body here, and putting off unwisdom, makes for itself another form newer and fairer: a form like the forms of departed souls, or of the seraphs, or of the gods, or of the creators, or of the Eternal, or of other beings.

The soul of man is the Eternal. It is made of consciousness, it is made of feeling, it is made of life, it is made of vision, it is made of hearing; it is made of the earth, it is made of the waters, it is made of the air, it is made of the ether, it is made of the radiance and what is beyond the radiance; it is made of desire and what is beyond desire, it is made of wrath and what is beyond wrath, it is made of the law and what is beyond the law; it is made of the All. The soul is made of this world and of the other world. . . .

As they said of old: Man verily is formed of desire; as his desire is, so is his will; as his will is, so he works; and whatever work he does, in the likeness of it he grows.

Hermes, December 1978

Calm and unmoved the Pilgrim glideth up the stream that to Nirvana leads. He knoweth that the more his feet will bleed, the whiter will himself be washed. He knoweth well that after seven short and fleeting births Nirvana will be his.

Such is the *Dhyana* Path, the haven of the Yogi, the blessed goal that Srotapattis crave.

Not so when he hath crossed and won the Aryahata Path.

There Klesha is destroyed for ever, Tanha's roots torn out. But stay, Disciple . . . Yet, one word. Canst thou destroy divine COMPASSION? Compassion is no attribute. It is the LAW OF LAWS – eternal Harmony, *Alaya*'s SELF; a shoreless universal essence, the light of everlasting Right, and fitness of all things, the law of love eternal.

The more thou dost become at one with it, thy being melted in its BEING, the more thy Soul unites with that which IS, the more thou wilt become COMPASSION ABSOLUTE.

Such is the Arya Path, Path of the Buddhas of perfection.

Withal, what mean the sacred scrolls which make thee say?

"*OM*! I believe it is not all the Arhats that get of the Nirvanic Path the sweet fruition."

"*OM*! I believe that the Nirvana-Dharma is entered not by all the Buddhas".

"Yea; on the Arya Path thou art no more Srotapatti, thou art a Bodhisattva. The stream is cross'd. 'Tis true thou hast a right to Dharmakaya vesture; but Sambogakaya is greater than a Nirvanee, and greater still is a Nirmanakaya – the Buddha of Compassion.

Now bend thy head and listen well, O Bodhisattva – Compassion speaks and saith: "Can there be bliss when all that lives must suffer? Shalt thou be saved and hear the whole world cry?"

Now thou hast heard that which was said.

Thou shalt attain the seventh step and cross the gate of final knowledge but only to wed woe – if thou would'st be Tathagata, follow upon thy predecessor's steps, remain unselfish till the endless end. Thou art enlightened – Choose thy way.

Behold, the mellow light that floods the Eastern sky. In signs of praise both heaven and earth unite. And from the four-fold manifested Powers a chant of love ariseth, both from the flaming Fire and flowing Water, and from sweet-smelling Earth and rushing Wind.

Hark! . . . from the deep unfathomable vortex of that golden light in which the Victor bathes, ALL NATURE's wordless voice in thousand tones ariseth to proclaim:

JOY UNTO YE, O MEN OF MYALBA.

A PILGRIM HATH RETURNED BACK "FROM THE OTHER SHORE."

A NEW ARHAN IS BORN.

PEACE TO ALL BEINGS.

The Seven Portals
H. P. Blavatsky

978-0-9793205-3-8

0-9793205-3-4

www.ingramcontent.com/pod-product-compliance
Lightning Source LLC
Chambersburg PA
CBHW021042090426
42738CB00006B/151